HESS

HESS

The Missing Years 1941–1945

David Irving

GUILD PUBLISHING LONDON

This edition published 1988 by
Book Club Associates
by arrangement with
Macmillan London Limited
London and Basingstoke

Phototypeset by Wyvern Typesetting Ltd, Bristol
Printed in Great Britain by Butler & Tanner, Frome and London

Contents

Part One

Germany

1 A Prisoner of Mankind

Semi-blind, his memory gone, he languished for forty-six years in prison, and spent over half of that time in solitary confinement. At first he was detained in cells with blackened windows, sentinels flashing torches on his face all night at half-hour intervals; and later in conditions only marginally more humane.

Occasionally, mankind remembered that he was there: at a time when "political prisoners" were being released as a token of humanity, the world knew that he was still in Spandau, and timid souls felt somehow the safer for it. In 1987 the news emerged that somebody had recently stolen the prisoner's 1940s flying helmet, goggles and fur-lined boots – and fevered minds imagined that these, his hallowed relics of 1941, might be used in some way to power a Nazi revival.

The prisoner himself had long forgotten what those relics had ever meant to him. The dark-red brick of Spandau prison in West Berlin was crumbling and decaying around him, and the windows were cracked or falling out of mouldering frames. He was the only prisoner left – alone, outliving all his fellows, his brain perhaps a last uncertain repository of names and promises and places, grim secrets that the victorious Four Powers might have expected him to take to the grave long before.

The prisoner was Rudolf Hess, the last of the "war criminals". In May 1941 he had flown single-handedly to Scotland on a reckless parachute mission to end the bloodshed and bombing. Put on trial by the victors he had been condemned to imprisonment in perpetuity for "Crimes against the Peace". The Four Powers had expected him to die and thus seal off the wells of speculation about him, but this stubborn old man with the haunting eyes had by his very longevity thwarted them.

Few questions remained about the other Nazis. Hitler's jawbone was preserved in a Soviet glass jar, Ley's brain was in Massachusetts; Bormann's skeleton was found beneath the Berlin cobblestones, Mengele's mortal remains were dis- and reinterred; Speer had joined the Greatest Architect. Dead too were Hess's judges and prosecutors. Hess himself was the last living Nazi giant, the last enigma, unable to communicate with the outside world, forbidden to talk with his son about political events, his diary taken away from him each day to be destroyed, his letters censored and scissored to excise illicit content. The macabre Four Power statute – ignored, in the event – ordained that upon his death the body was to be reduced to ashes in the crematorium at Dachau concentration camp. The bulldozers were already standing by to wreck Spandau jail within hours of his decease, so that no place of Nazi pilgrimage remained.

For forty years this Berlin charade was the sole remaining joint activity of the wartime Allied powers, a wordless political ballet performed by the western democracies and high-stepping Red Army guards. Every thirty days the guard was rotated. Each time that the British or the Americans or the French came to hold the key they could in theory have turned it and set this old man free. But they did not, because the ghosts of Churchill, Stalin and Roosevelt were themselves the jailers. In the name of a Four Power agreement that had long since been dishonoured, these ghosts kept Hess behind bars: and so Hitler's deputy lived on in Spandau, mocking history and making a mockery of justice itself.

Despite everything, he became a martyr to a cause.

Mankind dared not turn the key to set him free: and mankind did not know why.

Like Hitler himself, the subject of this narrative had been born beyond the frontiers of Germany. Walter Rudolf Richard Hess opened his eyes to the light of Egypt on 26 April 1894. He found himself in the wealthy family of a young German merchant, Johann Fritz Hess, in Ibrahimieh (Ibrâhî-mîya), a suburb of Alexandria.

Fritz Hess was thirty; he had inherited an import business founded by his father, Christian, and was a respected member of the German colony in Egypt. Thus the boy Rudolf spent his first fourteen years amid the silks and ceramics and servants of a palatial villa. Every two years the family left these patrician surroundings for a six-month stay at the family's hunting estate at Reicholdsgrün in the Fichtelgebirge mountains of central Germany.

His mother was Klara Münch, daughter of a textile manufacturer in Thuringia. Rudolf was fond of both parents, but it was she who taught him to pray, and his first memory, at the age of three, was when she bore her husband another son, Alfred. Rudolf was given a toy gun drawn by two horses as a present: the gift interested him more than the new arrival. Eleven years after that, he gained a baby sister, Grete.

The East Prussian philosopher Immanuel Kant had written, "I shall never forget my mother. She implanted in me and nurtured the first seed of good; she opened my soul to the lessons of Nature; she aroused my interest and enlarged my ideas. What she taught me has had an everlasting and blessed influence upon my life." Chancing upon these words in 1949, Rudolf Hess would reflect, "This holds true not just for the mother of Kant." He never forgot his mother. With her he would set forth into the

Egyptian desert before dawn to watch nature awakening in the darkened palm groves: his young nostrils caught the puzzling odour of burned gunpowder, his infant's eyes made out the shape of Arabs holding ancient muzzle-loading muskets. Sometimes his mother took them westwards into the Libyan desert, into the midst of an ocean of flowers which flooded the desert during the few weeks that it could boast of a spring, before the sun's furnace scorched off the last raindrops and the ghibli entombed the anemones and narcissi beneath its hot and drifting sands.

Fifty years later, when his horizons were encompassed by the confines of his cell at Spandau and an outer prison wall, he would still remember Egypt: he would write to his aged mother about how he was tending a hundred tomato plants or more:

> I have arranged their irrigation along the lines of Musa's system in the garden at Ibrahimieh, down by the tennis court: I stand here lost in thought, opening and closing the little canals as though . . . it were the Rhine–Main–Danube canal of the future! . . . In some book or other – was it Keyserling's *Journal of a Philosopher*? – I was reading about the splendours of a garden in southern climes, and suddenly I could see Ibrahimieh all over again with its blossoms and scents and all the indescribable and intangible things that went with it: the redhot *hamsin*; the cool sea breezes, heavy with their salty tang; the winter tempests, the sea foaming with white horses as far as the eye could behold, the screech of the seagulls; and the dull thudding of the waves that used to lullaby us to sleep. And then again, I recall the lukewarm moonlit nights and the eternal barking of dogs from out in the desert which made the all-pervading silence seem by contrast even more profound.

"How often", he reminded his mother in this 1949 letter, "you sat with us children on a bench, with Egypt's starry canopy above, telling us all you knew and singling out each of the bright stars by name. Even now I can't hear the names of Vega, of Cassiopeia, or of Aldebaran without thinking momentarily of you and of tranquil nights long, long ago."

His other ineradicable memories were of his father – of his severity, which was so intimidating that the two brothers never dared to romp around in the morning until he left for work.

Their education was the finest that money could buy. A private tutor gave them their first lessons; the tutor would remember Rudolf later as being attentive and earnest. The boy's inclinations were to study maths and science, but Fritz Hess needed an heir to take over the import business, and that was the purpose of the expensive grooming. He sent Rudolf to the German School at Alexandria in 1900. From 1906 he was given two years of private tuition, and then his father enrolled him at the Protestant College at Godesberg on the Rhine.

That too was one of Rudolf's early memories – leaving Egypt in 1908. As the coastline slowly fell out of sight and the Port of Alexandria's historic Column of Pompeius and the lighthouse built by Alexander the

Great slipped below the horizon, Fritz Hess said to his elder son: "Take a good long look at that land. You're bidding it farewell for several years to come."

From Godesberg he progressed in 1911 to the French-speaking Ecole Supérieure de Commerce at Neuchâtel in Switzerland, where he was initiated into the mysteries of accounting. He found this field of intellectual enterprise uninspiring – a depressing conclusion that a two-year apprenticeship to an export house in Hamburg served only to confirm.

Fortunately, the world war intervened in August 1914: with light hearts and patriotic souls he and his brother both volunteered for the infantry. On the 20th he was in uniform, and he went to the battlefields of France with the 1st Bavarian Infantry Regiment. His personnel records confirm that he saw action that autumn on the Somme and in the Artois. He showed a reckless disregard for injury: in France he was wounded at Verdun on 12 June 1916, but fought on; in Rumania he was injured in his left arm on 25 July 1917 at Oituz Pass, but stayed with his unit; two weeks later he was finally felled by a rifle bullet in his left lung during a charge by the 18th Bavarian Reserve Infantry Regiment at Unguereana. He nearly bled to death when the field dressing came adrift as he was manhandled down the mountain on an ammunition cart.

After a long convalescence in Hungarian and Saxon hospitals, he was allowed home on leave in the Fichtelgebirge. In March 1918 he volunteered as a fighter pilot, but the war had only one month left to run when he reached his operational unit, the 35th Fighter *Staffel*. He was demobilized with the rank of lieutenant a month later but had acquired a taste for flying that was to obsess him for the next quarter of a century.

He arrived in Munich in February 1919, depressed and embittered at the "treason" of the government in Berlin which had signed the Armistice. A Red "Soviet" regime had seized power in Bavaria. In Munich Hess ran errands for Baron Rudolf von Sebottendorff's secretive anti-Marxist, anti-Semitic Thule Society, and distributed inflammatory leaflets railing against the "Jewish" Soviet Republic of Bavaria.

They were strange and turbulent months for him. He narrowly escaped a Red massacre of hostages by turning up for a Thule meeting late – in time to see his less fortunate friends laden on to the truck which took them to their execution. He was wounded for a fourth time, this time in the leg, while manning a howitzer during the street battles fought by General Franz von Epp's ragtag army to liberate Munich on 1 May 1919.

His army personnel file records that on 7 May he joined a volunteer unit of Epp's Freikorps; left it on 15 October; was temporarily recruited by the local airfield at Schleissheim on 29 March 1920; flew an aeroplane to a Bavarian unit stationed in the Ruhr on 6 April, and finally resigned his commission in Munich on the last day of April 1920.

Hess now chose to enrol in the university to study history and economics. Here he had already found a new "father". A year before, a comrade on the training airfield at Lechfeld, Max Hofweber, had told him about his rare, gifted commanding general Dr Karl Haushofer. Intrigued, Hess had persuaded Hofweber to arrange an introduction, and they met on 4 April 1919 – beginning an intimate friendship that was to prove fateful to both of them.

Born on 27 August 1869, Haushofer was twice Hess's age, but he perceived in the young army veteran an uprightness, a courage and an intellect that were clearly wasted on the business training he had had so far. He took Hess under his wing, persuaded him to start up an interior-design business with Hofweber – Munich Wohnungskunst – and encouraged him to visit when he could. The young man had come round for his first tea at the Haushofers' on 28 January 1920. Hess found himself drawn naturally into the Professor's famous lectures on geo-politics and willingly acted as his unpaid assistant.

The tall, statuesque ex-general and professor with the beaky nose and beady eye was just the kind of father Hess would have preferred (his own parents were still in Egypt). The Professor took him into the family home: within a year, Hess had become like an adoptive son to him. They went everywhere together, on walks and outings and even trips to Switzerland. Seduced in turn by Hess's sense of moral rectitude and industry, Haushofer dedicated odes to his young friend and pupil, and told him of dreams that had come to him – rather as an over-romantic mistress might woo her mate.

In the summer of that year, 1920, Hess first saw Adolf Hitler and his embryonic National Socialist Party meeting in the Sternecker-Bräu beerhall. Enthusiastic about this new figure in his life, who obviously provided Hess with yet another authoritative father figure, he persuaded Haushofer to go with him to the new party's meetings that June, and on 1 July enrolled himself as Member no. 16. But Hess failed to persuade the Professor to fall in too behind the "tribune" (as he referred to Hitler, the party's first chairman).

What kind of pupil was Hess, a man in his mid-twenties? "He was a very attentive student," Professor Haushofer would reminisce a quarter-century later, "but his strength was not so much intelligence as heart and character, I should say." Hess worked diligently, but the political activities of the student bodies and officers' associations often lured him away. Even so, in Haushofer's view he was better educated than the essentially self-taught Hitler.

During Haushofer's lectures from 1920 onwards Hess absorbed uncritically the Professor's teaching on Germany's geographical need for more living space, passing them on to Hitler. Hess often used Haushofer's words to express himself. In 1921 he entered a competition with the following essay, answering the question, "What kind of leader does Germany need to regain her greatness?"

In the interests of the liberation of his nation, the leader does not shrink from using the weapons of his enemy: demagogy, slogans, street meetings, etc. Where all authority has vanished, only popularity creates authority. . . . The deeper the dictator's original roots are anchored in the broad masses, and the better he understands their psychology, the less the workers will mistrust him and the more followers he will win among these, the most energetic ranks of the people.

He himself has nothing in common with the masses: he is a personality in his own right, like every great man.

When necessity dictates he does not recoil from bloodshed. Great issues are always decided through blood and iron. And our issue is: to go under, or to arise anew.

Whether or not the Reichstag continues to babble, this man will act. . . . To reach his goal, he will crush even his closest friends. For the sake of the great ultimate goal he is able to endure seeming, temporarily, in the eyes of the majority, like a traitor to his nation.★

The lawmaker, acting with awesome harshness, does not shrink from punishing with death those who expose the finest part of the people to starvation – the profiteers and usurers. The Stock Exchange's gamble with the nation's wealth is ended. The betrayers of the people are banished. A terrible Day of Judgement dawns for those who betrayed the nation during and after the war.

The leader remains free from the taint of Jews and Jewish freemasons. Though he uses them, his gigantic personality must continually override their influence. He knows the peoples of the world and influential leaders. According to need he is able to trample them under foot or to braid threads with delicate fingers to the shores of the Pacific itself. One way or another, the enslaving treaties must fall. The new Grossdeutschland, embracing all who are of German blood, shall arise.

The edifice must not be tailored to the measure of its builder, lest the whole structure collapse upon his departure, as were the empires of Frederick the Great and Bismarck.

No independent personalities can possibly grow in the dictator's shadow – men who might in the future guide the steed on which a freshly risen Germany is riding.

Wherefore the leader achieves his last great deed: instead of draining his power to the last, he lays down its mantle and stands aside to serve his nation like a Trusty Eckehard.

Hess won first prize for these lines.

Something of his philosophical nature glimmered through the advice he entered soon after, on 24 April 1921, in the Haushofer family album:

Always assume that fate will play tricks on you, whether human or inanimate.

★ Haushofer told him once, Hess wrote at Nuremberg in 1946, "that when the stakes were high you must be prepared to be branded as a traitor for a while by your own people – to which I would add: or as a madman".

Come to expect those pinpricks of misfortune. Then you will see fewer disappointments in life than others, and more pleasurable surprises.

Give back blows that are harder than you get; and believe in your own final victory as you trust in that of your people.

– R.H., on a day when the mountains would not reveal themselves, when the waters poured forth from the skies and the old tree stumps were washed away. The world was beautiful after all!

When – according to Hitler's gloating narrative in *Mein Kampf* – over seven hundred Marxists tried to disrupt his Party's meeting at the Hofbräuhaus beerhall on 4 November 1921, there were only some forty-five Hitler "stormtroopers" to defend him. Hess was among them; he took a leading part in the ensuing brawl and suffered a skull injury, probably from the barrage of heavy beermugs and chairlegs that flew across the hall. In a ninety-minute battle they evicted their enemies, and none too kindly either.

Out of brawls like this emerged Hitler's Storm Detachment (Sturmabteilung), the SA. It began as a loosely organized private army of muscular young men who kept order at Hitler's meetings – and not infrequently disrupted those of the left. Hess not only joined it in 1922 but raised within it an "NS Students' Hundred" which later became the Student Battalion. Meanwhile, the fights grew bloodier, because the Communists did not intend to allow the right to prevail.

Often Professor Haushofer saw Hess come into the lecture theatre with a bandaged and bloodstained head, but never did his studies fall behind. In the university too he gave as good as he got, quoting Friedrich Schiller's poetry with such deadly effect in one argument with the law professor Rothenbücher that the latter hinted urgently to Haushofer that this turbulent student was too dangerous to remain in the academic world. Haushofer, no mean critic, found his pupil's work faultlessly prepared – years later he still recalled one paper delivered by the young man on the economic history of his native Alexandria.

The fighting went on. On May Day in 1923 Hess and his "troops" fought their way into a Communist procession, seized the red hammer-and-sickle flag and burned it – Hess justifying his action to the police who arrested him by saying that any public display of the flag which had led to the army's mutiny and Germany's military downfall was an outright provocation to any decent German. As the man of action supplanted the academic student, Hess haunted the various semi-official vigilante and paramilitary organizations of post-Versailles Germany, helping to mount guard on the War Ministry and patrol the streets.

If he continued at university, it was now only because he was preparing himself to serve Germany's Messiah, and he saw in Adolf Hitler all the talents that that man would need.

·   ·   ·

Hess had taken into the little Munich design firm a good-natured
twenty-three-year-old student, Ilse Pröhl, to handle the secretarial load;
economic circumstances had brought her from Berlin in April 1920. Ilse
had first set eyes on the young, unruly Rudolf in Schwabing, Munich's
bohemian quarter. He was wearing the bronze lion of General von Epp's
Freikorps on one arm and had just returned from an operation against
Communist revolutionaries in the Ruhr. "He laughed seldom," she
recalled in a letter twenty-seven years later, forgetting perhaps that civil
wars are the saddest expression of military enterprise. "He didn't smoke,
he spurned alcohol, and he had not the slightest notion that even after a
lost war young men could find happiness in dancing and good company."
He took her to Haushofer's lectures and dragged her along to the street
meetings and beerhall rallies. She too fell under Adolf Hitler's spell. "All
in all," Rudolf wrote to her on 24 October 1923,

> I am an odd mixture and this is also the cause of all those stresses that
> make life so hard for me sometimes. Today a need for repose, for
> tranquil and secluded study, heeding nothing of politics or the clatter of
> war, a yearning for a people around me with Culture from head to toe,
> for Mozart, piano and flute; and then tomorrow a march through storm
> and stream, a dive into the fray, public demagoguery and close to the
> negation of everything I held holy yesterday: today absurdly soft,
> tomorrow coarse, and rowdy. I don't know what to make of me.

A right-wing dictatorship had been set up in Bavaria under Gustav von
Kahr. It drew strength in part from the army and police, but also from the
nationalist paramilitary bodies like Hitler's SA, which skirted round the
constrictions of the Versailles treaty. Hitler tried to win Kahr for the
cause. After one visit to Kahr, Hess, who had accompanied him, wrote
these lines to the dictator:

> The nub of the matter is that H. is convinced that a resurgence is only
> possible if we succeed in bringing the broad masses, particularly of the
> workers, back into the nationalist fold. . . .
>   I myself know Mr Hitler very well since I speak with him almost on a
> daily basis and I'm close to him as man to man too. He is a character of
> rare decency, full of heartfelt goodness, religious, and a good Catholic.
> He has only one aim: the good of his country, and for this he sacrifices
> himself quite unselfishly.

This at least was how Hess saw Hitler in 1923. That summer Hitler
believed that he had persuaded the Kahr regime to stage a "march on
Berlin", but months passed and nothing stirred.
    Tired of waiting, Hitler decided to start the revolution himself. He
invited the unsuspecting Bavarian leaders to address a mass rally in
Munich's Bürgerbräu beerhall on 8 November: his plan was to seize both
hall and audience with his stormtroopers. By this time he trusted Hess –

five years his junior – implicitly, and asked him to accompany him in full uniform that evening. Hess went straight round to his friend and mentor, Professor Haushofer, and, without being able to tell him why, invited him to come too; the Professor smelt a rat, and made his excuses. Not so Kahr's foolish ministers. Fuelled by greed and oiled by their own folly, they fell right into Hitler's trap.

With Hess at his side, Hitler seized the hall and began blackmailing the politicians into joining his revolution. To Hess he gave the job of arresting the ministers, Messrs Knilling, Wutzelhofer and Schweyer. Hess stood on a chair and read out their names like a schoolmaster. These and other hostages he conveyed courteously but firmly to the suburban home of a publisher, and then – as news broke that same night that the *putsch* was in difficulties – further afield into the hills south of Munich.

At midday on the 9th the *putsch* collapsed. Hitler and his columns paraded defiantly with bands and bayonets and banners from the beerhall right into Munich's centre where they were met with a hail of gunfire from the *Landespolizei*. A dozen of Hitler's men fell dead.

Perhaps Hess could have done more. That is after all why hostages had been taken. But either they escaped or he set them free – history is uncertain. A wanted man, he went into hiding. For a few days the Haushofers concealed him in their Munich apartment, then like the SA's commander Hermann Göring and several other failed putschists he took refuge in Austria.

Hitler and his accomplices were put on trial early in 1924. Hess remained in exile, but surrendered to the authorities in the trial's closing days. It was common sense rather than any kind of exhibitionism that motivated him: Haushofer had smuggled a letter to him warning that the favourably disposed court in Munich would transfer the trial of Hess to Leipzig, where a far stiffer sentence might result. He got off relatively mildly. The Bavarian court sentenced Hess to eighteen months in Landsberg prison.

Hess had a small, quiet, whitewashed cell with a tranquil view across the countryside to the distant Alps. A former aviator friend was one of the warders. His cell was comfortably furnished, he had bookshelves, a modern reading lamp and writing desk.

Hitler had attracted a five-year sentence in the same fortress-like jail. Surrounded by friendly and admiring warders he and his twenty followers used these months to the full. They met each day at 10 a.m. around a long table in the common room, where Hitler held court beneath a swastika flag. The warders turned a blind eye, and Hitler and his accomplices conducted business as before.

They turned the same blind eye when Hess's young secretary Ilse came to see him, bringing books and gifts – the old policeman yawned, turned away and pretended to fall asleep so that the young couple could be effectively alone.

The prison's records show that between 24 June and 12 November

1924 Professor Haushofer came eight times to see Hess – always on a Wednesday – and stayed the whole morning and afternoon. Haushofer almost envied him these peaceful, contemplative surroundings. He saw Hitler too, but stressed years later, "My visits to Landsberg were meant for Hess as he was my pupil." In fact visitors were not supposed to see more than one prisoner, and so far as possible Hitler avoided being buttonholed by the wordy academic.

To Hess Haushofer brought books to improve his mind – Karl von Clausewitz on war, and the improved second edition of Friedrich Ratzel's *Politische Geographie* – but he could see that neither Hess nor Hitler had grasped the essentials of geopolitics despite these private "tutorials". "I remember well", reminisced the Professor in 1945, "that whenever Hess understood something and tried to explain it to Hitler, Hitler would come out with one of his new ideas about an autobahn or something completely irrelevant, while Hess just stood there and said nothing more about it."

The intimacy between Hitler and Hess dated from these months of shared imprisonment. He began to act as the Führer's secretary, and Hitler is said to have dictated some chapters of his turgid manifesto *Mein Kampf* to Hess, since he himself was unable to type.

One day that summer Hitler came into Hess's cell and read out a passage from the book describing the life and death of their fellow soldiers in the First World War. "The *Tribune*", wrote Hess to Ilse Pröhl on 3 July 1924, "finally read slower and slower and more and more haltingly. His face expressionless, he groped around his seemingly boundless concept; the pauses grew longer and more frequent until he suddenly put down the pages, dropped his head into his hands and sobbed out loud." After a while, continued Hess, Hitler pulled himself together and burst out: "Oh I shall exact a pitiless and terrible revenge on the very first day I can! I shall take revenge in the name of all whom I shall then see before my eyes." For Hess this was a turning-point in his life. "I am more beholden to him now than ever before," he wrote at the end of this letter to Ilse. "I love him!"

Some of these surviving letters which Hess wrote from the prison are typed, while others are written in the neat, flowing handwriting that would neither age nor change over the next sixty years. All show Hess acting as Hitler's adjutant, or pondering radical new legislation.

"Dear Herr Heim," he would write to Heinrich Heim,★ a twenty-four-year-old Munich lawyer, on 16 July 1924:

> I kept hoping to be able to send you a reply from Mr Hitler to your friend's letter together with my own thanks for the kind loan of the two volumes of [Kurt Meyer's] *The German Race* [*Das Deutsche Volkstum*]; but at present Mr H. does not want anything to do with everyday politics. I made a last try with the letter this morning, in vain.

★ Heinrich Heim, born 15 June 1900; joined the Deputy Führer's staff in 1933, became Martin Bormann's adjutant in 1939 and was the author of the famous records of *Hitler's Table Talk*.

He has now withdrawn publicly from the [Party] leadership because he does not want to accept responsibility for what goes on outside without his knowledge and against his will; nor is he in any position to mediate from within here in the eternal squabbles. He considers it pointless to get embroiled in all these petty nuisances.

He's convinced that after he regains his freedom he will be able to steer everything back on to the right tracks. Above all he will then very rapidly put a stop to everything tending to religious differences, and unite all forces for the fight against Communism, which is deadlier than ever and preparing under cover for its grand coup.

Compared with this, in my view the all too familiar bickering that your friend describes in the nationalist movement pales into insignificance.

I believe that only too soon the moment will come when everybody who is not already against us will fall in behind Hitler in the desperate struggle against the Bolshevik plague. Let us hope that he will be set free soon enough.

Whatever the follies of his supporters, the personality of Hitler – the gigantic significance of which I have only really grasped here – will prevail. . . . In the autumn Hitler's book will appear, and this will give the public at large a picture of both the politician and the man. . . .

Many thanks incidentally for that work by Kurt Meyer. I gather I may keep it for a while. I read with particular interest the section on German literature, and as a geopolitician I am glad to see that he has not neglected the environmental influences of terrain and geography.

Your paper on "Compulsory Labour Service" is arguably the best I have read on this subject; the obstacles, primary and secondary consequences, and associated possibilities are well set out.

Hess enclosed a reprint of an article by Hitler from *Germany's Renewal*. "If you have it already," he wrote, "you might pass it on to Miss Pröhl" – whom Heim had now taken under his care.

In mid-September Hess sent him a "monster of a law" which he had drafted on nationalization, and asked him to run his expert lawyer's eye over it to eliminate "legal howlers".

I have built up the external shape of the credit system so that natural growths are damaged as little as possible, which in turn will permit of some competition within the monopoly, since parallel organizations will continue to exist in the form of banking, Giro, and co-operative associations that are only loosely tied at the top in the Reich Bank. I don't know how practicable the whole thing is but nor do I see what objections there could be.

For a while Hess and Hitler hoped to be released on 1 October 1924. Three days before that date, Hess composed a farewell slogan for his fellow prisoners: "Germany shall live, even if Pettifogging Justice has to go to the Devil!" He added a dedication "to my fortress comrades in memory of the days and months we spent together behind walls and bars because German judges kowtowed to the opposite principle."

The emotionally charged months shared with Hitler in Landsberg prison cast Hess and all the others in a mould which the years would never break. Nineteen-year-old student Walther Hewel, a member of the Adolf Hitler Shocktroop that had seized the Bürgerbräu, described them in frequent letters. "Again two days I'll never forget," he wrote on the first anniversary of the failed *putsch*.

> Saturday evening [8 November 1924] we sat and sang old soldiers' ditties and swapped anecdotes about the 8th and 9th. Everybody had some story the others hadn't heard. We wallowed in memories of those eager, happy hours.
>
> At 8 p.m. Hitler, Lieutenant-Colonel [Hermann] Kriebel, Dr [Christian] Weber and Rudolf Hess [the leaders of the *putsch*] joined us to the strains of the Hohenfriedberg March played by the prisoners' band.
>
> 8.34 p.m.: we duly commemorated the historic moment when the trucks arrived with the Hitler Shocktroops.
>
> The short speech that Hitler delivered was just beyond description. It wrenched us inside-out. Those few words from him had each of these betimes rowdy and boisterous men going back to their cells subdued. For half an hour none of us could get out a single word.
>
> What people outside would have given to hear this man speak on this evening! Hitler stood in our midst in the little room and addressed us as though we were seven thousand people in the Circus [*Krone*]. . . .
>
> Today, Sunday, Hitler came over to us at 1 p.m. and said simply: "Men, at this moment one year ago your comrades were lying dead among you!"
>
> Then he thanked us for being so loyal to him then and now and shook our hands.
>
> When he had gone round the whole circle he stepped back.
>
> "And now, to our dead comrades! *Heil!*"
>
> The *Heil* that burst out of twenty throats could have rent those walls in twain.

"The man who will lead us out of hardship is Hitler," wrote Hewel that December. "A short time after his release he will have the millions around him once more just like before the great betrayal – but more resolute and numerous than ever."

2 The Private Secretary

Between the discharge of Rudolf Hess from Landsberg on the second day of 1925, two weeks after Hitler who had secured his own premature release, and the Nazis' accession to power eight years later he was one of the moral mainsprings behind the Party's revival and its accretion in popularity: athletic, good-looking and widely acclaimed for his personal probity, he became something of an antipole to the political toughs and street gangsters by whom even then the image of the Party was tarnished.

Hitler made him his personal secretary at 300 Reichsmarks a month. Indeed, in the baggage that Hess had stowed in the borrowed Mercedes-Benz in which Ilse had fetched him from the Landsberg prison gate were the scores of stenograms in which he had jotted down his hours of conversation alone with his fellow convict Hitler, and these would serve as guidelines over the coming years as Hess drafted the Party's pamphlets, posters and proclamations. The Party was re-established, and volume one of *Mein Kampf* appeared in July. "We'll need two years to reconsolidate the Party, more or less," Hitler said to Hess, thinking far ahead. "After that it may take five, eight or ten years before we've pulled it off in the Reich!"

It served the Party's purpose well that, abandoning his hopes of earning a doctorate, Hess became an assistant on Professor Karl Haushofer's staff at the Deutsche Akademie, a body that had been founded in Munich on 5 May 1925. Here he researched the problems of the German minorities abroad, and the theory and practice of geopolitics. He read more deeply in the teachings of Ferdinand von Richthofen, Friedrich Ratzel and Rudolf Kjellén, and struck up an intimate relationship with the Professor's twenty-two-year-old son Albrecht.

It speaks volumes for Hess's open character that he took a liking to this brilliant young man. Albrecht had just earned his doctorate *summa cum laude* and was about to embark on journeys to the Americas and Asia. An enthusiastic and gifted pianist, like Hess himself, the younger Haushofer was of a poetic and romantic disposition; their friendship blossomed through the years although it very soon became plain that Albrecht, son of a half-Jewish mother, had no liking for the National Socialists as such.

Above all, he was an expert on Britain, and often wrote on Anglo-German relations in the journal, *Zeitschrift für Geopolitik*, that his father had founded in 1924.

Albert Krebs, the Party's then gauleiter in Hamburg, wrote later that Hess was no "primitive simpleton or hidebound fanatic", but a man "bordering almost on the pathological" in subtle sensibilities. He could listen calmly to contrary opinions; his thoughts followed "impeccable and legal" lines. But it was Hess who innocently created the image of an infallible Führer. When he spoke of "our Führer" the millions would adopt the phrase precisely because Hess himself was so intensely believable. Hess created too the fateful Führer principle, which stated *inter alia* the notion that everybody to whom orders were issued must accept implicitly that those orders were properly issued, by people properly empowered to issue them. As Krebs added, Hess was one of the very few National Socialists close to Hitler who never dreamed of abusing the Führer principle to further his own political ambitions or to feather his nest. Josef Goebbels, the shrewd Nazi gauleiter of Berlin, came to much the same view at the time. He wrote in his diary after spending the evening alone with Hess on 13 April 1926 that he found him "most decent, quiet, friendly, clever and reserved". Goebbels added, perhaps even pityingly, "He is a kind fellow."

A "decent" Nazi might not have much economic prospect in the late twenties. The Party was struggling, its own future uncertain. But – partly at Hitler's humorous prodding – one evening at the Osteria Bavaria restaurant, a favourite Munich haunt, Rudolf Hess proposed marriage to young Ilse, the student who had faithfully stood by him for seven years, never dreaming that sixty years of extraordinary excitement and bitter hardship were to follow. She had been more than a little jealous of the masculine intimacy that had flourished between Rudolf and Professor Haushofer; yet the old man witnessed their wedding on 20 December 1927, and Hitler also attended the ceremony.

Hitler and Hess campaigned tirelessly all round Germany, and slowly the Party gained in strength and popular support. It gained its first twelve seats in the Reichstag. Hess was not much of an orator himself, sweating blood over even the humblest speech – but he used his flying skills instead. He obtained a 12,000-Reichsmark loan to buy a small plane from a young aircraft designer called Willi Messerschmitt, painted a black swastika and the name of the Party newspaper, the *Völkischer Beobachter*, beneath its wings and buzzed rival political meetings. On 10 August 1930 he circled low for more than two hours over a republican meeting in the Exhibition Park in Munich, making it impossible for the indignant leftists to hear the visiting Reichstag deputy or to sing their fraternal songs.

POLICE STATEMENT *Munich, 23 September 1930*

Summonsed to appear, the private secretary of Adolf Hitler,
Walter Richard Rudolf Hess

born 26 April 1894; married; Bavarian national; parents, Fritz and Klara
née Münch, businessman and -woman of Alexandria, resident in
Munich, Löfftz Strasse 3, III, deposes as follows:

"I am a member of the National Socialist German Workers Party and
private secretary to Adolf Hitler. The M-23 airplane D.1920 with the
slogan *Völkischer Beobachter* is my private property. . . . I am paid by the
newspaper for advertising flights. . . . I was aware before take-off that a
Constitution Festival was being held by the Reichsbanner Black–Red–
Gold in the Exhibition Park. . . . I had no reason not to fly over the
ceremony as it is the newspaper's intent to advertise subscriptions not
only to its political friends but also to those more remote, even to its
opponents. . . . I might point out that I carry out advertising flights
over friendly political demonstrations too. . . .

I have a previous conviction for aiding and abetting high treason. . . .
I have a wife to support.

In that September's election the Nazis won 107 seats; 6,371,000
Germans had voted for them, but the bloodshed and street violence,
particularly in Berlin, had alienated many liberal observers. "Dear
Doctor," Hess pleaded with Albrecht Haushofer a month later, before he
went to England:

You'll probably be asked in England for your views on us and the
situation in Germany at large; please reply in similar vein to H.'s
[Hitler's] remarks to the correspondent of *The Times*.★ Describe us as we
are – as a wall against Bolshevism; if we weren't, the majority of our
voters would – in consequence of the catastrophic economic results of
the Treaties – have been on the radical left while the rest would not have
voted at all, which would again have done the left a favour. . . . As for
the meaning of Bolshevism, you can tell the British all about that from
what you saw before your very eyes.

But don't on the other hand give voice to misgivings. You won't do
any good whatever, and you'll be damaging the only anti-Bolshevik
movement in foreign eyes. Because even assuming your doubts were
justified you would be frustrating all the hopes vested in this Movement,
and Germany would be beyond salvation. The Movement is the last
hope for millions of people! And believe me, your doubts are unfounded
– I can assure you of this from what I know myself. You are labouring
too much under the impressions from Berlin, which is in an altogether

★ Hitler stated in an interview published on 15 October 1930 in *The Times* that the Nazis
intended to repudiate reparations obligations. "A National Socialist Germany would never sign
cheques it could not honour. It would not make the political payments, because it would not
honestly be able to; but, like any honest merchant, it would honour all obligations to repay
private foreign loans and investments. If the world insisted on the political payments being
made, then Germany would go under."

different position. A number of Communist provocateurs there undoubtedly managed to infiltrate our ranks, and the hysterical Berliners were easy meat for them. But we're hot on their trail and they're being thrown out on their ear, one after the other.

I'm writing you this in the conviction that we're talking not just about the Party but about Germany, and that it is of universal importance – perhaps for the whole of Europe that is threatened by Bolshevism – how our National Socialist movement is assessed abroad and particularly in Britain. And you will probably be coming into contact with influential men over there.

Its finances swollen by the mushrooming sales of Hitler's book – the second volume had now been published – the Party opened an imposing headquarters building, the Brown House, in the centre of Munich on the first day of 1931; a few weeks later Hess proudly showed off his first-floor offices to his old professor, Karl Haushofer. They were right next to those of Hitler, Goebbels, Gregor Strasser, head of the Political Organization section, and Ernst Röhm, commander of the Sturmabteilung.

Although neither allowed the other the familiar *Du*, Hess was closest to Hitler at other times too: it was Hess who telephoned from Munich one day later that year to break the news that Hitler's beloved niece Geli had shot herself with Hitler's pistol and in his apartment.

Hess willingly hitched his star to Hitler's; he worshipped him like the Messiah, and Hitler knew he could count on him. "Once," reminisced Hitler years later, "the police raided the Brown House. There was a steel safe in my room there, filled with important documents. I had one key with me in Berlin, Hess had the other. The police demanded that he open the safe. He said I'd have to do it and he was very sorry but I was in Berlin. So the police had no choice but to seal it and await my return."

The next day Hess rang his Führer: "You can come!"

"Uh? That's not possible!"

"No," he said. "It's okay: it's empty!"

Since Hitler still could not grasp what had happened, he said cautiously: "Take it from me, I can't tell you on the 'phone. But you can come."

"Are the seals still on it?"

"Yes, unbroken!"

Hitler laughed. "Hess", he said later, explaining the mystery to his staff, "was always very handy at do-it-yourself. He'd spotted that you could unscrew the handles without breaking the seals."

The safe was opened, emptied and relocked, and the seals replaced intact. Hitler appeared for the ceremonial opening of the safe – of course he huffed and puffed, he talked of civil liberties, he promised there was nothing in it. When the police then threatened to break into the safe he relented and opened it, to the guffaws of his staff and the discomfiture of Munich's finest.

"I told you there was nothing in it!" triumphed Hitler.

Hess's role became that of the visible conscience of the Party. The public felt that, as long as he was still there, nothing evil could be afoot. When Gregor Strasser began to disrupt the Party in 1932, Hitler used Hess as a buffer. Already suffering from nutritional and nervous ailments probably directly related to the strains deriving from Nazi political life, Hess fobbed off the radical Strasser with letters that began with phrases like, "As I am tending my magnificent specimens of carbuncles, far from the sound of battle, I can't see you personally, nor will Mr Hitler have dreamed of telling you his real desires when he saw you. So he's asked me to tell you this. . . ." Hitler streamlined the Party, swept out the left-leaning Strasser and the other opposition elements and set up a Politische Central-Commission under his trusty henchman Hess. This put Hess in charge of directing Party strategy.

Whether in prominent seats at Wagner's opera *The Mastersingers* or at the secret meeting with former Chancellor Franz von Papen at the Cologne home of banker Baron Kurt von Schröder on 4 January 1933 – the overture to the final seizure of power later that month – it was Hess who stood next to his Führer. When that glorious day came, he was to be seen at the window next to Hitler and Göring, saluting the torchlight victory parade. But it could not be overlooked that Hess was not included in any role either in the first Cabinet that Hitler formed on 30 January 1933 or in the enlarged Nazi government that took power after the general election in March 1933 – a few days after the Communist Van der Lubbe had set fire to the Reichstag building in Berlin.

Rewarding Hess for thirteen years of dogged devotion, Hitler signed a decree on 21 April 1933:

> I appoint the director of the Political Central Commission, Rudolf Hess, as my deputy and authorize him to decide all matters concerning the direction of the Party in my name.

But Hess was not satisfied with purely Party affairs and told Hermann Göring, whom Hitler had just appointed Prime Minister of Prussia, that he wanted a hand in the affairs of state too. Göring, seeking allies, arranged for him to move into the palace in Wilhelm Strasse that really belonged to him as Prime Minister of Prussia, and persuaded Hitler to empower Hess, by a decree dated 29 June, to attend all sessions of the Reich Cabinet. A few months later, on 1 December, the Cabinet enacted a law "to ensure the unity of Party and State", which granted to Hess the dignity of Cabinet rank, as a Reich Minister without Portfolio.

To handle the expanding task of managing the Party, with all its funds at his disposal, Hess set up his own Office of Deputy Führer with Martin Bormann, a thick-necked ex-farmer, as chief of staff from July 1933. Bormann was 5 feet 7 inches of muscle and brain, driven by sexual and political ambition. Aged thirty-three, he had joined the Party in 1927 and had managed its relief fund for the last three years. Women were fascinated by his ruthless manner and domineering charm; with his patient wife Gerda he would father ten children (Hess was satisfied after ten years of marriage with one).

When later that year the journalist Alfred Leitgen interviewed Hess for the Berlin illustrated tabloid *Nachtausgabe* it was Bormann who persuaded him to join the staff as Hess's press officer. Hess instructed him to watch the Party's image in the foreign (and primarily the English-speaking) press; winning Hess's confidence, Leitgen shortly accepted the post as his personal adjutant – an acceptance which he would later have cause to regret.

As he set about the self-imposed task of reshaping and unifying Germany, on 3 May 1933 Hess authorized Robert Ley to set up a monolithic Labour Front in place of the warring and often Marxist-dominated labour unions. On 10 July he set up a Universities Commission: its job was to cleanse and purify the streams of higher education of unpatriotic and Marxist influences; a year later he would take control of the Party's student organizations, and a few months after that he would abolish all its rivals by decree. On 16 April 1934 he would create a body to censor all publications relating to Party history – and, as irony would have it, this was the body that would, in time, order the name of Rudolf Hess to be expunged from all books and official publications throughout the Reich. Continuing the cleansing process, Hess ruled that former Freemasons could not hold Party office.

Hitler had turned over to him responsibility for tending the twenty million *Volksdeutsche* – ethnic Germans trapped beyond the present frontiers by the Versailles Treaty or by other quirks of geography; the *Reichsdeutsche*, native Germans living overseas, were the responsibility of the Party's Auslands-Organisation (AO), run by Gauleiter Ernest William Bohle, who had himself been born in Bradford, England, and was in theory Hess's subordinate.

Since this new task revolved around issues of political geography Hess resumed close contact with the Haushofers. It was a risky step, because they were a marked family, given that the *materfamilias*, Martha, was half-Jewish: already on 10 March an armed Nazi gang had ransacked the Professor's house for hidden weapons. On 16 July, however, Hess had visited him to discuss "Aryan affairs", as Martha guardedly recorded, and on 19 August he personally signed a "letter of protection" for her two sons, Albrecht and Heinz, which safeguarded their professional futures; three weeks later, after he intervened with Dr Goebbels as Minister of Public Enlightenment, Albrecht was appointed to the chair of geo-politics at the Berlin College of Politics.

Later that year, on 27 October 1933, Hess would invite the Professor to preside over a new *Volksdeutscher Rat* (Council), seven of whose eight expert members were non-Party members. It angered the hardline Nazis that this council pursued non-Party policies, and soon Gauleiter Bohle demanded a seat on the council. Karl Haushofer appealed to Hess, but Hess's health was often indifferent and he felt powerless to defend the *Volksdeutsche* council's original neutrality. By the autumn of 1934, Bohle had muscled his way in. In January 1935 the Professor tried once more to persuade Hess to act: Hess was charming as ever, promised to help, but did nothing. He had grown politically impotent in the face of Bormann's hunger for personal power.

Albrecht meanwhile began to work as a secret emissary abroad for the Deputy Führer – partly out of patriotism but also because of the continued leverage that Hess was able to exert, thanks to his personal relationship with Hitler, on behalf of friends who were endangered because of their religion or politics. Thus the summer of 1933 found Albrecht Haushofer attending talks in Danzig and negotiating secretly with US Ambassador Thomas Dodd, and putting out feelers in Britain on Hess's behalf. That August saw them both acting in tandem to protect Dr Heinrich Brüning, often called "the last of the Weimar Chancellors", when his life was endangered by the SA rowdies in 1933.

> . . . a matter of great delicacy [wrote Albrecht Haushofer in confidence to Hess on 24 August 1933].
>
> As you well know there are people throughout your organization who have not been able to reconcile their eagerness to do something with the true interests of the whole community. I have learned that a personage who is living completely withdrawn in the interior but who still has a truly great name, H——h B——g, has cause to fear for his personal safety. The author of these fears, so I am told, is the SA Standartenführer 3, Schöneberg.
>
> I need hardly say what repercussions an accident to B's person would have abroad.
>
> Can you do something internally to apply restraints?

Hess could and did; on 7 September Albrecht Haushofer wrote thanking him for his timely intervention "in the B. affair". After living in Germany under Hess's personal protection until June 1934 Brüning emigrated to England just two weeks before the bloodbath which otherwise would probably have included him among its victims as well as his interim successor, General Kurt von Schleicher.

The events leading up to 30 June 1934 – the Night of the Long Knives – showed how little influence Hitler's puritan deputy had from his headquarters in Munich over the rowdies and extremists on the left wing of the Party all over Germany. The bloated and unruly two-million-strong SA "army" commanded by their former beerhall-*putsch* crony, the homosexual Ernst Röhm, was running out of control. Ever since the "seizure of power" they had stormed town halls, banks and insurance firms, and turfed non-Aryan executives out into the street.

In strings of decrees during 1933 Hess had tried to halt this trend. He was then architect of a little-known law passed in May 1933 guaranteeing the freedom of religious thought. He forbade SS, SA or other Party men to "intervene in the internal affairs of economic institutions". The SA paid no heed. Pointing out that every workplace was vitally needed, on 7 July Hess prohibited any Party operations calculated to harass the big chain-stores or force them out of business (they had previously been a target of Nazi propaganda). But the SA's operations went on: nothing, it seemed, could damp down the fires of revolutionary ardour. Röhm in fact was already acting as though he were the number two in Germany. It was plain that he had even greater ambitions, and Hess was determined to protect his Führer from them. On 9 September he forbade Party functionaries to hold diplomatic receptions; Röhm ignored him, and threw gala dinners for the Berlin diplomatic corps that were more lavish than those of the Foreign Ministry. On 22 January 1934 Hess published in the Party newspaper a warning that there was "not the slightest need" for the SA or other component organizations to "lead an independent existence". In a speech he warned, "You want to be more revolutionary than the Führer – but the Führer alone determines the tempo of the revolution!" Still Röhm ignored him.

Early in March a worried SA commander, Viktor Lutze, confidentially brought to Hess eye-witness accounts of Röhm's plans to overthrow the regime. Anxious to conciliate, Hess urged the Party's gauleiters at a meeting in Mecklenburg on 25 May to go easy on the SA. But events now took their course: Röhm had made too many enemies, and SS chief Heinrich Himmler, Göring and the army joined in an unholy alliance to force Hitler to cut him down.

What happened then is well known. Hess's precise role in the massacre of 30 June 1934 was often misrepresented by the malicious or ill-informed in later years, mostly on the basis of the history published by the author Konrad Heiden.* From the account of his adjutant Alfred Leitgen, who was with Hess in Bavaria that day, it is plain that he pleaded with Hitler *not* to shed the blood of their closest friends. "The Röhm *putsch*", Leitgen stated afterwards, "was probably one of the worst strains on Hess. He was in Munich at the time. . . . He fought tooth and nail with Hitler to save some of those men, and refused to be intimidated by even the most violent outbursts from Hitler. He saved a lot of men's lives – we'll never know how many." Their argument lasted several hours, as Leitgen, in an adjacent room, could hear. "Hess was deeply affected by this eruption of personal brutality in Hitler. His pronounced – I would say almost

---

* Konrad Heiden, *Adolf Hitler. Das Zeitalter der Verantwortungslosigkeit. Eine Biographie*, published in Switzerland in two volumes, 1936–7, and in English-speaking countries as *Der Führer*. Heiden – according to Julius Schaub, Hitler's personal adjutant, a pseudonym for a Jewish émigré – siphoned his scuttle-butt from disgruntled Nazi official Otto Strasser, who had fled in 1933 to Switzerland. Like Hermann Rauschning's totally spurious *Gespräche mit Hitler* (Zürich, 1940) Heiden's work was used as a basis for formulating the Nuremberg indictment in 1945, and is a favourite source-book of uncritical historians.

feminine – instinct was hurt in every respect. In those few days he aged years."

As though unable to look his former comrades in the eye, Hitler left it to Rudolf Hess to sweat out the consequences. On 4 and 5 July Hess addressed soothing words to the Party's Reichsleiters and gauleiters at Flensburg, and on the 8th its political heads at Königsberg in East Prussia. "Special thanks of the Movement", he said in a broadcast speech there, "are due to the SS, who in these days honouring their slogan Our Honour Is Our Loyalty carried out their duties in exemplary manner." He likened the massacre to ancient decimation – "that is, the execution of every tenth man, irrespective of whether he was guilty or innocent". However, he found it hard to explain to them the killing of men like Gregor Strasser, their former Organization Leader. He could not even explain it to himself. Moreover, his office had to deal with the influx of protests from the widows and children.

He was not at ease in this. Nora Villain, widow of the murdered SA doctor Erwin Villain, was notified simply that the Deputy Führer was not aware of the individual details and had forwarded her letter to the Gestapo. "Dear Mr Reichsminister," another woman, the fiancée of SA-Standartenführer Herbert Merker, wrote to Hess on the 12th: "My fiancé has been in the Columbia House [Gestapo HQ] since Sunday. Neither he nor his many comrades have been questioned to this day. . . . I beg you to return him to his unit at once so that informers don't use his absence to destroy SA unity." When it turned out that a Hitler Youth, Karl Lämmermann, had been shot as a homosexual on the perjured testimony of three others, Hess did authorize a Hitler wreath for the funeral, but not a rehabilitation. And then there was SA-Standartenführer Gottlieb Rösner, who wrote to Hess about one Karl Belding – missing and presumed dead since the 30th. The Gestapo had sent his widow a box with his "rusty house keys and an emptied purse". "As you can imagine," protested Rösner, "the wife and child are horrified."

Incongruously, Karl Haushofer of all people sent to Hess a fulsome letter of congratulations on the "great" deed, dated 1 July; but this merely documented the public's mood of relief at the end of the SA.

A few days later, on 27 July 1934, Hitler decreed that with the aim of streamlining Party and state his deputy should have a say in the drafting of all future legislation. Major laws like that introducing conscription on 16 March 1935 would bear Hess's formal signature. Yet he hardly had time to scrutinize them. He was taken by surprise by the Nuremberg Laws that September, which excluded Jews from professional and public life in Germany. These had been drafted by the lawyers and civil servants working at the direction of Wilhelm Stuckart in the busy, distant warrens of the Ministry of the Interior; for Hess, Göring and the other ministers called on to co-sign them they were a cuckoo's egg which they would find hard, in later years, to explain away.

The explanation for Hess's non-intervention was simple: his influence was waning. His timetable was swamped with ceremonial occasions as Hitler's deputy, such as awarding the Mother's Cross to the more fecund of Germany's females. His desk was stacked with provincial (Länder) legislation: that same year saw the Law Concerning Municipalities (Gemeindeordnung), attaching a Party delegate to every mayor's staff; no civil service official or Labour Service leader could henceforth be appointed without his consent.

During 1934 and 1935 Hitler put more and more distance between himself and the Party that had carried him into office.

He discouraged every hint by Rudolf Hess that the Party should move its headquarters to Berlin, and allowed only a small liaison staff at the Chancellery itself. The three Party-controlled departments located in Berlin were, however, of some importance: apart from Bohle's Auslands-Organisation there was Fritz Todt's department planning Germany's revolutionary new autobahn system and the Ribbentrop Bureau (Dienststelle) founded by Joachim von Ribbentrop, the ambitious businessman whom Hitler had appointed his specialist on international disarmament questions. It was to this latter office that Hess secured the attachment of his academic-misfit friend, young Dr Albrecht Haushofer.

The volume of work in Munich and Berlin was staggering. Without the organizing skill and dynamic energy of Bormann, Hess probably would not have coped. He took on two extra personal secretaries – Hildegard Fath in Munich, and Ingeborg Sperr in Berlin.

Miss Fath was engaged to one of his relatives. She came on to his staff on 17 October 1933; the tragic death of her fiancé on the last day of the year brought her into the Hess family's circle, and only here did she find the real Rudolf Hess, because at home he could unbend, relax and show a wit and intellect that his over-official, tense (*verkrampft*) manner had concealed. She described his sense of duty as fanatical. Paced – and increasingly outpaced – by the relentless, ruthless Martin Bormann he pushed himself beyond the normal limits of patience and endurance, biting back his anger at each misfortune or ugly symptom of the Party's lawlessness. He never lost his temper, and this was perhaps his real trouble: his one row with Ilse occurred when she had overspent their humble weekly allowance. The family house at Harlaching, on the fringes of Munich, was only modest; he had no weekend house.

His kindness to animals was almost ludicrous: grief-stricken when his brother Alfred's dog was shot by a stranger, he was visibly hurt when Miss Fath gently mocked his tears. And he was sad that he had no child of his own as yet, because he regarded his sexual appetite as normal and he led an active life. He went skiing, climbing and walking in the hills, although his old lung injury left him short of breath on the steeper slopes.

In 1933 he had begun staying for weekends at a clinic in Bavaria. It was here that Geoffrey Shakespeare, an under-secretary at the British

Ministry of Health, often met him over the next three years, because his son attended the same clinic. In 1933 he had inspected the Munich Housing Scheme, and so met Hess more formally. The Deputy Führer – who was, Geoffrey Shakespeare found, the most popular man in all Germany after Hitler himself – told him he was taking English lessons, as he had decided to do all he could to cement his country's friendship with Britain. Shakespeare often went chamois-stalking with him after that, and attended his social functions when he was in Bavaria. Shakespeare saw the uncomplicated foundations upon which Hess's life was constructed. He was "entirely devoted to Hitler, who is his God"; an intensely patriotic man of "superb courage" but no great intellectual gifts; a simple soul with "a queer streak of mysticism", and a "glance and countenance" that gave the impression of an unbalanced mind. But if Hess betrayed one fixed idea when they met it was this: "That there was no reason why Germany could not exercise supreme power in Europe, without lessening the power of the British empire in the world".

His health cracking under the guilty strain of being Deputy Führer, Hess had begun attending the clinic with serious problems which he blamed at the time on his gall bladder – excruciating abdominal cramps, in respect of which the doctors, however, found neither evidence nor cure. Unable to sleep, he deliberately drove himself to the point of exhaustion, dictating speeches – like the great Sport Palace speech on 7 January 1935 before the Saar plebiscite – sometimes until 2 a.m. "Once," wrote Ingeborg Sperr, who joined his staff on 1 May 1934, "I had to stand in for Miss Fath in his private home in Munich and I saw him trying out a new means of getting to sleep: he would go to bed at 5 p.m., and get up at 3 or 4 a.m. to go for a walk, because that was what some nature-healer had recommended to him."

As he lost faith in the orthodox physicians who had failed to produce the rapid cure he demanded for his complaints, Rudolf Hess moved into the camp of "alternative" medicine. Dr Ludwig Schmitt, a graduate of the universities of Tübingen and Munich, who would be his last regular doctor from 1936 to 1939, saw it happening. A decade later, still vexed at losing a powerful patient, Schmitt talked freely about Hess, claiming to have observed a tendency towards schizophrenia in the Deputy Führer; Hess was, in his opinion, "mildly psychopathic". "On one occasion in my office," Schmitt claimed, "Hess broke down and wept over Röhm's death, blaming himself for it." Hitler had planned to spare the SA commander, according to Schmitt, but Hess confessed to him that he had insisted on Röhm's death. He was worried too about Bormann and Dr Ley undermining his position with Hitler; he hinted that his two powerful underlings were misappropriating funds from *Mein Kampf* sales and the Volkswagen dividends – but he was powerless to take action against either.

Hess took a close interest in public health issues. Puzzled at the failure of orthodox medicine to develop cures for cancer, he argued that healers beyond the pale of medical orthodoxy should also be given a hearing – an indulgent attitude that attracted Homeric laughter from the professionals. He became involved in this issue initially through the ethical problems raised by advertising censorship (which came within his purview). "He could not", explained Leitgen, "see why he should ban advertising by naturopaths [*Heilpraktiker*] when it was allowed to astrologers, water diviners and other seers."

The regular doctors had certainly failed Hess. Although he maintained an athletic lifestyle, he tired frequently. He tried dieting – cutting out eggs, jams, and dried foods and caffeine – but his stomach cramps persisted. The doctors regarded them as typical hysterical symptoms; Schmitt wrote him off as a hypochondriac. Dissatisfied, Hess would turn in 1939 to the nature healers – unqualified men offering nature's cures: the chiropractors and irido-diagnosticians. Discussing this latter "science" with an American doctor years later Hess asked, "Do you know about the studies of the size of the pupil of the eye?" He explained, "I mean diagnosis based on the size and shape of the pupil. . . . A scientist – he wasn't a medical man – and I studied it a long time: by the change in the pupil you can not only tell what is wrong with anyone, you can tell where his illness is." The American surgeon confessed himself ignorant of this, and expressed sincere appreciation when Hess offered to arrange a session – although perhaps seance would have been a more fitting word. The American privately looked forward to meeting the man who could sell such an idea to anybody, even to the gullible Deputy Führer. Hess's own secretaries sniggered each time the two *Naturheiler* arrived, and called them his "sorcerers" (*Zauberer*).

Occasionally he went on journeys, and the separation from work and worries did him good. "On one vacation journey with him," wrote Miss Sperr, however, "I saw an 'eye-diagnostician' giving him medication that he had concocted himself, and massaging him. I was baffled by it all – this man made an extremely primitive impression."

When Hitler quietly ridiculed his deputy, Hess earnestly sent him a copy of the correspondence between Fredersdorf and Frederick the Great concerning such alternative medicines – as though medical science had made no advances in two hundred years. Of course Hitler's own choice of physician, the unsightly and controversial Dr Theo Morell, was hardly one of whom Germany's eminent physicians could approve; the same was true of Himmler (who placed himself in the hands of a Swedish masseur) and Ribbentrop.

By 1941, the year in which this book's main event took place, Hess's medicine cabinet was stuffed with homeopathic and nature-cure medicines. They had been furnished by Dr Kurt Schauer of the homeopathic clinic at Höllriegelskreuth, south of Munich, and by a Mr Reutter – evidently the "eye-diagnostician" – of Hohenzollern Strasse. When Hess set out on his famous flight, his uniform pockets would be filled with their potions, including an elixir obtained by the Swedish explorer Dr Sven

Hedin from a Tibetan lama – said to work wonders with the gall bladder – and glucose and multi-vitamin tablets that Hitler's portly doctor Theo Morell had given him, as well as an amazing assortment of drugs needed to ward off "all assaults of the devil", as the British Medical Research Council put it after examining the haul. "He seems to have protected himself (1) against the pains of injury by opium alkaloids; (2) against the discomfort of headaches by aspirin, etc; (3) against the pains of colic by atropin; (4) against the fatigue of flying by Pervitin [an amphetamine stimulant]; (5) against the sleeplessness following Pervitin by barbiturates." Amongst his effects were also "mixtures of unknown products made up along homeopathic lines – i.e., so dilute that it is impossible to say what they are."

Hitler ordered the arrest of everybody who had contributed to this state of affairs, beginning with the doctors themselves. Ludwig Schmitt would be among those arrested and consigned forthwith to Sachsenhausen concentration camp as a "personal prisoner of the Führer" accused of having used witchery to rob him of his deputy. "One thing is plain," foamed Hitler at the Party's confused gauleiters assembled on 13 May 1941 at his mountain home, brandishing his deputy's fourteen-page farewell letter, "Hess was completely in the hands of astrologers, eye-diagnosticians and nature-healers! And now he has gone to Britain – in the mad hope of seeing his English friends and making peace between Germany and Britain!"

3 The Wailing Wall

There is no reason to suppose that the Deputy Führer was unfamiliar with, or frowned upon, Hitler's aim of enlarging Germany's living space to the east. "With Hess," remarked his adjutant Alfred Leitgen, "the aversion to the Asiatic–Bolshevik ideology was so marked as to be almost pathological." For this historic task, Japan and perhaps even Britain had to be wooed and won.

On 7 April 1934 Hess very privately met the Japanese Naval Attaché Admiral Yendo on Professor Haushofer's glass-walled porch at 18 Kolberger Strasse and made a semi-official overture to him (aware that both the German army and the Foreign Ministry strongly preferred China to Japan). While Martha Haushofer poured the tea, the Professor interpreted. Initially both men were guarded in their remarks, but then Hess threw caution to the winds: "Well, I can inform you – and I'm speaking in the name of the Führer – that we sincerely want Germany and Japan to draw together. But I must stress that this can't involve anything that might jeopardize our relations with Britain." Yendo's face split into an enthusiastic smile that revealed all his gold teeth, and Haushofer relaxed. In his unpublished memoirs he described this meeting as the first step taken towards the Anti-Comintern Pact that the two countries signed in November 1936.

Simultaneously, with the help of his brilliant and widely travelled – but increasingly anti-Nazi – diplomatic adviser Albrecht Haushofer, Hess wove a thick web of threads towards the British. Had not Hitler himself written in *Mein Kampf*, "No sacrifice should have been too great in winning Britain's friendship"? It was a labour of love for Hess: born under British rule, in Egypt, he had a deep and natural predisposition towards their empire. Albrecht Haushofer too respected Britain, though for more pragmatic reasons. He had harped on Anglo–German relations in the monthly *Zeitschrift für Geopolitik*. "The ultimate decision on the fate of Europe", he wrote in April 1935, "lies today in English hands, just as it did in the tense years at the turn of the century . . . when the British empire and the Kaiser's Reich, after vain attempts to steer a common course, began to drift apart."

For four years Hess and the younger Haushofer arranged private meetings with British visitors – dozens of whom flocked to Hitler's Berlin in the mid-thirties eager to witness the revolution at first hand. Secret German transcripts (destroyed by Allied command after the war) recorded Hitler's meetings with these Englishmen, including Leo Amery, Lord Londonderry, Lord Beaverbrook (three times), Stanley Baldwin's secretary Tom Jones, Sir Thomas Beecham and others.

Called upon to explain his actions, two days after Hess's flight in May 1941, Albrecht Haushofer would list for Hitler the names of those on whom he had personally worked between 1934 and 1938 in Britain: from "a leading group of younger Conservatives" he mentioned Lord Clydesdale (who inherited the title Duke of Hamilton in 1940); the Prime Minister's Parliamentary Private Secretary Lord Dunglass (later known as Sir Alec Douglas-Home); Harold Balfour, Kenneth Lindsay and Jim Wedderburn, under-secretaries at the Air Ministry, Education Ministry and Scottish Office respectively; Hamilton's brother, he pointed out, was related to Queen Elizabeth and his mother-in-law the Duchess of Northumberland was Her Majesty's chief lady-in-waiting; close to the same circle were Lord Derby, Oliver Stanley, Lord Astor and Sir Samuel Hoare. Furthermore, Haushofer bragged, he had obtained access to Lord Halifax, the Foreign Secretary, and his deputy R. A. Butler. He named too Lord Lothian, who had visited Hess and Hitler in Berlin on 23 January 1935, and he identified William Strang and Owen O'Malley, both department heads in the British Foreign Office, as being closet supporters of an Anglo-German entente.

According to his adjutant, Hess's basic political concept was that the Nordic countries had a duty to avoid fighting any more wars with each other, if their influence throughout the world was not to be totally destroyed. So he always made time to receive visitors from Britain, particularly if they were old soldiers like himself. He never forgot the visit that the British Legion's president, General Sir Ian Hamilton, paid to Berlin. General Hamilton, veteran of the disastrous Gallipoli landings in 1915, made plain to Hess that he too felt it would be suicidal for the white race if Britain and Germany fell out once more. Each time Hess looked at the oily career diplomats of the Wilhelm Strasse, he regretted that it was not left to veterans like himself and General Hamilton to decide foreign policy: "Hess's view before the war", recalled Leitgen afterwards, "was that establishing friendly relations with foreign countries should be left to war veterans."

At that time, Karl Haushofer was to write, Ribbentrop shared Hess's roseate view of Anglo-German relations. Together with Hess, he and their young England expert Albrecht Haushofer attended the dinner that Hitler gave for the visiting British diplomatists Sir John Simon and Anthony Eden on 26 March 1935. A few weeks later, Ribbentrop signed the Anglo-German Naval Agreement in London; Hess and Hitler hoped that this was only the first step towards a full alliance.

In May 1935 the Swedish count Eric von Rosen, Göring's brother-in-law, invited Hess to explain the new National Socialist Germany to his country's high society. Speaking to 1500 people packed into the biggest hall in Stockholm and visibly delighted to be in the land of his idol, Rudolf Kjellén, Hess delivered a speech that glittered with elegance and style. He repeatedly emphasized his personal desire as a war-scarred veteran himself to restore peaceful coexistence among all nations. He showed sympathy for the problems of Hitler's former critics, who had been taken by surprise by the speed and durability of the Hitler revolution as it spread through German economic, scientific and family life.

Hitler's creed, he explained, was rooted in the sense of sacrifice and comradeship born during the war – during which, however, "some people" at home had swindled and profiteered their way to fortunes. "I myself", he added, "was not an anti-Semite until then; on the contrary I defended the Jews against their persecutors and opponents. But the facts of 1918 and later years were so self-evident that I became converted to anti-Semitism, try though I might not to. . . ." "National Socialist legislation", he continued soberly, "has now introduced corrective measures against this over-alienization. I say corrective, because the proof that the Jews are not being ruthlessly rooted out [*ausgerottet*] is that in Prussia alone 33,500 Jews are working in manufacturing and industry, and 89,800 are engaged in trade and commerce; and that with only 1 per cent of the population Jewish, 17.5 per cent of our attorneys and in Berlin nearly half the registered doctors are still Jewish."

Turning to the violent face of Communism, Hess revealed that in the same province, Prussia, 640 police officers had died at the hands of the Spartacists and Bolsheviks. Nearly six million Germans had voted for the Communists in 1932; millions more would have *become* Communists if they had won the election! Europe had Hitler to thank for averting that grave risk. "I had the good fortune to hear him speak way back in 1920 before but a dozen of his followers and I knew at the end of that speech: if this man can't save Germany, nobody can!"

A few minutes later Hess commended to them his reasons for trusting Hitler. They said as much about his own character as about that of his Führer.

Was it by chance that he came?
    I think not. I think there is a providence that sends to nations that don't deserve to go under – that still have a mission to fulfil in this world – the man to preserve them from disaster. But such a man must then be given absolute power.
    You may object that it is not good to put all power in the hands of one man. You may object that in the end even an Adolf Hitler runs the risk of exercising his solitary dominion arbitrarily or imprudently.
    I can but reply: the conscience of one upright personality is a far greater check upon the abuse of office than all your Parliamentary organs

of control or division of powers. And I know from my knowledge of Adolf Hitler the man that there is nobody more beholden to his conscience and, on the strength of that conscience, to his people than he. His conscience – his responsibility to his God, to his people and to history – that is his ultimate authority.

He does weigh the correctness of his actions by addressing himself to his people direct, holding plebiscites from time to time. And they will confirm his leadership, again and again! He knows that his honour is inseparably bound up with all his actions. He cannot hide responsibility behind the decisions of irresponsible Parliamentary majorities.

A later history will write of what Hitler has done to consolidate not only Germany's future, but that of the whole of Europe.

Hess in turn attracted the same kind of blind devotion from his personal staff. "Instilling confidence," Leitgen said later, "that is what I would have called his forte."

While Ribbentrop and Bormann merely exploited their chief's popularity to further their own ambitions, his private staff would have walked over coals for him. "We all, his employees," wrote Miss Fath in November 1945, "liked him very much and as far as I know the men of his staff and the political leaders liked and admired him too." She dealt with the letters arriving at the humble Hess household at 48 Harthauser Strasse in Harlaching. "Most of them", she said, "were from people who did not know him personally, but they were full of trust that he could help them in their troubles – or of thanks for help he had already given." The fan mail after his Christmas or New Year speeches was enormous. It struck her very forcibly that whenever he dictated a letter of reproach Hess invariably added some charitable suggestion for improvement – he "built a bridge", and never wittingly gave offence.

"He was so kind and noble that one felt obliged to be the same way," Miss Fath recalled, still pained from the shock of seeing him handcuffed and in a prison cell. She described one occasion when he got home so late that his supper had to be warmed again and again; Ilse Hess scolded him for making the cook and serving-maid stay up so late. Afterwards the maid whispered to Miss Fath: "Please tell him we're quite willing to work any time of day or night for him. We never mind that. We're glad to do something for him." "Perhaps," reflected Miss Fath, "that was his mistake: he was *too* kind; he presumed everybody else was as honest and upright as himself."

His incorruptibility extended to his dealings with his family. He wanted to help his father's import business in Alexandria but told him that the result must be an increase in foreign-currency earnings and that the application must therefore go through proper channels. However, Egypt was now swarming with troops, since Mussolini had invaded Abyssinia, and Hess hoped that this would be good for his father's business. "Perhaps," he wrote to his father on 24 October 1935, "the current Arab animosity towards the Italians will result in them buying more German goods."

This letter – which was intercepted by British Intelligence – gives a good picture of Hess as dutiful son and Deputy Führer in 1935. It showed that he had persuaded Hitler to leave his friend Eberhard Stohrer as Ambassador to Egypt and to receive the young diplomat in person. "Stohrer has told me of the [Alexandria harbour] fortifications at El Mex, Abu Qir, and so on. . . . It must be very interesting over there nowadays! I'd be most interested in the British warships in the harbour particularly since I know the part played at Jutland by some of them like [the battleship] *Queen Elizabeth* and her sisters."

"There is now", Hess continued in this private letter to his father, "widespread envy of Germany's position. She has nothing more to do with the League of Nations farce, but is able to stand aside without fear of being dragged defencelessly, kicking and screaming, into some squabble or other. Our rowdier friends sneak glances at us, appraising us as a really noteworthy ally – if we were ready for such a role. But I don't really think there's going to be a war over it. The last one is too vividly in memory all round."

No, Hess was not one of the more bellicose members of Hitler's entourage.

As for his family, he reported to their father that brother Alfred (who worked for Bohle's Auslands-Organisation) was recovering in Berlin from a stomach operation. With a trace of fraternal glee Rudolf wrote that top surgeon Professor Ferdinand Sauerbruch had insisted that Alfred cut down on smoking; their much younger sister Grete was looking good and had returned from Hindelang looking slimmer with her bad knee fixed "thanks to some jabs from Dr Gerl" – a local doctor there (of whom more will be heard anon).

"Ilse is acting as 'supervising architect' at Harlaching most of the time. You've probably heard by now that our perennial plan of enlarging the house is taking shape. I'd have preferred to postpone it but it has really become urgent. Above all I need a bigger dining room, because now and then I have to invite a large number of officers – for instance, it will soon be Wehrmacht officers – and we couldn't handle that in our present dining room. I need a bigger study too because whenever a lot of people have visited me so far I have had to use the drawing room and then there's nothing for our own use."

Meanwhile, he was having to live in Berlin, where Ilse visited him for relaxation at weekends – "it's a topsy-turvy world!" Berlin was a city that he detested; but he hoped the chaos was worthwhile – it would enable his father and mother to come over for a few months in the spring of 1936, and live in the apartment he was adding on to Harlaching for them. "I'm really looking forward to going to the theatre with you after your life in Egypt's artistic and cultural desert."

Hess was a moderate among immoderate men. On 25 October 1934 he had issued a decree reserving to himself the sole right to act in the Party's name in Reich and Länder affairs. In the new law books were ordinances signed by him protecting the little man against the Party. He provided the long-stop to deflect some of the grosser nonsenses of the zealots: the real lawlessness would begin only after his departure.

Outrages had of course already begun but he tried to abate, prevent, ameliorate – both in the particular and in general. Alarmed by widespread abuses of the 20 December 1934 Law Against Malicious Attacks on State and Party, he issued on 3 September 1935 regulation No. 184/35 sharply modifying that law's force. "The Deputy of the Führer has introduced his right of joint decision," stated Bormann, signing the document, "specifically because he wants to avoid offenders being sent to prison for months for each petty offence." Hess's new regulation required gauleiters to report to him all such cases independently of any legal proceedings, to enable Hess to quash them or issue a simple reprimand instead.

In the worsening climate of hatred against the Jews, Hess's secret actions also spoke far more eloquently than public words. He never forgot the Haushofers, nor what he owed to them. Three days after the Nuremberg Laws were passed in September 1935 he privately telephoned the Professor to reassure him that neither his half-Jewish wife nor either of his sons need have any fear so long as he was there to protect them.

Six weeks earlier, on 2 August, Hess had issued a secret circular decree No. 160/35 prohibiting any kind of excesses by Party members against "Jews or Jewish provocateurs" and insisting on the most rigorous prosecution of anybody causing criminal damage or bodily harm to Jews, or guilty of riotous assembly against them. He believed in turning the other cheek. When a Jewish terrorist murdered Bohle's representative in Switzerland, Wilhelm Gustloff, in February 1936 Hess again issued secret orders to all Party and state officials "to prevent outrages against Jews". "It is for the Führer alone to decide what policy to adopt from case to case," ordered Hess. "No Party member is to act off his own bat."

A confidential speech by Hess to senior Party officials at Nuremberg in September 1937 touched upon their campaign against Jews, freemasons and the feuding clergy. "We are a soldierly movement," he said, "and we must keep discipline in this too!" He titillated them with the example of German firms who still employed Jews as their representatives abroad – "really magnificent specimens from East Galicia", he said, using the same word (*Prachtexemplare*) as when describing his carbuncles to the late Gregor Strasser.

"At the same time German import firms abroad", he said – mindful of his father's firm in Alexandria – "gradually went to the dogs." "There were cases", he continued, "where these allegedly indispensable Jews acted for foreign rivals at the same time and even participated in the boycott of German goods!" Gradually the Party had got its way and exports were booming. "AEG", stated Hess, "has written to the Party that replacing its Jewish agents with German ones has led to 'a major boost' in sales which has more than covered the costs of the changeover. . . . Auto-Union has stated much the same." Nor, he added, were freemasons to be trusted, and he related a horror story about the "half-Jewish freemason" who had represented a major German bank in Spain and had tried to torpedo trade negotiations there. Their enemies, boasted the Deputy Führer, using another military metaphor, were being forced to abandon one position after another. "Even if things seem to go slowly sometimes, what are a few years compared with a development which will determine the course of German history for centuries and which, in the field of race legislation, will still be showing results in thousands of years?"

According to the Party's 1937 handbook his responsibilities were manifold and important: he directed the NSDAP's internal organization and cultural activities, its Auslands-Organisation, its technical office and its Main Archives, as well as departments supervising national health, genealogical research, censorship, constitutional and legal issues, foreign policy, guidelines on race, and university appointments.

But all this was only on paper. In practice he had become the movement's "wailing wall", as he put it at Nuremberg that September; he hankered after the old days of illegality. "Sometimes I wish I could sit down as I used to in the bygone days of our struggle, brewing venom, drafting posters or leaflets, and pasting them up or handing them out with my own two hands: I think I'd be sleeping much better if I was!"

As it was, he had become the Party's status symbol: displaced increasingly by boorish and pushy subordinates, but still wheeled around the countryside to bedazzle the masses, reassure the bankers and industrialists, and placate the nervous foreign diplomats. If there were shortages or unpopular measures to be introduced, Berlin counted on Hess to make them palatable to the masses. Speaking at the dedication of the new Adolf Hitler Hall at Hof, Bavaria, in October 1936 he had reiterated Göring's slogan: GUNS INSTEAD OF BUTTER! "We shall be prepared, if necessary," he said on this occasion, "to consume in future a little less fat and pork and fewer eggs – because we know that the foreign exchange which we shall thereby save will be turned over to our rearmament programme." Statements like these – uttered at a time when Germany was surrounded by heavily armed nations – were all that later prosecutors could hold against him.

The same prosecutors made only grudging reference to his strenuous attempts to find peaceful solutions to Europe's problems. Through the medium of Dr Albrecht Haushofer he had remained active in secret diplomacy, although the focus of interest shifted from the *Volksdeutsche* problem to the English-speaking powers.

Hess had met Konrad Henlein, the leader of the Sudeten German party, as early as 19 September 1934 at his parents' home in the Fichtelgebirge mountains. In what would prove a fruitless attempt to settle Berlin's differences with Prague he had sent young Haushofer to see President Eduard Beneš twice in December 1936, offering a non-aggression pact with Czechoslovakia in return for concessions to Henlein's Sudeten Germans.

Responding to SS pressure Hess had set up on 27 January 1937 the Central Office for Ethnic Germans (Volksdeutsche Mittelstelle) under SS Obergruppenführer Werner Lorenz, to centralize political efforts among Germans abroad. This inevitably reduced the authority of the previous bodies working in this field, as well as introducing a sharper note into the methods employed, particularly in the south-east.

While these events had transpired, Rudolf Hess had encouraged Albrecht Haushofer to strengthen his links with the British.

Haushofer was at this time in an ambivalent mood, experiencing worsening qualms about working for the Nazis. He quietened his nagging conscience by reassuring himself that his immediate chief, Hess, was "clean" in every respect. "Looking at the tasks I have been set since 1933," he wrote to Hess in a bitter, reproachful letter in June 1936, "I have – even under microscopic self-appraisal – a spotless conscience." For the moment, the young academic enjoyed the Deputy Führer's confidence – and, of course, his continued protection, which was the other part of the equation.

And that was how, indirectly, the *via dolorosa* of Rudolf Hess began. That summer of 1936 Berlin hosted the Olympic Games. Among the British Members of Parliament invited to the opening ceremony on 1 August were Harold Balfour, Jim Wedderburn, Kenneth Lindsay and Douglas, Marquis of Clydesdale. (These were of course the "British contacts" that Haushofer would identify to Hitler, after Hess's flight in 1941.)

The handsome young Scot, Lord Clydesdale – later Douglas, Duke of Hamilton – was a former amateur middleweight boxing champion. A flying instructor in the Royal Auxiliary Air Force, he had been chief pilot of the British expedition to fly over Mount Everest three years earlier. In this respect he had much in common with Rudolf Hess, an aviator of equal skill and courage who had planned at one time to be the first pilot to cross the Atlantic in the opposite direction to Charles Lindbergh.

However, Hess was not formally introduced to this intrepid Scottish officer either on this occasion or during the following days and there is no evidence that they even met. He certainly had one talk with Lindsay but when, on the 12th, Hitler invited the English diplomat Sir Robert Vansittart to dinner at the Chancellery, both Lord Clydesdale and Hess were certainly present; if they exchanged glances or even polite remarks neither could remember it later. On the 13th, Göring whisked Clydesdale away from Berlin to cast a professional eye over his infant air force.

All the closer was the link that was almost immediately established between "Douglo" Hamilton and Hess's expert, Albrecht Haushofer. It happened like this. The Scottish aristocrat's young brother David Hamilton chanced to meet Haushofer at a Berlin function. The British MPs invited Haushofer to dine with them and he explained his dual position as an academic and as a diplomatic expert with direct access to both Hess and the Foreign Ministry.

Clydesdale – perhaps on authoritative instructions from Whitehall – wrote to Albrecht Haushofer that winter. The latter replied on 7 January 1937, and thus the link was cast: together with his father, the old professor, Albrecht Haushofer met Lord Clydesdale at their Bavarian estate on 23 January. A few weeks later the Scotsman sent to the Professor a copy of his memoirs, *The Pilot's Book of Everest*.

Several times that year Albrecht Haushofer visited Britain. In a letter to his father on 16 March 1937 he wrote, "I'm off there tomorrow, and I'll be guest at first of the young airman who visited us in Munich, L.C. [Lord Clydesdale]." He lectured at Chatham House to the Institute of International Affairs in April, and stayed at the Hamilton estate, Dungavel, in Scotland. It was the first time that he had seen Dungavel, or that Hess – to whom he reported afterwards – had heard of it.

A profound friendship grew between the two men; leaving for America on board the liner *Europa* the German academic thanked his Scottish host ("My dear Douglo") on 30 June, but displayed his concern over the steadily worsening European situation (the Spanish Republicans had just bombed a German battleship in the Mediterranean). It was what Haushofer had seen of the British and their attitudes that alarmed him the most. He warned Hess about them, and he composed a pessimistic article for the *Zeitschrift für Geopolitik*. "One cannot avoid the conclusion", he wrote, "that they [the British] regard neither Italy nor Japan (nor even the Soviet Union) as Public Enemy Number One. They are once again glaring across the North Sea" – at Germany.

Rudolf was now forty-three, and about to become a father for the first time. Ilse, uncomfortably aware of her rotundity, wrote a gossipy letter to her mother-in-law Klara Hess in Egypt that October: "By the way: in a day or two we're having a splendid visit. Just imagine, the Duke of Windsor and his wife! And they say she's just about the most elegant and mondaine lady of the century. You can imagine how mondaine *I'm* looking right now! I think I'd have preferred Mussolini – he'd have a greater understanding for my present circumference than the Duchess of Windsor!" (The Duke had been forced to abdicate the British throne ten months earlier after announcing his plan to marry an American divorcee.)

In this letter – which was also intercepted by British Intelligence – Ilse described how they were going to enlarge the mountain lodge at Reicholdsgrün, what with Klara and Fritz coming over from Egypt, Rudolf himself, the new baby, the nanny, Alfred, Grete, the maids, adjutants, driver and personal detectives.

In Harlaching too the little villa was to be enlarged again, to accommodate the extra staff for Rudolf and Martin Bormann, a garage and pumps for ten cars, a telephone exchange, and all the other paraphernalia that a Deputy Führer was deemed to need.

Evidently Klara chided her about the cars because Ilse wrote again on 3 November: "We're not suffering from megalomania, Mama: we haven't any more cars. . . . We haven't even got a new one. It irks Rudi that his chief of staff Bormann has ten, and all brand new."

The Duke and Duchess of Windsor paid their compliments to Hitler on 22 October, and dined with the Hesses at Harlaching a few days later.

> Despite all my worries about the Duchess [recorded Ilse Hess at the time] because her Paris–American fashion-consciousness had been noised ahead of her, she was a lovely, charming, warm and clever woman with a heart of gold and an affection for her husband that she made not the slightest attempt to conceal from us strangers, so we all fell for her.
>
> It's a pity, but the British have passed up not only an exceptionally clever King but also a fine woman as Queen.
>
> Of course, it's something that just can't be forgotten by this sharp-witted woman, who's certainly got ambitions for her husband, that under the law in Britain . . . it might still have been possible for him to remain King *with* her, but his task was made impossible by dark intrigues, and of course in part by his own sound attitude on social issues and his pro-German inclinations. . . . At the end we were the only ones talking, everybody was listening and we forgot to leave the table.

She added the latest gossip from Berlin. Now Emmy Göring was pregnant too: "The Görings are hoping for a girl; Goebbels wants his son to be a politician – I'd like a boy too, but not a politician. It's rare for father and son to prosper in the same field – the child is always overshadowed by his father."

Ilse got her boy, after a difficult and painful confinement, on 18 November 1937: "Thank God," she wrote at the time, "Nature has equipped us all with a wonderful power to forget!"

The news reached Rudolf up at the Berghof, the Führer's imposing new house with its commanding views of Germany and Austria from the Obersalzberg. Hess grinned from ear to ear – one of the famous goofy grins that had endeared him to the Germans. He had never doubted that it would be a boy. The stars were favourable, and the moon had been full all night long before the birth.

He proposed to call him Wolf Rüdiger – he had called Hitler "Wolf" during the years of political struggle, and Rüdiger was one of the heroes in the Nibelungen saga. He would also bear the names of his two godfathers, Adolf and Karl (both Hitler and Professor Haushofer would attend the bizarre Nazi "naming ceremony", in which earth and water from every Gau in Germany was sprinkled on the infant, a few weeks later).

Proud beyond words to have given Fritz a grandson at last he looked at the little boy's big forehead, he whistled to make him laugh, and he decided from the shape of one ear that he was going to be a musical genius: behind his back, however, the infant genius fell asleep when classical music was played, and only came alive to the sounds of jazz.

Gifts and greetings to "the little Minister" poured in from all over Germany. "We have managed so far", wrote Ilse, "to keep our own life free of this hot-house atmosphere, so we'll probably manage with our child too."

Wolf Rüdiger would never become a politician; but he would spend fifty years in the shadow of his father – campaigning bravely for Rudolf's release from imprisonment, and would suffer a paralyzing heart attack when his father died.

4   The Bystander

Hess was not consulted about any military plans. His later prosecutors would use phrases like: "Until his flight to Britain he was Hitler's closest personal confidant," and "The relationship between these two men was such that Hess must have had cognizance of the plans of attack while they were taking shape." The prosecution at Nuremberg would also announce portentously that when Hitler set up his secret Cabinet Council on 4 February 1938 he made Hess a member; but the council was a sham – it never met!

Hess attended not one of Hitler's historically significant planning conferences – which were more monologues than conferences anyway. Colonel Fritz Hossbach's record of the Berlin conference of 5 November 1937, Captain Fritz Wiedemann's notes on Hitler's secret speech of 28 May 1938, Captain Wolf Eberhard's minutes of Hitler's speech of 15 August 1938, Colonel Rudolf Schmundt's record of the Reich Chancellery conference of 23 May 1939, Admiral Wilhelm Canaris's version of Hitler's bellicose Obersalzberg speech of 22 August 1939 – all of these and other key documents have survived, yet none of them records the Deputy Führer as being present. The evidence suggests that Hitler had left Hess in charge of the Party, like a caretaker in a closed-down factory; nobody consulted him, but he was too genuinely popular to be dispensed with.

Did Hess not at least recognize in Adolf Hitler the greatest tyrant of the twentieth century? To answer this, we have Hess's own innocent word-picture, rendered in a private letter to his mother, of how he saw this man in his own habitat – written at a time when, we now know, Hitler was on the point of taking absolute power over the armed forces and embarking upon operations into Austria and Czechoslovakia. On 15 January 1938, Hess wrote this long, worshipful account of life with Hitler; he sent it to his mother with the latest snapshot of the little boy, who was to be registered as "believing in God" – "which is", wrote Hess, "somewhere beyond Protestant or Catholic".

On 23 January the Führer is coming to have his first look at his godchild.

He'll be spending the evening with us. Probably Grete and Inge will come back from Berlin with me as they've not been with the Führer for years. I've got to travel up to Berlin tomorrow evening to attend the Führer's big dinner for [Yugoslav Prime Minister Milan] Stoyadinović. It's the first time I've been up there since Christmas. I'm glad to say I've been able to give Berlin a miss for four weeks.

But I have been up to the Obersalzberg twice for a few days with the Führer. As there was wonderful snow I was able to go skiing a couple of times.

On his rest days up there the Führer likes to stay up far into the night: he watches a film, then chats – mostly about naval things if I'm there as they interest both of us – then reads a while. It's morning before he goes to sleep. At least he doesn't ask to be woken up until 1 or 2 p.m., in contrast to Berlin where he doesn't get to bed any earlier but is up again after only four or five hours.

After a communal lunch he and his guests usually take a stroll of half an hour or more to a tea pavilion built a year ago with a magnificent view over Salzburg. . . .

It's really cosy sitting at the big open fire at a large circular table which just about fills the equally round building. The illumination is provided by candles on holders around the walls.

[Heinrich] Hoffmann [Hitler's photographer] and his missus are usually there – he plays the part of the court jester; there's always one of the Führer's doctors, Dr [Karl] Brandt or Dr [Werner] Haase, as well as the press chief Dr [Otto] Dietrich, [adjutants Wilhelm] Brückner, [Julius] Schaub or [Fritz] Wiedemann; often [Sophie] Stork, whom you know, is there with Evi Braun and her sister [Gretl]; and sometimes Dr [Theo] Morell with his wife [Johanna] and Professor [Albert] Speer – Speer is usually there about the new buildings being planned.

After one or two hours up there we walk on for about ten minutes to a group of cross-country vehicles waiting to drive us down.

We all have supper then around 7.30. The Führer occupies himself until then with plans to rebuild Berlin, Munich, Hamburg and Nuremberg. The architectural plans are spread out on a big table in his cavernous reception room and illuminated by special lamps. With draughting equipment and ruler he makes a few amendments to the finished plans based on his data. He sketches many of the buildings himself, then has proper designs drawn up.

He's not thinking small, either: the new street across Berlin with the new ministry buildings along it is to be 150 yards wide with the transit traffic in the centre and service roads on either side; at one end there'll be the huge central station, then it goes off at an angle to the new airport which will be the biggest in the world. Nobody is allowed to talk about the other buildings planned for Berlin yet; it's going to be a really impressive Reich capital.

The poor Finance Minister's hair stands on end. . . .

But we're assuming that hordes of foreigners will come just to see all these gigantic buildings and construction works, and this will rake in the foreign currency. In centuries to come the world will gaze upon these buildings, and remember their creator Adolf Hitler, the founder of National Socialism – which may by then become a self-evident foundation for many of the world's nations.

So Hess prattled on, enthusiastically describing to his mother, on the edge of the Egyptian desert, the new central stations being planned for Munich and Cologne, and the suspension bridge to span the Elbe at Hamburg high enough to allow the biggest ships to pass beneath: all these modern pyramids being built by a German pharaoh fearful of his own mortality – not that his deputy saw in Hitler any of the negative allures of the despots of ancient Egypt.

You probably know [Hess wrote in that same letter] that a large terrain on the Obersalzberg worthy of the Reich head of state has been purchased bit by bit and gradually shut off from the outside world. It's a real blessing that the Führer can now go for strolls without having people trailing after him asking for autographs and without coming across little groups everywhere waiting to see him and lining all the paths.

Not that the thousands of visitors who make their pilgrimage to the Obersalzberg each year won't get any chance to see the Führer: because once a day at a fixed time the people are allowed to file past him. It's always a moving sight, particularly the Austrians among them who are often weeping with emotion and can't get a word out when they are at last standing in front of the Führer.

All the greater is the contrast offered by the Germans: on their faces is written the same cheerful spirit that is spreading across the whole Reich. . . .

Often there are foreigners present, and they just goggle at this evidence that the German people are not groaning under this dictator's lash at all ∿!*

The prominent foreigners are now received at the Berghof, among them Lord Halifax recently and Lord Rothermere before him; the Italian Foreign Minister Count [Galeazzo] Ciano was also up there, and delegates of the international war veterans who were meeting in Berlin.

When the weather's fine you can't imagine a better place for the German head of state to receive visitors. Even if the talks are held indoors, which is usually the case, you've got a clear view through a gigantic window taking up one whole wall of the Great Hall across to the Untersberg mountain, like a colossal painting.

Private letters like these, which were never intended for publication, confirm the picture of Rudolf Hess as a home-loving idealist and as the unquestioning disciple of a modern Messiah.

Hess evidently hated it when duty called him to the Reich capital. "The

---

* In the Hess family letters this wavy line ∿ denotes a chuckle.

Boss is back in Berlin," wrote Ilse on 28 January, "for the 30th [fifth anniversary of coming to power] etc. I do hope he doesn't have to go up there too often, or stay too long. Otherwise his little son is not going to recognize him, and he's going to have to keep getting used to his Papa again."

As the events of 1938 and 1939 began to cast their long foreshadow, Hess slipped out of the active political scenery, his place at important headquarters discussions assumed occasionally by Albrecht Haushofer instead. He became an actor on a constantly widening stage. When Hitler marched into Austria in March 1938 Haushofer was at the Berlin Foreign Ministry, while Hess was down in Vienna, meeting the cheering crowds with Hitler. Hess figured as joint signatory of the Reich law assimilating Austria on the next day, 13 March – an action which Hitler legalized by a favourable plebiscite one month later. Together with the Ministers of the Interior and Justice Hess signed the regulation extending the hateful Nuremberg Laws to Austria on 20 May.

With Austria now part of the greater German Reich, Hitler's plan was to envelope and dominate Czechoslovakia, enforce his remaining territorial claims on Poland, and then conquer Lebensraum in the east. Hess attended none of the resulting military and political conferences.

Only rarely do the important documents reveal glimpses of him during the mounting Czech crisis. Albrecht Haushofer meanwhile stayed that April with Lord Clydesdale at Dungavel again, and told him that Hitler was now demanding the return of the Sudeten German territories from Czechoslovakia. Haushofer wrote to Clydesdale twice in May, and he was present when Hess conferred with the Sudeten leader Henlein once again. Hess's personal involvement in the Munich crisis was limited to authorizing a document formally placing the NSDAP organization at Wehrmacht disposal if mobilization went ahead.

He attended the last Party rally, in September 1938, and had Professor Karl Haushofer as his guest. Haushofer thrilled to the night-time spectacle of the "cathedral arch" formed by massed searchlights, and exchanged remarks with Ilse Hess about the full moon and the rising planet Jupiter. "Little Wolf Rüdiger", Ilse told him, "was born under Jupiter, Mars and Venus" – and the Professor considered this intelligence noteworthy enough to mention in a letter that night to Martha.

Hess was acutely aware of his declining influence. His inability to halt the Party's campaign against the churches was the most obvious proof of this. Wolfgang Bechtold, an editor on his staff, saw him at this time as a desperately shy, retiring person who shunned publicity. "Hess", wrote Bechtold, "had gathered a small group of personal associates and friends with whom he would discuss strange matters such as astrology and herbal cures." The realization that Bormann was supplanting him in Hitler's favour stirred the first dangerous feelings of inferiority. The ruthless, power-hungry Nazis were replacing the pioneers and patriots who had founded the Party. It was out of Rudolf Hess's personal control.

When another Jew, Herschel Grünspan, fatally wounded a German embassy official in Paris, violent pogroms broke out all across Germany. Jewish businesses and synagogues were burned and wrecked and many Jews were murdered: again Hitler and Hess intervened to stop the violence. That same night (10 November 1938 – "The Night of Broken Glass") Hess's office sent out telegrams to all the gauleiters ordering them to protect the Jews and their property, and he issued secret decree No. 174/38, which to the lasting shame of West Germany's otherwise reputable historians none of them has yet seen fit to quote:

FROM: OFFICE OF THE DEPUTY FÜHRER   IMMEDIATE ACTION!
Ordinance No. 174/38   *Munich, 10 November 1938*

On express orders issued at the highest level of all there is to be no arson whatever against Jewish businesses or the like, under any circumstances.

Hess ordered the Party courts which came under his jurisdiction to prosecute the Party officials accused of excesses, and sent his secretary Miss Sperr to witness one of the hearings and report whether they were being conducted with proper severity.

He also wrote out on the 14th a renewed "letter of protection" for Professor Haushofer, who had attended with Hitler as joint godfather the "naming" of the Hesses' first and only son at Harlaching four days before:

The retired general, Professor Dr Karl Haushofer, is of proven Aryan descent; his wife Martha née Mayer-Doss is not Jewish within the terms of the Nuremberg Laws, as I have determined from genealogies produced to me.

I forbid anybody to molest them or search their home.

Over the next weeks, Hess privately did what he could to intercede for lists of Jews brought to him by Haushofer – the first such names, of Julius and Else Schlinck, were handed to Ilse Hess on 8 December.

A few days after Grünspan's halfwitted crime and the no less demented outrages by the Nazi rowdies, Hermann Göring as head of the Four Year Plan chaired a secret conference in Berlin on the economic effects of the pogrom and penal measures against the Jewish community. Hess, as usual, was not present: he never was at internal conferences of government affairs.

Subsequently, however, he issued from Munich regulations designed to mitigate the damage done in turn by Berlin's decrees: Hess announced that the Jewish problem as such would be "submitted to an ultimate solution" – at that time Berlin was planning an enhanced emigration drive – but he emphatically forbade any steps that might disrupt Germany's exports or other important foreign trade relations.

. . .

During 1939 Hess was a mere bystander. He watched helplessly as Britain, provoked by Hitler's seizure of Czechoslovakia in March, issued her ill-considered guarantee to Poland.

Occasionally Rudolf Hess's path crossed with that of the Haushofers, but there was a growing estrangement between them. Hess had just asked the Professor to see Count Pál Teleki, the New Hungarian Prime Minister, in Budapest when Hitler's sudden occupation of Prague made it pointless. Hess knew that foreign policy was dictated by Hitler directly to Ribbentrop, who had been his Foreign Minister since February 1938. And after a final blazing row at Hess's home on 10 November 1938 Hitler no longer respected Professor Haushofer's opinions – the old Professor had warned the Führer not to bank on Italy, and had criticized his bellicose speech at Saarbrücken one month before.

From Berlin, the Professor's pessimistic son Dr Albrecht Haushofer had maintained his secret contacts with the British ruling aristocracy. On 28 November Lord Clydesdale had gone there to warn him about Britain's rising sense of outrage. From all that he saw in the inner councils in Berlin, by July 1939 the younger Haushofer was sure there would be war – a prophecy which "inordinately affected" his father, reading this in Albrecht's letter on the 8th. "Until the middle of August," Albrecht predicted knowledgeably to his mother on 12 July, "nothing will happen. From the middle of August onwards everything is to be prepared for a sudden war. Now as before O'Daijin [Hitler] wants only a local war . . . he is not sure whether the West will remain quiet."

Escaping the muggy heat of central Germany's last pre-war summer, Albrecht took his class on a cruise off the western coast of Norway. Here, amid the tranquil fiords and leads, he penned a long, furtive letter in English to Lord Clydesdale ("My dear Douglo"). Dated 16 July, this gloomy letter explained why he had trodden carefully since Munich; it argued once again the German case on the Treaty of Versailles and warned that "the great man of the regime", meaning Hitler, was not now preparing to "slow down". The letter in fact bordered on treason, and Haushofer knew it: for that reason he posted it from neutral Norway to England. "To the best of my knowledge," he continued, "there is not yet a definite time-table for the actual explosion, but any date after the middle of August may prove to be the fatal one. So far they want to avoid the 'big war'. But the one man on whom everything depends is still hoping that he may be able to get away with an isolated 'local war'."

The rest of the letter Lord Clydesdale probably dismissed as unhelpful. Haushofer predicted that although the German people were still disunited they would stand solidly behind Hitler in any war over the Danzig Corridor (a broad strip of territory across Germany, giving Poland access to the sea). "A war against Poland would not be unpopular," he added. But there was still time, he hoped, to avert an explosion. Perhaps Britain might get to work on Mussolini and Mr Chamberlain might accept that the German claims on Poland were not unjustified. Albrecht Haushofer concluded by asking Lord Clydesdale to destroy the letter and to send him a simple picture postcard as a sign that it had arrived.

Lord Clydesdale took it round first of all to Morpeth Mansions, where Winston Churchill had his Westminster flat. Churchill was a firebrand, a backbench Member of Parliament implacably opposed to the policies of appeasement. He sat dripping wet and wrapped in a bath towel, reading the pages through, then handed the letter back to his visitor. (He would forget all about the letter until Rudolf Hess himself arrived.) "There's going to be war very soon," he said.

A postcard went off to Berlin, signifying to Albrecht Haushofer – whom cowardly Gestapo murderers, in the ruins of Berlin in the closing days of the war, would shoot without trial as a traitor – that the letter had been received.

In Germany, tempers frayed. A few days further into that summer, Albrecht's younger brother Heinz passed on to the Deputy Führer some cases of glaring injustice to act upon. Hess wrote back an uncharacteristically prickly letter. He lectured Heinz that any criticism of the "system" amounted to criticism of himself: he counted himself, with pride, responsible for its triumphs; true, in any revolution the pendulum did swing to extremes, and it might take time to settle down. "You know full well", Hess wrote, "how I do my utmost to intercede wherever I am told of individual cases of undesirable side-effects." He mentioned the case of the SS official Odilo Globocnig, accused of massive corruption. Hess had instituted an investigation and the corruption charges had been found to have been exaggerated, but Hess had still obtained Globocnig's dismissal from office (he later headed the mass-extermination operations in the East). Unrepentant, Hess invited Heinz Haushofer to picture the "undesirable side-effects" if the Bolsheviks had triumphed in 1933 instead of Hitler – "a man", he marvelled, "who dares to walk a path that often goes to the very brink of war".

In fact Hitler wanted to go beyond the brink. He wanted a short war, for reasons of domestic politics as much as for the attainment of any imperial goals.

Visiting the Haushofers' mountain home early in August Hess reassured them that the war would be just "a little thunderstorm". On 22 August, he disclosed to them that Stalin had agreed to sign a pact with Hitler (he made no mention of the pact's secret protocol dividing the spoils in Poland and the Baltic States between Germany and the Soviet Union: probably he was not aware of it).

The "notebooks" kept by Hess's rude and bullying *Stabsleiter* Bormann during the last days of peace show the final stepping-stones towards disaster.

22 *August:* Führer's conference with commanders-in-chief and generals [on the Berghof].

23 August: Ribbentrop flies to Moscow to conclude German–Russian Non-Aggression Pact.

24 August: 2.00 a.m. public announcement of the pact. 3.30 p.m. [Hitler] flies from Ainring [near Salzburg] to Berlin.

Hess, however, went south to Graz, where he addressed the seventh annual rally of the Auslands-Organisation the next evening. "We shall follow the Führer's flag, come what may," he declared. "The power to blame for Poland's irresponsibility is Britain. The more reasons they give to justify their hostility towards Germany, the less we are inclined to believe them. . . . While we stand ready to follow the Führer, we are fulfilling the will of Him who sent us the Führer. Therefore I say again: we Germans are with the Führer whatever the future may bring."

Bormann was certainly with Hitler:

25 August: The Reichstag session set down for the 26th is dropped; the Party rally is not cancelled, just postponed. From the 25th onwards German mobilization is very quietly proceeding.

26 August: Daily conferences, from dawn to dusk.

27 August: There'll be no Reichstag session for the moment; after a short speech the Reichstag deputies are sent back home by the Führer.

28 August: [Sir Nevile] Henderson [British Ambassador] returns from London; the negotiations go on.

29 August: Henderson receives new letter from the Führer; in spite of the talks the German mobilization still goes quietly on.

30 August: On Thursday the 31st our mobilization will be complete.

That day Hitler appointed Hess a member of a six-man "little Cabinet", the Ministerial Council for Reich Defence that would pass laws while he was at the front. This appointment too would be held against Hess at Nuremberg; in fact its sessions were dominated by the blustering, forceful personality of Field Marshal Hermann Göring, and Hess never attended.

On 1 September 1939 Bormann entered: "4.30 a.m., the struggle with the Poles began. Reichstag: the Führer announces the steps he has taken." Hitler was wearing his field-grey tunic for the first time; Hess, saluting him, wore the Party's brown shirt and broad leather belt. Aware of the gradual erosion of Hess's authority over the last years, Hitler closed his speech with a promise intended as a sop to his blindly loyal deputy. In the event of his death, he announced, Hermann Göring should succeed him; if some misfortune should befall Göring too, then Hess would follow as Führer. His old teacher Professor Haushofer sent his immediate congratulations to Rudolf Hess upon thus becoming "third highest man in the Reich".

Field Marshal Göring was less enchanted to hear "that nincompoop" named as his successor, and afterwards told Hitler so. Hitler smiled. "But Hermann," he pointed out, giving his own interpretation of the Führer principle. "When *you* become Führer of the Reich – *pfui!* You can throw Hess out and choose your own successor."

5   The Little Thunderstorm

"My entire work is undone," lamented Hitler to Rudolf Hess after the British joined in his "little thunderstorm"; and the Führer's young secretary Christa Schroeder heard him add, "My book has been written in vain."

It was true: how often in *Mein Kampf* had Hitler underlined his aspirations for a common cause, even a great alliance, with Britain! Hess had believed him implicitly. And yet, even now, Britain was keeping out of the actual fighting, seemingly standing back while Hitler's armies invaded Poland from the west, and Stalin's equally rapacious armies then poured in from the east.

Hess's name all but vanished from the newspapers, although he put in an honourable appearance on behalf of the Party at the state funeral of General Werner von Fritsch, the army's melancholy and grievously wronged former Commander-in-Chief, who had sought death in action in Poland a few days earlier. On 8 October he was one of the ministers formally signing the decree dismembering Poland and restoring to the German Reich the territories that had been confiscated in earlier years. This document too would be held against Hess at Nuremberg, regardless of the irony that the Soviet government sitting in judgement upon him there had itself signed that secret protocol with Nazi Germany in August 1939 encouraging and sharing in precisely this "war crime".

Over the next year, there was little public trace of Rudolf Hess. He withdrew into his family, particularly now that his son had been born, and came home as frequently as his official duties permitted. "He liked to invite some relatives," recalled Miss Fath five years later. His parents had come over from Egypt: all their worldly goods had been forfeited under the Treaty of Versailles in 1919, and now they had again lost everything. "From the beginning of the war they lived entirely in his household, more in Berlin than in Munich. He was a very tender son, and did for his parents as much as he could do. His father liked to see cheerful plays, operettas and films; his mother's interests were more in nature healing and philosophy."

He became briefly controversial for an Open Letter to an Unmarried

Mother, published in the newspapers at Christmas. Army officers angrily read into its vague language a public encouragement to SS officers to impregnate the womenfolk of troops while their husbands were away at the wars, to boost the Reich's strategic birthrate. (He had been misquoted.) Hess delivered his Christmas broadcast that year from on board a German warship.

He would have liked to be able to fly, but Hitler had forbidden him to pilot an aeroplane for the time being. His job was too far from either the battlefields or the real responsibility of war. As the war progressed he became moody and monosyllabic; his secretaries saw him brooding at his desk, with nothing of consequence to do. Hitler was at his field headquarters. Göring had taken charge of the government. Apart from running the Party and participating in Party court actions against malfeasors like Gauleiter Julius Streicher (in February 1940) there was little for Hess to do.

He found more time to indulge his interest in the occult and in strange medicines. Credulous and gullible, he devoured the horoscopes which had somehow survived the Führer's hostility to such frivolous pursuits. Meanwhile, hungry for more power, Martin Bormann scrawled contented entries in his notebooks, which revealed his sniping against his chief:

23 February: 12.30 p.m., journey to Munich with the Führer's train.

24 February: Celebrated Party's Foundation Anniversary. Afterwards at Café Heck; Führer's dispute with R.H. [Hess] about nature healers and mesmerizers.

25 February: 12.20 p.m. departure with Führer's train for Berlin; I have a lengthy conversation with the Führer on the topic of "superstition and medicine" and VIPs.

Hess's part in the actual war was still minimal. The German naval files contain scattered evidence of his personal interest in the technical problems of naval blockade and mine warfare; but if the Admiralty gave him a polite hearing, it was only out of deference to his high station. And all the time he itched to be back in the cockpit of a fighter plane, as he had been when the First World War ended.

Norway and Denmark were occupied by German troops to forestall Churchill's own plans to invade Scandinavia; in May Hitler unleashed his armies on France and the Low Countries. The British Expeditionary Force, embarking at Dunkirk, barely escaped the catastrophe, and by late June France had been laid low. The photographs show Hess at the Armistice ceremony with Hitler at Compiègne.

To general astonishment Hitler had formulated terms that seemed magnanimous when compared with the terms imposed on Germany at Versailles; but Hitler wanted the needless war in the west to end – not because he desired to pocket the spoils, but because he had designs on the east. He had already started discussing with his general staff a redeployment of his armies against Soviet Russia – though whether defensively or offensively nobody as yet could say.

Hitler uttered frequent comments in these weeks that indicated the unchanged warmth of his private feelings towards the British and his desire for peace with them at almost any price. "Mein Führer," Hess had asked him over lunch in the Reich Chancellery, just before the French campaign, "do you still think about England as you used to?" "If the British knew", snorted Hitler, "how little I am asking of them!" – and he signalled that lunch was over.

In a speech to his generals at Charleville on 2 June, he said: "We can easily find a basis for peace agreement with Britain." He said the same to his staff. "The Chief plans", wrote his confidential secretary Christa Schroeder on 25 June, "to speak to the Reichstag shortly. It will probably be his last appeal to Britain. If they don't come around even then, he will proceed without pity. I believe it still hurts him even now to have to tackle the British. It would obviously be far easier for him if they would see reason themselves. If only they knew that the Chief wants nothing more from them than the return of our own former colonies, perhaps they might be more approachable."

Hess sat in on these private conversations, and was deeply troubled. In one conversation (with his own dispossessed parents in mind) he told Hitler he hoped that Germany would demand back from Britain everything taken by them under the terms of Versailles. Hitler shook his head. "This war may yet bring about the friendship with Britain that has been my aim all along," he said. "You don't impose harsh conditions on a country you want to win round to your side."

But in London a different Prime Minister was now in office – a politician for whom there could ultimately be no talk of withdrawal. Although in May and June even the British Cabinet records showed Prime Minister Churchill briefly but seriously contemplating the idea of "accepting Mr Hitler's terms", he invariably kicked himself out of these bouts of melancholy overnight, and a veil was drawn over these episodes; the contemplative passages in his Cabinet records remain blanked out to this day, although revealed in private papers of some of the participants.

Hitler made his "last appeal to reason" in the Reichstag on 19 July. It was rejected; on 20 July Churchill began a different kind of war altogether – summoning his bomber force commander privately to his country house and ordering him to prepare to unleash the heaviest bombers that British genius and skill could manufacture to discharge their cargoes of high explosives and incendiaries over the centre of Berlin as soon as he gave the word.

Hess could see that time was running out. On 2 August he described to Albrecht Haushofer the Führer's concern about the undesirable turn the war was taking. Given that Hitler was loath to force a "showdown" with

Britain, who were the Britons of vision with whom Germany could talk? This was the question that Hess put to his widely travelled friend.

Hitler had no intention of staging an opposed invasion of England. Several times that August he allowed selected commanders to deduce that "Sea Lion" was just bluff, a means of putting political pressure on the British government to see things his way. The naval staff recorded this on the 14th, and that same day Hitler laid bare his feelings about Britain to his new field marshals. He promised that he would use his army "only if we are absolutely forced to".

> Probably two reasons why Britain won't make peace [Field Marshal Wilhelm von Leeb's diary quoted Hitler as saying]. Firstly, she hopes for US aid. . . . Secondly, she hopes to play Russia off against Germany. . . .
> But Germany is not striving to smash Britain, because the beneficiaries will not be Germany, but Japan in the east, Russia in India, Italy in the Mediterranean, and America in world trade.

"This is why", concluded Hitler, "peace is possible with Britain – but not so long as Churchill is Prime Minister."

The next day Rudolf Hess summoned Albrecht Haushofer to Langenbeck for another secret talk about putting out feelers to Britain: an idea was forming in his mind.

The Battle of Britain had begun lamely, with Göring's squadrons trying to neutralize the British air force and its airfields. London had still not attracted any raids. The British and German records show that Hitler had prohibited any attacks on British towns at all, and had totally embargoed London as a target.

This was known to Churchill from deciphered German air-force orders. At 9 a.m. on 25 August, however, speaking from his Sunday-morning bed at his country house, he personally telephoned bomber headquarters and ordered them to raid Berlin that night with the heaviest possible force. Berlin too had not been attacked before, but he had personal, political, tactical and strategic reasons for desiring to provoke enemy retaliation against his own capital city.

The RAF attack on Berlin that night changed the picture dramatically.

Since Hitler failed to respond, Churchill ordered a further raid on the night of 28–9 August, which killed several Berliners. Hitler angrily left the Obersalzberg the following afternoon and flew back to Berlin, where he discussed this unpleasant development with his ministers and generals. On the next day General Georg Thomas of the Wehrmacht High Command recorded: "The Führer's back here, very indignant about the British raids on Berlin. Has authorized planning to begin for a heavy attack on London from tonight."

But then he refused to lift the embargo, aware that bombing London would finally strangulate the faint flutterings of peace hopes that he kept hearing. Diverse high-level British feelers had already reached Berlin since June, mentioning Lord Lothian in Washington, Lord Halifax and his Under-Secretary Rab Butler at the Foreign Office. Hitler may well have suspected that this was precisely why Churchill wanted him to begin blitzing London: he was determined not to fall into his opponent's cynical trap, but it was not easy to ignore the clamour for reprisals.

Reluctant to lift the embargo on bombing London even now, at the end of August 1940 Hitler authorized renewed covert approaches to the British. Berlin lawyer Dr Ludwig Weissauer was sent to Stockholm with instructions to establish contact with Victor Mallet at the British Legation, and reveal the generous German peace offer: Germany would withdraw all forces from France and the Low Countries and retain only those regions in Poland and Czechoslovakia which had earlier been Germany's; and Germany would assist the British empire against any enemies. (From Mallet's diffidently phrased telegram to London inquiring if he was permitted to receive Weissauer it is plain that he had deduced that the Führer himself was behind the offer, and that he thought that Britain should listen. They turned him down.)

Simultaneously the Deputy Führer, Rudolf Hess, arrived unexpectedly at the Haushofer household in Bavaria at 5 p.m. on the last day of August, evidently looking for Albrecht; his young friend was on diplomatic business in Vienna, so Hess embarked on a long, long conference with the old professor instead, which included a secluded three-hour walk in the forest where nobody could overhear them. It was 2 a.m. before they parted.

Arriving back in Munich on 3 September, Haushofer typed a letter to his son. The urgency was now apparent, although Hitler had still not lifted the bombing embargo. "As you know," wrote the Professor, "everything is set for a very harsh assault on the Isles in question – so all the top man has to do is press the button." The question which both Hess and he were asking was: was there no other way? Hess had imparted to him a certain line of thought, which Karl Haushofer now passed on to his son ("because that is obviously why it was told to me"). "Wouldn't you say", he asked, "that there's a way of talking over such possibilities with a middle-man on some neutral ground – perhaps with the old [General Sir] Ian Hamilton or that other Hamilton?" – meaning Lord Clydesdale, who had recently succeeded his father as Duke of Hamilton.

Thus Hess had got it off his chest. Before he returned to Berlin, the Professor had told him that it occurred to him that he had recently had a letter from an old family friend in Lisbon – a Mrs Violet Roberts, daughter-in-law of the former British Viceroy of India, Lord Roberts of Kandahar, and that she had marked her letter "Address your reply to Mrs V. Roberts," with a postbox address in Lisbon.

Hitler – Hess – the Haushofers – Mrs Roberts's postbox in Portugal: the first exiguous threads of the political drama were becoming visible.

It was none too soon. On 4 September Hitler addressed ten thousand Berliners at the Sport Palace in the capital. They had suffered more British raids, and he now promised to give measure for measure. "If they proclaim that they will attack our cities on a grand scale," he announced, "we shall *wipe their cities out!*"

Churchill reacted by bombing Berlin again two nights later.

Expressing anger and sorrow to his staff, Hitler lifted the Luftwaffe's embargo on bombing London: on 7 September, for the first time in the war, several hundred German planes raided the British capital's port and working-class East End. That night the City's skyline was a mass of fires.

In Hess's imagination danced one infernal image, and it would haunt him for years to come. Explaining his motives for undertaking his perilous mission a few weeks later, he admitted that it had been his toughest decision, "But . . . in my mind's eye I kept seeing – in Germany and Britain alike – an endless line of children's coffins with weeping mothers behind them, and then again, the coffins of mothers, with their children clustered behind them."

As the news agency reports of London in flames rattled off the teleprinters throughout the 8th, Hess asked Albrecht Haushofer to meet him in Austria immediately. Hess, the born aviator, had made up his mind to undertake a desperate mission: he saw no reason why he should not succeed where all the professional diplomats had failed. When war had broken out he had volunteered for Luftwaffe duties. Hitler had not only refused, but had asked for an undertaking that he would not fly. Hess had promised not to, adding, "For the next year."

Now, in September 1940, the year was up. The First World War fighter pilot, the daredevil who had planned to fly the Atlantic like Lindbergh, the begoggled Nazi hero who had won the "round the Zugspitze" air race in 1934, would undertake the aeroplane flight to cap them all. He would single-handedly rescue the peace: stop the senseless bloodshed: save Germany: extricate his Führer from the military impasse and restore him to his Berghof and his drawing-board and to his bridges, buildings and autobahns.

He instructed Miss Fath to obtain daily bulletins on the meteorological conditions over the Channel, North Sea and British Isles, either direct from the air force or from her colleague Miss Sperr, of his liaison office in Berlin.

As the bombing of London continued, Hess retired to Bad Gallspach near Linz in Austria: evidently his cramps had returned. The two-hour talk that Hess had here with Albrecht Haushofer on 8 September was noteworthy for the latter's hopeless pessimism – the infectious product of years of intercourse with pettifogging diplomats like Ernst von Weizsäcker and Ulrich von Hassell. For all his geopolitical expertise, the conversation also displayed Haushofer's inability to grasp that America's material wealth could not avail Britain if Hitler's submarines prevented convoys from crossing the Atlantic, and that the British naval blockade of

Germany would be broken if Hitler invaded Russia. We have only Haushofer's contemporary version of their talk ("On 8 September, I was summoned to Bad G . . .") but it says all that we need to know.

Hess immediately asked about possibilities of conveying the Führer's sincere wish for peace to leading British personages. "It's clear", he pointed out, "that if the war goes on, the white race will be committing hara-kiri. . . . The Führer neither had nor has any desire to destroy the British empire. Is there anybody in Britain ready to talk peace?" Haushofer – so he claimed – used blunt language in his reply: it was not just the Jews and freemasons, but virtually every Englishman who regarded any treaty signed by Hitler as worthless.

"Why?" asked Hess, genuinely puzzled.

Haushofer pointed to the broken treaties that littered the last decade. "In the English-speaking world," he said, "the Führer is regarded as the devil's deputy on earth." When he added that the British would rather convey their empire piecemeal to the Americans than allow Germany to dominate Europe, Hess heatedly asked why: the diplomat pointed out that Churchill himself, being of half-American blood (like several members of his Cabinet) would have few qualms in that respect. Reverting to Hess's original question, he said, "My view is that the British who have property that they stand to lose – the more calculating elements of the 'plutocracy' – are those likely to be ready to talk about peace. But even these will only regard peace as a temporary truce."

"Do you think", asked Hitler's deputy, "our feelers haven't been getting through to them – that we've been using the wrong language?" It was obvious that he was referring to Ribbentrop.

"It's true", said Haushofer, "that Mr von R. and others fulfil the same role in British eyes that Duff Cooper, Eden and Churchill do in ours." But it was a matter of fundamentals, he insisted, not personalities.

Hess persisted, and asked him for names: Haushofer unwillingly listed the pro-German British diplomats he had met at the British Foreign Office over the years: Owen O'Malley, now at Budapest; Sam Hoare, now at Madrid; and Lord Lothian, now at Washington. "The final possibility", he suggested, "would be a personal meeting with my closest friend, the young Duke of Hamilton, on neutral territory: Hamilton has immediate access to everybody who's anybody in London, including Churchill and the King." Having volunteered that suggestion, he pointed out how difficult it would be in practice to make contact – and gloomily added that it was bound to fail whichever way they plumped for.

"I'll think it over," said Hess, before retiring for the night. "I'll tell you if you're to do anything."

Stricken by sudden apprehensions, Haushofer said that he would need detailed instructions and – if he was to make any such trip by himself – he wanted "guidelines from the very top". Aware of the risks he was already taking, he wrote a cautious memorandum on their talk (which he asked his father to store away carefully a few days later):

From the entire conversation [this document ended] I formed the impression that it had not been conducted without the Führer's prior knowledge, and that I would probably hear no more about it until he and his Deputy had talked it over again.

From this moment, Hess was determined to establish contact with the Duke of Hamilton through Portugal. He would be asked either to come to Lisbon to meet Albrecht, or to state in strict confidence where he would be in the immediate future so that they could send a neutral gentleman to him with a message of "great importance".

Albrecht's pessimism had not, however, eluded Hess, nor his insistence on getting written clearance from Hitler. Still at Bad Gallspach on the 10th, he set out his line of thinking in a letter to the old professor instead, gathering up the threads they had begun to spin during their long walk on the last day of August: he suggested that they send an Auslands-Organisation agent to hand to the Professor's friend Mrs Roberts a letter addressed to the Duke, and inform her whom she could safely hand any reply to in Lisbon. "Meanwhile," concluded Hess, "let us keep our fingers crossed. If this beginning comes off, the horoscope they gave you for August will have come true – because it was during our long quiet walk on the last day of that month that the names of your household's young friend [Hamilton] and old ladyfriend first came to you."

Another week passed while Hess's letter made its way through the posts to the Professor at his Alpine hut and then onwards to his son Albrecht, who was now back in Berlin – a week during which the death toll in London mounted under the merciless bombing.

More apprehensive than ever, Albrecht Haushofer wrote hesitantly to his parents on the 18th: "I want to think the whole thing over for another twenty-four hours then I'll write direct to T." – Tomodachi was the Haushofers' codename for Rudolf Hess. He continued: "The way he has in mind really won't work. I might be able to phrase a letter to D.H. in such a way as not to put our old ladyfriend in any kind of danger; but first I must make it quite plain to T. that my ducal friend is no more able to write to me without the permission of his seniormost authorities than I for my part can write to him." He dropped another clear hint that he was waiting for authorization from Hitler in the letter that he wrote to Hess the next day, 19 September: he wanted instructions, "if not from the Führer himself, then from some person getting them straight from him."

It was a four-page letter whose sheer verbosity betrayed the panic of the academic suddenly called upon to be a man of bold decision. He had, he wrote, considered the technical problems of getting a message to the Duke. It would have to be phrased so innocuously that there was no chance either of its being intercepted or destroyed, or of its putting Mrs Roberts or the Duke at risk. Albrecht was sure the Duke would be swift enough on the uptake. "I can write a few lines to him without my address or full signature – an 'A' will suffice – so that *he alone* recognizes that there is something more serious behind my wish to meet him in Lisbon than a personal whim."

He advised against including anything else – suppose an old lady in Germany received such a letter to be forwarded to a third party whom it asked to disclose where he planned to be on a certain date – particularly since Albrecht Haushofer shrewdly guessed that Hamilton was now either "directing the air defence of an important sector of Scotland" or holding down a top Air Ministry job in London. "I think", he gently chided the unworldly Deputy Führer, "it doesn't take much to imagine the leer with which our own [Wilhelm] Canaris or [Reinhard] Heydrich [chiefs of military Intelligence and secret police respectively] would view any promises of 'secrecy' and 'confidentiality' offered by such a letter. . . . Both the old lady and the air force officer would be in for a pretty rough ride!" Moreover, he argued, Hamilton obviously could not fly to Lisbon without being given leave – "that means that at least their Air Minister [Sir Archibald] Sinclair or Foreign Secretary Lord Halifax would have to be in the know."

So Albrecht's suggestion was simple: he should write an innocuous letter to his friend the Duke via Lisbon, suggesting that they meet there. "If nothing comes of it, one can always make a further attempt – assuming we find a suitable third party – via a neutral, who will be asked to convey a personal message." He felt bound to add that he considered the chance of success for any approach by the Führer to Britain's upper classes was "slim" for the reasons he had already stated orally.

Still in Berlin, that same day Albrecht typed a draft letter to the Duke. It expressed elegantly phrased condolences on his father's death and the loss of his brother-in-law the Duke of Northumberland at Dunkirk, then added, with exquisite circumlocution: "If you remember some of my last communications before the war you will realize that there is a certain significance in the fact that I am, at present, able to ask you whether there is the slightest chance of our meeting . . . perhaps in Portugal." He suggested a short trip to Lisbon, assuming that the Duke could make the "authorities" understand and grant him leave.

It was a well-phrased letter, but hope was not written large in Albrecht Haushofer's vocabulary. Sending a copy to his father to run his eye over on the same day, he added in English, a language fashionable among the more erudite anti-Nazis, "The whole thing is a fool's errand – *aber dafür können wir nichts*" – there is nothing else we can do.

Hess was impatient for action – each night the lines of coffins in his imagination grew longer: on the 17th, 18th and 19th the Luftwaffe had dropped 334, 350 and 310 tons of high explosive on London. On the 22nd he telephoned instructions to Dr Haushofer to go ahead with the Hamilton letter – he was to hand it to Rudolf's brother Alfred at the Auslands-Organisation headquarters; an AO courier would carry it immediately to Mrs Roberts in Lisbon. That was the plan.

Albrecht Haushofer very reluctantly did as he was bidden.

"Everything went off okay," he reported to Hess from Berlin on the 23rd. "I can report mission accomplished inasmuch as the letter that you desired" – a phrase he could not emphasize enough – "was written this morning and has gone off. Let's hope it avails more than a sober assessment allows us to expect!"

Haushofer entrusted a copy of the Hamilton letter to the safekeeping of his father, adding, "Well, I've made it pretty plain that it's an operation for which I did not provide the initiative." He had "not the slightest belief", he pointed out, "that it had any chance of bringing peace." That being so, why had Albrecht Haushofer gone along with the charade? The answer accepted by his biographers as the most credible can be sought in his known contacts with individual anti-Hitler plotters like Fritzi von der Schulenburg, Johannes Popitz, Ernst von Weizsäcker, Ulrich von Hassell and the lawyer Carl Langbehn (most of whom would come to a sticky end like himself). He hoped to be sent to Lisbon with a full "legitimation" by the gullible Rudolf Hess; once there, he would re-establish contact either with the British Secret Intelligence Service (SIS) agents that he had unquestionably been meeting during his pre-war visits to London, or with the German émigrés like Erich Ollenhauer, George Frankenstein and dozens of others who were accepting regular pay, career prospects (and even knighthoods) from the German Section of the SIS in return for working for their native country's defeat.

Hess, unwittingly, was outsmarting Albrecht Haushofer: because, as the days turned into weeks and no reply came from the Duke, he began planning more intensively to make the trip himself.

Early in October, Hess began drafting his own letter to the Duke. Since his own English was fragmentary, he telephoned Gauleiter Ernest Bohle, head of the AO, to invite him to come round. A slender, dark-haired official of 5 feet 10 inches, Bohle was nine years younger than Hess, but no less fanatical in his pro-British sentiments. He arrived at the Deputy Führer's private office at 64 Wilhelm Strasse at 9.30 p.m., consumed with curiosity; but even Hess's adjutant, Alfred Leitgen, was unable to tell him what it was all about.

Hess closed the door behind the Gauleiter. "Mr Bohle," he said quietly, "I have called you in to ask if you'd do a very secret job for me." Explaining that it was about ending the fighting with Britain, he charged Bohle not to breathe a word to his other boss at the Foreign Ministry, Ribbentrop. After pledging him to secrecy, he sat the Gauleiter at a typewriter and asked him to translate a letter into English. It was addressed to the Duke of Hamilton. Bohle gained the impression that Hess was planning a meeting in Switzerland – although it was not apparent how the Duke was supposed to get there. "At the suggestion of Dr Albrecht Haushofer," it began, he (Hess) was addressing to him this plea for Anglo-German understanding. The letter pictured the terrors of bombing and outlined Hitler's familiar peace proposals, based on a return to the status quo with Britain and talks on the former colonies; its "descriptions of the coming war in the air if the hostilities continued were downright prophetic", Bohle would recall later.

Over the next three months Hess called him in several more times to translate additional pages. Once Hess asked if he would act as interpreter – and Bohle, who had interpreted at the Hesses' dinner party for the Windsors, eagerly agreed.

Was Hess planning to take Bohle with him on his flight? And what happened to this secret letter from Hess to the Duke? Bohle's recollection is too substantial to be discounted; but the letter has not surfaced in British archives, nor did the Duke admit in his communications with Churchill's ministers after Hess arrived that one existed. In fact, a few days after Hess's flight, the Duke secured – to the displeasure of the government – an audience with the King: so Hess's letter may well repose among the Royal Archives at Windsor, along with the two later letters that he wrote to His Majesty while he was Churchill's personal "prisoner of state".*

By early November 1940 British troops were landing in Greece, German air raids had killed fourteen thousand Britons, and Rudolf Hess decided not to wait any longer for a reply from Lisbon. Probably encouraged by Hitler, who was in Berlin with him, Hess made up his mind to carry out his alternative plan. On 4 November he wrote a farewell letter, ready to leave it for his family to find after he had taken off. "My dear ones," this brief letter began:

> I firmly believe that I shall return from the flight I am about to make and that the flight will be crowned with success.
>
> Should I not return, however, the goal I set myself was worth the supreme effort. I am sure you all know me: you know I could not have acted any other way.
>
> Your Rudolf

Albrecht Haushofer meanwhile had given up. With perceptible relief he wrote to his mother on the 12th: "Nothing from L.," meaning Lisbon. "Probably nothing will come, either."

Much of what happened in those months before Hess's last flight must remain speculative. Was Hitler really taken unawares by it? (Members of both men's staff gained the vague impression that Hitler was only play-acting.) Were the British half-expecting Hess *himself* to come? (Czech exile leader Eduard Beneš recorded that SIS officers told him they were expecting *somebody*.)

The diaries of Albrecht Haushofer and his father – the principal links in the chain between Hitler, Hess and the British – were removed by Allied officers from the Haushofer mountain lodge on the Partnach Alm in May

---

* The Royal Archives at Windsor has declined to provide access to His late Majesty's papers on the Hess incident.

1945 and have not been seen since. And the British Air Minister's personal file on the Duke of Hamilton has had all the evidence relevant to the instructions given to the Duke in the three months before Hess's flight removed (and unusually unobtrusively – i.e. without even the usual "Withdrawn"-sheets inserted in the three-month-long gap).★

German investigators trying to reconstruct Hess's motives a few weeks later learned of his "inner conflict" at finding Germany and Britain at each other's throat, and of his mental turmoil at being excluded from active service; his "daredevil flying" was well known, and it had caused the Führer to forbid him to fly. Finally, the investigators learned of his "penchant for the mystical, for visions and prophecies". From his farewell letter of 4 November, it is a reasonable deduction that planning this dramatic, single-handed flight became a compulsive obsession.

It developed a momentum of its own. Since August, the weather reports over Britain had been furnished to him each day. Every augury and oracle seemed to be urging him on. An elderly woman peddled a horoscope to him: it seemed to be telling him to go. Fascinated, he instructs Miss Fath to send the details of hour and place of birth which the old crone needed in order to elicit further and better particulars. These omens, when they came, confirmed to those with the requisite occult insights that it was not only the duty but the destiny of the Deputy Führer to fly to Britain to end the war.

Fired by this holy sense of mission, Hess asked Ernst Udet, the former air ace who was now Göring's Director of Air Armament (General-luftzeugmeister), to make a Messerschmitt plane available to him for "pleasure flights" at Berlin's Tempelhof airfield.

It is an indication that Hitler had not sanctioned any notion of his deputy flying off to anywhere that Hess ducked when Udet replied that he would have to get Hitler's approval first for him to be given a plane, and then, after nagging Udet almost to distraction, quietly abandoned the request. "The Führer's permission," he commented two years later, "I might as well have turned myself straight in to be arrested!"

He turned his attention south instead.

One day, recalled his happy-go-lucky friend Professor Willi Messer-schmitt, Hess turned up at his Augsburg aircraft plant and asked to be given flying tuition on their Messerschmitt-110, a new long-range twin-engined fighter plane. The company proudly took one out of its production for him. After a few practice flights, of increasing duration, Hess began coming up with odd demands for the modification of his plane: the range was too limited; it needed fuel tanks built into the wings; it ought to have better radio equipment. The company humoured him; after all, he was the Deputy Führer. Director Theo Croneiss, whom Hess had known since First World War squadron days, ordered the improvements made.

★ The existence of the instructions is clear from the family documents published by his son, James Douglas-Hamilton, in *Motive for a Mission* (London, 1972).

By early January 1941 all seemed ready but this "motorized Parsifal", as Professor Haushofer would call him without a trace of malice, was still tinkering with his chosen chariot. A typical docket in Professor Messerschmitt's factory files reads:

MR HESS'S ME-110   *7 January 1941 Mtt/ke*

Mr Rudolf Hess's Me-110 has an old-type heater without cut-off valve between radiator and heater. I think it necessary to have the valve post-installed now. Please see if this is possible and suggest ways of doing it.

That day and the next Hitler briefed his field marshals and generals on the Obersalzberg, setting out his strategic plans for the spring in the Balkans and North Africa. Britain, he said, was only remaining in the war because she trusted in Russia and America to come in soon: and he told them of his plans to invade the Soviet Union.

Hess, of course, was not present. Far from it – he had decided to leave for Scotland.

On the 10th, he asked his personal adjutant Karlheinz Pintsch to drive him as usual to Messerschmitt's factory airfield at Augsburg. But this time, before climbing up into his Me-110, he handed to his loyal, unquestioning adjutant two envelopes – a letter addressed to Hitler, and sealed instructions to be opened in four hours' time, if Hess had not by then returned.

After two hours' flying, the weather thickened and Hess aborted the mission. He landed at Augsburg to find that Pintsch had opened the instructions: they revealed that his chief, the Deputy Führer, had "flown to Britain".

If he were not to be branded a traitor Hess had to take Pintsch into his confidence too. His intention had been, he said, to fly to Scotland, land at Dungavel, show the Duke of Hamilton the visiting card given him by Albrecht Haushofer, and ask to be taken to the King. To see the King! With one swift flight – which might, he admitted, cost him his life – he would have by-passed the warmongers at 10 Downing Street. Thus Hess intended to end the war.

It says a lot for the trust that Hess inspired in his staff that Pintsch unquestioningly joined his circle of conspirators, and made no attempt to betray his master: but there was one unexpected sequel.

Two weeks later Max Hofweber, the Deputy Führer's old First World War comrade from Lechfeld airfield, came up to Berlin for a gossip with him. The Party chief excused himself after a while. Hofweber struck up a conversation with Pintsch – and learned to his horror of Hess's abortive attempt to fly to Britain. Pintsch swore him to secrecy.

Appalled at the consequences if Hess tried again, Hofweber drove through the night down the autobahn to Munich and spoke with old Professor Haushofer – the one wise man who could stop Hess from going ahead with what seemed like a mad act. Haushofer promised to try, and met Hess some days later. To conceal his source of information, the Professor all too deviously told him that he had had a "dream", in which he had seen Hess striding through the tapestried halls of English castles, bringing peace to two great nations. He had hoped to use this story of a "dream" to prise the truth out of Hess; but Hess just listened, fascinated to hear this further occult evidence of the rightness of his mission – and said nothing.

Some months earlier Hess had begun drafting and redrafting two letters for Hitler. One was short. The other, running to some fourteen pages, he had evidently begun in October; it would be contemptuously described by his arch-rival Ribbentrop as "a long and crazy manuscript". It set out to Hitler the peace proposals that he intended to discuss with Britain. It seems to have had four sections, each typed by a different hand. Laura Schrödl, the official secretary he had shared with Leitgen since February 1936, typed the pages concerning compensation to be paid to the Germans abroad who had lost property in the war – one of his obsessions; she had been aware of his planned mission since September. Hildegard Fath, warned like Laura Schrödl to strictest secrecy, typed a few pages; Hess and Pintsch typed the rest.

Hess would tell the Duke of Hamilton that he had set out four times all told, and been defeated on three occasions by bad weather. But this was not the only reason for the delay between November 1940 and May 1941.

His preliminary long-distance flight experiments had shown the need for more mature preparations than he had anticipated. Through Hitler's personal pilot Hans Baur he obtained an illicit copy of the map showing the forbidden air zones. He experimented with different navigational systems, tried direction-finding the Kalundborg transmitter in Denmark, asked Gauleiter Terboven to obtain similar DF data for him, instructed Messerschmitt's senior radio boffin, Mr Mortsiepen, to install a specially modified radar set, then finally opted for a radio receiver that would enable him to "ride" part of the way on the navigation beams (*Leitstrahlverfahren*) laid across the North Sea by the Luftwaffe bomber squadrons. Ironically, it meant he would have to await the next big air raid on England.

There was also a political reason for the three-month delay to Hess's flight "trials": the Italian army in North Africa was suffering severe reverses; it had begun a long retreat from Egypt to Tripolitania that only the arrival of the small German force commanded by Lieutenant-General Erwin Rommel and his counteroffensive in April would halt. Then Hess waited a few days more, until the German victory in mainland Greece was complete at the end of April 1941, since he was reluctant to make any peace attempt, even in secret, that might be interpreted in Britain as a sign of weakness.

Hess discussed the position during two long stays with Professor Haushofer from 21 to 24 February and 12 to 14 April, without revealing what he himself was plotting to do. On his explicit instructions Albrecht Haushofer continued his own efforts to reach his British friends, as he mentioned in conversation with former ambassador Ulrich von Hassell on 10 March, talking of "the urgent top-level desire for peace".

In those spring weeks vague peace feelers did appear from the other side. After preliminaries by Hassell, Albrecht Haushofer received a greetings message from Professor Carl Jacob Burckhardt, of the International Red Cross in Geneva, who asked him to come to Geneva and passed on – according to Haushofer's contemporary statement to the Gestapo – "cordial greetings from old friends in England". Was this a camouflaged reply from the Duke of Hamilton? It seemed so to Hess. A former high League of Nations official, Burckhardt was known to favour a compromise peace and to have excellent contacts in London.

From Madrid meanwhile, other peace soundings had come from Sir Samuel Hoare, the Ambassador. Rather curiously, the German Deutschlandsender broadcast on 23 April this formal statement: "Reports concerning a journey to Spain by Hess are denied by authoritative German quarters." The files reveal no explanation for this.

Three days later, at a secret meeting with the Haushofers in his Harlaching villa, Hess gave traditional diplomacy one last chance. Albrecht told him of the message from Burckhardt; Hess gave him permission to go, and the young man met Burckhardt on 28 April. "In reality," wrote Martha Haushofer in her diary after her son's departure, "I do not rate the prospects very highly, nor does Albrecht."

Albrecht Haushofer wrote after the interview with Burckhardt, "I found him torn between a desire to promote the possibilities of European peace and acute anxiety lest his name be bandied about in public. He asked me to keep the matter top secret: a few weeks before, he said, he had had a visit in Geneva from a person well known and respected in London's leading Conservative and City circles." This person spoke of the desire of important Englishmen to review peace prospects. His views on a post-armistice Europe were close to Hess's – the British interest in eastern and south-eastern Europe was purely nominal; western Europe would have to be restored; but Germany could have her old colonies back. Albrecht suggested that Burckhardt arrange a meeting with this person in Geneva.

In Berlin on the last day of April Hitler was dictating to his Wehrmacht generals orders for Barbarossa, the attack on Russia, to begin on 22 June. Hess was still in Munich, receiving Salvadore Merino, leader of the Spanish Falange syndicates, at the old Brown House. Later that day, Hess drove to Augsburg and made one more attempt at the flight. This was probably just a final "dress rehearsal", because he took none of the steps (last letters and so on) that he took ten days later; and he still wanted modifications to the plane on which his life – and the future of Europe – might depend.

On 1 May, again visiting Messerschmitt's Augsburg factory to deliver at a mass meeting there the principal speech on Germany's Labour Day, he bestowed on the Professor the Pioneer of Labour award, then took him aside and asked for the answers to questions ("by Monday" – 5 May) that should have left the aircraft expert gasping:

2 May 1941 [Works memorandum]

1. Mr Reichsminister Hess asks what radius curve will be flown if the autopilot is thrown right over; additionally, he asks how true the radius will probably be, and how great the wind influence is likely to be. I can't rightly figure out what it's all about but I forgot to ask what he's up to.★

2. Please see to it, if not already done, that in his plane the second seat's oxygen bottles are fed into those of the pilot. Also, an oxygen mouthpiece is to be put into the plane beside an oxygen mask.

3. He wants the Pitot back-pressure calibrated and a graph showing what a reading of 410 or 450 km really means over 500–60,000 km.
TDM/Mtt/Mo *Signed Messerschmitt*

So Hess had his wits about him. In fact after his arrival British analysts would search every German broadcast since Hitler's birthday (when Hess himself had delivered the principal speech from the Führer's headquarters near the Yugoslav frontier) and find no evidence of any differences with the Party or progressive mental disorders. As Bodenschatz said, to use the navigational *Leitstrahl* Hess must have been fully alert. It was a difficult plane, and a hazardous flight: Udet, one of the First World War's greatest aviators, would try to reassure Hitler that Hess could never have completed such a risky flight. Göring too reassured Hitler, when the time came, that the Deputy Führer must have ditched and drowned. Hitler disagreed. "The Führer believes in Hess's ability," wrote one of his staff when they first heard the news of his departure. "When Hess gets his teeth into something," said Hitler expressionlessly, "he does it properly."

The Nazi victory in the Balkans was complete. Shortly, Hitler's airborne troops would descend on the remaining British stronghold, the Mediterranean island of Crete. As Hitler marched into the Kroll Opera House at 6 p.m. on 4 May to report on this great military victory, in a speech broadcast live around the whole of Europe, English radio monitors heard the Reichstag deputies rising to their feet and cheering; Hitler was flanked by Hess, Göring, Dr Wilhelm Frick, Minister of the Interior, and Himmler. Hitler's speech contrasted the Wehrmacht's prowess with Churchill's discomfiting, bumbling retreats in Greece and North Africa. It had the deputies in fits of laughter.

Just as he did after Norway and Dunkirk, Mr Churchill – he also began this campaign – is trying to say something that he might yet be able to

---

★ Field Marshal Erhard Milch, Göring's deputy, told Bodenschatz in May 1945: "Messerschmitt knew all about it, definitely; knew exactly what was going on, and so did [Director Theo] Croneiss. The plane had been specially fitted out for this purpose."

twist and distort into a British victory. I don't think that very honest, but in the case of this man it is at least comprehensible. If ever any other politician had met such defeats, or a soldier had encountered such catastrophes, he would not have kept his job six months – unless he was possessed of the same talent that alone distinguishes Mr Churchill, the ability to lie with devout mien and distort the truth so that in the end the most frightful defeats turn into the most glorious victories. Mr Churchill may be able to put down a smokescreen before his fellow countrymen, but he cannot eliminate the results of his disasters.

Hess listened attentively to these remarks about Churchill. He drew Hitler aside as the session ended. According to Hitler's recollection they spoke for half an hour. Hess inquired if he still stood by his programme outlined in *Mein Kampf*; Hitler – anxious to drive to the station where his train was due to leave at 8.15 p.m. for an inspection of the new battleships *Bismarck* and *Tirpitz* at Gotenhaften – answered shortly that he did. A week later Hess would tell British officers, "As recently as 4 May, after his Reichstag speech, Hitler declared to me that he had no oppressive demands to make on England." Laura Schrödl, his secretary, also recalled that long meeting in the Kroll Opera building. "Subsequently," she recalled, "he [Hess] left for Munich and attempted to start his flight then and there, but because of an engine defect he had to postpone it again."

Hess never saw Hitler again. His movements over the next days are uncertain. Hitler's train arrived back in Munich on the morning of the 9th, but it was Göring who met him on the platform, not Hess. Hitler spent ten hours in the Bavarian capital before going on to Berchtesgaden, without having bothered to see his deputy.

On Friday 9 May, Hess knew that the historic hour was approaching. That day he telephoned Dr Gerhard Klopfer, a legal under-secretary (Staatssekretär) on Martin Bormann's staff. "What is the position of the King of England?" he asked the legal expert, *tout court*.

"I can't answer that at once," said Klopfer, puzzled by the way the question was framed. "I'll get the information from a college professor and call you back."

Later that day, Hess received a letter from the Minister of Agriculture, Walter Darré. Göring's wire-tapping agency, the Forschungsamt, which was tapping Darré's (or Hess's!) line, heard him try to call Darré's number in Berlin; unable to raise the Minister, Hess wrote a letter:

9 May 1941

Thank you for your letter. I don't know who has been telling you I would fix that conference we agreed on for the middle of this month.

I am planning a major trip and don't know when I'll be back. . . . I'll get in touch with you again after my return.

Why should he not be returning? He was flying to an enemy country as a parliamentary, conveying terms of truce to an honourable foe. It was a time-honoured usage – which Hitler had himself accepted at Warsaw and in the subsequent campaigns – that such couriers are permitted to return to their own lines unmolested, whatever the outcome of their negotiations. Nor did Hess consider that he needed any special letters of authority: had Neville Chamberlain needed to produce such a document when he came to Berchtesgaden, Godesberg and Munich on behalf of his head of state to avert war in 1938?

No, Hess considered that his identity as the Führer's formally appointed deputy should be enough to enable him to talk on equal terms with King George VI.

Some days earlier, Albrecht Haushofer had returned from Geneva with instructions from Burckhardt to return to Switzerland soon, whence "he would be flown to Madrid and have a conference" with Hoare, the British Ambassador. For a few days they waited for word from Madrid, but time was running out fast. Karl Haushofer recalled, "When my son returned from Switzerland Hess spoke to him again, and it was after that he flew to England." That same night, after Hess's departure, a telegram came from the German Embassy in Spain, requesting, perhaps fortuitously, Albrecht's attendance in Madrid on the 12th. It was too late: by that time Haushofer and all of Hess's staff would be in Gestapo custody.

Tenth May 1941. It was a day of endings – the end of an obsession; the end of the months of trials and preparations; the end, it turned out, of Rudolf Hess's freedom. The day had begun warm and sunny but now, like Hess's life itself, it was half spent and beginning to cloud over.

Ilse had been off-colour for several days, and did not know why. Of course she had noticed that something was afoot – the conspiratorial meetings, the strange telephoned weather reports about locations referred to only as "X", "Y" and "Z", the travel bag packed and unpacked, the map of the "Baltic coastline" pinned next to Rudolf's bed (in fact it was the coast of Scotland); finally she had deduced that he was planning a mission to Marshal Pétain in France.

He had written a new farewell letter to his parents and brother, and one to Ilse with the wry remark that she would now be able to guess "the secrets of 'X' and 'Y'" which had bulked so large in their life of late. Hess also wrote to Heinrich Himmler, swearing that his men had known nothing of the plan. He had avoided implicating his friends. "I am very sorry to say", recalled Professor Haushofer four years later, "that he did not confide in me and actually lied to me in my flat, shortly before his flight. I told him that I had the feeling that he was hiding something from me. He kept the whole flying thing from me, and just told me that 'a plane had been presented to me by the Führer'." In a letter to Albrecht Haushofer, Hess apologized, explaining that he saw only one possible solution – "to cut the Gordian knot of this unhappy entanglement". He hid these letters with his testament among little Wolf Rüdiger's toys, where they would be found the next day.

That Saturday, Ilse stayed in bed reading. She still felt unwell. Looking into her room, Hess noticed that she was reading *The Pilot's Book of Everest*, by the Duke of Hamilton. They exchanged a few meaningless words about his good looks and his courage as an aviator.

Hess was now impatient to leave. Making this flight had become an obsession, and he knew it. Nine years later, he reflected:

> I had lived those months in a whirl of instruments, cylinder-head pressures, jettison fuel containers, auxiliary oil pumps, coolant temperatures, radio beam widths – which didn't even work when the time came – the heights of Scottish mountains and God knows what else! I had put on blinkers that shut out everything else around me apart from the broad reality of the war and daily politics. Today, I am glad to have been driven like that into finally taking the plunge over there – after a desperate struggle to extricate myself from an obstinate charger that refused to let me go. True: I achieved nothing, I couldn't stop this lunatic struggle between nations, I couldn't prevent what came and what I saw was coming.
>
> I was unable to bring salvation – but I'm glad that at least I *tried*.

The morning weather forecasts came in, and they were good for X, Y and Z. Heavy cloud layers were predicted over Scotland and some precipitation: "Lower cloud layers to the southern and eastern side of the mountains, thinning out". He telephoned his adjutant Pintsch: "This is the day," he said.

He had dressed in a light-blue shirt. Ilse liked it, because it matched his eyes, but his reason for wearing it was more prosaic – today he would be changing out of his casual light-grey suit and into a Luftwaffe captain's uniform expensively tailored for him in Munich.

He had thought ahead to the moment when he landed; if he came in non-combatant's clothes, the British would be entitled to treat him as a spy. Thinking ahead too, he had packed a wrist compass, so that he could find his way to the Duke's castle if he landed too far off; a flash-lamp and a box of Bengal matches; visiting-cards of both Haushofers, and an authentic-looking, properly postmarked envelope addressed to "Hauptmann Alfred Horn, München 9".

More detailed weather forecasts came. They now promised "ten-tenths cloud cover at 1500 feet" over the North Sea. He spent the whole morning playing with little Wolf Rüdiger – "Buz", as he was called in the family: it perplexed Ilse that her husband the Deputy Führer should have so much time on his hands that day to shuffle around the floor pushing trains with his boy.

Some time that morning he may have learned that the Luftwaffe was scheduled to make its heaviest raid on London (its farewell, in fact, before regrouping against the Soviet Union). That would keep the British night-fighter squadrons busy in the south.

At midday his lunch guest arrived – former Nazi chief editor and philosopher Alfred Rosenberg, born like Hess beyond Germany's frontiers, and educated in Moscow. The two men set about their cold-meat luncheon alone, since Ilse was still upstairs. Hess talked quietly with Rosenberg. The latter noticed only one thing that struck him in retrospect as odd – that after the nanny had taken Buz up to bed, Hess went upstairs on an impulse and brought him down again to play.

After Rosenberg left, Hess went upstairs to take leave as casually as he was able of Ilse and Buz. She noticed uneasily that he was now wearing not only the blue shirt, but breeches of air-force blue and flying boots as well.

He murmured something about having to be in Berlin. She asked a wife's usual questions – when would he be back? – but he answered with an evasion, hinting at Monday so unconvincingly that she smiled: "I don't believe you. Well, come back soon," she added. "Buz will miss you."

"I'm going to miss him too," he said, and took a last peek at the curly-haired boy as he sat on a white potty in the nursery.

By 5 p.m. the Luftwaffe's blind bombing beams had been switched on for the night's raid – they intersected just east of Regent's Park in London's West End. Soon afterwards the Deputy Führer's little Mercedes SSK set out with Hess and his adjutant along the autobahn out of Munich. Before reaching the airfield at Augsburg he told the driver to stop, and stepped out for a stroll in the Bavarian mountain crocuses with Pintsch. The cheap metal watch on his wrist showed that they were running a few minutes early. After a while, he asked to see the weather report again. "You've certainly got a good day for the flight," said Pintsch, trying to make it sound an everyday affair.

At the gate to Messerschmitt's Hunstetten airfield the sentries saluted the Mercedes and lifted the boom. A few minutes later the little Me-110 fighter plane, looking pathetically inadequate for the burden it was to carry to Scotland, was wheeled out. Hess watched as its tanks were filled, and checked for himself that none of the guns was loaded. It was important that he should arrive unarmed.

He gave his adjutant the letter that he was to deliver to the Führer, with the familiar instructions. He had to borrow a flying overall, since his own was under repair, so he wrote a note of apology to its rightful owner. At last he climbed into the cockpit, alone.

At 5.40 p.m., the two 1000-horsepower Daimler-Benz engines lifted the Messerschmitt 110 into the leaden skies. Their thunder could be heard by the handful of watchers long after the plane had vanished from sight.

Part Two

Britain

6 Fool's Errand

Hounded by the sirens' wail, harrowed by the deaths of ten thousand fathers and mothers, wives and friends, the British people were cold, miserable and unreceptive as that summer and autumn of 1940 drew in, replaced by a winter of even bleaker defeat and deprivation. They saw no respite from war, with its perpetual blackout, its censorship, its rationing, its bomb craters and its power cuts – and yet with rugged good humour they showed in countless ways which amazed the foreigners and inspired themselves that they were determined to see it through. That winter, they were whipped into a frenzy of nervous apprehension by their prime minister's stout broadcasts anticipating – but not fearing – Nazi invasion, and inspiring them to hate Herr Hitler and his satraps for each heartless bomb that fell upon Britain's soil.

"These cruel, wanton, indiscriminate bombings of London are, of course," Churchill had declared a week after the Luftwaffe's Blitz began in September 1940,

> a part of Hitler's invasion plan. He hopes, by killing large numbers of civilians, and women and children, that he will terrorize and cow the people of this mighty imperial city, and make them a burden and anxiety to the government and thus distract our attention unduly from the ferocious onslaught he is preparing. Little does he know the spirit of the British nation, or the tough fibre of the Londoners. . . .
>
> This wicked man, the repository and embodiment of many forms of soul-destroying hatreds, this monstrous product of former wrongs and shame, has now resolved to try to break our famous island race by a process of indiscriminate slaughter and destruction. What he has done is to kindle a fire in British hearts, here and all over the world, which will glow long after all traces of the conflagration he has caused in London have been removed.

By the spring of 1941 That Man seemed to be getting his way everywhere, and still the threat of Nazi invasion hung suspended over the Channel horizon, oppressing all but Winston Churchill himself: for he

alone had known since July 1940 (from his codebreakers) that it was
Hitler's bluff, and that 1941 would see the invasion of Russia, not of
Britain; he had not divulged this secret Intelligence even to Anthony
Eden, his new Foreign Secretary.

Early in November 1940, as the Nazi bombing offensive was approaching its bloody climax in Coventry, a curious letter reached Table II of the
first-floor desk of a Postal Censorship officer in London. He opened it on
2 November, and found in it another envelope, forwarded from Thos
Cook's office in Lisbon to their office in Berkeley Street, London.

At first it seemed to be anonymous – a note sent by "A" from a city
called "B", asking a Mrs Violet Roberts to forward an enclosed
three-page letter to His Grace the Duke of Hamilton and Brandon at the
House of Lords; the letter was described as significant to His Grace and his
friends in high office.

It was of course the letter from Albrecht Haushofer in Berlin. It had at
last reached London and been stopped – just as he had anticipated – by the
Censors. "My dear Douglo," it began, "Even if there is only a slight
chance that this letter should reach you in good time, there is a chance, and
I am determined to make use of it." He offered condolences on the deaths
of his father and brother-in-law, then continued with a paragraph that
Censorship Examiner No. 1021 quoted in his report:

> If you remember some of my last communications in July 1939 you – and
> your friends in high places – may find some significance in the fact that I
> am able to ask you whether you could find time to have a talk with me
> somewhere on the outskirts of Europe, perhaps in Portugal.
>   I could reach Lisbon any time (and without any kind of difficulties)
> within four days after receiving news from you. Of course I do not know
> whether you can make your authorities understand so much that they
> give you leave. . . .
>   But at least you may be able to answer my question.

The writer had assured the Duke that letters would reach him within
five days from Lisbon: he should mark the envelope containing his reply
only "Dr A.H." ("nothing more!") and send it, sealed in another
envelope, to a certain company address in Lisbon. "My father and mother
add their wishes for your personal welfare to my own," concluded
Albrecht Haushofer's letter. "Yours ever, 'A'."

Although there was nothing specific, Censor No. 1021 suspected that
the letter had originated in Nazi Germany – "B" might be Berlin; perhaps
the handwriting or punctuation gave off a Teutonic odour. At any rate, an
analysis sheet was made, photographic copies were laboriously prepared;
the original letter was passed to Military Intelligence department MI12
for MI5 (counter-espionage), the copies percolated throughout that
winter along the ponderous and dusty channels of British Intelligence

agencies, resting for weeks at a time in buff folders, accumulating dockets and sage comments as they went.

Albrecht Haushofer was identified as the sender but source material is sparse about who now decided what. One possible course was to set up an espionage "game" – to respond to him and arrange a meeting as suggested: another was to find out if the Duke or people around him were part of a Nazi fifth column in Great Britain. Kurt Wallersteiner, of the German Section of SIS, saw that its dossier on the Duke was soon "inches thick". Ex-President Eduard Beneš, in close touch with British Intelligence, learned that they did respond to the letter. Perhaps this was the subtle approach that went that April through Madrid and Professor Burckhardt to Haushofer. (Beneš wrote that the SIS were shocked by the size of the fish they eventually "hooked".)

Meanwhile, since the Duke was now, as Haushofer had predicted, a serving RAF officer, MI5 passed the intercepted letter to the Air Ministry's security branch. From there on 26 February 1941 Group Captain F. G. Stammers wrote a cautious letter to the Duke at his RAF station in Scotland: the Ministry was anxious for a chat with him about a particular matter when he was next in London.

In mid-March Hamilton faced Stammers across a desk in the Ministry. "What have you done", the Group Captain asked him pleasantly, "with the letter that Albrecht Haushofer wrote to you?" The most recent letter that Hamilton had *received* was in July 1939 – the one that he had shown to Churchill at the time; he had concealed this in a bank safe. Stammers pushed the photostat of the intercepted 23 September 1940 letter across the desk. "It seems to us", he said, "that this Haushofer is a pretty significant chap." Hamilton agreed – Haushofer, he explained, was closely connected with the Foreign Ministry in Berlin, which had often sent him over to London as a moderating influence during Ribbentrop's ambassadorship there. Hess was evidently not mentioned at this interview.

"We think", said Stammers as they parted, "that it might be of considerable value to make contact with Haushofer."

The British official files so far released are devoid of any reference to this Ministry meeting (which is documented in the Duke's family papers).

Two months passed. The SIS pressed ahead with its deliberations, and at 11.30 a.m. on 25 April the Duke again appeared at the Ministry, this time before Group Captain D. L. Blackford. "Jerry" Blackford, a tall, round-faced officer with a charming manner, was chief of Air Ministry security. A "Major Robertson" of Military Intelligence joined them. Together, they made it plain that they wanted the Duke to "volunteer" to fly to Portugal for an exploratory meeting with Haushofer. "I'll go if I am *ordered* to," said Hamilton, stressing the penultimate word.

"Chaps usually *volunteer* for this type of job," they replied.

It is significant that this was the moment when Professor Burckhardt in

Geneva began putting out feelers "from a high British personage" to the Haushofers. Evidently Hamilton smelt a rat – suspected perhaps that the SIS was planning to contact the Nazis without higher authority. After taking advice from learned friends, he wrote to Blackford on 28 April agreeing to go but only on two conditions. First, "I should not . . . like to hold any consultation with X without the knowledge of . . . H.M. Ambassador" (in which connection he wanted to see Sir Alexander Cadogan before leaving: Cadogan, Permanent Under-Secretary at the Foreign Office, controlled all SIS matters under Churchill). Secondly, a reason must be given to "X" why it had taken seven months to reply, otherwise Haushofer might infer that the British had "got the wind up" and suddenly *wanted* to talk peace.

The Duke's arguments could not be ignored. The plan would have to be shelved. Blackford wrote to the Duke at his airbase in Scotland a letter which makes plain that another agency *had* been behind it. "You will realise, of course," wrote Blackford, "that the Air Ministry are in no way concerned with the policy question involved and are only concerned with the problem whether or not it is practicable to open a channel with your assistance. I have, however, put your views to the Department concerned" – which he did not identify. He blamed the seven-month delay on "another Department having mislaid the papers", and added that in the view of Air Commodore Boyle, Director of Air Intelligence, "in the present circumstances a move of the kind suggested could not be made without Cabinet authority". If this letter meant anything at all, it was that the Cabinet had *not* been consulted by the SIS.

It was Saturday 10 May when Wing Commander the Duke of Hamilton and Blandford dictated to his typist at RAF Station Turnhouse, near Glasgow, a reply to Blackford's letter. He said he appreciated that the project had been temporarily shelved, and now regretted that what he called "a very good opportunity" had been missed owing to the delay.

If the proposition materialises and I am asked to go, I think that probably the best way would be . . . I would write to "X" – "I did not reply to your letter last autumn [23 September 1940] because I saw no opportunity of leaving this country at that time. It appears now that I may have a chance of arranging a meeting with you abroad some time during the next month or two. If you would still like to see me, will you let me know."

But events had passed out of his control. Late that night, as he was on duty in the RAF operations room of Turnhouse Sector, on the outskirts of Edinburgh, a radar unit located a single unidentified plane flying in from the North Sea. At 10.08 p.m. it crossed the coast close to Farne Islands. Almost at once the Royal Observer Corps (ROC) telephoned the Duke with a puzzling detail: the intruder was a German plane all right – but of a short-range type only once before seen this far north, a Messerschmitt-110.

The Duke did nothing to scramble a fighter plane (notwithstanding the impression he created by his report a few days later: "Normal action had been taken to intercept and shoot down the enemy aircraft"). It was not until half an hour later, as the mystery plane entered the next fighter Sector controlled by RAF Station Ayr, at 10.34 p.m., that action was allegedly taken to intercept the "raid", now formally assigned the control-number "42J". The station's records state, "A Defiant [fighter plane] of 141 Squadron attempted to intercept, but failed to do so." This entry, however, was written some days after the importance of the Messerschmitt's pilot was known, and the record book of No. 141 Squadron shows that the Defiant – piloted by Pilot Officer Cuddie with Sergeant Hodge as observer – took off on what was entered as a routine "night patrol" lasting fifty minutes. (The obsolescent Defiant would not have stood much chance of "intercepting" a 500-m.p.h. Messerschmitt anyway.)★

At 10.56 p.m. the ROC spotted the Me-110, losing height and now only three thousand feet up. Well below the scattered clouds, it was doubling back from Scotland's west coast over Ardrossan, a few miles up the coast from Ayr. After circling back once or twice as though looking for something the plane vanished from the radar screens just to the south of the city at 11.07 p.m. A local Home Guard unit reported that a plane had crashed at Eaglesham, just south of Glasgow and that the pilot was a German and had parachuted out and been taken prisoner.

Two officers from RAF Station Ayr – Flight Lieutenant Gemmel and Second-Lieutenant Fowler – set out at once towards Glasgow, curious to see the crashed plane and prisoner. The plane was indeed an Me-110, but there were two striking features: its fuselage marking VJ+OQ was a *delivery* code, not an operational squadron code; and its guns were not only not loaded but were packed solid with their original grease.

Mystified, the officers went off to search for the pilot. This officer had spent his last minutes of liberty before being apprehended by ploughman David McLean struggling to disengage his billowing parachute – not that he could have escaped, because his ankle was sprained and he had injured his back when the slipstream hurled him against the rudder of the crashing Messerschmitt.

Sipping tea in the deepest leather armchair in the parlour of the ploughman's cottage, he had shown a picture of a little boy to the family. "My son," he explained. "I saw him this afternoon but I don't know when I'll see him again."

Robert Williamson, the tin-hatted local constable, had arrived, as had a boozy Home Guard company commander, Mr Clarke, who was brandishing a lethal-looking Webley revolver. "I am Hauptmann Alfred

★ There were much faster planes, Hurricanes, at Turnhouse. The next day, reported the Duke, he "jumped into a Hurricane, the fastest aircraft available, and flew to Northolt".

Horn," the German pilot told them, wincing as a stomach cramp convulsed his gut. "I have an urgent message for the Duke of Hamilton. Please take me to him at once."

This extraordinary request percolated through the official channels to Glasgow and Edinburgh, although the laxity of Scotland's Saturday-night licensing laws had a befuddling effect. It reached RAF Ayr, which recorded: "He gave his name as Alfred Horn and claimed that he had come to see his friend the Duke of Hamilton. His English was good." It reached RAF Turnhouse too: the Duke was telephoned that Horn was "on a special mission to see him and had intended to land at Dungavel" – his home, only two minutes' flying time from where Horn had baled out.

With a self-control that would seem remarkable under any circumstances, but which bordered on the grotesque in this instance, the Duke decided to do nothing, and restrained his Intelligence officer Flight Lieutenant Benson from visiting the prisoner that night.

Why this seemingly inexplicable reluctance, given the extraordinary circumstances? Clearly the Duke of Hamilton wanted time to think: but was it about his official duty or his own personal reputation? It seems legitimate to rehearse here the evidence – some of it quite hard, some of it very tenuous indeed – that the pre-war ties that had variously bound Rudolf Hess, Albrecht Haushofer, and the Duke were of a more profound nature than has otherwise been suspected. Ten years of barren, childless marriage had preceded the birth of Ilse Hess's first child. There was, besides, something about Hess's personal history that led more than one medical expert who interviewed him to diagnose a latent streak of homosexuality, expressed at its bluntest by Nuremberg's prison Commandant, Colonel Burton C. Andrus, in a confidential 1945 memorandum which alleged that Hess and Hitler had enjoyed a homosexual relationship during the Landsberg prison episode of 1924 (see p. 12).

Some of these indications are only vague, others stronger; there was the oddly intimate relationship with the old Karl Haushofer (who would commit suicide in 1946, his illusions about Hess shattered); there were the poems, odes and dreams that the two men exchanged, resulting in an upsurge of jealousy in Rudolf's much younger bride; there was the year-long close confinement in Landsberg with not only Hitler but Ernst Röhm: ("*Ich liebe ihn*, I love him!" he had exclaimed in that letter to Ilse, written in July 1924 after the "turning point" experience of seeing Hitler weep). Röhm was an admitted homosexual whose butchery by Hitler in June 1934 would outrage what chief adjutant Alfred Leitgen would delicately call Hess's "pronounced – I would say almost feminine – instinct". Two months after the killing of Röhm, Hess was the first top Nazi to establish close and very private contacts with Konrad Henlein, the youthful Sudeten-German leader whom Heinrich Himmler's handwritten notes reveal to have been another closet homosexual. In 1941 Hess would talk about the deceased Röhm with a degree of hatred that suggested to the British army's chief psychiatric consultant John Rawlings Rees "the repression of homosexual trends". At the same time, it is significant to note, the Gestapo in Berlin began to investigate, according to what Heinz Haushofer has revealed to this author, rumours that there had been homosexual activities between his brother Albrecht and Hess or "the young and handsome" Duke of Hamilton, to whom Albrecht repeatedly referred in private correspondence as "my closest friend". Their friendship was so close, indeed, that Albrecht was sure even one year into the war that "an A. will suffice", at the foot of a letter, for the Duke to know whose hand had written it.

This is all that can – and perhaps should, given the impossibility of questioning any of the three principals concerned – properly be said about this aspect of the affair.

With the muzzle of that Webley wobbling in the small of his back, and almost blinded by the alcohol vapours wheezed at him by the Glaswegian clutching its ancient trigger, Hauptmann Horn was driven along the bumpy country lanes to the headquarters of the 3rd Battalion of the Home Guard in a Boy Scout hut in Florence Drive, Giffnock, a suburb of Glasgow. He hoped that the same merciful Deity which had yanked him clear of the crashing Messerschmitt now evidently had his finger wedged between the Webley's firing pin and percussion cap, just in case. They pulled up outside the headquarters at precisely fourteen minutes after midnight. For a few minutes there was uncertainty about what to do with this prisoner. RAF Abbotsinch, Glasgow's local airbase, was asked if they wanted to interrogate him. "No," came the reply. "Put him in a police cell for the night." The 14th Argyll and Sutherland Highlanders, eventually reached after twenty minutes' battling through blocked GPO telephone lines, gave the same advice. It was after all Saturday night and the Scots had better things to do.

The Home Guard's Battalion Commander felt uneasy, even embarrassed at this display of inefficiency to a Nazi prisoner who somehow seemed a cut above them all. "This officer is of some importance," he warned the army, and reported Hauptmann Horn's arrival to his own Area Command as well. What kind of Luftwaffe captain claimed to be forty-seven – older than some of these "Dad's Army" veterans? "It was obvious", the Colonel wrote a few days later, "that his uniform was new and of particularly good quality and had not seen service."

He ordered extra courtesies displayed to their captive, and a Home Guard major, James Barrie, to escort Horn to Glasgow in his car when the time came. Two detectives arrived, and helped to list* the prisoner's effects: these included a Leica camera, photographs of Horn and a small

---

* During the night three inventories were taken of the prisoner's personal effects. These were originally attached to each unit's report, in Scottish Command files (now Public Record Office, file WO199/3288A); sadly, all three lists are now missing – perhaps still "closed" because of what they might reveal. File 3288B is sealed for fifty years, but this *may* merely report disciplinary proceedings against Glasgow army officers for events on this extraordinary night.

boy, a quantity of drugs and medicines, a hypodermic syringe, and visiting cards of the two Haushofers.

The army said that the 11th Cameronians would send an escort, and twice the Home Guard battalion telephoned them to hurry up. Hauptmann Horn was already visibly tired, and in pain. The Polish Consul Roman Battaglia turned up to interpret, and two ROC officers arrived soon after; one of them, Group Captain Graham Donald – a machine-tool manufacturer in civilian life – took one look at the prisoner and suspected that he was not "Alfred Horn" at all.

After interrogating him for five minutes, he suddenly asked him to autograph a picture of an ME-110. The pilot carefully obliged: *Alfred Horn*. "Aren't you Rudolf Hess?" challenged Donald, feeling cheated. "You're his split image!"

Horn denied it, but admitted that the likeness had caused him enough embarrassment in the past. "I have called over to see the Duke of Hamilton," he explained. "I know him very well."

Donald invited him to prove who he was. At first the prisoner said that he carried no identity papers. Then he unflapped his breast pocket, smiled and produced a crumpled envelope. It was addressed to "Hauptmann Alfred Horn, München 9".

Donald was totally unconvinced. "I recognized him easily," he wrote a week later to his superiors. "My difficulty lay in getting one sensible individual up here with enough eyesight to bear out my identification! Fortunately I was able to contact the Duke of H. about 2 a.m. and finally things started moving, slowly." (Among Horn's property had been found a map, with Dungavel castle marked on it.) "On Sunday [the 11th] I d—d nearly 'phoned you to ask you to let Mr Churchill know personally, but . . . it would sound such a cock-and-bull story over the wires."

Two things intrigued Captain Anthony White, night-duty officer at the army's Glasgow Area headquarters: that the German should have arrived in an Me-110, and that he was asking to see the Duke. Around 12.30 a.m. he telephoned RAF Turnhouse and asked to speak to the Duke's Intelligence officer despite the lateness of the hour; but the Duty Pilot there came back on the telephone and said that Flight Lieutenant Benson was "not available". "We have the story already both from the ROC and from Ayr aerodrome," he added dismissively. "Benson will leave here for Glasgow at 8.30 in the morning."

White was astonished at RAF Turnhouse's lack of interest. "This is not an ordinary case," he said. "Is Flight Lieutenant Benson aware of the whole facts?"

"You have told me nothing new," came the response.

This was not the only lassitude of the night, and Glasgow Area asked for an investigation. RAF Turnhouse's delay was "most unfortunate", wrote Colonel R. Firebrace in his report at the time. "It can only be assumed that the decision to do nothing until morning was taken by Wing Commander the Duke of Hamilton," and that His Grace had "prevented" Benson from going post-haste to see the prisoner.

Captain White ordered a unit of the 11th Cameronians to relieve the Home Guard of their mysterious prisoner. By the time the message reached Lieutenant F. E. Whitby, Horn was being called a "difficult" prisoner; Whitby collected handcuffs from the Craigie Street police station and set off for Giffnock with orders to escort the prisoner to Maryhill Barracks in Glasgow.

At 12.45 a.m. White telephoned the barracks, though not without difficulty, as the switchboard operator there was in a drunken stupor and when awakened he found the duty officer Lieutenant B. Fulton in a similar condition in the orderly room – in fact in his pyjamas, fast asleep in bed.

"Pull yourself together," shouted White down the telephone at him when Fulton eventually came on the line. "Are you awake now?" Fulton claimed that he was. "You are to expect one German prisoner within one hour. I don't know his rank. Make all arrangements necessary."

Fulton told the Guard Room to prepare a cell and went back to bed.

Although the 11th Cameronians' headquarters at 35 Coplaw Street was only two and a half miles from Giffnock, it was twelve minutes past two before Lieutenant Whitby and two soldiers arrived at the Scout Hut. Major James Barrie, whom the Home Guard had asked to escort Horn to the barracks in person in recognition of his mysterious rank, was appalled to see the handcuffs and made Whitby put them away. "I've never heard of an officer being put in handcuffs," he pointed out; nor would handcuffs be used against this prisoner until Nuremberg, in 1945, when he was transferred to American hands.

They set off in Major Barrie's car across the city to the Maryhill Barracks in the north-west. It was once more shrouded in slumber. No military police were guarding the gate, which was apparently unlocked, and the Guard Room was deserted. After several blasts of the car's horn – it was now 2.30 a.m. – a lance-corporal appeared in shirtsleeves and braces.

Major Barrie was mortified that their foreign visitor should witness this display of laxity by the Highland Light Infantry. But worse was to come, as their Hauptmann Horn was now locked into a bare cell which even Lieutenant Whitby found "most unsatisfactory"; it contained a board bed with grimy mattress and grease-stained bolster.

For the first time Horn too became angry. "British officers in Germany would never be treated as badly as this," he protested.

Leaving him under guard, his officer escort went off to look for the night duty officer. They found Lieutenant Fulton still in bed; he neither saluted the Major nor called him Sir. He picked up his bedside telephone and called Glasgow Area command. "The prisoner has arrived. He's a Hauptmann."

Captain White's voice came back, "Where have you put him?"

"In the Guard Room."

"Get him out of the Guard Room. Get a proper bedroom for him and a bed. Give him any food he may require and see that his injuries are properly attended to by the MO."

Fulton tried desultorily by telephone and batman to locate a better room but failed. Lieutenant Whitby suggested he might try getting out of bed first, and eventually Major Barrie persuaded the barracks hospital to treat Horn's injuries and let him stay the night there. Second-Lieutenant Bailey arrived to drive Horn over there; this officer was dressed only in tartan slacks and glengarry (a casual Scottish cap).

At the small Maryhill Barracks hospital, it thus fell to Major C. W. Greenhill of the Royal Army Medical Corps (RAMC) to conduct the first of many medical examinations on the prisoner on British soil. It was now 3.30 a.m. He noted that Horn complained of an injury to his right ankle, pain in his upper lumbar region, and gastric trouble of old standing; Greenhill gave him a powder against the last, and a sedative at the prisoner's request.

Rudolf Hess, Deputy Führer of Germany, awoke on Sunday morning, 11 May 1941, to find himself in a side room of the detention ward of this little hospital at Maryhill Barracks, Glasgow. Barely twelve hours had passed since he had taken off at Augsburg to see the Duke of Hamilton. Now at 10 a.m. the Duke was shown in, accompanied by Flight Lieutenant Benson, his Intelligence Officer. Benson checked over the prisoner's property: the Haushofers' visiting cards must have caught the Duke's eye, and the fact that his castle Dungavel was marked on one map.

"I should like to speak to you alone," said the prisoner. The Duke motioned to Benson and the army officer on guard to withdraw. "I saw you at the Olympic Games in Berlin," continued the German. "You lunched with us. I don't know if you recognize me – but I am Rudolf Hess!"

Hess went on to tell the Duke that he was on "a mission of humanity", that Hitler wanted to stop fighting Britain and end the bloodshed. "My friend Albrecht Haushofer told me you were an Englishman who would probably understand our point of view." He had hoped, he said, to arrange a meeting in Lisbon: the Duke now realized that Hess was behind the Haushofer letter of 23 September, so recent in his own memory. "The fact that I as a Reichsminister have come to this country in person is proof of my sincerity and Germany's willingness for peace." He asked Hamilton to get together the leading members of his party (the Conservative Party) and talk things over with them.

"There is now only one party in this country," replied the Duke.

Hess persisted. "I can tell you what Hitler's peace terms will be! Firstly, he will insist on an arrangement whereby our two countries will never go to war again" – a sentence with uneasy echoes of the piece of paper which Chamberlain had brought back from Munich – and explained, when the Duke asked how that could be arranged, that Britain must simply abandon her traditional opposition to whichever was the strongest power on the Continent.

"Even if we were to make peace now," argued the Duke, sceptically, "we should be at war again within two years." Hitler, he pointed out, had chosen war at a time when Britain was anxious for peace, so there was not much hope of any agreement now.

"I want you to ask His Majesty to give me his word [*Parole*]," said Hess – meaning, to allow him to return to Germany. "Because I came here unarmed and of my own free will."

He had probably rehearsed this sentence before leaving Germany; how he was to return, since he had failed to land his plane in one piece, was not discussed. The Duke suggested that they meet again with an interpreter. Before he left, Hess asked him to conceal his true identity from the press, and to send a telegram to his aunt in Zürich stating that "Alfred Horn" was in good health.

Nonplussed by this extraordinary meeting – there was nothing in King's Regulations and Air Council Instructions to cover anything like it – the Duke notified the garrison commander that this was a Very Important Prisoner indeed – he must be removed from the danger of enemy bombing immediately, and placed under close guard.

He drove off to Eaglesham to inspect the crashed and gutted wreckage of the Messerschmitt. Given his own meetings with the SIS and Air Intelligence in recent weeks, he may have suspected that strange – even illicit – dealings were afoot. But his loyalty as an officer was to his King, and to nobody else.

Back at RAF Turnhouse, near Edinburgh, later that afternoon he told his commanding officer nothing except that he had something vital to communicate to the Foreign Office in London. At 5 p.m. he tried to reach Sir Alexander Cadogan there by telephone, but it was a hot Sunday afternoon and the Permanent Head of the Foreign Office was down at his country cottage, gardening. "Sir Alexander is an extremely busy man," the Duke was told.

He clung to the telephone for half an hour or more, arguing. He insisted on getting an interview with Cadogan at 10 Downing Street that same evening, but the Permanent Under-Secretary's secretary J. M. Addis was less than accommodating, and a stand-up long-distance shouting match developed between the official in London and the young Wing Commander in Edinburgh – in the midst of which a strange voice broke into the line: "This is the Prime Minister's secretary," it said. "The Prime Minister has sent me over to the Foreign Office, as he is informed that you have some interesting information. . . . I would like to know what you propose to do."

"Have a car at Northolt within an hour and a half," said the relieved

Duke, referring to an RAF aerodrome west of London. "I'll meet it there!"

At midday in Germany Hess's adjutant Karlheinz Pintsch had turned up at the Berghof, Hitler's mountain lair in Bavaria, and handed the Führer a letter from Hess. (The longer, fourteen-page one had already been delivered the previous evening but Hitler had put off reading it.) Hitler took the envelope from Pintsch and tore it open.

> Mein Führer [it began], By the time you receive this letter I shall be in Britain. . . .

"*Um Gottes Willen!*" he exclaimed. "For God's sake! He's flown to Britain." He handed the letter, shocked, to air-force general Karl Bodenschatz. The General saw that the two-page note announced that the writer had flown to Glasgow, Scotland, and intended to land on the private airfield of an English "lord" whom he had met at the 1936 Olympics. (Professor Messerschmitt later saw that Hess had added that he was "willing to give his life to the cause of making peace with Britain", while Miss Fath recalled that her boss had explained in the letter that he had planned this flight "to spare further bloodshed and create favourable conditions for concluding a peace".)

Both letters are lost, but Bodenschatz, talking in confidence to fellow generals in May 1945, recalled that Hess had added that he could not have gone to the Führer beforehand because he would not have been given a hearing, "since I regard the Russian affair as madness". He promised nonetheless to say nothing to the British about "the Führer's plans against Russia". If this was indeed said, and it is by no means certain, then it was perhaps fortunate for Hess that his wife Ilse destroyed the only copy (kept in his safe at Harlaching) when the French troops arrived in 1945. She noticed, she wrote years later, that it ended with the words, "And if, Mein Führer, my mission fails – and I must admit that the chances of success are slim – if fate decides against me, then it cannot harm either you or Germany. You can dissociate yourself at any time from me. Say that I went mad." It has to be said that (perhaps for obvious reasons) neither this advice nor the reference to a plan against Russia was in the text that Martin Bormann read out to the largely uninitiated Party chieftains assembled at the Berghof a few days later.

Among the listeners that afternoon were Poland's Governor-General Hans Frank, Reich Minister Walter Darré and Party official G. Schäfer. Frank reported to his staff afterwards: "The Führer said it is now clear that Hess was completely in the hands of astrologers, irido-diagnosticians and nature healers. He has gone to Britain, according to his fourteen-page letter to the Führer, in the mad hope of attempting to restore peace between Germany and Britain." Darré recalled two letters by Hess – one to Hitler, reporting in detail on his "five attempts since November

1940" to make the flight, and one to Haushofer, announcing that he was going to try it now. Schäfer also recalled the letter from Hess to Haushofer – "Both had had horoscopes cast: the astrologer had told Rudolf Hess that *he* was the man, and that he must fly to Britain on this particular day. From the letters he left behind it emerged that the stars were at their most propitious on the day he acted."

Mr Churchill was not at 10 Downing Street when his Private Secretary telephoned the Foreign Office that Sunday afternoon. He was not even in London – he never was, when signals Intelligence had tipped him off that the city was about to be bombed. He and his favourite ministers then fled to refuges distant from the capital. Having learned on Friday that the Luftwaffe was planning a heavy raid on Saturday night, 10 May, he had driven as was his custom one hundred miles to where he considered himself completely safe – to Dytchley Park, the stately home of a wealthy Parliamentary friend in Oxfordshire.

It was a prudent decision, because just after 7 p.m. that Saturday evening the headquarters of RAF Fighter Command had confirmed: "There is reason to believe KG100's target tonight will be London." KG100 was the Luftwaffe's target-marking squadron. By 7.45 p.m. the RAF had located the enemy's electronic beams flickering invisibly above London's streets: "KG100's target will be east of Regent's Park. Attack will be from 23.00 to 01.30, & there may possibly be a second attack at 02.30."

At 11 p.m. – almost the very moment that Rudolf Hess was abandoning his Messerschmitt above Scotland – the first of four hundred bombers had arrived over London. It was the biggest raid of the war: it wrecked much of the city, demolished the House of Commons, seared Westminster Abbey, and killed or injured 3000 unfortunate citizens.

Churchill was having a beastly war so far: Norway, Dunkirk, Greece, Libya – all these military disasters would probably be engraved on his epitaph. More fearful of a negotiated peace than of any imposed defeat, he had obliged his censorship and security agencies to keep a most watchful eye on the slightest signs of "defeatism" now. Just as Chamberlain had felt bound to keep wiretaps on the "warmongering" Winston Churchill in 1938 and 1939, so Churchill now kept his Whitehall underlings under surveillance: they had intercepted the Duke's long, cryptic call from Edinburgh, asking for Sir Alexander Cadogan. This explains why Churchill's secretary suddenly interrupted the Duke to ensure that it was the Prime Minister's car that awaited him at Northolt aerodrome. With his accustomed mastery of the English language, Churchill told his Foreign Secretary, Anthony Eden, the next day that he had "intercepted" the Duke and had had him taken to Dytchley.

In Scotland meanwhile Hess's right ankle was swelling and painful, but his gastric pains had eased. At 2 p.m. that Sunday, 11 May, an ambulance had removed him to the military hospital in Buchanan Castle at Drymen, on the Duke of Roxburghe's estate a few miles outside Glasgow. Four other German airmen were admitted at the same time. Hess was again registered under the name Alfred Horn and provided with special accommodation in one of the castle wings. "Active steps were taken to guard this prisoner," the hospital authorities recorded. Half a dozen officers guarded the ward in three shifts, two NCOs and twelve soldiers stood at the main entrance, and armed patrols swarmed the castle and grounds.

> We had this German air force officer a couple of days in hospital [one doctor described in a private letter routinely opened by Churchill's security authorities]. . . . We developed sentries with fixed bayonets everywhere, infantry officers with revolvers at their belts filling our Mess room, staff officers and all sorts of big-wigs following each other. We couldn't use the telephone because it was for "priority" use only – in fact we got very tired of our unexpected patient.
>
> I found him surprisingly ordinary – neither so ruthless looking nor so handsome nor so beetle-browed as the newspapers would have us believe. Quite sane, certainly not a drug-taker, a little concerned about his health and rather faddy about his diet, quite ready to chat. . . .
>
> He was treated just like any other officer patient, except that he was not allowed newspapers. At the moment we know nothing of why he came. . . .

A pall of smoke still hung over London as the Duke of Hamilton piloted his Hurricane into Northolt airfield that Sunday evening. An official saloon swept him westwards, away from the mutilated city, to the sixteenth-century baronial mansion where Churchill was weekending. A pompous butler received the Duke at the steps, allowed him time to wash, then showed him into a drawing room where Churchill was sitting next to his wealthy young host, Ronald Tree.

It is not improbable, whatever he maintained in his later memoirs, that the Prime Minister knew from his security agencies what information the Duke was bringing: he had had time to ponder the daunting implications of the parachute arrival of the Deputy Führer clutching an olive branch. He had eaten, and now he had the ease of mind to toss it off lightly. He would be Sir Francis Drake on the bowling-lawns of Plymouth Hoe, unhurriedly contemplating the onset of the Spanish Armada – or, in this case, its departure.

"Now, come," he bellowed to Hamilton, whose flying kit stood out rudely amongst the cigars, brandy and dinner jackets. "Come and tell us this funny story of yours." There were appreciative guffaws from Brendan Bracken and the other ministerial house-guests. But the Wing Commander declined to be drawn in public. After a quick dinner, he found himself alone with Churchill and Sinclair, the Air Minister ("who happened to be one of the guests," the Duke wrote, perhaps naively).

After telling his extraordinary story, he concluded with a warning that he was still uncertain whether their unexpected visitor was in fact Rudolf Hess, and he showed them the photographs that he had removed from the prisoner's wallet. Churchill agreed diffidently that it certainly looked like Hess – but then he turned to more important matters. He was Drake again: he had, in effect, a game of bowls to finish. "Hess or no Hess," he announced, "I'm going to see the Marx Brothers."

"This interview was short," wrote the Duke afterwards, without comment.

On the following morning – it was now Monday, 12 May – Churchill took the Duke with him back to 10 Downing Street.

For all his display of insouciance, in private he had cause for alarm at this uninvited meddling by Hess: he was banking on inflicting a humiliating defeat on the Nazis when they parachuted into Crete just eight days later; he had read the enemy's top-secret instructions for this operation and was confident of scoring, at long last, a great victory. Right now he could not afford peace – at any price.

He had telephoned Anthony Eden's house during the night, and asked for him to come round as soon as he got back to Number 10. Shown the photographs, the Foreign Secretary (who had met the Deputy Führer in March 1935) confirmed: "They do appear to be of Hess."

Churchill professed to be unimpressed: "I didn't believe the story," he said. He glanced at his desk diary; it showed an 11.30 appointment with the Night Air Defence Committee. He cancelled that, and called a conference with Eden, the Duke and the three Chiefs of Staff – whom he called in rather grotesquely one by one, almost as though he were afraid of them ganging up against him. "I want the prisoner identified," he finally said, "with all possible speed."

While Eden escorted the Wing Commander across Downing Street at one o'clock to check the photographs against Foreign Office files, the Prime Minister entertained to lunch the press magnate Lord Beaverbrook, who after a successful stint as Minister of Aircraft Production had become Minister of State. Beaverbrook had visited Hitler's Chancellery three times before the war. Churchill passed one of the snapshots wordlessly across the table to him. "It's Rudolf Hess!" exclaimed the Minister, with the broad grin of somebody who expects to be thanked for a favour. Churchill glowered.

Across the road at the Foreign Office, Hamilton was confirming to Sir Alexander Cadogan that it was obviously Hess. Cadogan sent for "C" – the Brigadier who headed the SIS – and Ivone Kirkpatrick, who had served at the Berlin Embassy before the war and now had an office at the BBC.

"I wonder how Hess managed to get hold of a plane?" mused somebody out loud.

"Hess", explained Kirkpatrick, "is the third most powerful man in Germany."

"Foreign Secretary," said someone (probably the mysterious Brigadier), amid suppressed titters, "you are the third most powerful man in
Britain: why don't you get a plane so that Kirkpatrick and the Duke can
go to Scotland and establish this man's identity?"

It was now evening. They took off at 5.30 from Hendon airfield in a De
Havilland aeroplane, a Rapide in name but with only one-third the speed
of a Messerschmitt and so little range that it had to refuel twice to make
the flight to Scotland.

They landed at RAF Turnhouse at 9.40 p.m., to news that Berlin radio
was announcing that the Deputy Führer, Rudolf Hess, was missing.

Down in London, a slip of paper had been passed to Churchill during his
five-o'clock Cabinet. A private secretary had written on it, "Hamilton
and Kirkpatrick are leaving by air for Scotland this evening. They will see
the aviator 'Horn' either this evening or tomorrow." After the Chiefs of
Staff meeting that evening, another handwritten bulletin was rushed to 10
Downing Street. The Deutschlandsender was announcing Hess's presumed death in an aeroplane accident. At 8 p.m. German radio broadcast
an official National Socialist Party communiqué: despite Hitler's
prohibition on flying, it said, Hess who had been suffering from a
progressive disease had taken off in a plane on Saturday and not been seen
since. "A letter which he had left behind unfortunately showed in its
confusion the traces of mental disturbance which justify the fear that Hess
was the victim of hallucinations."

This dispelled any lingering doubts about the prisoner's identity.

Eden telephoned Cadogan, and they met just before eleven o'clock at
the Foreign Office. Eden had already buttonholed "C" and the three men
went to see Churchill. Ensconced in the comfortable labyrinths of his
underground bunker, the Cabinet War Room, the Prime Minister had
already drafted an announcement guided more by the sense of history
than by the tactical demands of guile and psychological warfare. He read
it out to them, rejoicing in every syllable:

On the night of Saturday the 10th, a Messerschmitt-110 was reported by
our patrols to have crossed the coast of Scotland and to be flying in the
direction of Glasgow. Since a Messerschmitt-110 would not have the
fuel to return to Germany this report was at first disbelieved. However,
later on a Messerschmitt-110 No. — crashed near Glasgow with its guns
unloaded. Shortly afterwards a German officer who had baled out was
found with his parachute in the neighbourhood, suffering from a broken
ankle. He was taken to hospital in Glasgow where he at first gave his
name as Horn, but later on declared that he was Rudolf Hess *and that he
had come to England in the name of humanity hoping that a peace might be made
between Great Britain and Germany*. . . .

Cadogan, the experienced, cynical career diplomat, choked on these last words and crossed them out. "This won't do," he wrote in his private diary. "Looks like a peace offer and we may want to run the line that he [Hess] has quarrelled with Hitler."

The rest of Churchill's statement – which ended with details of the steps taken to identify Hess – was issued at 11.20 p.m.

The Air Minister Archie Sinclair had meanwhile sent a message up to RAF Station Turnhouse with instructions to await Kirkpatrick and the Duke; in view of the Berlin broadcast they were to proceed to Drymen hospital immediately. The castle was fifty miles from Turnhouse, and the country roads were in total darkness because of the blackout. It was after midnight before the two men arrived.

There were three hundred inmates at Drymen hospital. The Luftwaffe Hauptmann who had arrived there at 3.30 p.m. on Sunday was still known to the staff only as "Alfred Horn". He had been carried on a stretcher along passages and up winding stone staircases to a former servant's bedroom under the roof, and put to bed on an iron-framed bedstead. A bulb in a white enamel lampshade lit the room, crudely shaded by a yellowing newspaper.

At 9.45 on Monday morning Dr J. Gibson Graham, a lieutenant-colonel in the RAMC, had conducted a routine examination. The aviator explained to him that he had blacked out twice – once from the unexpected G-forces when the plane looped upside down, and again as the rudder smashed into his spine during his jump. He had come to his senses lying in the darkness of the field. "He complains", wrote the Colonel in his notes, "that his head feels confused from time to time, especially after any interview due to the strain under which he has recently been." The prisoner also felt a dull back pain at a spot identified by the doctor as over the twelfth dorsal vertebra, and an X-ray taken by Major A. Dorset Harper, the hospital's surgical specialist, confirmed a small chip fracture of the spinous process – although there were fortunately no signs of spinal concussion in the central nervous system. As for the swollen ankle, the X-rays showed that a small fragment of bone had become detached from the tibia.★

So Hess remained in bed, writing copiously, and secretly highly pleased with his accomplishments so far.

At a quarter past midnight the guard woke him up and brought in two visitors – the Duke of Hamilton and a suave gentleman with a neat moustache whom he did not at first recognize, Ivone Kirkpatrick. The latter questioned him on several incidents which they had both witnessed in Germany, and pronounced himself satisfied. "It immediately became

★ A chest X-ray on 13 May 1941 showed a rather small, centrally placed heart (such as in a typical case of Effort Syndrome). "The lung fields are clear." reported Dr Gibson Graham, "save that in the right upper zone there is a small calcified area." (Hess's military record, it will be recalled, maintained that he had been shot in the left lung in 1917; but there is no indication of this in the chest X-ray.) A telegram of 14 May confirmed, "No evidence [of] lesion old or recent in any other system."

plain", he reported to London a few hours later, "that there could be no doubt whatever about his identity."

Hess plunged at once into a recital of the brief he had been writing. Kirkpatrick listened with commendable restraint, given the lateness of the hour, and Hess felt quite at ease as he slowly unfolded what was basically a distillation of Hitler's many speeches. "From a long and intimate knowledge of the Führer," Kirkpatrick quoted him as saying, "which had begun eighteen years ago in the fortress of Landsberg, he could give his word of honour that the Führer had never entertained any designs against the British empire" – a point which, he said, Hitler had confirmed to him only a few days ago after the Reichstag speech. "There is no foundation", stressed Hess, "for the rumours now being spread that Hitler is contemplating an early attack on Russia." Kirkpatrick, who knew differently, deduced that Hess was "not very well informed" on German strategical plans.

As Hamilton and Kirkpatrick were leaving, after two hours or more of discussion, Hess stopped them. "I forgot one thing," he dictated. "Our proposals can only be considered on the understanding that . . . the Führer could not negotiate with either Mr Churchill, who has been planning this war since 1936, or his colleagues."

It was now 13 May 1941. The sensational news made the front-page headlines of the world's newspapers. The British government was baldly stating that Hess had fallen out with the Nazi leaders, stolen a plane and fled to Britain to escape the Gestapo.

Baffled by the opposing claim from Berlin that the Deputy Führer was mentally ill and suffering from hallucinations, Dr Gibson Graham examined him again at 10 a.m. Although the prisoner clearly regarded himself as an important personage, and was not inclined to unburden himself to a stranger, Gibson found all his vital signs normal. "The patient does not look ill," he reported that day. "While guarded in his conversation he did not strike me as being mentally of unsound mind. Such information as he gave with regard to his health was given in a rational and coherent manner." Gibson Graham ran a series of routine tests on the central nervous and reflex systems, found nothing abnormal, and concluded that he could be safely removed.

"He told me", Gibson Graham reported later, "that he had come to this country on a special mission, the nature of which I would learn in due course."

When Kirkpatrick telephoned Sir Alexander Cadogan from RAF Turnhouse at 10.50 a.m., he summarized the medical tests so far: "The doctors say that they can detect no sign of neurosis" (although a delusion might not, they warned, become apparent for some time). To Kirkpatrick himself the prisoner had appeared calm, "but slightly off balance". In the lengthy account that he now dictated to Cadogan of their interview, he spoke of what he called Hess's "monomania" – his single-minded obsession with his peace mission. "But the condition was attached", he continued, "that Hitler would not negotiate with the present Government in England."

Neither Cadogan nor Kirkpatrick deliberated for one moment on the merits of the proposals that the Deputy Führer had so laboriously brought to Scotland. Kirkpatrick suggested simply that they introduce Hess to a suitable Conservative dignitary not in Churchill's government, describe him as someone "tempted by the idea of getting rid of the present administration" and, in rooms fitted with hidden microphones, try to find out the secrets of Germany's future U-boat and aircraft programmes. Kirkpatrick advised against bringing Hess to London, let alone trying to establish any official contact with him.

Cadogan instructed the diplomat to stay where he was: further instructions would follow. "Frightful day," he entered in his leather-bound five-year diary in an unhurried pen-and-ink script that belied his real indignation at this Nazi interloper: "Mostly Hess – constant interruption. . . . Undoubtedly it is Hess. But can't see why he's come here unless he's mad. Drs [doctors] say he isn't."

He took Kirkpatrick's report over to Number 10 at midday. Churchill read it in silence, chomping on his cigar, then told Cadogan to settle how and where Hess was to be detained. "He wants him to be a State Prisoner," recorded Cadogan, baffled by the term. Cadogan consulted Sir William Malkin, the Foreign Office's Legal Adviser, then tried to contact Kirkpatrick with instructions to stay on in Scotland for a while.

After lunching with the King as usual – as was his Tuesday custom – Churchill sent this note over to the Foreign Office.

PRIME MINISTER'S PERSONAL MINUTE   *13 May 1941*
Serial No. M540/1

On the whole it will be more convenient to treat him as a prisoner of war; under W.O. [War Office] not H.O. [Home Office]; but also as one against whom grave political charges may be preferred. This man like other Nazi leaders is potentially a war-criminal and he and his confederates may well be declared outlaws at the close of the war. In this case his repentance would not stand him in good stead. [He crossed out the word "not".]

 2. In the meanwhile he should be strictly isolated in a convenient house not too far from London, fitted by "C" [head of the SIS] with the necessary appliances [i.e. microphones], and every endeavour should be made to study his mentality and get anything worthwhile out of him.

 3. His health and comfort should be ensured; food, books, writing materials and recreation being provided for him. He should not have any contacts with the outer world or visitors except as prescribed by the Foreign Office. Special guardians should be appointed. He should see no

newspapers and hear no wireless. He should be treated with dignity as if he were an important General who had fallen into our hands.

W.S.C. 13.5.41

A government "D"-notice that day forbade British newspapers to mention the Duke of Hamilton. But Berlin shortly announced that Hess's letters had revealed that it was the Duke he had been flying to see. In the United States the Hess mystery still dominated the headlines and radio bulletins: had Hess "escaped", as the BBC was claiming; or had he "privately brought some form of peace proposal" as Berlin was suggesting?

John Gilbert Winant, the Lincolnesque US Ambassador in London, tackled Eden in person but was served only platitudes: apart from assuring him confidentially that Hess was "of right mind" and "not here as an agent for his government" there was nothing that Eden was prepared to divulge.

Wall Street shivered. US industrialists were tooling up factories to produce the munitions of war – but by the time the production lines were complete Hess, they feared, might single-handedly have brought about peace in Europe. Telegrams warning of these "staggering implications" reached the Foreign Office from British officials in New York.

Their alarm was shared by the staff of President Franklin D. Roosevelt. The flight of Rudolf Hess had, one White House official secretly advised F.D.R. on the 14th, "captured the American imagination" like that of Charles Lindbergh – a comparison which would not have displeased the Deputy Führer. "No amount of conversation", this memorandum continued, "about economic penetration of South America or Nazi trade wars, or even the necessity for survival of the British Navy seems to have convinced the American people, particularly the middle and far West, that this country is in danger from the Nazis. But if Hess were to tell the world what Hitler has said about the United States, it would be a headline sensation." The official added a tantalizing postscript: this idea must be a "telephone job" between the President and Churchill. (The two leaders, with blithe disregard for secrecy, conducted their top-secret conspiracies mainly by transatlantic telephone.)

Telegrams from neutral well-wishers – addressed to Hess care of British archbishops, government officials and anywhere else thought likely to reach him – began to pile up in the racks of Churchill's Postal Censorship. Among them was one sent on the 13th by Count Eric von Rosen, who had hosted the 1935 lecture for Hess in Stockholm; another telegram, from Connecticut, articulated the feelings of millions of Americans at that time. "Courage," it adjured the now imprisoned Deputy Führer, "Christ too thought himself defeated. From a friend in America." All of these telegrams were stopped and destroyed.

In the painful isolation of his castle hospital room, the injured aviator

Rudolf Hess was aware of none of this outcry. He had hoped to negotiate almost immediately with a high British official, and then to return with the King's parole to Germany, to face either the hangman or a hero's welcome and the Maria Theresia Medal (traditionally awarded only to officers who disobeyed orders and were proven right). He had certainly given to junior listeners at Drymen – as the Lord Provost of Glasgow publicly stated a few days later – the impression that he had expected to be permitted to fly back to Germany.

Nervous and irritable, Hess objected to being under the supervision of a private soldier; the soldier was withdrawn. He asked for books – *Three Men in a Boat* by Jerome K. Jerome, *Sea Power* by Commander Russell Grenfell, and *Dynamic Defence* by Basil Liddell Hart – and demanded the return of his medicines, money and camera. All these requests were ignored. He asked for a piece of his crashed Messerschmitt as a souvenir. When Kirkpatrick and the Duke came on the 14th they undertook to see what they could do. They listened, seemingly impressed, to Hess's reminiscences of his epic flight. He had dived in his Messerschmitt, he said, from 15,000 feet and started hedgehopping across the border country; he had nearly gone down with the plane when he blacked out.

He made no remark at all on Russia. Instead Hess brought up the current anti-British Arab rising in Iraq, and for the agenda of the talks which he was confident would soon take place he mentioned a further provision which made sense only when the renewed confiscation of his father's property in Egypt was recalled. "The peace agreement", he said, "should contain a provision for the reciprocal indemnification of British and German nationals whose property had been expropriated as the result of war." He asked for a qualified interpreter to be present when the time came.

On Churchill's instructions his "State Prisoner" had been consigned to an intellectual darkness pending his debriefiing. Officers were forbidden to speak to him, he was allowed no newspaper or wireless. He did not even know if the world outside was aware of his deed. He had been formally assigned the status of a prisoner of war. While the Foreign Office would handle his contacts with the outside world, his security was entrusted to the War Office's Director of Prisoners of War (DPW), Lieutenant-General Sir Alan Hunter.

Charged with this difficult job on the 14th Hunter immediately sent Major J. J. Sheppard, one of his best staff officers, up to Scotland to prepare the prisoner's top-secret move to London, where he would be housed temporarily in the Tower. To the Prime Minister he described Sheppard, who had been awarded the Distinguished Service Order and the Military Cross in the last war, as a first-class "natural gentleman". At midday the General went over to the Foreign Office to discuss Hess with its permanent head, Sir Alexander Cadogan, and with the head of the SIS. In particular they had to settle where the Deputy Führer was to be permanently housed for his debriefing, and what special electronic apparatus was to be installed.

Simultaneously the Foreign Office issued propaganda guidelines to British embassies around the world. They were to stress that the Deputy Führer was sane, and emphasize that his previous loyalty to Hitler made it unlikely that he would have taken this "bold step" had he not been concerned for his own safety or, more probably, about the trend in Nazi policies; thus they were to portray Hess as having "sought sanctuary" in Britain. "Avoid over-playing Hess hero-worship," the confidential circular concluded, "or referring to him as a refugee. Remember he is after all one of thè architects of Nazidom. His status is that of a prisoner of war."

That evening Churchill called Eden, Cadogan and the head of the SIS over to Number 10 to discuss issuing a statement in Parliament. The Minister of Information, Alfred Duff Cooper, had pleaded that they could no longer delay. So far Nazi propaganda was making all the running. Eden left them at it after a while, and Churchill began to draft a six-page statement along the lines that Hess was not "mad" but had fled his Nazi fellows. Pacing up and down, he dictated, to the girl sitting at the special silent typewriter, "He is reported to be perfectly sane, and . . . in good health, as indeed seemed probable from the remarkable flight which he made." Hess, he continued, was not on a mission from the German government, but he had discussed the basis for peace. "He appears to hold these views sincerely, and he represented himself as undertaking a mission" – here he later inserted the word "self-imposed" – "to save the British nation from destruction while time remained."

Cadogan had hated every word so far. His timetable in ruins because of Hess, he resented having to listen to Churchill now. ("*How* slow he is!" he reflected.) He himself felt that any talk of Hess's "peace proposals" was wrong – it corresponded exactly to what Berlin had put out that afternoon. "Hitler", he remonstrated, "will heave a sigh of relief – *and* the German people! They'll say, 'Then it's *true* what our dear Führer has told us. Our beloved Rudolf has gone to make peace!'" They must lie, lie and lie again about him. The whole object of any statement must be, he noted in his diary, to get the Germans to fear that Hess was a traitor. However, Churchill brushed his arguments aside.

Since Cadogan remained hostile, Churchill changed tack. "It must not be forgotten", he continued, resuming the pacing and getting into a rhetorical stride that did more justice to style than to accuracy,

that Deputy Führer Rudolf Hess has been the confederate and accomplice of Herr Hitler in all the murders, treacheries and cruelties by which the Nazi regime imposed itself on Germany as it now seeks to impose itself on Europe. The blood purge of June 30, 1934, the long torments of Herr Schuschnigg and other victims of Nazi aggression, the horrors of the German concentration camps, the brutal persecution of the Jews, the perfidious inroad upon Czechoslovakia, the unspeakable, incredible brutalities and bestialities of the German invasion and conquest of Poland . . . are all crimes in which he has participated.

He also dictated a paragraph, which he later scratched out, "I have seen suggestions that I or some other Member of the Government should see him. But this would no more be possible than that I should see Herr Hitler or any other of the war-criminals himself, should they visit us in these peculiar circumstances."

Eager for support, Churchill kept telephoning Eden that evening, and invited Beaverbrook round to dinner to discuss his draft. When both men opposed it, he flew off the handle and telephoned Eden at midnight to come round at once. "I'm afraid I didn't sleep very well this afternoon," said Eden from his bed; but he again insisted that they keep the enemy in the dark about what Hess was saying. Churchill challenged him to do better. The Foreign Secretary did as demanded, the Prime Minister did not like it and said so. "Which is it to be," he growled. "My original statement – or no statement at all!"

"No statement," said Eden flatly.

"All right, no statement," snapped Churchill, and slapped the telephone on to its hook.

Churchill wanted Hess blotted off the newspaper front pages. He wanted no pictures ever to be taken of "Z", as he was henceforth to be known. When Duff Cooper pleaded for new photographs, arguing that Fleet Street was using pre-war photographs that showed the Deputy Führer in all his glory, Churchill declined. "I would send a photographic expert," promised the wretched Information Minister, "with instructions to take a series of pictures which would not present the subject in too flattering a light." Churchill told him to wait.

Churchill decided that from this moment Rudolf Hess would become his personal prisoner, a non-person, cut off from the outside world, and known only by the last letter in the Alphabet. On his instructions General Hunter and his deputy visited Aldershot, the main British Army base a few miles south of London, where they selected Mytchett Place, one of the War Office's most stylish properties, as Hess's future home. This would become "Camp Z". Hunter ordered its elegant furniture to be replaced, a double perimeter fence to be erected, and machine-gun posts and slit-trenches to be dug into the lawns.

That midday, 15 May, Churchill discussed the Hess case with the Cabinet in his room at the bomb-damaged Houses of Parliament. Cadogan found him "in v. good form". "The P.M.", he minuted, "instructed Mr Duff Cooper to lead the press on to the line that Hess is one of the 'war criminals' whose fate must be settled by the Allied Governments after the war." That was more like what the Foreign Office wanted. The PM also agreed with them that there should be no statement to the House of Commons as yet: "Hess should be held by the War Office as a prisoner of war. He was also a Prisoner of State and should be kept in isolation and only allowed visitors approved by the Foreign Office." Cadogan was smug. Churchill, he congratulated himself in his private diary, "has got over his tantrum and admits our view [is] correct". As the monitored conversations of German prisoners of war showed, they were baffled by the episode – just as Hitler's public must be.

Churchill passed on to the Foreign Office President Roosevelt's request that Hess be pumped for details of Hitler's plans against America; at lunchtime Cadogan telephoned Hamilton at RAF Turnhouse with corresponding instructions to return to Drymen hospital that afternoon.

There, the daily regime was almost imperceptibly harshening. Little by little, Hess was realizing that he was a prisoner. He was shaved by a hospital orderly in the presence of two army officers. He was not allowed to retain any cutlery in his room, and when he asked for a pencil sharpener even this was refused him.

It was small wonder therefore that when General Hunter's staff officer Major Sheppard arrived on the 15th he found Hess mistrustful and still a little shaken from his ordeal. The officers told Sheppard that the prisoner was conversing freely with them and deriving pleasure from relating the details of his flight to them; but they added that he would lie in bed often for hours sunk in thought and occasionally made notes.

Talking with Sheppard, the Deputy Führer confined himself to generalities. He evidently realized that he was slithering inexorably into the hands of the SIS – any new visitor might really be a Secret Service officer. He remained quiet, although restless at night, and unable to sleep without sedatives. Unfortunately the Scottish Command's medical file on Hess has been sealed for seventy-five years so we cannot state what medications he may have been given.

When Ivone Kirkpatrick arrived in the little room in mid-afternoon he likewise received a frostier reception, particularly when he tried to wheedle out of Hess details of Hitler's evil intentions against the United States. Hess limited himself to the statement that Hitler was not afraid of any eventual American intervention in the European war. "Germany has no designs on America," he assured Kirkpatrick, more than a little perplexed by the British diplomat's question. "The so-called German peril is a ludicrous figment of somebody's imagination" – he never guessed it was that of Roosevelt himself. He continued, "If we make peace now the United States will be furious: they really want to inherit the British Empire."

Generally speaking [recorded Kirkpatrick] it was difficult to get him to talk politics. He thinks he has told me all he has to say. . . . In particular he objects to be [*sic*] closely guarded. He says he came here at great risk to himself and having got here safely has no intention of trying to run away or commit suicide.

Kirkpatrick telephoned the Foreign Office with this meagre result at 5 p.m. – he had "got nothing fresh" out of their prisoner, he confessed.

Rather curiously, the Duke of Hamilton arrived late that day, 15 May, at the Foreign Office in London and insisted on seeing His Majesty the King. The august Permanent Under-Secretary advised the Wing-Commander to see Churchill first, but the Duke evidently would not wait; he certainly lunched with King George VI at Windsor Castle the next day. The Royal Archives decline to state what passed between them, but the RAF officer sent a letter to the King a few days later remarking, "It is clear that Hess is still an unrepentant Nazi who repeats *ad nauseam* the usual Nazi 'claptrap'."

It would take three or four days to get "Camp Z" at Aldershot ready for the prisoner. The SIS technicians has already moved into Mytchett Place, hiding sensitive listening devices in all the areas on the prisoner's side of the steel security grille, and connecting them to ultra-sensitive amplifiers in a secret room where every word could be engraved on discs.

At 3.30 p.m. on 16 May Churchill instructed Sir Alexander Cadogan and the SIS chief to bring the Deputy Führer in the utmost secrecy from Glasgow to the Tower of London during the night.

That same day Churchill sent these instructions to Cadogan:

PRIME MINISTER'S PERSONAL MINUTE   *16 May 1941*
Serial No. M550/1

Please make now a fairly full digest of the conversational parts of Hess' three interviews, stressing particularly the points mentioned by me in the statement I prepared but did not deliver. I will then send this to President Roosevelt with a covering telegram.

2. I approved the War Office proposal to bring Hess to the Tower by tonight pending his place of confinement being prepared at Aldershot.

3. His treatment will become less indulgent as time goes on. There need be no hurry about interviewing him, and I wish to be informed before any visitors are allowed. He is to be kept in the strictest seclusion, and those in charge of him should refrain from conversation. The public will not stand any pampering *except for intelligence purposes* with this notorious war criminal.

           W.S.C. 16.5.41

Orders went up to the hospital outside Glasgow to prepare Hess for departure for an unspecified destination at 7 p.m. He was not notified that he was about to be moved until a few minutes before then. "He was perfectly composed," reported the military hospital commander, Colonel R. A. Lennie, "and appeared to take his removal as a matter of course."

Before his stretcher was carried out to the waiting ambulance, Hess admitted to Lennie that he felt better, and thanked him courteously for the kindness shown at this hospital. He was elated at this sudden move, and puffed up with self-importance. As the army escort formed up he clearly enjoyed being the object of such tight security. Unable to suppress his curiosity about the destination, he asked if the journey was to be by train, and if the journey would last two or three hours. He guessed that he was bound for London – and half hoped that the negotiations were about to start at last. As the ambulance carried him through the darkening lanes and streets to Glasgow's central station he became calm – even resigned, in Sheppard's belief. Hess noticed approvingly that unlike most British women the ATS girl driver did not wear any lipstick. In a few days' time, he reflected, he might be back among the mountains of Bavaria, in freedom, with his wife and son.

The doctor, Gibson Graham, and Major Sheppard travelled down with him. Major Sheppard pondered on this prisoner's mental stability, and had his doubts. He noticed, for instance, that whenever a conversation developed from smalltalk into one that called for a considered opinion, the prisoner immediately averted his gaze. "His eyes take on a strange and distant look," Sheppard wrote the next day, "and he is then very cautious in his replies." That the Deputy Führer might merely be security-conscious did not occur to the Major. To him, Hess was "cunning, shrewd and self-centred". He was "continually on the alert to pick up any points in general conversation which might lead to information affecting his personal well-being".

"He is very temperamental," advised the Major, "and will need careful handling if he is to be outwitted."

7   The Tower

With all the nervous eagerness of a man no longer in his prime who has pulled off a feat of personal courage for which he is about to be rewarded, Rudolf Hess settled into the first-class seat allotted to him on the London, Midland & Scottish Railway Company's night sleeper to London. It was late on 16 May 1941. He was quite flattered to find that he was under a heavy escort: Lieutenant-Colonel Gibson Graham, Major Sheppard, six Scottish officers of the Highland Light Infantry and the Cameronians, and seven other ranks (back in the train's third class) making up the party.

But when he was escorted to his first-class sleeping berth at the onset of night, there was the first complication. He found that an officer had been placed in his berth with him, and that the lights were to be left on. The Deputy Führer felt that such concern for his security was unnecessary. "I can't sleep if I am being watched all night," he said, his voice rising sharply. He demanded to be left alone, and in total darkness. "I shan't try to sleep if I am being watched." The requests were courteously refused. This visibly disconcerted him – according to Dr Gibson Graham he became "violent", although the word is probably an exaggeration, given Hess's lameness; not even the distinctly hostile Major Sheppard made any mention of "violence" in his "Report on the Conduct of 'X'". The doctors offered Hess a sedative, but he took only a small portion and sulked, wide awake, for the greater part of the night-long journey.

The news of his arrival had of course leaked out in the capital, and a small knot of Londoners formed on the station platforms. But the train had been delayed two hours by an air-raid warning in the Midlands, which gave the army time to divert to a quiet siding and to "eliminate" a Gaumont British newsreel van which tactlessly appeared at the railway station.

The officers loaded Hess into an unmarked ambulance, which carried him across north-east London to the Tower. Peeping out of the darkened windows he was silently nonplussed at the absence of the heavy blitz damage of which Dr Goebbels' propaganda had made so much. "[Hess] remained very quiet in the ambulance," reported his escorting officer, "and did not utter a word until installed in his new quarters when he expressed himself as being comfortable."

In the Tower of London, he was ushered into officers' quarters in the Governor's house where Dr Gerlach, the German consul in Iceland, had recently been interned. It was next to the White Tower. Hess still expected to be in England only a few more days, and enjoyed every moment. "From my window," he reminisced, confined in a different prison cell, seven years later, "I could see the guards parade each day, displaying enormous stamina and a drill that would have done them proud in Prussia. They even had a military band, though I could have done without the bagpipes – as could many of the English, or so they confessed to me. But the Scottish officers who had accompanied me were so proud of their national music – and of their whisky ∿! – that they became extremely touchy over any criticism of it."

Information Minister Duff Cooper had banned all reports on what Hess said, and Eden had concurred in this up to then. Churchill telephoned Eden to inquire, "Would it not be all right to raise the ban on *speculation* about Hess provided that we warned everybody that all speculation is unauthorized?" Eden agreed, and the editors were told to start speculating.

On the day after his arrival, the 18th, Hess asked his captors in the Tower if he might speak with the Duke of Hamilton and Ivone Kirkpatrick. Both men were indeed in London. That same evening the thirty-eight-year-old Duke of Hamilton was with Sir Alexander Cadogan, "looking more and more like a Golden Spaniel", as the diplomat noted. But Hamilton would never be allowed to see Hess again. An officer told Hess that they would note his request but could not carry it out immediately. Hess took offence at this unexpected rebuff. However, he settled back confidently to wait for the great encounter with the British leadership: why else would they have transferred him to this castle apartment? At 6 p.m. Major Sheppard recorded that Hess was placid and comfortable, and had taken his food. "Appears quiet and rational," he wrote in his report, which would be on Churchill's desk within a few hours. And even the ultra-critical doctor Gibson Graham found that Hess *was* behaving rationally. He was able to walk around his Tower room, although with a perceptible limp.

But on the 19th Hess composed a letter to Germany which showed the British officers, who did not forward it, that he was fully expecting that he would be quietly liquidated, that his death would be portrayed as a suicide, but that it might still yield some fruit in bringing about peace between Britain and Germany, which would bring revenge on Churchill and his warmongers. Only his draft of this remarkable letter survives, with its date torn off at the top:

I am anxious that you should know of the following:
In the letter which I left behind for the Führer I mentioned the

possibility that news of my death might come from Britain. I told him that no matter what cause of death might be given – suicide, for instance, or death during an altercation – or even if the suspicion arose that my death had been engineered by elements in Britain opposed to peace, people in Germany were not *in any way* to let themselves be influenced by it.

Even if my death were to occur under the oddest circumstances, it would be *all the more proper* to conclude a peace with the elements in favour of it. This would in a way be my last wish. In the long run my death would probably be beneficial to the cause, as the British would then for the first time, after peace had been restored . . . [a passage is torn off here] my death might be able to play a big propaganda role.

"I am sure", continued Hess in this craftily contrived letter, "that the Führer is in full agreement with this line of thinking and will conform with my wishes. By the way," he added nonchalantly, "in my letter I gave him my word that in no circumstances would I commit suicide. He knows how I loathe that."

To the Scottish officers still guarding him, the imputation that Churchill might be contemplating anybody's liquidation was sacrilege. They idolized the Prime Minister, while this man was the devil's deputy. By the fourth day of this sojourn in the Tower Major Sheppard, whose own dislike of the Nazi prisoner had been evident from the first moment, found Hess less communicative than ever.

Hess, obviously concerned about his new predicament, was surly and asking to be left alone. He wanted to compose his thoughts and analyse each fresh situation.

"I believe", wrote Sheppard after escorting Hess on to his next place of imprisonment, "by the very nature of his make up, which reflects cruelty, bestiality, deceit, conceit, arrogance and a yellow streak, that he has lost his soul and has willingly permitted himself to become plastic in the hands of a more powerful and compelling personality." Making no attempt to conceal his own hostility, Major Sheppard decided that the "peace envoy" claim was a blind, designed to camouflage Hess's flight. Hess, he had observed, had written copious notes during this stay at the Tower, evidently his "case for submission through intermediaries to the British Government". This, argued Sheppard, surely indicated that the peace mission was a last-minute deceit.

At 10 Downing Street, Churchill was still under pressure to issue some kind of public explanation of the Hess case. Inspired by the feckless Duff Cooper's ministry, rumours were flying that the Duke of Hamilton had actually been in correspondence with Hess. Whitehall, faced with several courses of action, opted for the traditional course of English statesmanship: to do nothing.

On 13 May Churchill had promised a further statement to the House, and his Cabinet colleagues met at 5 p.m. on the 19th to discuss it. Cadogan loftily wrote in his diary: "P.M. still hankering after his stupid statement about Hess. Insisted on reading it with great gusto to the Cabinet."

With the exception of Churchill's servile Air Minister, the Liberal leader Sir Archibald Sinclair, they unanimously opposed his statement, feeling that Herr Hess had received far too much publicity already.

After the Cabinet, Ivone Kirkpatrick came in to report on his meetings with Hess. Not for one moment was there any talk of considering the German proposals to end the bloodshed. Cadogan wanted to draw Hess out by *pretending* to negotiate, and Churchill agreed; when the Permanent Under-Secretary suggested that they use Lord Simon, the Lord Chancellor – a former appeaser – for this role, Churchill heaved with laughter and bellowed his agreement. "The very man!" he shouted, and the Prime Minister's guffaws were echoed around the Foreign Office by Anthony Eden for several days afterwards.

"We'll wait and see what 'C's' men report," inked Cadogan into his secret diary, referring to the camouflaged MI6 officers who would now be subtly introduced to Hess as "companions".

Thus the only parliamentary exchanges that ensued about Hess were on the 22nd, when a Question planted by the government enabled Sinclair to state flatly: "The Duke has never been in correspondence with the Deputy Führer" (he could hardly reveal that the Haushofer letter had been intercepted before it reached the Duke). In the bland exchanges that followed, Major Vyvyan Adams – one of the Churchill pre-war clique – postulated the witty theory that "the motive of this highly undesirable alien [Hess] was not to call upon the noble Duke but to consult a really good German doctor!"

Shortly, Hess would make the acquaintance of enough doctors and psychiatrists to test the mental equilibrium of even the sanest aviator.

Fearful of the spooks that he had himself created, of "Nazi invasion", of "Gestapo parachutists in nun's garb", and – more appositely, in view of British Intelligence techniques – of "hidden Nazi microphones" everywhere, the Prime Minister decided that Hess should be watched over by handpicked officers of the Scots and Coldstream Guards.

Saturday, 17 May, had therefore seen a curious little gathering of red-hatted and red-tabbed colonels in the middle of the presumably un-"bugged" croquet lawn at Pirbright camp, home of the Guards Brigade. Speaking in low whispers Colonel Sir Geoffrey Cox, Quartermaster-General of the London District, was discussing the establishment of the hush-hush "Camp Z" with Lieutenant-Colonel T. E. G. Nugent, Brigade Major of the Guards Brigade, Lord Stratheden, Commander of the Coldstream Guards training battalion, and Lieutenant-Colonel A. H. C. Swinton, Commander of the Pirbright camp. They picked their seven best young Guards officers for the unusual job:

Captain H. Winch as Guard Commander, Lieutenant the Hon. S. E. V. Smith as adjutant, Second Lieutenants W. B. Malone, J. Mcl. Young, P. Atkinson-Clark of the Scots, and T. Jackson and R. Hubbard of the Coldstream. Over the next two days three hundred sappers erected barbed-wire barricades and machine-gun pits around the perimeter of the chosen site, and the first twenty-four Guardsmen arrived.

As General Hunter reported to Churchill, they could not make the final move until the afternoon of the 20th, owing to the time needed to test and install what he delicately called "certain technical apparatus" at Camp Z. (The circumlocution was necessary, because the Geneva Convention forbade electronic eavesdropping on prisoners of war.)

Camp Z's commander would be a Scots Guards officer, Malcolm Scott. Rushed down from Edinburgh to the Prisoners of War Directorate at Hobart House in London at midday on the 18th, Major Scott was promoted to lieutenant-colonel and handed these top-secret orders by Alan Hunter's deputy, Colonel Coates:

OPERATION ORDER NO. I   MOST SECRET

1. You will proceed to Camp Z at 1200 hours on Sunday May 18th instant to take Command.

2. This camp is a special one and will be guarded by a contingent of Coldstream and Scots Guards from Pirbright.

3. You will be responsible for the custody of the prisoner at Z and for the security of the camp. You will be responsible for the health and comfort of the prisoner. Food, books, writing materials, and recreation are to be provided for him. He is not to have newspapers nor wireless.

4. He is not to have any contacts with the outside world whatsoever.

5. He is not to have any visitors except those prescribed by the Foreign Office, who will present military permit A.F.A.M. with the stamp of the D.D.P.W. [Deputy Director, Prisoners of War] on the left, signed by Sir Alexander Cadogan, Permanent Under Secretary at the Foreign Office, and on the right, the Foreign Office stamp. No matter who the visitor may be he must not be allowed inside the perimeter of your camp unless he produces this authority.

6. The prisoner will not be allowed to send any letters whatsoever from your camp without first having submitted to D.P.W.

7. All correspondence addressed to the prisoner, arriving at your camp, will be submitted in the first instance to D.P.W.

It remained only to "Bring in the Prisoner".

At 2.30 p.m. on 20 May 1941, two private cars pulled up at Tower Wharf in the Tower of London – a twenty-four-horsepower Wolseley with Pirbright commander Colonel Swinton and three Scots Guards officers, followed by a Lincoln carrying Captain Winch and his three officers from the Coldstream.

The last few miles of the journey up from Pirbright had taken longer than anticipated because acres of the City of London were still blocked by wrecked buildings after the Blitz (which the route taken by Hess's ambulance earlier had deliberately avoided). As a security measure the City police had been left in the dark about Hess's move from the Tower. The Guards officers had also been ordered to make themselves unobtrusive, but it did not help that each officer was carrying a loaded pistol and that there were seven Tommy guns between the two cars. All security steps were rendered nugatory when a colonel drove up resplendent in red tabs and hat, and accompanied Sir Geoffrey Cox to the north door of the Governor's House, where the same ambulance that had brought Hess shortly arrived as well. Watched by a hundred pairs of idle Cockney eyes, the Nazi leader was stretchered out to the ambulance. Then with the Lincoln in front and the Wolseley bringing up the rear of the cortège, the ambulance set off across Tower Bridge and wound its way through the smoking slums of south London and out into the country lanes of Surrey to Camp Z.

It was 5.45 p.m. when they arrived. "Z", as Rudolf Hess would henceforth be known, hobbled painfully upstairs and went to bed. The unique handwritten diary of Camp Z's Commandant, never before published, reveals the growing strain on this lonely man – cut off at first from all news of the outside world and his family – as the British secret service began its efforts to prise out of him whatever information he had about the innermost councils of Nazi Germany.

20 May 1941

The ambulance containing "Z" arrived. . . . "Z", who was accompanied by Colonel Graham, R.A.M.C., was escorted to his room and went straight to bed where Major-General Hunter interviewed him and introduced him to all officers of the guard and the personal companions.

Major-General Hunter addressed all officers on their duties.

20.00: "Z" was served with dinner in his room.

23.00: The Officer on Duty, 2nd Lieut. W. B. Malone, took up his position within the grille for the night.

Hess said that he was comfortable, but again asked to see the Duke of Hamilton and Ivone Kirkpatrick. He began writing a letter to the Duke, but after giving it to one of the officers recovered it and began to formulate it differently.

Among the new faces that General Hunter immediately brought upstairs to meet Hess were three enigmatic "Companions" – in fact hand-picked members of the SIS (otherwise known as MI6). All spoke fluent German. Major Frank E. Foley, CMG, a short, round-faced Somersetshire man, had built up the SIS network in Berlin from 1920 to the outbreak of war in 1939 disguised as His Britannic Majesty's Passport Control Officer; now fifty-six, he was greying and bespectacled, but with a German wife and many friends from pre-war Berlin he was the ideal leech to "suck" the Deputy Führer dry of any secret information. Helping him were "Captain Barnes" and "Lieutenant-Colonel Wallace" – probably Lieutenant-Colonel Thomas Kendrick who had run the SIS in Vienna, also disguised as a PCO, until his unmasking and expulsion in August 1938. These SIS officers had seen their respective consulates swamped with Jewish visa applicants as the Nazi persecution began and Foley in particular, a Zionist sympathizer, in whose memory an olive grove now stands in Israel, had recruited most of his agents from Jewish circles. "The number of Jews saved from Germany", wrote one of them, "would have been tens of thousands less had Captain Foley not sat in the consular office in the Tiergarten Strasse." Now their dream had come true: they had what they saw as one of the top persecutors within their grasp.

8 Camp Z

At 1.15 a.m. on the first night after Hess's arrival at Camp Z the Guard Commander Captain Winch was told a shot had been fired outside the perimeter fences. The floodlights were switched on, and soldiers rushed to investigate. Nothing was found.

Since the sound had come from about 600 yards away Colonel Scott, the camp Commandant, finally dismissed it as of no consequence. The episode did, however, show how strained were the nerves of the officers guarding the Deputy Führer: steeped in their government's own propaganda about the enemy, they were obsessed with fears that Hitler's dreaded "Fifth Column" might intervene, or that he might parachute stormtroopers into Aldershot to rescue, or even assassinate, their captive. (In fact although Hitler had growled to his staff, "Hess is a dead man!" there is no record in Nazi files of any mission to liquidate his luckless deputy.)

Until purchased by the War Department in 1912, Mytchett Place, Rudolf Hess's new permanent residence, had been a ramshackle, run-down mansion of the type which abounds in that part of southern England. Set well back from the road in rambling, unkempt grounds, at a patch of moorlands known in the fourteenth century as "Mucheless-hette", it was an unpleasant outpost of Windsor Forest. The building of the house itself had been begun in 1779. Until now its only claim to fame had been one afternoon in September 1939 when Their Majesties had been entertained to tea by the Major-General then in residence. They must have hurried on.

Even to the psychiatrists shortly assigned to tackle Hess, there was something indefinably sinister about its atmosphere – a setting for an Edgar Allan Poe mystery story. It is unlikely that Hess, peering out of his darkened ambulance windows, will have understood the significance of the newly diverted roads, or glimpsed much of the freshly excavated slit trenches and machine-gun positions or the heavily patrolled double-perimeter of barbed-wire barricades, as he was driven up to the house, but the bare wooden floors, the ill-matched, heavy furniture hastily brought together by the War Office cannot have lifted up his soul as he gazed about his new home.

During that first night Second Lieutenant William "Barney" Malone of the Scots Guards, a burly, dark-haired former borstal housemaster, looked in at hourly intervals. Awakened at 8 a.m., the prisoner asked for "bacon and fish" for breakfast but suddenly refused to eat them and would not touch the mug of tea either – confiding to "Barnes" of all people that he suspected that the "big black man" (Malone) was a member of the secret police and might be trying to poison him.

The Commandant recorded:

9.00: "Z" reported to have had roughly five hours' sleep.

"Z" served with breakfast in his room but ate very little of it. He appeared to be nervous of attempts to poison him.

13.00: "Z" came down to lunch which he took with the three Companions and [the doctor] Col. Graham. He was in much better spirits and apologised to the doctor afterwards for his suspicions at breakfast.

After lunch Hess returned to bed – his damaged ankle probably still hurting. When he returned to the downstairs mess at 8 p.m. he was wearing his full uniform as a captain of the German air force. It provides a clue to what thoughts were unwinding in his mind. There is no doubt that he had guessed that the "Companions" were in fact officers of the British secret service. Coming from Nazi Germany, with his own insight into the methods which regimes employ, he believed himself to be at mortal risk. Consciously or unconsciously he evidently wanted to remind his captors that even if they chose to violate his rights as a self-appointed parliamentary they could not deny that as a Luftwaffe officer who had arrived openly, in uniform and in an unarmed plane, he was entitled to be treated according to the Geneva Convention. He had now taken in the fact that there was no knob on the inside of his bedroom door; that his room and the mess downstairs were enclosed within a steel grille; that he was a prisoner of the secret service of Hitler's deadliest enemy; that he might have to rely on his wits alone to stay alive.

22 May 1941   [Commandant's diary]

08.30: "Z" came down to breakfast. He stated that he had had a good night but has an obsession that the guard officers are planning to murder him. He spent all morning in his room and came down to lunch at 13.00 dressed in plain clothes. After lunch he walked in the garden with his Companions and the doctor [Gibson Graham]. . . . He had [dinner] as usual with his Companions who reported that he seemed much easier in his mind and franker in his conversation.

23 May 1941

10.15: He went into the garden with his Companions but only stayed there a few minutes and then went up to his room with Capt. "Barnes".

It is noticed that "Z" will talk very freely with the doctor and seems to trust him but all other officers are treated with suspicion. . . . "Z" is still apprehensive that the guard officers are out to murder him. He was unconvinced that they are really officers of the Brigade of Guards, maintaining that a uniform means nothing.

Unfortunately, the verbatim transcripts of these early conversations – there were at least two dozen – between Hess and his captors have been retained in British secret service archives. But it is clear Hess suspected that as soon as he had been "squeezed dry" for Intelligence purposes he would be liquidated as a "war criminal", probably in the guise of a suicide. "He told me", recorded Dr Gibson Graham, reporting on these first days at Camp Z, "he was convinced he was surrounded by Secret Service agents who would accomplish his death either by driving him to commit suicide, committing a murder staged to look like suicide, or by administering poison in his food." When Gibson Graham tried to allay his suspicions Hess merely shifted them to another group of captors. And when the food was served in the mess from a common dish, he was careful not to select the chop placed closest to him.

Uncertain what to make of him, Graham quite properly decided that an expert psychiatric opinion was called for, and stated this request in letters to the authorities on the 23rd and 24th.

The Deputy Führer's well-being was not high on the list of official requirements.

The Foreign Office – personified by Eton-educated Permanent Under-Secretary Sir Alexander Cadogan – had given to MI6, the secret service, which came directly under his purview, the job of penetrating Rudolf Hess's mind, to the point of destruction if need be. This is clear from Cadogan's private diaries, only the non-Intelligence parts of which have hitherto been published. A prior requirement of this task was that the prisoner be stripped of his self-esteem. Every conceivable means that was legal within the Convention was adopted to this end – depriving Hess of all outside information (newspapers, neutral visitors, radio); isolation in a military compound (the sounds of machine-gun fire, of parade-ground drilling, of military engines); slamming doors.

Already alarmed and demoralized by the prospect of failure, Hess started to crack. As the fissures became visible, Camp Z's officers adopted a callous unit of success, measuring his current self-esteem in pounds, shillings and pence.

The records of the psychiatrists who were, over the coming months, the witnesses of this process of degeneration provide one of the most harrowing parts of the whole Hess incident. These specialists' role was ambivalent from the start. Their science has been, ever since the writings of Professor Sigmund Freud, a subjective and controversial one – its findings as much a factor of the patient's relationship to the analyst as of the latter's personal animus towards him. In 1941 military psychiatry was in an innovative phase, ranging from the experimental use of amphetamines for assault troops and of "truth-drugs" for Intelligence purposes to the techniques of electro-convulsive therapy. By 1945 the frontiers of psychiatry would have been pushed so far that its American practitioners secured the brains of Benito Mussolini and Nazi labour leader Robert Ley for laboratory examination; in 1946 they would request that the Nazi war criminals at Nuremberg should be shot through the heart, to enable an unspoilt examination of their heads.

Shortly after his transfer from the Tower of London to MI6's "Camp Z" Hess began to notice that the food and medication he was being given left him with a distinctly unusual sensation. Since the sensation recurred several times over the next weeks, he was able to describe it clearly in later depositions.

> As far as I think I am able to observe, the symptoms . . . are as follows: a short time after taking it, a curious development of warmth rising over the nape of the neck to the head: in the head, feelings which are similar to headache pains, but which are not the same: there follows for many hours an extraordinary feeling of well-being, physical and mental energy, joie de vivre, optimism. Little sleep during the night but this did not in the least destroy my sense of euphoria.

He also observed "withdrawal symptoms" when the substance was not being used – without any cause, a plunge into pessimism, verging on a nervous breakdown, followed later by lengthy periods of exceptionally rapid exhaustion of the brain. On the first occasion when he suspected this mysterious substance had been slipped to him, the contra-indications were so strong that he feared, he said, that he would indeed become insane "if they succeeded in giving me further quantities".*

24 May 1941   [Commandant's diary]

Air raid warning 23.45 to 00.45. "Z" was restless throughout, but later went to sleep and slept heavily till 07.30.

After breakfast he walked for some time with Major Foley [of MI6]. After tea . . . he had a long talk with the doctor in the drawing room. He stated that he had given his word to the Führer that he would not commit suicide. This, presumably in a letter he left behind him.

In fact the content of Hess's letter to Hitler, though lost, is known well enough to state with certainty that it contained no such promise; he hoped

---

* Over two years later, Major Foley's colleague Robert Bruce-Lockhart, head of the Foreign Office's Political Intelligence Department, privately visited Lord Beaverbrook, who had by that time also interviewed Hess (pp. 178–84 below). The Cabinet Minister let him read his dossier. "In Max's [Beaverbrook's] view," wrote the Intelligence officer, "Hess was not a mental case when he came to this country. . . . Max thinks he was probably given some kind of drugs by our people to make him talk." *The Diaries of Sir Robert Bruce Lockhart*, vol. ii: *1939–1945* (London, 1984).

that the threat of such a letter's publication in Germany would give his captors second thoughts – because in effect thousands of British prisoners were hostages in Hitler's hands.

Unimpressed, Gibson Graham remarked to Colonel Scott, " 'Z' is daily decreasing in stature. I estimate his worth now at not more than £2 a week."

After coming out to watch the next morning's 10 a.m. parade on the drive, Hess suddenly and without comment broke into the goose-step, marching up and down the path – "Apparently", as Lieutenant Malone wrote in his illicit private diary, "the idea was meant to convey that he was not impressed."

25 May 1941   [Commandant's diary]

"Z" . . . appeared to have been upset by something and was gloomy and morose, speaking little to anybody. He remained in his room all the afternoon but had a short walk with Capt. "Barnes" in the evening in spite of the rain.

   In the morning I held a C.O.'s parade which he saw in the distance and pretended not to be impressed. However he gave a ludicrous exhibition of modified goose-step in front of his [MI6] Companions presumably to show he was equal to the occasion.

   Brigadier Stuart Menzies ["C", the head of MI6] visited the Camp from 17.30 to 19.00 and remained with the Companions throughout. He did not interview "Z".

26 May 1941

He was unable to take any exercise as it rained solidly all day. Apart from meals he spent all day in his room reading. He has been very depressed and dejected and Col. "Wallace" thinks he is beginning to realise that the State of England is very different from what he had been led to believe.

"The patient", Dr Gibson Graham also recorded, a few days later, "became very depressed and thought that he must have been misinformed regarding the urgent desire of Britain for an understanding with his Government."

Given the strains of life at Camp Z – the Tommy guns hidden under sofas, the three mysterious Companions constantly in attendance, outranking all others in the dingy mansion and impressing on visitors the need for utter secrecy – it would not be surprising if the doctors and custodians were themselves overwhelmed by ill-defined forebodings about the prisoner. Hess himself kept obstinately recovering composure. Challenged about the imbalance of powers, since Britain was being aided by the United States, he cockily reminded Dr Gibson Graham that the fall of France had left Germany with enhanced mineral and industrial resources too. Tasked thereupon with the Nazi concentration camps, Hess "laugh[ed] sarcastically", as Dr Gibson Graham recorded, and reminded him: "You should know, you invented them." (Churchill's own memoirs of the Boer War had referred to the British "concentration camps".) Tackled finally about Hitler's occupation of Prague in March 1939 – despite the Munich Agreement – Hess referred to the airfields that the Czechs had begun building to enable Russian bomber squadrons to operate against Germany. "But the general impression one got", Gibson Graham summarized a few days later, "was of a man under strain and intensely worried."

Colonel Scott's record did not reflect this:

27 May 1941

It was a very wet morning and he was unable to go out. But it cleared after tea and he went out in the garden with Capt. "Barnes" and the doctor and had a sharp walk. He seems calmer and in a better temper.

He complains of his food, saying that it is over-seasoned.

"Barnes", "Wallace" and Foley were reporting their recorded conversations with Hess direct to MI6 and the Foreign Office. In the plush surroundings of the Ambassadors' Room of the Foreign Office, on the afternoon of 28 May, Anthony Eden called in three or four of the country's top diplomatic correspondents for a private briefing. After the newspapermen had settled into deep chairs and a settee with cups of tea and biscuits in hand, Eden spoke about Hess. One thing stuck in the memory of *The Times* representative, A. Leo Kennedy: "Hess", said Eden, "was very earnest about his mission." Although the Deputy Führer would not admit it, he seemed to have crossed swords with Joachim von Ribbentrop, the Foreign Minister. Hess had also seemed surprised to find how relatively well off the British were. Kennedy left the Foreign Office convinced, as he wrote in his diary, that Hess had flown to Britain "to try and get a peace plan over" – which, the journalist concluded, he would certainly not have done without Hitler's personal consent.

This was immaterial to British Intelligence. They were interested only in Hess's secret knowledge. Their agents, and in particular Lord Swinton's little-known Security Co-ordination Committee which orchestrated the efforts of MI5, MI6 and the other Intelligence agencies in the United Kingdom, were becoming deeply involved in the case. ("It should be on record", minuted the Air Ministry on its Duke of Hamilton dossier, "that an influence on the framing of the replies in this folder was Lord Swinton's organisation.")

Moreover, Churchill wanted Hess's resistance broken. The time had come to start feeding to him poisoned morsels of information about the outside world – beginning with the naval victory that had at last tilted the scales of Churchill's unbroken record of defeats.

28 May 1941   [Commandant's diary]

"Z" had rather a restless night and woke at 05.00 and didn't have much sleep after. He came down to breakfast and had a long walk in the garden afterwards.

He seemed in a better mood but at lunch was told by the "Companions" of the sinking of the *Bismarck* [Germany's newest and finest battleship had been destroyed the day before]. This news completely bowled him over and he retired to bed directly after lunch complaining of backache.

According to Dr Gibson Graham this was "entirely nerves" – he was introducing a physical ailment to camouflage his mental turmoil.

28 May 1941   [Lieutenant Malone's diary]

When asked if he would like a lunch of light food sent up "Z" said, "No, I will go down and have lunch with you. Exactly the same food. That is my request." When I went down to the anteroom Colonel "Wallace" and "Barnes" were most annoyed. They are very bored with "Death's Head." Wallace" now says, "He's worth thirty-five shillings a week – no more."

Apparently he went off to his room in a huff because of the *Bismarck* and they were banking on an all-day retreat.

He has been terribly afraid that a member of the Secret Service would creep inside his bedroom at night and cut an artery to fake a suicide, and is very tricky about meals – apparently he left a letter saying he would not commit suicide so that if he was bumped off over here Hitler would know that it was not suicide and then would take reprisals against our prisoners of war. At dinner tonight he insisted on Colonel "Wallace" helping himself to fish first, and then did not himself take the next piece, but the next but one in the dish. The Commandant was much amused because "Z" ordered a hair net to sleep in at night!

I find it difficult to realize that this rather broken man who slouches into his chair careless as to his dress, whose expressions are unstudied, who is incapable of hiding his emotions, who swings in mood from cheerfulness to depression in a few hours, whose body reflects his mental pain and whose mind is clouded with delusionary ideas (he sees Hitler's face in his soup, says [Colonel] Kendrick [of MI6]), who believes in second sight and dreams – that this man was the Deputy Führer of the Reich! He is such a *second-rater*, with none of the dignity, the bearing of a great man.★

Two hours later Hess went downstairs, announcing that he felt better; teasing him, Gibson Graham said he would be provided with dinner alone – Hess pleaded to be allowed to eat from the common dinner. Hess's only other request that day, recorded Scott contemptuously, was for a hairnet.

★ From a remarkable diary kept by Second Lieutenant W. B. Malone, extracts of which were first published by the *Observer*, London, in September 1987.

Zusätze zu den Personal=Notizen:

20.2.16 *an Haltentgründung n*

8.3.16 *krank ins Kriegslaz. I.*

    21.3.16 *ins Kriegslaz. -*

    24.4.16 *zur Genesung*

    29.4.16 *zur Truppe*

20.5.-2.6.16 *nach Reicholdsgrün*

12.6.16 *bei Douaumont*

    13.6.16 *ins Res.-Laz.*

    28.6.16 *ins Res.-Laz.*

    14.7.16 *zur Ersatz-Tr.*

25.7.17 *auf den Höhen*

    (li. Oberarm) – bei

8.8.17 *bei der Erstürmung des Ungureana p̃p̃ verwundet*

    (Gew.-Geschoß – Lunge lks)

    9.8.17 *ins Kriegslaz. 21 c / Bezdivasarhely,*

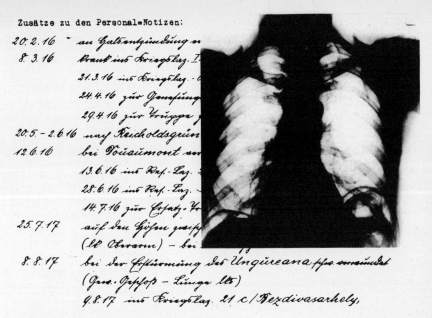

DENTAL TREATMENT CARD.   Army Form I 5033.

Date of First Examination 30/9/41   Place _____   Dental Officer *J. M. Barnes Capt. A.D. Corps*

Army Number	Rank	Name	Squadron, Battery or Company	UNIT	Age	Date of Enlistment	Period of Engagement
		JONATHAN					

Dental Centre	Reference Number	Date	TREATMENT	Initials of Dental Officer
		30/9/41	Inspection	J.M.B.
		2/10/41	6⌋ Crown. Stoned to prevent wear to occlusal surface of 6⌋. ⌊3 porcelain crown has chipped lingually. Stoned off sharp edge and reduced height of ⌊3 to ease pressure. Scaled and polished all teeth	J.m.B
			(OVER)	

BRIDGES

M.O.D. Inlay NOTATION

8765432 1 | 1 2345678
8765432 1 | 1 2345678

CROWN

BRIDGES

Sc

REMARKS.
ORAL HYGIENE = GOOD

NOTE—THIS CARD MUST NOT BE FOLDED.

Wt. 38406/1918 850,000 1/40 "J.&C.M." 51-5035

On 8 August 1917 Hess's personnel file shows (left) that a rifle bullet had pierced his left lung. X-rays in Spandau prison (right) failed to show the scar, leading to speculation about the prisoner's true identity. The Spandau authorities declined to compare a 1941 dental chart on 'Jonathan' (i.e. Hess) with their current records as requested by the author in 1987.

The events of this day and the next persuaded Gibson Graham that Hess was "definitely over the border that lies between mental instability and insanity".

Shaken at the news of *Bismarck*'s loss with so many friends aboard, Hess had at first retained a frigid aloofness towards the Guards officers. Second-Lieutenant Bill Malone in particular had until now aroused his suspicions; Hess had confided a few days earlier to MI6 agent Captain "Barnes" that he felt Malone might be some sort of English "Gestapo" plant, to be treated with caution. But during this painful afternoon Malone talked about skiing, and this struck a sympathetic chord; by evening, when Malone came on duty shortly after Hess trailed disconsolately up to his room, he felt he could trust the officer after all. As bedtime approached, Hess asked for a sedative. At about 10.30 p.m. Dr Gibson Graham came upstairs and gave him something, but it left Hess more restless than ever, and Malone saw him moving about in bed and rising to go to the lavatory.

At 2.20 a.m. the unhappy prisoner appeared at the duty officer's room inside the "cage". "I can't sleep," he told Malone. "Could you get me some whisky – just a small one?" Since Hess was purportedly teetotal the request surprised Malone. (It may well be that Hess, puzzled that Gibson Graham's "sedative" was not working, had decided to try alcohol instead.) Reluctant to wake Dr Gibson Graham at such an hour, Lieutenant Malone handed him a tumbler of very dilute whisky.

Hess drank it. "The whisky was not too small?" he inquired, plaintively. "It was enough?" Malone said it was, but offered to get a sleeping mixture too. Hess declined it.

Twenty minutes or so passed, then Hess again appeared in Malone's room, nervous, distressed, unable to sleep and anxious to talk the hours away. "Speaking in a stage whisper," as Malone reported a few hours later to the Commandant, "which never rose above a murmur, he ran through his reasons for coming to England and wishing to see the Duke of Hamilton." Hess finished by asking Malone to contact the Duke, to ask him to arrange an audience for the Deputy Führer with the King. "If you do this," said Hess earnestly, "you will in due course receive the thanks of the monarch for a great service to humanity."

Malone evidently held out little hope to him, because Hess continued by setting out his belief that the secret service, at the behest of a "clique" of warmongers, had hidden him out here at Camp Z so that the Duke of Hamilton could not find him. And now they were trying to drive him to insanity – or to suicide.

"That's nonsense," said Malone.

Hess persisted: "During the past few days a devilish scheme has been started to prevent me from sleeping at night and resting during the day. Last night noises were continuously and deliberately made to stop me sleeping – doors were loudly opened and shut, people ran up and down uncarpeted stairs, the sentinel kept clicking his heels." Malone pointed out that the sentry outside the cage wore rubber shoes. "Yesterday", Hess went on, unabashed, "an enormous number of motor bicycles were stationed close by with their engines running, to prey on my nerves. And special aeroplanes were sent over to disturb me. This is all an obvious plot to break my nerve." Malone tried to explain that with a large military training camp only a few hundred yards away such sounds were perfectly normal, but Hess shook his head hopelessly and flapped his hands about on the arms of his chair.

Looking grim, he retired to bed, then reappeared in Malone's room a few minutes later. "Excuse me for what I said just now," he said, his eyes haunted and hollow with sleeplessness. "I am in a very nervous condition, I didn't mean all I said."

"He returned", wrote Malone in his own meticulous diary, "to the question of the Duke of Hamilton.

'If you would get in touch with him and tell him where I am you would do a great service to your country. Your King would thank you. I have come here simply to stop this carnage, this terrible waste. No German who went through the last war wanted this war. I have come to no purpose. I have failed.'"

Hess had become shrunken, described Malone in the same note – "an old, almost wizened man, as he finished, slumped in the armchair opposite me in white dressing-gown with red facings, one bandaged ankle crossing the other. An impression of shaggy eyebrows, deep animal sad eyes, a look of anguish and torture on his face. He flapped his hands listlessly from the elbow on to the sides of the armchair."

He was still lying in bed, wide awake, when Malone went off duty the next morning. Hess asked his replacement, Lieutenant Jackson, if there was indeed a training ground for motorbicyclists nearby – just to check if he could trust Malone's truthfulness.

29 May 1941   [Commandant's diary]

"Z" . . . breakfasted downstairs, but the Companions couldn't get a word out of him. . . . Rang up Col. Coates at 15.00 and explained the position. Col. Coates rang up at 17.45 to say that Col. Graham would be relieved over the weekend by a Psychiatrist which is all to the good.

That evening Colonel Scott came to dinner with Hess in "A" Mess. Hess accepted a glass of port from the Colonel, then asked to speak privately with him. Scott asked Major Foley – of MI6 – to come and interpret. Hess now asked for the locks on the inside cage to be changed to the *inside* since they were supposed to be for his "protection"; he asked too for at least a summary of the news in future (he had deduced why they had sprung the *Bismarck* bombshell on him); he wanted to be allowed out into the garden whenever he chose. He offered his word of honour not to escape, and explained that he felt entitled to state these requests since he

had come here of his own free will and had thrown himself on the chivalry
of His Majesty the King.

> Having finished this conversation I walked with him & Major Foley in
> the garden [recorded the Commandant]. He, "Z", seemed easier in his
> mind and talked freely on many subjects.

It was a disturbing case. Churchill had affirmed in his draft statement of
12 May, "He is reported to be perfectly sane." Dr Gibson Graham stated
the same in his closing opinion: "No evidence of mental instability was
noted at the beginning of my care of Rudolf Hess." But such evidence
now seemed to accumulate with each day that passed here at Camp Z, and
on 29 May Gibson Graham again recommended psychiatric investigation.

Colonel Coates put the matter to the Cambridge-educated Dr John
Rawlings Rees, consulting psychiatrist to the British Army since 1938.
Given the rank of colonel, the balding, portly, pipe-smoking Rees lived in
a modest bed-sitter in the famous Tavistock Clinic in North London.
Four years older than Hess, he would publish *The Shaping of Psychiatry by
War* in 1945 and eventually rise to the summit of his profession, becoming
director of the World Federation of Mental Health. He would remain in
medical charge of Hess for as long as he remained on British soil.

Rees in turn selected, as an immediate replacement for Dr Gibson
Graham, a major in the RAMC, Henry Victor Dicks. Dicks had been
born in 1900 in Pernau, Estonia – at that time a Baltic province of
Germany – to an English exporter and shipowner. His mother was
German, and he spoke both that language and Russian like a native; he had
served as an interpreter for Military Intelligence on Churchill's anti-
Bolshevik expedition to Murmansk in 1919, and subsequently with the
British mission to General Denikin's White Russian armies. He had
joined the British Army as Command Psychiatrist, London District, after
publishing *Clinical Studies in Psychopathology*, a popular textbook, in 1939.
Considered one of the most brilliant psychiatrists of his generation, Dicks
had obvious linguistic advantages, but given his Jewish origins it is plain
that there could be nothing but hostility between himself and his subject,
the Deputy Führer of Nazi Germany. Dicks's own interests were already
in the persecution of minorities, and in what later became known as the
Holocaust – on which he would publish a book.* Dicks, in fact, had sold
his soul to the higher needs of the SIS. "In 1941," he would recount, in
Fifty Years of the Tavistock Clinic,** "I was seconded for the extraordinary
and highly secret duty of looking after [Hess]. As a result of this
experience, a good contact was made with Military Intelligence which
took me off the [current] developments . . . into a hush-hush realm."

The relationship between doctor–interrogator Dicks and patient–

---

* *Licensed Mass Murder* (London, 1972).
** London, 1970.

Deputy Führer Hess, was illustrated by an incident involving Hess's request for reading material (in these early weeks he was forbidden newspapers). He was told that poetry by Goethe, textbooks on world history, on higher mathematics and on medicine were unobtainable. Eventually Dicks provided him with some volumes of Goethe – and an English novel about a little boy of just Wolf Rüdiger's age. "Every page", recalled Hess, writing four years later, "was to remind me of my child and I was to be reminded that there was hardly any hope of ever seeing him again."

From the moment that the SIS doctor Dicks set foot inside Camp Z, on Friday, 30 May 1941, the antipathy between Hess, the Nazi peace-emissary, and this Estonian-born psychiatrist was corrosive.

Gibson Graham had imparted to Rees his conclusions that Hess showed marked hypochondriacal tendencies with delusions of persecution, and described how Hess was "misinterpreting simple incidents" and giving them a sinister meaning. It is clear from Colonel Rees's immediate report that he did not share Gibson Graham's diagnosis. Despite the language difficulty (unlike Dicks, Rees spoke no German) he formed the impression from their friendly talk that Rudolf Hess's depression could be adequately accounted for as the result of his "sense of failure" and that it did not give any indication of a seriously diseased state of mind: "He has the facies [facial expression] and the slow manner of speaking of a man suffering from a depression."

Evidently to satisfy his personal curiosity, Colonel Rees asked Hess why he had flown to Scotland. Rees, with years of peacetime clinical experience in dealing with neurotics, delinquents and criminals, told the War Office afterwards: "I got a strong impression that the story was in general true." Hess had spoken hauntingly and convincingly of the need to halt the bloodshed: Germany was so powerful in submarines and planes that Britain could not but lose; the Führer, however, had always loathed the idea of fighting Britain. Since the Blitz had begun in September 1940, Hess continued, the needless slaughter and destruction had preyed on his mind. So he had borrowed a plane and flown here to make contact with the large group of Englishmen who wanted peace. Rees was taken aback by the honesty of the man – he had until now believed quite differently. "Hess's lack of fluency in English makes it difficult, I should judge, for him to tell a convincing story that is completely untrue, and at times when he spoke of the slaughter, etc., there was emphasis and feeling in his voice that I felt sure was not simulated."

As they strolled about the enclosed garden, Hess told Colonel Rees of his discontent. Why was he not allowed books? He could not understand why his captors were starving him of news. He could not even understand the bars and locks to cage a man who had "come with a flag of truce", a man of "flag rank". Why was he no longer allowed to speak to Kirkpatrick and the Duke of Hamilton?

It was plain to Colonel Rees that despite his "obvious" intelligence, the prisoner had a pathological – almost pathetic – reluctance to understand his current position. Anxious and tense, the German twice remarked to him, "The King of England would never let these things happen." By this, he meant the barbed wire, the sentries, the grille whereby the "warmongers" in Whitehall were restraining him. Colonel Rees saw him, in fact, as a suicide risk despite his "alleged promise" to the Führer.

31 May 1941   [Commandant's diary]

There were two air raid warnings during the night – the sirens being particularly loud. They seemed to worry "Z" who got up and paced the landing and his sitting room but went back to bed at 06.00. . . . He came down at 12.00 and walked in the garden with Capt. "Barnes".

Major Dicks, the new doctor, reported for duty and spent a great deal of the evening and after dinner walking in the garden with "Z".

The contrast between Rees, who had been fundamentally impressed by Hess's sincerity and intelligence, and Dicks, the hostile psychiatrist, could not have been more marked. A secret planning conference between Dicks, Colonel Scott and the Companions had preceded the first meeting. Dicks was instructed to adopt the role of a regular doctor, not a psychiatrist, with the task of helping Camp Z to manage Hess, and the MI6 officers to extract useful information from him.

Major Dicks was then brought upstairs into "Z"'s drawing room. Dicks's immediate reaction was: "a typical schizophrenic". The erstwhile Deputy Führer was seated at a table littered with papers – he was composing a letter to the British Cabinet – his skull-like face, in Dicks's words, wearing a profoundly unhappy, grim expression, with his eyes staring into infinity. Frontally, his face was gaunt, hollow-cheeked, pale and lined, but conveyed an impression of baleful strength. In profile, however, Dicks perceived the receding forehead, the exaggerated supra-orbital ridges bristling with thick bushy eyebrows, the sunken eyes, the irregular "buck" teeth, the weak chin and receding lower jaw, and these told him instinctively all he needed to know about Rudolf Hess. "The whole man", he wrote, "produced the impression of a caged great ape, and 'oozed' hostility and suspicion."

As they were left alone together, it was plain that the feeling was almost mutual. While Hess – already aroused by the easy German spoken by the Companions – took in Dicks's Central European features and lisping, heavily accented German, the Major assembled further reasons to dislike Hess – such as the prisoner's misshapen ears, which a cruel heredity had positioned far too low in relation to the level of his eyes. In a subsequent examination he would find the palate of Hess's mouth to be narrow and arched.

Thwarting every attempt by Dicks to draw important secret Intelligence out of him, the prisoner remained civil towards this three-faced companion – the psychiatrist masquerading as a doctor to extort secret data from him for MI6. He talked of his own interests in health and welfare, and mentioned with some pride the Rudolf Hess rehabilitation centre which he had founded in Dresden for disabled industrial workers, and talked with equal fervour about the complexities of his secret flight to Scotland. He cunningly asked whether the BBC had interviewed the crofter who had found him (he was probing to find out how much the British public had been told of his arrival and mission).

As they walked downstairs and out into Camp Z's little garden, Hess again blamed his imprisonment on Churchill and the "narrow clique of warmongers" who were preventing him from getting his message to the people who wanted peace: the Royal Palace and real British aristocracy epitomized daily for Hess by the other handsome young Guards officers like Lieutenant Malone whom he could see through the grille. But he himself was trapped inside with Dicks and the German-speaking Companions: these were the ones who were thwarting his mission to save the world from war. And might not one of them, some day, take a bribe to let some hate-filled German émigré kill him?

Dicks tried hard to extract material from him that first day, but Hess would not even oblige him with the names of the flowers they trod on. In the distance, a bugle sounded. Recalling what Dr Gibson Graham had told him of the goose-stepping episode, Dicks remarked on the childishness of military practices. "Somebody or other once said you can do anything with bayonets except sit on them."

"Yes," responded Hess. "That was Napoleon. But he did try, and still made a mess of things in the end."

That night Dicks examined Hess in bed. He now found "in addition to the stigmata of degeneration already noted" – the forehead, ears, chin, and so on – that the prisoner was of round-shouldered, narrow-chested physique. Hess confided to him that he was finding difficulty in sleeping, and asked for the return of his Phanodorm sedatives, as well as a list of nature-cure and herbal remedies with which Major Dicks was unfamiliar. In his initial summary, he used the words "paranoid", "hypochondriac" and "cranky treatment".

"What a dull dog!" was the comment of one Guards officer to Dicks, speaking of Hess. And another said, "I think this man is worth about two pounds ten shillings in the open labour market!"

Any assassin would have been hard put to poison Hess. Regardless of the mocking comments and injured feelings of his Companions, he went to extreme and even absurd lengths to protect himself. That first evening, 31 May 1941, Dicks saw Hess wait until the soup course had been served, then calmly switch his plate with the senior officer's; he took slices of beef from half-way down the stack, and stubbornly refused to touch the wines brought in from the officers' mess or to drink their coffee or tea. "I have to be careful when and what I drink," he remarked ironically.

His precautions verged upon the paranoid, that is true; but to him they were an essential, if tedious, prerequisite to staying alive. He was a man with a mission.

1 June 1941   [Commandant's diary]

"Z" had a rather restless night. . . . Several shots were fired during the night by the French Canadians [based] in the neighbourhood. . . . Spent most of the morning in his room but after lunch walked in the garden and also sat out for a considerable time – in fact till about 18.00. . . . Major Dicks now has charge of the case. He is still treated by "Z" with a certain amount of suspicion.

2 June 1941

"Z" had a restless night so did not get up for breakfast – in fact he stayed in bed till 12.00. . . . He complained of his lunch again being over-seasoned and now says that it is a deliberate attempt to starve him. He went straight to his room after lunch and wrote hard all the afternoon and didn't come down till 17.30 when Major Dicks went up & brought him down to walk in the garden.

3 June 1941

"Z" . . . had a very good night. The doctor gave him a drug [Phanodorm] which "Z" himself had asked for, which seemed to have the desired effect. He went for a short walk after breakfast which was not announced, as it should have been, by the Companions – with the result that he was seen by three civilian workmen who were building an incinerator in the camp lines. It rained hard for the rest of the day so that "Z" was unable to do anything but sit in his room and write his long journal. It cleared up a bit after dinner & he had a short walk with Major Foley. A corporal from Pirbright came over to cut his hair which seemed to make him happier.

In these first days of June Hess alternated between hours of depression, seemingly baffled by his plight, and exalted hard work on the letter to the British Cabinet. "On the question of whether he has the power to negotiate," recorded Lieutenant Malone in his private diary, "he takes up a God the Father, God the Son attitude – 'I know the Führer and the Führer knows me.'" Questioned again by Dicks about his mission, Hess refused to be drawn. "I shall disclose my intentions only to properly authorized representatives of His Majesty's Government," he said, and resumed work on the document, carefully setting out in indelible pencil a statement which even Dicks had to admit contained arguments that were "models of clarity, of exposition and logical argument". As the days passed, he betrayed to the MI6 officers an unforgiving impatience to be brought face to face with a minister of the requisite rank.

On the 4th, the depression seemed to be deepening to a suicidal level. Second-Lieutenant Jackson reported to Colonel Scott that the German had repeatedly climbed out of bed and retired to the lavatory, sometimes for half an hour at a time. He spent the afternoon sitting morosely under a tree in a position that seemed most uncomfortable, refusing to speak to anybody. What thoughts were besieging him? There was no clue: but that evening he again went out, walking up and down in an agitated way, seemingly counting the steps. The microphones overheard him muttering, "I can't stand this any longer." He refused the spurious "company" offered by the MI6 Companions and on retiring at 10 p.m. he turned to wish them "Goodnight". He had never done that before.

At 10.30 p.m. the senior MI6 officer, Colonel "Wallace", went to tell Scott that he, Foley and Dicks all suspected that Hess was planning to kill himself that night. Scott ordered Lieutenant Malone – who had a broad experience of mental cases – to replace Lieutenant Hubbard on duty inside the grille.

Evidently during one of Hess's outings they had searched his room and found he had written a letter to his wife Ilse – for the first time (it would be January 1942 before she received any letter from him, however). The letter contained a quotation from Goethe's poem "The Divine" ("*Das Göttliche*"):

> According to eternal, iron, great
>   Laws
> Must we all
>   Complete the cycles
> Of our being.

Hess understood and liked these lines, and he quoted them in several letters over the next years.

The official records show that by this time the Foreign Office had finalized its plans for a "pseudo-negotiator" to visit Hess. The Lord Chancellor Lord Simon, a tall, bony Liberal intellectual who had been Foreign Secretary six years before and who had met Hess in Berlin in 1935, had a smattering of German and agreed to go along with the unpleasant scheme of tricking Hess into betraying his country's secrets in the belief that he was bringing about world peace. Uneasy about what he was being asked to do, given his reputation as an "appeaser", Simon asked for written confirmation; Eden supplied it on the 27th. "The Prime Minister and I", he wrote, "would be grateful if you could see your way to interview the man of whom we spoke. We feel sure that it is in this way that we are most likely to obtain advantages helpful to the common cause. We do not rate the chances high, but we are confident that this is the best method we can devise."

FOREIGN SECRETARY TO PRIME MINISTER   *27 May 1941*

I saw Simon yesterday, and I think that he will be willing to undertake the work of which we spoke. He has asked for 24 hours to consider the matter. We are agreed that he should make it plain [*to Hess*] that the Government know of the interview, but that it would be unwise for him to indicate close collaboration with you and me – rather the reverse. . . . All this will be kept Most Secret and only Cadogan and I in this Office are aware of the project.

That evening Eden told Churchill of his conversation with the Lord Chancellor. Now it was Churchill's turn to feel queasy: that Simon should interview Hess he agreed – but with strong reservations.

At the same time [Eden emphasized to Simon on 28 May] he asked me to place it on record that His Majesty's Government are of course not prepared to enter into negotiations for peace either with Hess or any other representative of Hitler. Our policy remains as publicly stated on many occasions. Though of course we know that you fully understand the position, the Prime Minister felt that you would like to receive this letter.

It was a curious postscript, which showed that Churchill realized that by letting Simon get near to Hess he might be playing with fire.

For his part Simon, being a lawyer, still wanted everything set down in writing, and submitted his own advance description of his mission to Eden for approval. "Utmost secrecy", instructed Eden in a handwritten reply, agreeing with the Lord Chancellor's document, "will be observed. . . . I agree that you must say that you have come with the Government's approval though I hope it would not be necessary to emphasize this too much." He concluded, "Both Winston and I are most grateful to you."

Two weeks would pass, however, before Lord Simon finally agreed to the dangerous meeting with the Deputy Führer. His reluctance is clear from the diary entry that Sir Alexander Cadogan wrote after briefing the Cabinet on 29 May: "J.S. [John Simon] had called in the morning – he is getting rather cold feet about interviewing Hess." Cadogan applied a "hot-water bottle", and admitted to himself that there probably was a risk involved ("but P.M.", he added with a callous dry humour, "says he doesn't mind"). On the 30th Cadogan briefed the King's Private Secretary on the plan to let Hess and Simon meet.

With that gentle irony for which the British foreign service was renowned, Cadogan added an entry about his own minister, Anthony Eden, three days later: "He and Hess are psychological cases."

On the following day, 3 June, Cadogan talked over the whole Hess affair with "C", the head of MI6; later that day he heard that Simon had sent for Henry Hopkinson, Cadogan's private secretary, and agreed to take the job on. At seven the next evening "C" came to discuss with Cadogan the "arrangements" for this fresh attempt to trick Hess into revealing state secrets. "Simon", noted Cadogan, "has undertaken the job & will start on Monday!"

MI6 showed to Lord Simon all the transcripts of the Hess conversations, and provided him with notes suggesting which information he might try to worm out of the captive. "Generally speaking," Cadogan wrote, briefing Churchill in secret on the Simon plan,

> Hess has stuck to the line which he took in his original interviews with the Duke of Hamilton and Mr Kirkpatrick, namely, insistence on the certainty of German victory and the senselessness of continuing the struggle. He still maintains that it was his own personal idea to come to England and that he was not sent by the Führer. He still professes anxiety to get into touch with the leaders of the Opposition in this country who, he supposes, represent a strong Peace Party.
>
> When he found himself in his new quarters behind barbed wire and bars he began to profess great anxiety: he complained that he had fallen into the hands of a clique of the Secret Service and began to complain that his mission had failed and that there was nothing for it but to put him into a prisoner of war camp like an ordinary prisoner of war.
>
> He went through several days of increasingly severe depression, so much so that the Medical Officer became anxious for his reason and feared that he might attempt suicide.
>
> He was accordingly told that it might be possible in the course of a few days to arrange for him to interview some responsible person.

The news that a "negotiator" was coming to Camp Z had a startling effect on Hess.

5 June 1941   [Commandant's diary]

He came down to breakfast at 09.00 hrs in a highly excitable state. During the day, however, he calmed down considerably – possibly on being told officially that a high representative of the Foreign Office is to visit him on Monday next. He stayed in his room, complaining of a headache from after lunch till 16.30 after which he walked in the garden for some time.

At dinner and afterwards he was most talkative and explained his fear of poison saying that he trusted all of us here but was afraid of "emigrants" bribing the staff to poison him.

He stayed up later than ever before – drank a glass of port and went to bed at 23.45.

He is very anxious to have a calendar showing the phases of the moon [Hess was a keen astrologer].

Over the next four days of waiting Hess went into a kind of nervous relapse, as the same diary shows:

6 June 1941

"Z" . . . complained of a headache which the doctor says is entirely nervous and spent most of the day writing in his sitting room.

7 June 1941

"Z" had another restless night and did not come down to breakfast. All day he was in an agitated state probably due to his approaching interview on Monday. . . . He only went out for a very short time between the showers of rain.

Hess certainly knew the identity of his forthcoming visitor, because the Guards officer John Young saw a note in his diary that the Lord Chancellor was coming. "The greatest secrecy is to be preserved," wrote Young's fellow officer Malone, "as the PM is deadly afraid that Hess's peace plan will get known [and] split the country (there have been Peace Demos in Liverpool)."

In a visibly bad mood, on 8 June Hess walked up and down the exercise yard at a furious pace, his hands clasped behind his back, his face grey, his head bowed. At lunchtime he whipped Colonel "Wallace" 's plate of meat away from him, declaring: "Would you be so chivalrous as to let me have this?"

8 June 1941

"Z" had another bad night. He did not get up till very late. Came down to lunch, refused to eat either soup or fish and when the meat came round instead of helping himself he snatched Col. "Wallace" 's plate and helping. He has again, in fact, a very vivid fear of poison. He refused to speak a word to anyone, refusing tea or dinner & retired to bed like a spoilt child in a towering rage. The whole performance was an exhibition of nerves and at the moment it seems unlikely he will be in a fit state for tomorrow's conference.

All this suggested to Major Dicks the "neurotic alibi" as described by Adler. The Companions felt it more likely that Hess was engineering a hysterical breakdown to avoid having to meet a superior intellect: that the British government had, in effect, called his bluff. But then Dicks performed a standard British Army intelligence test on him, under the guise of playing a paper game. It was called Raven's Progressive Matrices Test, and after twenty-five minutes the psychiatrist found that Hess had filled in columns A to D without a single mistake, putting him firmly in the upper 10 per cent of intelligence distribution. So perhaps a profile study of foreheads, chins and earlines was not a foolproof guide after all.

The fears that Hess would feign a collapse to dodge the all-important confrontation with Lord Simon proved unfounded when the day came. Simon and veteran SIS officer Ivone Kirkpatrick arrived at Camp Z on 9 June 1941. To avoid any unauthorized eyes recognizing either Simon or Kirkpatrick, the sentries were taken off the gate, the soldiers were cleared out of the drive and entrance hall and the provost sergeant on the inner gate was ordered to allow through the big chocolate-coloured

Packard when it arrived. Kirkpatrick, one of its passengers, afterwards wrote, "We drew up at the door and were met by the two special officers, both of whom I already knew." Simon found the whole charade somehow distasteful. As Major Dicks later related, "There was never any intention of accepting [Hess's] proposals for peace. . . . The main purpose of this interview was to try to induce him to give away the German position and plans."

Hess, who had all too naively risked his life to fly to Britain, did not realize this.

9 June 1941   [Commandant's diary]

"Z" spent a very restless night, but having spent some time and taken infinite care in dressing up in uniform, seemed to regain a portion of his former self.

The two doctors "Guthrie" and "McKenzie" [disguises assigned to Lord Simon and Ivone Kirkpatrick to fool the guard] arrived at 13.00 and went straight to lunch in "A" Mess [with the Commandant and guards].

"Z" lunched in his room with Capt. "Barnes". His lunch, however, only consisted of some glucose tablets. He returned all else.

At 14.00 the stenographer arrived and a few minutes later three officers of MI5 [counter-espionage] with the "witness" [Kurt Maass, a German consular officer asked for by Hess from an internment camp].

Wearing the full Luftwaffe captain's uniform and regalia in which he had set off from Augsburg four weeks before, Hess waited in his upstairs drawing room to receive them.

9 The Negotiator Comes

Thus, on 9 June 1941, Hess was allowed to state his case to a high British personage. The two sides could hardly have been more unequal. Hess was alone and entrapped, a simple man of Parsifal-like honesty, who had flown to Scotland wearing a cheap steel watch and the most ordinary of linen underwear, impelled by the naive belief that if man had begun the carnage, then mortals could halt it.

Lord Simon was cut from a different cloth. Yes, he vaguely remembered meeting Hess during the Berlin talks of 1935. A tall arrogant ex-barrister, he had in recent years, like Churchill, accepted very substantial interest-free "loans" from an Austrian-born multi-millionaire who had made his fortune mining gold on the South African Rand; as with the Prime Minister, the payments would only become public knowledge when converted into gifts in the benefactor's will, published in *The Times* in February 1944 (Simon had received £10,000, Churchill twice as much). Simon had shifted belatedly from appeasement to the opposite camp. Churchill had appointed him Lord Chancellor, the head of Britain's legal profession, and in that august capacity Lord Simon would be among those who, like Churchill, would clamour in 1944 and 1945 for the summary liquidation without trial of the enemy leaders. Truly, it was a time when British justice was among the finest that money could buy.

On the morning of Hess's confrontation with Lord Simon, Churchill asked John Martin, his secretary, why he had not received "C"'s report on Hess yet. The reply came from Major Desmond Morton, his Intelligence liaison officer. Morton, a florid, gin-swigging veteran of the First World War trenches, had been Winston's "mole" inside the Intelligence community since the early thirties. He was one of the band of illicit helpers who had fed secret Intelligence data – always anti-German, and often wildly inaccurate – to Churchill while he was still in the political wilderness. Churchill had rewarded him in 1940 with a key position, liaising with MI6 and the codebreaking organization.

"I have read all the detailed conversations with Hess," he reported to the Prime Minister on the morning of 9 June 1941.

My chief preliminary deductions are:

(a) Hess came here without the prior knowledge of Hitler.

(b) While not "psychotic", i.e. "mad" in the medical sense, he is highly neurotic and a very stupid man.

(c) He is not in the inner councils of Hitler or his Generals on high strategy, but may unwittingly possess knowledge of which he himself is unaware.

(d) He is really completely misled about the morale of this country and has little or no knowledge of how it works and is governed.

(e) He has hitherto really believed that he could bring about a rapprochement between England and Germany. . . .

Morton undertook to report to Churchill again after the interview between Hess and "the High Representative" of His Majesty's Government.

Hess had prepared assiduously for this meeting. He had set out in writing (and signed) Hitler's peace terms, as he knew them:

BASIS FOR AN UNDERSTANDING

1. To prevent future wars between the Axis and England, spheres of interest [are] to be determined. The Axis' sphere of interest is Europe; England's sphere of interest is her Empire.

2. Return of the German colonies.

3. Compensation of German nationals who, before or during the war, had their residence inside the British Empire★ and, as a result of measures taken by a Government of the Empire or through some other circumstance, such as public disorder, looting or the like, suffered damage to their persons or property. Corresponding compensation by Germany in respect of British nationals.

4. Armistice and peace only if concluded simultaneously with Italy.

"The above points, substantially," continued the Hess document, "have been indicated by the Führer *repeatedly* in conversations with me as the basis for an understanding with England. No further points have been mentioned."

The document would be in Churchill's hands the next day; it remained undisclosed to the British people until twenty years after he died.

With this paper in his hand, Hess received the little delegation in his upstairs room at 2.30 p.m.

The three hours that followed are fully recorded for history, as the first section of the transcript is preserved in Churchill's files and the rest in Lord Simon's. The two ministers – German and British – talked at cross-purposes, for each had a different aim. Moreover, the interpreter frequently failed to convey the true sense of Hess's remarks, effectively blunting their emotional appeal. Ivone Kirkpatrick, who spoke fluent

---

★ He may again have had his parents' home in Egypt in mind. See p. 4.

German, spotted this; but he was virulently anti-German, and told Cadogan afterwards that nothing useful had transpired – "Hess recited all the rubbish that he's treated us to for the past month." Simon, reporting to Cadogan two days later, was, however, swayed. "Very interesting," recorded the Foreign Office official. "He has very definitely formed the impression that H[ess] is telling the truth – strange though it be."

"Herr Reichsminister," began Simon, flattering Hess with his full title, "I was informed that you had come here feeling charged with a mission and that you wished to speak of it to someone who would be able to receive it with government authority." Reading from his briefing notes, he continued, "You know I am [the Lord Chancellor] and therefore I come with the authority of the government and I shall be very willing to listen and discuss with you as far as seems good anything you would wish to state for the information of the government."

Perhaps he had not expected the lengthy historical sermon that Hess now launched into, recited sentence by sentence – probably from a prepared text – which the interpreter intervened to translate. It is the authentic voice of Rudolf Hess, so let it speak in full.

> I am extremely grateful that [the Lord Chancellor] has come out here. I realize that probably nobody really understands why I came, because the step I took was so extraordinary that I really can't expect otherwise. So I'd like to begin by setting out how I came to do it.
> I had the idea when I was with the Führer in June last year, while the French campaign was still on—

After a brief interjection by the Lord Chancellor asking whether he had said that *he* had reached this decision, Hess continued:

> I have to admit that when I went to the Führer I was convinced that in the long run we were bound to defeat Britain, sooner or later, and I represented to the Führer that we should obviously now demand back from Britain all those material assets, like our merchant fleet, that had been taken from us by the Treaty of Versailles.
> The Führer at once contradicted me. In his opinion, he said, this war might become the origin of reaching at last the understanding with Britain that he has been striving for ever since going into politics.
> And I can testify that for as long as I have known the Führer – ever since 1921 – the Führer has always said that as soon as he came to power he would bring about a rapprochement between Germany and Britain – that he would *do* something.
> He told me in France [Hess was reverting to June 1940 in his narrative] that even if victorious you don't impose harsh terms on a country you want to live in harmony with.
> That's when I had the idea that if you in Britain only knew this it should be possible for Britain to be willing to reach an agreement.
> Then came [he now reached 19 July 1940 in his time-table] the Führer's

offer to Britain after the conclusion of the French campaign. The offer was turned down, as you know. This made me more determined than ever, under the circumstances, to put my plan into effect.

The record shows that Hess now paused for a long time. He had begun feeling very exhausted of late, and did not know why.

"Over the next few months," he said, when he finally spoke again,

there then began the aerial engagements between Germany and Britain. By and large they caused heavier losses and damage to Britain than Germany. I gained the impression that in consequence Britain could no longer make any concessions at all without losing face badly. So I said to myself it was time to put my plan into effect – because once I turned up in Britain the British could take it as reason [*Anlass*] enough to cultivate negotiations between Germany and Britain without any loss of prestige.

It all sounded so simple. But Hess was talking to lawyers and diplomats, not men of flesh and blood at all. Kirkpatrick started quibbling with the interpreter about the meaning of the word *Anlass*. Hess pressed on:

My impression was that quite apart from the question of the terms of an agreement, there was a degree of general mistrust to be overcome in Britain.

I have to admit that I found myself facing a very tough decision – in fact the toughest I've ever taken. But I think that what helped me to take it was that in my mind's eye I kept seeing – in Germany and Britain alike – an endless line of children's coffins with weeping mothers behind them, and then again, the coffins of mothers, with their children clustered behind them.

Lord Simon was clearly more moved by Hess's sincerity than Kirkpatrick was.

I deduce from the conversation as a whole [reported Simon afterwards] that Germany does not want a greatly prolonged war. Hess, interpreting Hitler's mind, insists that this is because of the appalling suffering it would involve to civilians. (H. was eloquent on "women and babies" and showed me the photographs of his own wife and child.) But H. throughout maintained that if the war went on, we were doomed.

Hess asked if he might bring up a number of points which he believed had a psychological bearing on Anglo-German relations. "I shall have to go back a bit," he said. (If Kirkpatrick knew what was coming and groaned, the protocol does not show it.)

After Germany was defeated in the World War we had the Treaty of

Versailles imposed on us. Now, no serious historian still thinks
Germany was to blame for the World War. Lloyd George said the
nations stumbled into the war. I recently read what one British historian,
Farrer, wrote about King Edward VII and his foreign policy at that time;
this historian Farrer states that the main responsibility for the World War
belongs, as far as the pre-history is concerned, to Edward VII. After the
collapse Germany was saddled with this Treaty which was a frightful
misfortune not just for Germany but the whole world. Every attempt
that Germany's politicians and statesmen made to obtain concessions
before the Führer came to power was a failure.

To start with the Führer tried to obtain concessions and the granting
of the most elementary rights by negotiation. He first of all demanded a
"200,000-man army" for Germany. Refused! A few planes, tanks, heavy
guns – refused! He suggested at least abolishing gas [warfare] by
international convention, and the abolition of bombing raids on the
civilian population as well. Refused! He then proposed the international
abolition of bombing planes altogether.

All this was uncomfortably true, as Kirkpatrick was aware: but it was not
new.

After this experience there remained no other course of action open to
the Führer but to make what progress he could on his own. He began by
attempting to normalize relations with his neighbouring countries. The
relationship to Italy was already determined, a matter of history. He
signed a pact with Poland [in 1934]. He abandoned Alsace-Lorraine to
France for ever and guaranteed the frontiers. He made one offer after
another to Britain in one shape or another. The only offer accepted by
Britain was the Naval Agreement [of May 1935], and that this agreement
was subsequently repudiated [by Hitler in April 1939] was entirely a
consequence of the fact that Britain, despite this agreement, continually
tried to work against Germany and alongside our enemies. Under these
circumstances the Führer could not agree that Germany must labour
under a permanent handicap with regard to England.

There followed the union with Austria [in March 1938]. This was just
putting the principle of democracy into practice, since afterwards [April
1938] 95 per cent of the population voted for it.

Then came the Czech crisis. The French [Aviation] Minister Pierre
Cot had stated that in a future war by Britain and France against
Germany Czech territory would have to be used as an air base. Further to
which, ethnic Germans over there were being brutally treated, and this
gave us the leverage [*Handhabe*] to intervene. ["And I can assure you
these brutalities were not invented," he said in reply to a query by
Simon. "I can swear to that."]

Then came Munich [September 1938]. The Führer afterwards told me
how glad he was, he thought it was the beginning of a rapprochement.
But unfortunately information arrived from Britain immediately
afterwards that Chamberlain had remarked that he was merely trying to

win time to rearm; *The Times* reiterated this on Chamberlain's death [in November 1940]. On top of which, Britain's foreign policy has historically always been to form a coalition against the strongest Continental power and attack it sooner or later. I expect you know here that General Wood, addressing the U.S. [Senate] Foreign Relations Committee in 1941, stated under oath that Mr Churchill had told him in 1936, "Germany is getting too strong; it has to be destroyed."

It turned out moreover that the Czechs [*Resttschechei*] were still getting financial backing from France and Britain to help further rearmament. As a responsible statesman the Führer had no choice but to eliminate this serious menace in the heart of Germany.

After this discursive – and not entirely disingenuous – presentation of recent history, Hess turned to the dispute with Poland which had led to Hitler's attack.

Poland. The Treaty of Versailles had created the [Danzig] "Corridor". Imagine what Britain would do if a corridor went right across England – for example so that Ireland could get at the North Sea! Nonetheless the Führer was ready to settle this matter by negotiation and on 5 and 6 January 1939 he made corresponding proposals to [Polish Foreign Minister Josef] Beck, both in person and through his Foreign Minister [Ribbentrop]. The proposals were firstly to return to us the wholly German city of Danzig; secondly, Poland was to retain the Corridor – Germany desired only two extra-territorial routes across the Corridor: a railroad line and an autobahn; and the Führer would have guaranteed the frontier. The German public was shocked at this proposal – only a man with the Führer's authority could have made it. In mid [or March?] 1939 the proposal was repeated once more to the Polish Ambassador [Josef] Lipski. Poland was of course willing to accede and was restrained only by the influence exercised by Britain. Poland was even ready to entertain the German terms immediately before the war began – in the last eight days – but then the signing of the Mutual Assistance Pact with Britain took place [on 25 August 1939]. The Poles themselves – members of the Polish Foreign Office – confirmed this afterwards.

Once again, it was the brutal treatment of ethnic Germans that triggered our intervention. Neutral journalists were there and they confirmed these atrocities. I could produce photographs including pictures of German children dying with their tongues nailed to a table.

Then came the war, and Britain and France declaring war on us.

The Führer made his first peace offer to Britain and France after the Polish campaign [October 1939].

In the ensuing months the Führer received reliable Intelligence [through code-breaking] on British plans to invade Norway. There was confirmation that the object of these plans was to occupy certain parts of Norway as a base for operations against Germany. Significantly, when the Führer drew the appropriate conclusions and moved into Norway [in April 1940] our troops were welcomed as if they had been the expected Englishmen. There was even a nephew of Churchill up there [Giles Romilly] who told people that the British were coming. He was a journalist [on the *Sunday Express*]. . . . Before we moved in there was the *Altmark* and *Cossack* affair [February 1940] and [Churchill's] minelaying in neutral Norwegian waters: these were the two first territorial violations of international law in this war, apart from [the British planes] overflying [Holland and Belgium] and bombing raids.

After a confused reference to further Intelligence about British plans to invade Denmark, Hess proceeded:

We were moreover aware of the Entente's plans in Belgium and Holland. The idea was to attack the Ruhr through Belgium and Holland as soon as the arms build-up behind the Maginot Line was adequate. We became aware that maps had already been printed for the purpose, and we later indeed found them. French and British billeting staffs had already been into these countries. We obtained the directives for refuelling the motor transport of the Entente in these countries, and all this was doubly confirmed by the documents [of the French General Staff and Allied Supreme War Council] that we found at La Charité [a railway station outside Paris]. I have gone into such detail because I know the important psychological part all this plays against us over here.

As for violations of international law and as for the breaking of treaties, etcetera, I believe from what I know of English history that Britain would have acted the same way as us given the same situation, and even in the absence of the causes that we had. I need only remind you of [Admiral Nelson at] Copenhagen! The phrase, "to copenhage", comes from Britain, not Germany. I could draw up an endless list of Britain's breaches of treaties and violations of international law down through history. Remember Lawrence of Arabia! It's common knowledge that he resigned his rank of colonel because he could not approve of Britain not keeping her word to the Arabs. It ill behoves Britain to reproach others for repressing smaller nations. We have not suppressed any little nations. The Czechs are relatively well off now they have had to disarm. One thing is plain: Germany has never yet treated any nation as the Boers, Indians and the Irish [have been treated]. There's no Amritsar episode in our history! Nor did we set up any concentration camps for women and children, as you did for the Boers.

Nor has the German people forgotten that they signed the Armistice on the basis of [President Woodrow] Wilson's Fourteen Points, but that they were not adhered to: the Armistice was broken in one point, namely the internment of the German fleet. And as you know the Treaty of Versailles was also broken in one of its most fundamental points, that on *disarmament*. According to the Treaty, the other powers were also obliged to disarm after a given time, just like Germany. People often point out to me that Britain reduced her army and air force too, but her real power is her navy, and if the thirteeen heavy warships which Britain retained, first-class warships, had been taken as the equivalent for

Germany's army – because for Germany it is the army that is paramount – then we ought to have had an enormous army with all kinds of modern weaponry. . . .

I only mention all this because it's the kind of allegations you bring up against us. And I think that if we are to discuss things frankly as man to man we ought to put these recriminations aside.

Kirkpatrick translated the sentence for Lord Simon.

"I myself am convinced," continued Hess,

that leading Englishmen who know the real situation don't voice these reproaches. But they do play a major part between our two peoples, and the mistrust that the German public feels towards Britain is certainly no less than the mistrust the British feel against them.

Again and again [Hess was unconscious of the irony] the German public asks: what kind of guarantee does Germany have that Britain will adhere to treaties any better than in the past, and particularly her more recent history? And on top of this is the bitterness in Germany where the German public knows that the Führer for his part did not want any bombing war, any war of bombs against the civilian population. When the war began the Führer proposed [in the Reichstag on 1 September 1939] that such raids should be eschewed.

For a second time Rudolf Hess paused: it did not require much imagination for Simon and Kirkpatrick to guess what harrowing picture was again in his mind's eye.

Despite this, there was an increasing number of raids by the British air force on Germany's civilian population. The British retort, "Rotterdam!" I must point out that Rotterdam [bombed with heavy casualties by the Luftwaffe on 14 May 1940] was within the so-called "Fortress Holland". And this heavy raid had the result of preventing much more bloodletting in Holland: it was because of it that Holland capitulated.

The argument was specious and unhelpful, but Hess pressed remorselessly on:

The British air raids on the other hand cannot claim to be preventing further serious bloodshed.

Despite these attacks on the German civilian population the Führer hesitated, then hesitated again. But after a while the mothers who had lost children, and families who had lost next-of-kin came and besought the Führer not to wait any longer with his reply. The victims were nearly always in towns and villages devoid of the slightest military importance. When the Führer at last had to accept that despite his hesitation and despite his warnings the British would not see reason, then he took action along the lines laid down by Admiral ["Jackie"] Fisher: "Mercy has no place in war: when you strike, strike hard and everywhere you can." [On about 4 or 5 September 1940 Hitler gave orders to the Luftwaffe to stand by for mass raids on London.]

But I can confirm that it troubled the Führer badly, again and again, when he ordered these raids. His heart ached – I saw it with my own eyes. The whole time he was full of sympathy for the British people who were sacrificed to this mode of warfare.

Simon and Kirkpatrick exchanged glances. When Hess resumed, "I'd now like to analyse the situation as we in Germany see it—" the Lord Chancellor hastily but politely intervened: "May I just interrupt here to say – with the permission of Herr Reichsminister, because I listened closely to his account of the German view since it began: I have not interrupted – I wish to be a good listener, which is the compliment I wish to pay him, and that is why I have come."

Hess nodded. "Yes," he said in English.

"He will of course understand", continued Simon, in some embarrassment at having listened to the whole speech without comment, "that I could not accept this account of the war. And I hope he will plainly understand that, if I do not contradict . . . it is not because I agree, but because . . . the real purpose why I have come is to hear from him about his mission."

Flashing a toothy smile, Hess waved aside the interpreter. "No need to translate. I understood."

"That's really a matter", said Simon, "that will ultimately be decided perhaps by history – perhaps not in very few years."

"Certainly," said Hess affably. "I only said all this so that [the Lord Chancellor] can see how we, the German people, see the position."

"No doubt Herr Reichsminister will understand also . . . that the British people too are a proud nation – *Herrenvolk* – and will not easily accept such reproaches. . . . I wish to hear what are the proposals he has come to make here. I think that is why he has come."

"My decision to fly here", said Hess,

was influenced by the fact that among Germany's leaders there is the absolute conviction that Britain's position is hopeless. Things go so far that our people just keep wondering what on earth can Britain be hoping for that she keeps on fighting this war. All our aircraft plants are still intact, and since war began a large number of new factories have been or are being completed. Our production has grown so much that last winter we were hard put to find storage for all the finished aeroplanes, because the squadrons didn't need any – our losses were relatively slight, about one day's production.

"Air personnel", explained Hess to Simon, "which is now coming along is moving about on approximately as large a scale as the entire English expeditionary force in France."

The Lord Chancellor pressed him for figures, but Hess would not give them, saying merely, "In view of my personal relations with the aviation world – Messerschmitt is a friend of mine, and I know all the factories and Luftwaffe commanders – I do have some idea of what will happen to Britain sooner or later. And that is one of the reasons why I have come."

"Then your message is", pondered Lord Simon, "that you believe there will be in future a far more violent and terrific overwhelming attack on this country?"

"Yes."

Hess began to talk about the development of the U-boat campaign.

"Nothing", scoffed Simon, "amuses the British people as much as German figures about sinking British tonnage. It makes them laugh."

"Maybe," retorted Hess. "But I am convinced the day will come when the English people will no longer laugh about it."

"The day may come, the day may come," mocked Simon. "But if your German official figures are correct, you know, it's a pity we're not all dead."

Emphasizing that he had no intention of sounding threatening, Hess warned that Hitler would proceed to starve the British Isles if the British did not see reason.

Following SIS instructions Simon tried to draw Hess on Hitler's U-boat production locations. "Might I just ask, Herr Minister," he murmured with extravagant politeness, "if it is convenient, a question about this? We in this country are under the impression that we have bombed, very heavily and successfully, the U-boat yards, say, at Kiel—"

Hess interrupted with an easy laugh: "I don't think people here are quite clear as to the real effect of such air raids. You can't tell anything from aerial photographs, and as for agents' reports we've had our own sad experiences of them." Since Simon pressed him about Kiel, Bremen, Hanover and Wilhelmshaven, the Deputy Führer admitted, "As I told you, those aren't by any means all our U-boat yards. . . . Let me assure you, the submarine warfare the Führer is envisaging hasn't even begun."

The Cabinet Minister now asked Hess to state precisely whether he had come with or without Hitler's knowledge.

"I learned the terms", began Hess, launching into a long narrative about his mission, "on which Germany would be willing to do a deal with Britain from the Führer himself, in a whole series of talks with him, and I must emphasize in saying this that those terms have always remained the same since the outbreak of war. As for the mission I have chosen for myself [*die von mir selbst gewählte Mission*], whenever it seemed I might be able to risk making the flight, again and again I asked the Führer about the terms so I could be certain nothing might have changed in the interim. I adopted this plan last June and tried to carry it out on 7 January; I wasn't able to effect it before then for a variety of reasons – among them the bad weather and the difficulty of getting an aeroplane from the factory. . . . I waited the whole time. Virtually from December onwards it would have been possible. Then I waited for suitable weather – it was winter, and there was risk of icing."

He handed over the document entitled "Basis for an Understanding", and discussed it paragraph by paragraph with his visitors.

It was 5.30 p.m. when the unique – and, alas, fraudulent – interview of British Lord Chancellor and captive Reichsminister Without Portfolio ended.

Fearful of being left to the uncertain mercies of Major Dicks and the Companions, Hess asked to see Lord Simon alone. "He repeated to me", reported Simon to Churchill afterwards, "his fear that he was being poisoned. He asserted that noises were deliberately made at night to prevent him sleeping. He thought he might be assassinated."

Again hidden microphones recorded every word of their dialogue. "The idea which you have," the British Minister was heard rebuking Hess, "that there is something intentional, deliberate, about it, is absolutely unfounded."

"I can't prove it," admitted Hess timidly.

"But you can take it from me now. . . . I would not deceive you for any purpose at all," said Simon, guiltily concealing that he had been sent to Hess for a reason very different from the one which he claimed. "You have got the idea that clever people might be interfering with your food – it is fantastic nonsense!"

Hess interpolated a polite "Yes".

"It is really fantastic nonsense. You have got the impression that there is mixed up here some sort of secret service with the officers! It makes me wonder what happens in Germany, but it does not happen here. . . . It simply isn't true, any sort of double dealing like that at all."

"I had the impression", explained Hess in clumsy English, "that the soldier who always sleeps with me had the intention to give me something different. I did not touch them . . . and I always eat from the common stand and drink from the common water. . . . But mornings I get the milk – milk [meant] only for me – and I get a feeling, pains, in my—"

"It's perfect nonsense!"

"If you will not believe me I will go off my head and be dead. . . ."

"It is ridiculous because nothing of the sort happened."

"But there are in England surely some [people] who don't desire an understanding between England and Germany?"

"I am sure I don't know."

"May I show you my wife and son?" pleaded Hess, tugging the photograph out of one pocket.

"I shall be very pleased to see them," said Simon, aware that the hour was getting late.

"*Please*," shrieked Hess, "*save me for them!* Save me for peace, and save me for them!"

He explained to Simon that he did not trust Dr Dicks at all. His predecessor had been very *sympathisch* – "But this doctor, he – I can't trust him."

Simon told him to pull himself together. "You ought to behave like a soldier and a brave man," he said.

"Yes," replied Hess, suppressing his indignation. "I have courage. Otherwise, I would not be here."

The distasteful duty done, Lord Simon left Camp Z – "In a driving downpour," described Malone in his private notes, "in which the Commandant stood at the outer gate keeping sentries away."

Major Dicks, the SIS doctor, found Hess, still wearing his Luftwaffe uniform, in a state of virtual collapse – every ounce of energy drained from him; he refused the tea, milk and cake offered to him. When Dicks then brought up a glucose drink, Hess stared into his eyes, then challenged: "I will have it if you have some first."

9 June 1941   [Commandant's diary]
At the end of the conference he asked for a private word with "Dr Guthrie" [Lord Simon] and in this harped upon his fear of poison.

"Dr Guthrie" told him in no uncertain words that his suspicions were an insult to the British Army officers who were deputed to look after him.

This was later rubbed in by Major Dicks who was asked by "Z" to give his word of honour that no attempt at poison was contemplated. Having received this assurance and shaken hands on it he set to and demolished a whole dish of cake and asked for more which was provided.

For the rest of the evening he seemed relieved, was somewhat arrogant and truculent and strutted about the lawn after dinner with Major Foley.

Churchill discovered Lord Simon's six-page "preliminary report" inside the top of the despatch box of papers handed to him by his Private Secretary. The Lord Chancellor, he found, had concluded that Hess had come on his own initiative, in an attempt to negotiate a peace and thereby restore his prestige in Germany. Realizing now that he had failed, Hess feared that he had made a fool of himself. He was continuing to ask for a meeting with *der Herzog*, hoping that even now this gentleman, the Duke of Hamilton, could put him in contact with the people opposed to the warmongering Churchill "clique"; but he now saw that in Churchill's England "there is no Opposition to which he could display his wares". "Hess", averred the Lord Chancellor, "is quite outside the inner circle which directs the war: he does not, apparently, know anything of strategic plans."* And he added, "He gets information, I imagine, mainly

---

* At the Nuremberg war crimes trials, of course, the indictment against Rudolf Hess would allege precisely the opposite.

from personal contacts with Hitler who confides in him many of his innermost thoughts." Buried in Lord Simon's report was one dangerous notion to which Churchill took immediate exception, as indeed he had to since he based Britain's entire war effort on the need to defend the empire from a Nazi onslaught. "It is clear to me", Simon had written, "that Hess' 'plan' is his genuine effort to reproduce Hitler's own mind, as expressed to him in many conversations."

PRIME MINISTER TO FOREIGN SECRETARY   *14 June 1941*
Personal Minute, Serial No. M645/1

I have read the [Simon–Hess] transcripts which seem to me to consist of the outpourings of a disordered mind. They are like a conversation with a mentally defective child who has been guilty of murder or arson. Nevertheless I think it might be well to send them by Air in a sure hand to President Roosevelt. Pray consider this. . . .

I see no sufficient foundation for [Lord Simon's] assumption that [Hess] is in fact reflecting Hitler's inner mind, although no doubt he gives us some of the atmosphere of Berchtesgaden, which is at once artificial and foetid.

I do not see any need for a public statement at the present time, and meanwhile [Hess] should be kept strictly isolated where he is.

Churchill, of course, was aware of many things that Anthony Eden was not. He could afford to ignore any offer of peace that Hess (or even Hitler) might make, because his codebreakers had now furnished him with the hardest evidence that Hitler was about to unleash his massed armies and air force squadrons against Russia, and a few days later Hermann Göring himself would secretly inform Britain, through a Swedish friend, of the precise "Barbarossa" date.

So who needed Rudolf Hess? Desmond Morton read Lord Simon's report and wrote to the Foreign Office urging that an official propaganda statement be issued to prove, if need be with extracts from the conversations, the "ignorance, stupidity, falsity and arrogance" of the Nazi leaders. "I submit", wrote Morton, "that the time has now come to cash in on this wind-fall. . . . The longer we wait the rottener the apple."

The Foreign Office needed little bidding. "We must decide how best to exploit H.," Cadogan mused in his diary, and added the decision: "Mendaciously."

Hess had hung his Luftwaffe captain's uniform back on its peg, and with it his self-esteem.

His humiliation as a Reichsminister and Deputy Führer was complete. He was a prisoner, under constant surveillance even in his most intimate moments. He had come to speak to the English, but his only succour was a spurious "doctor" – a psychiatrist of German descent – whom he did not trust. Apart from the rare visits of the New Zealand-born Lieutenant Bill

Malone – whose father had died on the beaches of Gallipoli and who thus had no cause to love Churchill – the only companionship was the uncertain variety offered by the strangely uniformed officers assigned to him by MI6.

He could feel his mind beginning to crumble, hear voices urging him this way and that.

Over the next week it dawned on him that he had been tricked – that the interview had been arranged only in an effort to draw secret Intelligence out of him. He was sure that he had not revealed any, but what of the future? As he later said, he was in no doubt of the perils that he had exposed himself to by venturing into the enemy camp. While he doubted that the British – the object of his and Hitler's obsessive infatuation – would stoop to torture, he fully expected them to use truth drugs.

These were thoughts that occurred to him in the rare lulls of his otherwise increasingly tempestuous introspections. He no longer expected to be returned to Germany – far less to return home as the man who had brought peace where the professionals had failed.

10 June 1941   [Commandant's diary]

"Z" had a much better night, only waking once at 05.00, when he opened his window, drew his curtains and slammed his door. . . .

11 June 1941

"Z" . . . went so far as to take his coat off, take a spade and make an attempt to dig one of the flower beds. It was very obvious that he had never held a spade before. He was somewhat exhausted by this labour & after lunch retired to his room to lie down. . . . He is still very truculent & his Companions find meals with him a great trial. He is still, in spite of the assurances given him, very apprehensive about poison and refuses to see any reason on the subject.

12 June 1941

Asked for a bottle of whisky in his room which had to be a new, unopened bottle – (still fear of poison). He was in quite a cheerful mood & was reported by his companions to have actually laughed twice.

One way or another, he expected shortly to be dead. He could hear the mocking voices of Colonel Scott and Gibson Graham asking if he had made provision for his next-of-kin, and he wondered how and when he was going to die. He was frightened of being driven insane: he did not feel it right that a man of his position, Deputy Führer of Germany, should offer such a picture to foreigners. A decision was forming within him not to await a total breakdown, but to quit this life voluntarily while he still had such a decision within his gift, should the same strange, fraught symptoms recur. But perhaps the evil forces beyond his Companions and the "doctor" would get to him first? He decided to wait no longer. In the privacy, as he thought, of his upstairs room Rudolf Hess began to write out farewell letters to his relatives. In one, expressing his utter loyalty to the true cause of National Socialism, he addressed these gloomy words to Adolf Hitler: "I die in the conviction that my final mission, even if it should end with my death, will somehow bear fruit. Perhaps, despite my death, or even because of my death, my flight will have brought about peace and a reconciliation with Britain." Re-reading these farewell letters, he was proud that they showed such calm and deliberation. (They were of course never forwarded – they appear to have remained in the hands of Major Dicks.)

13 June 1941   [Commandant's diary]

"Z" had a very good night – did not come down to breakfast but asked for milk & biscuits in his room at 10.00 hrs. He spent the whole day up to 18.00 in his room when he came down for a short walk in the garden. He had a long walk after dinner not going to bed till 23.00.

    The only incident during the day was a short & sharp battle with Sgt. Ross over his underclothes. . . . A tug-of-war ensued . . . and eventually he was allowed [by the duty officer, Lieutenant Malone] to keep the underclothes for the present.

14 June 1941

"Z" . . . was in a "difficult" mood all day and paced the terrace like a caged lion, refusing to answer when spoken to. His only request was for an enema which was duly purchased for him by Capt. "Barnes". He retired to his bathroom with his treasure but emerged eventually without apparently having received any consolation from his new toy and spent the afternoon in his room in the deepest gloom.

    After dinner, however, he condescended to go into the garden and play dart bowls with Capt. "Barnes" and even went so far as to make a joke.

A few hours later, in the early hours of Sunday 15 June, the real crisis developed. At 1 a.m. Lieutenant Jackson woke the Commandant to say that "Z" was in a greatly agitated state of mind, demanding to see Malone at once. Lieutenant Malone was on outside duty and could not be reached, so the Colonel sent Major Dicks up to see Hess. The "doctor" was the last person Hess wanted to see; he stormed and raged at him.

Lieutenant the Hon. Stephen Smith, Scott's adjutant, came up to the little sitting room, and talked to the prisoner until 2 a.m. Smith made a full report to Scott:

He was in his dressing gown and pyjamas and looked very drawn & pale, eyes sunk deep in his head.

    I said that I had heard that he had asked for an officer of the Guard.

He was in a state of extreme nervousness and did not make much sense in English.

I therefore told him that I spoke German.

He said that he had got to know and to trust Mr Malone, that he feared that he might not live through the night, and that he wished to give certain last letters to Mr Malone.

I said that Mr Malone was a soldier like the rest of the guard, was on duty and could not leave his post.

I said that I could do anything for him that Mr Malone could do and that he could trust me.

He said that he trusted all the members of the Guard but that he was "in the hands of the Secret Service", was being poisoned, and we could do nothing to stop them.

I adopted the pompous tone which always goes down with Germans and said that his life and security were in the hands of the Brigade of Guards and were *ipso facto* secure.

He said that I didn't know what was going on.

I said that I was the adjutant, that I did know, that the Germans were not the only efficient soldiers and that we, the Guard, had the fullest control over all that went on here.

Hess had then said that he would like to drink some whisky, but that the whisky brought to him the night before by the "doctor" had been poisoned. When Smith nonetheless took a swig of it, Hess clutched his arm and begged him not to risk his life. The adjutant then sent the duty officer to wake the staff and obtain a new bottle of whisky; Hess poured out some of it for himself and drank it. Appreciably less nervous by this time, he vanished into his bedroom and reappeared with a medicine bottle on the label of which he had marked a skull and crossbones, the poison symbol in Germany. This, he told Smith, contained a sample of the poisoned whisky from Major Dicks – would he get it analysed privately, without telling Dicks?

Stephen [recorded Lieutenant Malone in his diary] finished the bottle and what was left in the main bottle then sent for another bottle which they both tucked into. Stephen got very "angry" finally and tried the shouting technique and assumed a *"verstehen?"* bluster which calmed "Z" down.

The adjutant told Malone that Hess had the mentality of a poorly educated cheap little clerk, and added that he was quite sure that Hess was mad.

As the hour was getting late [Smith reported to Colonel Scott] I got more and more terse. I told him that with the exception of the three [MI6] officers and the doctor who attended on him there was no person in the house other than selected soldiers from the Coldstream and Scots Guards regiments.

He contradicted this – whereupon I told him in German parade-ground terms that I would not be called a liar by him. "I do not permit this – is it understood?"

He jumped to his feet and apologized, shaking my hand.

Half an hour later Hess was back in bed, fast asleep and snoring.

The next morning, Hess took his full Luftwaffe uniform off its peg – a pale-blue tunic with rather darker trousers, silver epaulettes and gold stars – dressed carefully and asked for Colonel Scott to be sent up to him. He asked now to be sent to hospital at once, as he was on the verge of a nervous breakdown – "before it is too late", were the words Scott noted in his diary – and he asked for Lieutenant Malone to be relieved from his outside duties to allow him to talk for half an hour with him. At his request, Scott also sent "one of the Guard officers" – Lieutenant Jackson – off to Pirbright to fetch Luminal or some other sedative. Major Dicks was obviously not pleased at this development, because later that morning Scott telephoned Colonel Coates at the War Office. "I suggest that Colonel Rees comes down here for a consultation with Dicks," the Commandant said. "Dicks is now of the definite opinion that 'Z' is insane."

Hess bounded forward and gripped Bill Malone warmly by the hand, startling the Lieutenant, as it was the first time the Deputy Führer had done this.

The rest was familiar – the allegations about the poison being fed to him on the instructions of a "small clique" who wanted to prevent him from bringing about peace. The interview with Lord Simon appeared to have persuaded him that Churchill was aware of this, but not the other members of the government. "I am convinced", he said, "that the Cabinet as a whole is anxious to negotiate for peace. You Guard officers are being hoodwinked. No steps that you can take for my safety are going to defeat the anti-peace clique's machinations." He was prepared to believe, he said, that the Companions were decent men in themselves, but they were carrying out the clique's orders.

Malone reminded him that this was England, not Germany; that the British did not do things like this. "He had an astute answer to every objection and argument," the Lieutenant reported to Colonel Scott later that day. In fact Hess indignantly repudiated Malone's suggestion that he was basing his suspicions on his experience of Nazi methods. "You are to go to Germany when the war's over", he instructed Malone, "and tell Himmler from me that if such methods are in fact being used they are to cease immediately!"

Hess now related what he recalled of the effects of the milk he had drunk four days before Simon's visit. He believed in all seriousness that he was being fed a drug that would either kill him or drive him insane. Thus, he confided to Malone, a swig of the whisky yesterday had brought on the same symptoms as the milk. "Poor Mr Smith!" he said. He was certain that Stephen Smith was going to suffer for having taken a drink of it.

"What if Mr Smith survives?" asked Lieutenant Malone in a bantering tone.

"Then," said Hess readily, "I can only ascribe my condition to the pills the doctor has been giving me to make me sleep: they have precisely the opposite effect."

He showed to Malone the one-ounce bottle with the pencilled skull-and-crossbones, and an envelope with some pills. "Would you get these secretly analysed?" he asked. Since Malone seemed to concur, Hess then produced two unsealed envelopes, one addressed to his wife and the other to "Mein Führer". "I want you to have them forwarded through official channels as soon as I die," he said. "I don't expect they will be allowed to get through," he added, handing duplicates to Malone. "So will you deliver these personally when the war is over?" He finally handed to Malone his wallet, containing a sheaf of photographs of his little boy Wolf Rüdiger.

Malone was uneasy about what was going on, and made it plain that he was going to have to report to Scott that the prisoner had handed him these duplicates and envelopes.

"I beg of you," pleaded Hess, his eyes more gaunt than ever, "keep them secret – in the interests of humanity!"

Malone thought it over, then said that as a Guards officer he could not do so: but he would ask official permission to retain them. "If they refuse," he said, "I'll give them back to you."

A clammy feeling of helplessness swept over the prisoner. He thumped the floor with his foot, he flailed the chair arms with his hands, then resigned himself to Malone's suggestion.

It is clear from Malone's account that he tried heroically to calm the worried man, but failed. "He seemed aware that his mental balance was disturbed," he wrote a few hours later, "describing the symptoms which led him to believe that his nerves were being 'destroyed'. He begged to be taken to a hospital for treatment, and said that when he was in hospital in Scotland and in barracks [i.e. at the Tower], he was happy and felt well."

Through the grille door, Hess watched the Guards officer walk down the Victorian oaken staircase. "Mr Malone!" he called out on an impulse. The Lieutenant came back up to the locked gate. "Would you let me have back the letters I just gave you? It's no use you having them if you'll have to report the matter."

But for the grace of God, this day, 15 June 1941, would have been the last in his life. For this day, three diary entries hold our attention briefly, like searchlights converging on a plane:

15 June 1941   [Second-Lieutenant Malone's report]
Later in the morning when I again saw him he asked me to go to

Germany at the end of the war to inform his people that he had "died the death of a brave man". I promised that . . . I would do as he wished.

15 June 1941   [Commandant's diary]

"Z" . . . went to bed early and was given one tablet of sedative, the remainder of the box was kept by me. He was very angry at this and tried to snatch the box.

15 June 1941   [Sir Alexander Cadogan's diary]

"C" [head of MI6] came in about Hess, who's going off his head. I don't much care what happens to *him*.

We can use him.

There's a meeting tomorrow between Winston and [Lord] Simon about him, at which I hope to be present and to get decisions on how to treat and how to exploit him – alive, mad, or dead.

Once already that day, Hess had confronted Major Dicks, standing by the table in his upstairs room with his fists clenched, exclaiming, "I am being undone, and you know it!"

Dicks tried not to show concern. "How do you mean – undone?"

"*You know it! You know it!*"

It happened then in the dark hour before dawn. At five minutes to four, dressed in his pyjamas. Hess walked into the duty officer's room, inside the grille, and told Lieutenant Young, "I can't sleep, so I've had a little whisky."

It seemed an innocuous remark. Five minutes later the Military Police warder on the grille's gate heard the prisoner's voice coming from within his room, asking him to fetch the doctor. Roused from his bedroom on the far side of the landing, Major Dicks put on a dressing-gown and stumped over to the grille with more sleeping tablets. The warder unlocked the gate and stood aside to let Dicks through. Hess's bedroom was right opposite it.

Suddenly Hess was there, rushing out of the darkness of his room towards the opened gate – he was no longer in pyjamas but in his full Luftwaffe uniform. Flying boots thudding across the floorboards, a look of despair in his eyes, he tossed Dicks inelegantly out of the way and into the warder's path. An army sergeant running up the stairs drew his service revolver. Dicks screamed, "Don't shoot him!"

Too late anyway, because "Z", Churchill's Prisoner of State, had leaped into the air, clearing the stairwell balustrade like an Olympic hurdler. His brain was throbbing; he could hear voices all round him; he wanted to end it all now – for Germany's sake. He spun over, trying to make sure that it was his head that hit the floor below.

10 Conversations in an Asylum

Unanaesthetized, wide awake, Rudolf Hess lay in the stairwell surrounded by soldiers, guards and others he could not identify through the screaming pain.

Lieutenant Young, the ashen-faced duty officer, the provost sergeant and the Military Police sergeant were joined by Colonel Scott, wakened by the thud and shouts. The prisoner was conscious enough to feel his left thigh shattered, his spine damaged. He was groaning, according to Major Dicks, who was standing by, "Morphia, give me morphia!"

As he had pitched himself over the bannister, his left leg had tangled with the oak balustrade and this had thwarted his suicidal intent.

Colonel Scott watched as Dicks injected what he said was morphia, and was puzzled that it "did not seem to have much effect and [Hess] kept crying for more, appealing in turn to myself, Major Foley and the duty officer to order the doctor to do this". Dicks had in fact not given Hess any morphia at all, and refused to do so until a surgeon could come: morphia might mask the symptoms of serious internal injury. Instead, he had administered a hypodermic of distilled water. Hess realized the deception and told him so, but with an air of resigned inevitability rather than bitterness. For a moment, the poisoning suspicions had left him, because he accepted without complaint the hot tea required to treat his shock.

Major Foley could envisage the international consequences if Hess should die in British hands. He telephoned "C" in London to say that Dicks was insisting on a surgeon specialist. Brigadier Menzies, as Colonel Scott, Camp Z's army Commandant, noted, "sanctioned the request". It was a significant nicety, because it confirmed that Hess was in fact totally in the hands of MI6, the secret service, and not of the Brigade of Guards.

Scott at once ordered Stephen Smith, the adjutant, to take a car to the Cambridge Hospital – a nearby military hospital – and pilot the senior surgeon out to the secret Camp Z location. Only then did Scott try to contact the Prisoners of War Directorate at Hobart House in London. "C" meanwhile telephoned the news of Hess's near-suicide to Sir Alexander Cadogan, who took it calmly. After that morning's Cabinet, at which

Lord Simon reported on his talk with the Deputy Führer, Cadogan
wrote:

> [I] rode Prime Minister off his idea of announcing the broken thigh –
> which wd. be simply silly.
>   He agreed that in regard to H[ess] "mum's the word".

"That's what I wanted," concluded this heartless Permanent Under-
Secretary, "and I will now get on with my propaganda."
    The surgical specialist Major J. B. Murray, a Fellow of the Royal
College of Surgeons, had arrived with the necessary apparatus at Camp Z
at 5 a.m. Scott saw him give "another injection of morphia" (in fact, the
first) then put the leg into a temporary Thomas's splint. Hess trusted the
newcomer implicitly, his docile manner surviving even the cutting open
of his uniform breeches. The Guards officers carried him upstairs and he
was put to sleep on an army bed, with an officer instructed not to leave his
side.

Lifting through the shifting strato-cumuli of morphia into the sunlight
realm of consciousness above, Hess opened his eyes, and found darkness
around him again. His eyes adjusted to the gloom, and he saw Bill
Malone, the friendly Guards Lieutenant, sitting next to the bed.
    "Mr Malone," he said, in a voice as natural as though they had been
conversing for some time. "Will you please get me a glass of fresh water?"
Malone carried his glass to the water bottle, but Hess said: "From the *tap*,
please!" He sipped the water. "*Gut!*" He paused shortly, then inquired:
"And how is Mr Smith this morning?"
    Malone replied that the Lieutenant had slept well as far as he knew.
    Commenting only "Better!", the prisoner confided after a while to
Malone about the farewell letter he had written to his family. "I was
certain that I was on the verge of a complete and lasting nervous
breakdown," said Hess in a matter-of-fact voice. "I had seen the onset of
this nervous trouble and I knew what it would end in. It all began with
that glass of milk ten days ago. The second attempt was two days ago, by
means of the whisky – either that or the pills were much more successful –
and the reaction was so severe that for a time I knew I was completely out
of my mind." He told Malone that he had expected a third attempt to be
made and that it would succeed in driving him permanently insane.
    "Surely you didn't mean to kill yourself?"
    "I certainly did, and I still will," said Hess, dimly aware of the pain now
burning inside him. "I cannot face madness. It would be too terrible for
me to bear, and for others to witness. By killing myself I would be acting
like a man – I know that of late I have been behaving like a woman,
dämlich," he said, and explained what he meant. "When I first came here I
got up at eight each morning. But then came that period of 'no sleep', 'no
sleep', 'no sleep'. I began to go to pieces under the influence of drugs."

Malone reminded him about his "promise to the Führer" not to kill himself, and was probably not surprised by the answer.

"I give *you* my word of honour that I made no promise. I only wrote as much in a letter to the Duke of Hamilton, because I knew that it would be seen and would stop anyone who might plan to kill me."

Aware of the reprisals that might follow in Germany against British prisoners, Malone warned the Commandant immediately that Hess still planned to kill himself and that the cunning and ingenuity of would-be suicides made "Z"'s safekeeping an unfair responsibility for young Guards officers.

Colonel Coates at the War Office telephoned Scott to order him and Dicks to see Colonel Blake, the Army's Assistant Director of Medical Services. Hess would probably be unable to move for five months, while the fracture healed. There were clear security and secrecy problems involved in getting Hess X-rayed. The army agreed to send the equipment to Camp Z, and to send two first-class medical orderlies from the mental ward of the Connaught Hospital. Reporting this tragic episode to the War Office that afternoon, Colonel Scott echoed Malone's opinion:

Z's case has now definitely become one that can only be dealt with by trained mental specialists from an asylum. . . . I cannot subject young officers to the strain & responsibility of sitting with a patient who is insane. Apart from the two medical orderlies now arrived, there is no-one in this camp who is used to the diabolical cunning shown by a patient of this sort, or who is trained in the various methods whereby we can defeat the object of a madman determined to commit suicide.

At 5 p.m. a truckload of medical equipment arrived. Two hours later the radiographer Major Rigby confirmed the fracture, high up in the left femur, and found a small crack in one of the thoracic vertebral spinous processes as well.

Before surgery could begin, Scott was telephoned by Colonel Coates at the War Office. "I've got Colonel Rees with me," he said. "It's urgent for Rees to see 'Z' *before* he gets the anaesthetic."

To help kill the pain, Dicks had given Hess Veganin tablets through-out the day. Hess found that they were ineffective. (Dicks later suggested that the tablets came from the new surgeon: "Major Murray supplied some tablets which he said were very helpful. In this case they did no good.")

It was 8 p.m. before Rees, the army's consultant psychiatrist, arrived at Camp Z. He evidently took a leisurely dinner before going up to see Hess. To Rees's annoyance, the prisoner refused to speak with him until he had been given something to help him empty his bladder. Rees promised him a catheter would be passed, but both Dicks and Murray frowned on this, as it might prove habit-forming. When Hess now asked for atropine to relieve him, Dicks merely smiled and said, "Tomorrow perhaps."

Dicks was not alarmed. Urine retention was a common post-traumatic symptom, he said later; but Hess blamed it squarely on those tablets that the doctor had called "Veganin", and since nothing was available to help Hess's discomfort Rees told the doctors to go ahead with surgery.

At 9.45 p.m. Hess was put under anaesthetic and the surgeon realigned the fragments in an operation that lasted until midnight: Major Murray drove a steel Steinmann pin into the tibia, then trussed the limb into what was called a Balkan frame, with ropes, weights and pulleys that would be left on almost continuously for the next few months. With the final photographs taken, Rees and the other doctors left soon after midnight. The next morning Rees would report to Cadogan, who was ultimately responsible for the secret service and its custody of Hess. Hess, Cadogan entered in neat, pedantic handwriting, "is definitely paranoid, and we have got another – and a rather awkward – lunatic on our hands for the duration." As though exculpating Major Dicks and the Companions, Rees emphasized that this persecution mania must have developed before Hess's departure from Germany.

When Hess reawakened in the early hours of that morning, 17 June, he found two new medical orderlies and Sergeant Waterhouse in his room, and Lieutenant Peter Atkinson-Clark on duty as well. Moreover he was now in grim discomfort from a full bladder. According to Major Dicks, it was Hess who urgently appealed to him to get that catheter – a slender flexible tube which a skilled doctor can pass into the bladder through the penis. According to Hess's subsequent depositions, "He [Dicks] returned two hours later with Second-Lieutenant Atkinson-Clark, the young duty officer, with the intention of giving me a catheter." This ugly episode began at 1.30 a.m., after what had been a very long day for everyone concerned. (Dicks later pointed out, "I had been on duty for twenty-one hours.") Seeing Dicks bearing down on him with the instrument, Hess realized that the doctor intended to administer it without any anaesthetic (Dicks explained later, justifying this, that Hess had just had a prolonged anaesthetic and morphia). Trussed and almost helpless, his nerves as shattered as his leg, Hess heard Dicks announce that he was going to insert the catheter by force whether he wanted it or not, and ordered the Lieutenant and the male nurse Corporal Everatt to pinion the prisoner's arms (Dicks: "I asked the orderly to hold the patient's hand . . .") whereupon Hess, lashing out with his right leg, screamed, "Help! Help!" until officers and orderlies poured out of doors all round the landing on the other side of the grille. Dicks snapped that he was a coward, and grinned approval as Lieutenant Atkinson-Clark sneered, "We are treating you the way the Gestapo treats people in Germany."

At 6 a.m. Hess passed water naturally. For months after, he would see the episode as proof that Major Dicks was the "enemy within".

It was one of southern England's hottest summers. As the thermometer rose that day, feelings against Hess ran high too, from the

Commandant – whose career would have been wrecked if the suicide had succeeded – down to the lowest orderly.

17 June 1941 [Commandant's diary]

He remained quiet during the day. Capt. "Barnes" had lunch with him.

At 20.00 "Z" sent a message down to say that he refused to eat any meals unless an officer had his meal with him. No notice was taken of this request and Sgt. Waterhouse later reported that after several refusals to eat anything he eventually relented, asked for dinner and made a hearty meal of soup, fish and a sweet.

Major Foley reported that he had had instructions from London to let him read *The Times* daily.

"This is the first occasion", remarked Colonel Scott, "on which he has been allowed any news."

Had MI6 been stabbed by conscience, a fear that the programme to reduce the prisoner's self-esteem had gone too far? Until MI6's own papers are accessible, in the twenty-first century, it will be hard to say. Significantly, he was not allowed any other newspapers yet, or to listen even to a gramophone, let alone the radio. On the other hand, the change was unlikely to have been made to "prime the pump" and extract more Intelligence morsels from him, because MI6 shortly withdrew "Barnes" and "Wallace", leaving only Major Foley with the Deputy Führer.

On 18 June Scott went up to see the prisoner. Hess had had an agonizing night, with the sultry heat adding to the discomfort caused by the thirty-five pounds of weights straining at his broken leg. He treated the Commandant to a long diatribe against Major Dicks, who was out to kill him, he said. He pleaded again for atropine. "If I don't get it, I will go foolish tonight," he said, using a literal translation of the word *narrisch*.

"You're talking nonsense," snapped the Colonel. "Your accusations are an insult to the British Army."

"You don't realize," persisted Hess. "*I know*."

He looked long and hard at the Colonel, standing at the foot of his bed. "You are responsible for my security. It is your duty to see that I don't go foolish, by getting the atropine for me. But you must get it yourself. The doctor will only give you something quite different, and a poison to keep me awake."

"Whom do you trust," asked the Colonel, humouring him. "Major Murray?"

"No, he's only a surgeon. He knows nothing of my" – here Hess struggled for the right English word – "'interior economy'."

"Do you trust Colonel Rees?"

"Is he coming down today?"

"Yes," said the Commandant.

Rees arrived at 3 p.m. and spent over an hour upstairs with Hess. The prisoner told him everything – about the plot against his life and sanity, and how he had tried to kill himself because he would rather be dead than insane in this country; he talked of going on a hunger-strike. He was so engrossed with these ideas that he told Rees he had little interest in reading *The Times* yet. "On Monday when I talked to him," Rees told the War Office, "the Intelligence Officers and Major Dicks constituted the gang who were driving him into insanity. I was regarded as his one hope. . . . There is no doubt, therefore, that Hess's mental condition which was", he added in exoneration of his colleagues, "somewhat masked before, has now declared itself as a true psychosis (insanity)." It was probably incurable, but they might consider trying "continuous sleep treatment" or "electric convulsion therapy" (a controversial treatment even now, in which electric shocks are transmitted directly to the brain). To Rees, the outlook seemed rather gloomy:

> [Such] a man is often apparently normal until some new circumstance comes along when he breaks down again into his deluded, mentally hunted condition. Although Hess is secretive about most of his history it seems clear that there must have been similar attacks of this mental trouble previously though probably they have been more marked this time owing to his circumstances.

Rees recommended that a total of six mental nursing orderlies should be assigned to Hess, to keep him under round-the-clock observation to prevent suicide attempts, and that Dicks should be replaced eventually by a more junior psychiatrist.

18 June 1941   [Commandant's diary]

Later in the evening "Z" told the doctor [Dicks] that both Col. Rees and myself were suffering from a "Mexican drug" and were therefore not responsible for what we did – he could see it in our eyes. He was sorry for us and if he knew the antidote would be only too glad to divulge it to us.

He then said he would take no more medicines from the doctor whatever they were.

19 June 1941

"Z" spent a quiet day having had about three hours' sleep during the night. Capt. "Barnes" lunched upstairs with "Z" who was in quite a good mood and ate a good lunch.

Capt. "Barnes" received orders to report back to his headquarters [MI6] and left in the afternoon. . . .

An electric fan was procured as [Hess's] room was almost insufferable.

Rather curiously, Scott's diary adds: " 'Z' at his own request has been cut off all medicines and drugs and is very much better for it. It appears that his fear of poison in the drugs given him outweighed any effect they should have had."

Taken off Major Dicks's medication, Hess recovered his spirits, an improvement which lasted for several days.

20 June 1941 [Commandant's diary]

"Z" slept well and didn't wake up till late. He was still in quite a cheerful mood and had no complaints during the day. The duty officer [Lieutenant Hubbard] both lunched and dined with him and reported that "Z" had a very good appetite.

Col. "Wallace" left to-day to return to his duties at Cockfosters [Military Intelligence interrogations centre, outside London]. Major Foley is now alone as representative of M.I. [Military Intelligence].

Rang up Col. Coates who told me that instructions are being sent tomorrow placing the whole of the security within the grille under the doctor and six medical orderlies.

By a freak of which the British government would probably not have approved, the seventeen handwritten diaries kept by those six RAMC orderlies around the clock, from June 1941 to October 1945 – what might be called the Missing Years of Rudolf Hess – were shipped with him to Nuremberg, and are thus now physically outside his erstwhile captors' control. One of these patient NCOs, Corporal Riddle, would believe shortly that he had seen the first signs of hallucination by the prisoner. With another, Corporal Everatt, a clean shaven, quiet man of medium build who was always immaculately turned out, Hess formed a particularly trusting relationship. The diaries, covering over two thousand closely written pages, show that Hess was not left unobserved for one moment of those years, that every heartbeat, temperature degree, sleeping minute, ounce of urine, grain of food was recorded – that every snigger, sigh or startled movement was noted and analysed.

21 June 1941 [Lance-Corporal Everatt's report]

On taking over at 05.45 hrs Patient had had a fairly good night. Awake and talking until 06.45, he then slept until 07.15 hrs, passed urine 20 ozs and slept fitfully until 09.10 hrs. He then had toilet and treatment to pressure points. Did not want any breakfast. Spent the morning reading. Visited by M.O. [Dicks] at intervals and visited by Major Murray at 11.00 hrs. States he feels comfortable, but would like something to occupy his mind. Has been very cheerful this morning, passed further amount of urine.

When Everatt was relieved at 2 p.m. Hess tried to sleep, but the room was too hot so he spent the afternoon writing. He felt stabbing pains near the fracture, and slept only briefly and fitfully.

On 22 June 1941 the heatwave showed no signs of abating. None of the German troops who invaded the Soviet Union that dawn, on a front that extended from the Arctic Ocean to the Black Sea, would forget the heat, the dust, the flies.

Outside Aldershot, Major Dicks came in to see the prisoner: Hess was as comfortable as the Balkan frame and weights permitted. While hidden microphones listened for every nuance of the reply, the doctor mentioned the news about Russia. Hess said quietly, "So they have started after all," and turned a wry smile on the Major.

22 June 1941   [Commandant's diary]

He seemed to suffer a lot from the heat.

22 June 1941   [Lance-Corporal Everatt's day report]

On taking over at 13.00 the Patient was upset by the heat of the day and could not rest. Given s.w. [soap-and-water] enema, good result, and given a tepid sponge, and treatment to pressure points. He then settled for a time but could not find sleep for any length of time and could not concentrate on reading or writing but did a small drawing of his left foot, but soon tired of that. Visited by M.O. at intervals during the afternoon.

Not so restless this evening, but sits with a far-away look in his eyes, appears to be thinking of home, but will not say.

23 June 1941   [Orderly's night report]

02.30 hrs: Patient still restless & cannot sleep at all. Started making a few remarks, why he didn't manage to die a week ago. . . .

05.00: Patient still had no sound sleep at all.

23 June 1941   [Lance-Corporal Everatt's report]

06.00: on taking over the Patient had had very little sleep and was not too happy with himself and things in general.

"He then read *The Times*," observed Everatt, "and appeared brighter & cheerful." The newspaper's main headlines read "GERMAN ARMY ATTACKS RUSSIA: WIDESPREAD RAIDS ON AIRFIELDS: FULL BRITISH AID FOR RUSSIA: PRIME MINISTER'S DECLARATION OF BRITISH POLICY". Hess persuaded Bill Malone to lunch with him.

23 June 1941   [Commandant's diary]

"Z" . . . suddenly looked old and grey. He complained that he couldn't read, as all print appeared double – neither could he concentrate. He again put this down to a drug being administered in some way by the doctor.

It was at about this time that a search of his belongings revealed a secret hoard of sleeping tablets – though whether Hess had been saving them to kill himself, or to have analysed later, was not yet clear. More tediously, he was also insisting on having an *officer* to share his meals – and he meant that literally: share. Nor would he accept an orderly fulfilling this role, evidently reasoning that lance-corporals in wartime Britain might be expendable, while Guards officers were not.

To add a note of unrequired comedy to the Hess incident, the Duke of Hamilton let the government know that he was going to issue a writ for libel about Hess. The London District Committee of the Communist Party had spoken of him in a pamphlet as having enjoyed a "close friendship" with the Deputy Führer and had classed the Duke among "industrialists, bankers and aristocrats who had served to build up Hitler". On 8 June the Party's General-Secretary Harry Pollitt threatened in the far-left *Reynolds News* that he would demand Hess be produced as a witness.

Any interference with such an action would be deep contempt of court, but Churchill's Cabinet felt above the law. Labourite Cabinet Minister Herbert Morrison pleaded with the Air Minister to blackmail the Duke into dropping the action. A behind-the-scenes panic began. Cadogan wrote to the Treasury Solicitor: "The decided view of my Secretary of State [Eden] . . . is that it is out of the question that Hess should appear." Minutes flew between Air Ministry (the Duke's superiors), 10 Downing Street, the Foreign Office (whose prisoner Hess indirectly was), and the Treasury.

Desmond Morton, Churchill's bilious intelligence adviser, sent him an alarmed three-page memorandum urging that Hess's production be disallowed "on general grounds of public interest". Colonel Rees's report of his latest interview with Hess was, suggested Morton, the most cogent reason. "It is clear from this report that Hess is suffering from a delusional mania, and there is no knowing what he might say under cross-examination."

Reading this on 22 June, Churchill needed no second bidding: Hitler might have invaded Russia that very morning, but this – the possibility that Hess might show his face and tell his story in the law courts in the Strand, only a few hundred yards from the newspaper head offices in Fleet Street – was really serious. He sent this minute to David Margesson, his War Minister:

PRIME MINISTER TO SECR. OF STATE FOR WAR   *22 June 1941*
Personal Minute, No. M.669/1

We should of course refuse to allow Hess to be produced as a witness, but I see no reason why the Duke of Hamilton should not defend his honour in the Courts, especially if he proceeds by criminal action.* The case would of course have to be heard in camera.

---

* As Churchill knew, an action for criminal libel could end with a prison sentence. Such actions are very rare but he himself had successfully brought one against Lord Alfred Douglas whose pamphlet accused Churchill of making a Stock Exchange killing out of the Battle of Jutland. Lord Alfred Douglas went to prison.

Margesson reassured Sinclair the next day, "I will see that Hess is not permitted to appear as a witness."

But the Duke, like many a would-be litigant, would not swallow his pride. RAF Turnhouse's operations book shows that on 24 June he temporarily handed over command to another officer, and left for London. Two days later he flounced into Sinclair's office at the Air Ministry and said that he had every intention of going on with the case. To withdraw now would harm him. He wanted his day in court.*

Hess, of course, was in no condition to appear anywhere.

Tormented by the stabbing pain in his leg, bleary from fatigue and racked by suspicion, he struggled through these days, living from one minute to the next, as orderlies, surgeons, Guards officers, the hateful Major Dicks and nameless visitors paraded past his pulleys, weights and bedside paraphernalia. He tried to write, but words failed him; he wanted to read *The Times* but could not concentrate.

23 June 1941   [Commandant's diary]

He stated that he had thoroughly thought out for twenty-four hours beforehand his attempted suicide [and] that he had dived head first over the staircase well. . . . The suicide idea seems to be definitely in his mind again and if his present depression increases another attempt may be made in the near future.

24 June 1941

"Z" had a poor night, was restless and depressed. All day he was in a bad mood and threatened again to commit suicide as soon as he got the opportunity.

During the day War Office prisoner-of-war experts inspected Camp Z. Even though Hess seemed to be about as mobile as a trussed turkey, they would not put it past him to burst free: a wire cage would have to be erected across the staircase well.

25 June 1941   [Orderly's night report]

Patient appears to be very depressed, possibly through lack of sleep.
    02.30 hrs complains of pain in right leg.
    03.15 hrs patient is getting hysterical & out of hand, says the pain he cannot stand it any longer. He asked for doctor & I thought it advisable under the circumstances to inform him of patient's action. Doctor gave ¼ gr[ain of] morphia.

25 June 1941   [Commandant's diary]

At 03.30 the duty officer and the medical orderly on duty thought it fit to call the doctor. The doctor reported that "Z" was in a hysterical

---

* He did not get it – the case was settled out of court on 18 February 1942.

condition and a raving lunatic and in such a state at any moment might attempt to tear the splint from his leg. He therefore decided to inject ⅜ grain of morphia in spite of the risk that by so doing he might be inducing "Z" to become a drug addict.

"Z" then became quiet and slept. [Later:] He speaks very little now and is sullen and morose.

The morphia allowance was stopped the next day, but the corporals informed Colonel Scott that the fear of poisoning seemed to be returning.

Lieutenant Bill Malone was one of the few men the prisoner felt he could still trust. " 'Z' said", wrote the Scots Guards lieutenant in his diary on 28 June, "that he was still sure that attempts were being made to poison him – for instance, the glucose he had been taking was doped. Very hesitantly he asked whether I would take some of the glucose. It was a great risk for me. I said certainly, filled a tumbler with glucose and topped up with water. This I drank off at a gulp. Then he produced a tablet and asked whether I would take it – he said this was the tablet which prevented him from passing water."

Malone did as bidden, while Hess watched with an expression that Malone described as eagerness mixed with apprehension.

28 June 1941   [Commandant's diary]

"Z" . . . became very much more talkative with Malone.

Underneath there seems to be a very great admiration for England. He was full of praise of the education system (especially as regards public schools) which he admits is superior to the German.

It seems a possibility that when he is allowed to read Hitler's & Goebbels' explanations of his flight to England there may be a revulsion of feeling on his part against Nazi Germany and some useful propaganda may result. . . .

Poisoning still an obsession and Malone was asked to sample his glucose tablets, which he did.

Four new medical orderlies (making six in all) reported for duty and Major Dicks lectured them on their duties and the importance of secrecy.

Corporal Everatt found Hess "rather impressed" by the influx of new men. One of them, Corporal F. R. Farr, wrote in his night report that Hess "appears sociable, is co-operative, and seems to appreciate attention given to him". On 29 June, however, Corporal Riddle, whom Major Dicks would recall later as an experienced and sensitive man, made the first record of a disturbing symptom that he believed he had witnessed during his tour of duty – "that the patient whilst in the state of anxiety observes the corners of the room in a very mild hallucinated state: grimaces, but no gesticulations present."

Hallucinations? For a man of Hess's rare physiognomy, with staring, deep-set eyes, it would be easy to be mistaken. Some of the other orderlies

– coached, perhaps, by Dicks and Riddle – also began to notice these symptoms.

30 June 1941   [Orderly's day report]
Short periods during which he appeared preoccupied and gazing with a fixed stare. He has spent a good deal of his time reading *The Times*.

30 June 1941   [Orderly's evening report]
Scanting at the paper & books, to be interrupted by sharp suspicious looks at different parts of the room.

30 June 1941   [Commandant's diary]
Major Foley had further talks with "Z" . . . in an attempt to allay his poison phobia. "Z" seemed to be reassured and promised that if ever he had any further suspicions he would send for Major Foley whatever time of day or night it might be.

    After these talks he seemed very much easier in his mind and became quite talkative to the duty officer at dinner.

    Lieutenant Atkinson-Clark, the Guards officer involved in the violent "catheter incident", had been withdrawn from Camp Z soon after.

    Normal days were rare, and the false hopes were often dashed. Hess became increasingly capricious, and stirred dim recollections of the occult. He congratulated Corporal Riddle: "Your hands must be electrified!"

    Major Dicks did not possess the requisite powers, evidently, and by early July he was losing what little patience he had. At 2.30 a.m. on 1 July he was again roused, this time to give, very reluctantly, further morphia to Hess after he complained of excruciating gall-bladder pains. Dicks found the patient's pulse was normal. "It's obvious", he told the Commandant scornfully, "that his fears of poison having been allayed he has invented another complaint. This is only what I'd expect in 'Z's' particular form of insanity." But *was* he insane?

1 July 1941   [Commandant's diary]
Later in the day . . . he stated [to Major Foley] that he had quite lost his suspicions of the officers of the staff here and realised that the whole of this poison phobia was manufactured in his own mind.

1 July 1941   [Corporal Farr's day report]
Visited by Major Dicks and Major Foley during the morning, but patient was sleeping each time so was not disturbed.

    He asks for *The Times* during the morning but threw it down as if in disgust after about two minutes and murmured, "Retreat! Retreat!" . . . Facial appearance is drawn and pale.

In 1933 Hitler appointed Rudolf Hess Deputy Führer. By 1966 Hess, alone and facing over twenty years of solitary confinement in Spandau prison, was a spectral shadow of his former self.

One of the Nazi Party's most popular orators, Hess was equally at home in the workers' canteens or touring the election battlefield at Hitler's side.

In September 1934 the Nazi Party held its annual rally in the new Nuremberg arena. Hess posed with SA Commander Pfeffer von Salomon and Hermann Göring for film cameras taking footage for Leni Riefenstahl's Triumph of the Will.

After he parachuted into Scotland from a crashing Messerschmitt 110 fighter in May 1941, Hess was imprisoned in the secret Camp Z at Aldershot. Air photographs were taken to test its camouflage.

Senior MI6 official Frank Foley (top left) tried to squeeze every secret out of Hess; the Duke of Hamilton *(top right)* never saw him again, but both Lord Simon (bottom left) *and Lord Beaverbrook (bottom right)* were allowed into the secret world of Camp Z to talk to him.

Interrogated on 9 October 1945 by US Colonel John H. Amen at Nuremberg, Rudolf Hess – wearing his famous flying kit – said he could remember nothing but his own name. Amen failed to crack him.

In the dock at Nuremberg, 6 December 1945, Hermann Göring and Rudolf Hess share a joke. One week earlier, Hess had admitted that he had been faking his amnesia all along for tactical reasons.

Photographed in his cell at Nuremberg on 23 November 1945, Hess looked haggard and unwell. It was deliberate – he had been starving himself for weeks to obtain this effect.

Hess's death made front page news in every newspaper.

This photograph of Spandau prison, taken at very long range, was claimed in the press to show Hess walking in the grounds, on the left-hand side of the picture.

At 3 p.m. that day Corporal Riddle relieved Farr. At first he recorded that the Deputy Führer appeared to be much brighter, although his depression was still pronounced. "During that time he adopts a vacant stare," wrote Riddle, trying to find the right words to express what he was seeing, "expressions are shown by twitching his face & sudden outbursts of German phrases which give an impression of anger." Several times that evening – at two-minute intervals, in fact – Hess restlessly asked for the bed to be changed from sitting to lying positions.

On the 2nd, his mind seemed to be repairing, even though Everatt again saw "that very vacant stare". To Colonel Rees, visiting the little upstairs room just before six o'clock that evening, Hess expressed a wish to broadcast to the German nation. Rees was pleased by his apparent, though probably only temporary "return to sanity". The army psychiatrist's pleasure was not only professional, of course. "It might still be possible," he told the Commandant, "to get some useful information out of him."

3 *July 1941*   [Corporal Riddle's night report]
He soon fell asleep, peaceful in nature.

At 3.25 hrs he asked the attendant to place his hands on his side & said the electricity in them did him good.

05.00 he awoke with an outburst of phrases, but slept again straight away soundly.

3 *July 1941*   [Corporal Farr's afternoon report]
Comfortable and cheerful . . . has remained so throughout the afternoon, being more sociable and conversant. He has spent his time mostly reading, but short periods have been spent staring into the corner of the room in a preoccupied manner.

3 *July 1941*   [Commandant's diary]
Another distinct improvement in "Z".

The duty officer [Lieutenant Malone] reported that during dinner he carried on a long conversation on a variety of subjects connected with politics and the war in which, amongst other things, he stated that Hitler did not want his colonies back for their mineral wealth but as a training ground for young Germans to harden them & make them live an adventurous life.

"Z" talked quite rationally and not once did he mention his health, poisoning, or suspicions of officers. This is the first occasion upon which he has talked to Malone without mentioning himself and his health which up to now have been his all-absorbing and only interest and consequently only topic of conversation.

And so it went on. Incommunicative periods, during which he sat morose and sulky, alternated with long conversations, periods of near-fasting with episodes of ravenous appetite. He would devour the newspaper, putting aside the War News pages to read later. Sometimes the orderlies heard him mumbling to himself, at others they saw him staring vacantly: but what else could a prisoner do under the circumstances?

4 *July 1941*   [Corporal Everatt's day report]

The patient spent most of the afternoon reading books and papers, had several conversations with us . . . spoke of his early life in Egypt and his return to Germany. He has been much brighter and not lapsed into sullen moods. . . .

   Later this evening he appeared to be hallucinated. He sat for a while as if listening to voices and then smiled. When asked why he was laughing he did not answer at first, but when he did he said it was a book he had been reading that was passing through his mind.

Colonel Scott came up to see him in the morning with Major Dicks, but Hess answered only in sullen monosyllables. He asked for water-colours and a drawing block, but found it difficult to handle the brush or pencil in his reclined position. Fresh orders had now come from the secret service:

5 *July 1941*   [Commandant's diary]

Instructions were received from "C" through Major Foley that "Z" might now have the *Illustrated London News*, *Sphere*, and *Country Life* [all glossy pictorial magazines of British high society]. Old copies of these periodicals were taken up to him.

   The medical orderly [Lance-Corporal Riddle] reported that in the afternoon "Z" was lying gazing at the ceiling and at intervals laughing out loud which seemed to prove to the orderly's mind that "Z" was quite mad.

Since Major Dicks was particularly impressed by Riddle's reliability, the Corporal's Day Report is worth quoting:

Patient . . . showed a peculiar attitude although he attempted to be interested in painting which only lasted for twenty minutes.

   Earlier the patient showed acute signs of Hallucination being present by laughing & muttering in a quiet manner [accompanied] by looking in an unoccupied glare at the corner of the room. . . . This lasted for about one hour.

   [He] asked how long he would be in bed before being allowed to get up & seemed to be disappointed when answered in about nine weeks.

   Refused to eat dinner when accompanied by Lieutenant Hubbard.

   Asked for all the lunch to be locked up in the drawers & the key left near him.

The pattern was repeated the next day. After a cheerful start, he soon reverted to apathy towards his surroundings and vacant stares for long periods. He retrieved the locked-up dinner, and enjoyed it, spent the afternoon scantily reading, then showed more enthusiasm when he began to paint the flowers that Riddle had set up for him.

"Tomorrow may be better," he said, contemplating his first effort. He asked the Corporal to treat his head with his hands: "They are good for me, they're electrified. I will see that you get a very good present."

Riddle asked what he was thinking about.

"There's something wrong with my head," responded the Deputy Führer, with soulful, empty eyes. "I am *thinking* all the time, but I don't know what about."

Through routine internal surveillance operations – letter-censorship, wiretaps and informers – MI5 learned at the end of June that seventeen Polish and two British officers had hatched a plot to murder Rudolf Hess.

Since Hitler's defeat of Poland and France most of the exiled Polish army was stationed in Scotland. On 6 and 7 July Colonel Hinchley Cook of MI5 came down to Camp Z to discuss security against such an attack with Colonel Scott and local garrison commanders. "Code words were agreed upon," recorded Scott on the 7th, "as warnings that the suspects had left their present locations."

Hess of course was not told. He was in a cheerful mood that day but on the next day, depressed again, he asked for paper and envelopes, leading Major Foley to conclude that they might expect more letters of farewell to his wife, etcetera.

"What happened to the letters I wrote before my suicide attempt?" Hess asked.

"In this country," the Intelligence officer explained, "suicide is a crime, so we have sent forward your letters to higher authority as evidence."

The prisoner meekly accepted the explanation, and wrote more.

Scott, his attention still on the "Polish Plot", ordered the night guards to patrol the *inside*, not the outside of the perimeter wire and took steps to guard against a heavy car being used by the assassins to batter down the camp's double gates.

The days passed hot and sultry, with Hess often morose and unapproachable, but talking so normally and sensibly to those Guards officers he trusted, and on such a wide range of subjects, that the suspicion seems justified that his earlier "insanity" might have been a deliberate ploy. He was seen immersed in Sir Nevile Henderson's tragic history of the last months of peace in Berlin, *Failure of a Mission*. The title that the British Ambassador had chosen might equally apply to Hess's own attempt. The news of Hitler's historic battlefield triumphs in Russia buoyed him to believe that victory was not far off. "I should prefer to return to Germany," he remarked to Second-Lieutenant Tunnard on the

12th, his mind on peace – or perhaps the Duke of Windsor's exile – "rather than to accept the governorship of one of the colonies."

13 July 1941   [Commandant's diary]

"Z" was in a depressed mood all day. The doctor [Dicks] suspects that "Z" is taking another violent dislike to him.

However when Malone went up to dine with him dressed in "Blue Patrols" "Z" was greatly impressed and let himself go on several subjects.

He tòld Malone the whole story of Unity Mitford – how she had chased Hitler about wherever he went and eventually how she had, after the outbreak of war, tried to commit suicide by shooting herself in the "English Garden" in Munich.

The doctor who performed the operation on her was a personal friend of "Z"'s and told him that she would be quite insane for the rest of her life.

He then discussed music and, contrary to Major Foley's previous report, he appeared to be intensely interested in it and attended all concerts in Berlin when possible.

He shows a wide knowledge of many things – for instance he knew all about the bad echo in the Albert Hall, knows many surprising details of British life, customs, authors and the books they have written and so on.

He discussed religion at length – said that he himself was more religious than most, but said that Germany intended to do away with Christianity as being only a Jewish fable and replace it by a new German religion. He did not admit that Roman Catholicism was on the increase in Germany.

He spoke of [Sir Oswald] Mosley [leader of the British Union of Fascists] but said that although he had met him he had not seen enough of him to form an opinion of him.

He takes a great interest in architecture especially old English country houses and would like to have an illustrated book on the subject.

He asked whether it was because the men liked it that women in England used so much make-up.

Hess continued this revealing dialogue with the Scots Guards officer the next day. Hitler, he assured Bill Malone, did not desire world domination, as the dispersion of effort would result in a dangerous weakening of the German people. "He plans to control all of Europe, with the possible exception of Britain. This will provide enough problems to keep us busy for a long time."

Explaining that Hitler had no intention of destroying Britain – "He likes Britain and the British!" – Hess recited the Berlin end of the then unknown sequence of events whereby Churchill had launched the world into the horrors of saturation bombing. Hitler had delayed bombing London (Hess said "England") until the last possible moment in spite of the demands of his military commanders. "He only gave in when

England started bombing Germany" – Hess meant *Berlin*, which had been subjected to heavy RAF raids on Churchill's personal order from 25 August 1940, thirteen days before the first Nazi raids on London.

"His liking of England", revealed Hess, "was of long standing. This was partly based on his contacts with British visitors to Germany, all of whom he found to have an outlook on life and a bearing of which he entirely approved. He was particularly captivated by the Duke of Windsor, whom he considered to be the most intelligent prince he had ever met." (That had been at the Obersalzberg in October 1937.)

For centuries, Hess reflected, Britain's policy had been based on the destruction of the strongest power in Europe. Spain, the Netherlands and France had each been destroyed in turn. Now it was Germany's turn to be destroyed, as she had become the strongest. This, he said, had been King Edward VII's policy. "Churchill", he continued with ill-suppressed indignation, "worked unceasingly behind the scenes before this war to engineer the means for the destruction of Germany." Churchill's remarks to the American General Wood in 1936 proved it. The luckless Poles had been dragged into the maelstrom through the "encirclement" machinations of the British. "Polish diplomats told our Foreign Ministry", said Hess, "that they would have been perfectly willing to discuss the Corridor with us, but Britain dissuaded them."

What Hess had to say about propaganda techniques startled his listeners. "This", he told Malone, "was Britain's principal weapon in the last war. It did more than anything to break down our resistance. It came in thanks to the socialists and Jews, and it was far more effective than your blockade. To prevent you using this weapon a second time, we forbade our public to listen to British broadcasts."

When the war began, he continued, German morale would not have stood up to defeat. "This is a fatal flaw in the German character," said Hess. "It's one that I know is absent from the British: you can *take* failure, and that makes you superior to us. The trouble with us Germans is that we are extremely susceptible. It might be possible to let the Germans listen to the BBC now that they have been strengthened by victories and have confidence in the Führer: but it wasn't at the beginning."

He scorned Britain's own propaganda effort. "When the Ministry of Information was bombed," he said with a laugh, "I complained to Göring that this was a serious mistake!" Recently, he admitted, the propaganda had improved and he asked Malone if he knew who were the men who broadcast to Germany. Malone shook his head, and asked Hess if he knew the real name of "Lord Haw-Haw" – the Irishman William Joyce whose broadcasts from Berlin were listened to clandestinely by two million Englishmen. Hess did not know Joyce's identity, but mimicked "Where is the *Ark Royal*?" The words showed both that he himself had listened to Joyce's broadcasts (perhaps to improve his English), and that he knew it had been a mistake for Germany to claim the aircraft carrier as sunk.

Dilating immodestly on the Nazis' own propaganda successes, Hess said that every German soldier believed that British troops were ten times as brutal as themselves. He himself accepted that the British shot down "Red Cross planes" on sight (again on Churchill's instructions, German air–sea rescue planes were attacked although unarmed and displaying the Red Cross emblem); Hess added that lifeboats riddled with machine-gun bullets were evidence of Britain shooting up sailors in the water. Britain had been the first to disregard what he called "the rules" by mining Norwegian waters.

He declined to believe the German war crimes that Malone mentioned, like the sinking of hospital ships, but agreed that Polish priests had been shot (for espionage, he said). But Britain's "political morality" had improved, said Hess, adding spontaneously: "In this you are about fifty years ahead of Germany."

The conversation drifted on to weapons design. Hess, whose nights had been plagued by the sound of machine-gun fire from the nearby butts, said that Tommy guns had one disadvantage – their high rate of fire caused ammunition-supply problems in battle. "The morale effect of their *noise* more than makes up for that," he said. "The Führer is a great believer in the demoralizing effect of noise." It was Hitler, he revealed, who had had little sirens fixed to Luftwaffe bombs to increase the terror effect on troops.

"There is no longer any Communism in Germany," he said, shifting the topic again. "I am sure of this from my visits to the big factories. I saw the change for myself." In his imagination he saw the big, well-landscaped factories they had built in the Ruhr and around Berlin, the showers and recreation facilities for the workers; he saw the unemployed vanishing from the streets.

"The workers realized what we had done for them," he said, meaning the Nazis. "The provision of newspapers hammering home the ideals of National Socialism changed the ideas of even the older men." The direction of labour had not resulted in antagonism, he said, because it was better than being unemployed. "Our pact with Russia did not encourage Communism in Germany," he explained, "because the German people understood Hitler's reasoning in making the pact. They knew he wanted to avoid encirclement, and they were perfectly aware of Britain's efforts over the previous six months to persuade Russia to come in with her."

From Communism the Deputy Führer turned easily to the subject of Christianity. Both he and Hitler were more religious than most, but Christianity was, he argued – echoing words he had so often heard Hitler himself use – alien to the racial understanding of the German people. "I believe in a Hereafter," he said, "but not in a heaven including a God resembling an old man with a beard."

He talked again of Hitler's determination to replace Christianity with a new religion, to be devised by some man who had yet to come forward. Man as such was not satisfied with abstractions, but "externals and rituals" were necessary and would have to be devised. He believed this hostility to Christianity was why the Vatican had not openly praised the crusade against Russia; conversely, he inferred that Stalin had made a serious mistake in destroying religion in the Soviet Union without putting something in its place.

As for the Jewish problem, Hess was well informed about the solution proposed by Hitler. "The Führer", he disclosed to Lieutenant Malone, "has decided to banish all Jews from Europe at the end of the war. Their probable destination is Madagascar." (Madagascar, part of the French colonial empire, is a temperate island as large as Germany off the coast of Africa. German Admiralty and Foreign Ministry files contain the documents on Hitler's 1940 Madagascar plan.)

Before discussing his former colleagues Hess remarked in general upon their allies. The Chinese he admired as honest and dependable; their leader Chiang Kai-shek was a great man. But he felt the Japanese were untrustworthy, and he would not put it past them to make a lunge at Australia when it suited them.

He expressed dislike for his Foreign Minister. "There is no possibility whatever of Ribbentrop ever succeeding to the leadership," he said, "even if Hitler, Göring and I myself all die." Ribbentrop was too recent a Nazi member – a new Führer would have to come from the Old Guard. But, he added even-handedly, "Ribbentrop had no hatred of Britain any greater than any other Nazi leader."

Asked which Englishman he would like to meet, given the chance, Hess mentioned the half-forgotten General Sir Ian Hamilton. "He sent me his memoirs not long before the war, but I never had time to read them. And I'd like to read his book about Gallipoli."

In pleasurable reminiscences, the conversation meandered as the afternoon drew on. He mentioned that German battle casualties in Poland, France and Greece had been far lower than enemy propaganda maintained; and, talking of propaganda, he was contemptuous of the notion that the Gestapo itself had engineered the Bürgerbräu beerhall assassination attempt in November 1939. "If the Gestapo had planned it," he said proudly, "they would have used a more reliable timing device than two alarm clocks to detonate the bomb! The explosion happened only seven minutes after the Führer had left." Subsequently, Hess continued, border police caught the man who had installed the device in the deserted beerhall. He believed (probably wrongly) that the man, Georg Elser, was connected with the two British MI6 officers Stevens and Best, who were ambushed a few days later on the Dutch border by Gestapo officials pretending to be German generals disgruntled with Hitler. ("'Z' inferred", reported Malone, "that they were not sufficiently important to be executed for their activities which he seemed to think were puerile.")

Gradually the conversation ended. Hess admitted sadly that before his injury he had stood as close to the windows as possible to listen when the officers played Beethoven records in the anteroom.

"When I get out of this bed," he said, pointing at the Balkan frame and weights, which had now been reduced to twenty-four pounds, "I'm going to design a country house. I'm going to build it in Scotland after the war." (It was subtle flattery of the Scots officer Malone.) "Can you let me have some books of designs of English country houses?"

> *14 July 1941*   [Lieutenant Malone's report]
>
> "Z"'s references to relatively unimportant English names [and] his understanding of background evidenced in conversation demonstrate that his sources of information about England must have been considerable, that his memory and grasp of detail are excellent, and that he has made a close study of the English scene for a considerable time. He says that his English was learnt only at school, but it is far too good and colloquial for this to be true, and his use of peculiarly English phrases indicates recent coaching.

"Superficially he appears to be much better," concluded Malone, "and would seem quite normal to anyone who did not know of the events of the last few weeks." But beneath the waters of this surface improvement, he warned, there were still "jagged thoughts and treacherous suspicions".

The psychiatrist Major Dicks had never established this degree of rapport with the prisoner. On 16 July he was notified that he was being replaced (although he continued periodic visits to Hess thereafter). To this émigré psychiatrist, Hess remained an object of hostility until the very end – a crazed, degenerate sub-human doomed by a cruel heredity to eventual insanity. Despite their education, the Guards officers who shared their meals with the prisoner often failed to perceive this. For example, as the Commandant observed, Second-Lieutenant M. Loftus, who was replacing Tunnard, seemed to have gained "Z"'s confidence at once during the hour that he spent alone with Hess over dinner on 17 July. It is clear from other sources that Hess always told the unvarnished truth in these conversations. Loftus showed him a photograph taken from *Life* magazine – of Hess in all his glory, standing next to Hitler at the Reichstag meeting in Berlin shortly before his flight, or as the American caption had it, "six days before Hess deserted from Germany". Loftus apologized for the caption, but the Deputy Führer took it in good spirit. He was visibly distressed by the magazine's four pictures of damage caused by the 10 May raid to Westminster Abbey. "If the war goes on," commented Hess, "there won't be any fine old buildings left either in Germany or in Britain."

"Which of these men do you like best?" asked Loftus, pointing again to the Reichstag podium.

That was an easy one. "The Führer!" said Hess, chuckling out loud.

They swapped their favourite jokes about Göring. Told the unfavourable British verdict on Ribbentrop, Hess chivalrously remarked, "We all depend on the press for our popularity, and the reverse; it's the same in every country." As for the Reichsführer SS, Hess remarked that Heinrich Himmler was an agreeable fellow behind the bespectacled façade.

"Had you already made up your mind at the time of this Reichstag meeting – to leave Germany, I mean?"

"I had that intention as far back as Christmas," replied Hess. "I made two separate attempts. Both times I was forced back by bad weather." He had also experienced problems with the plane's controls (*Steuerung*) and radio. Only his adjutant, Karlheinz Pintsch, had been privy to his intention, but his friend Haushofer had told him that he had had a dream – a dream in which he had seen Hess alone in the air. "He also dreamed he saw me on a return journey," the prisoner added with a wry smile. "That was just before my final attempt – the one that succeeded."

Talking of psychic phenomena, Hess freely admitted that he believed in second sight, in predestination and in ghosts.

"Why did you try to kill yourself?" asked the young Lieutenant.

"Because I was afraid I was going mad," replied Hess, simply and without affectation. "I flew to Britain to stop the war – or at any rate to stop the indiscriminate bombing of civilians. After I failed, I began to feel I had been deluding myself all along and people might think me mad in Germany." He promised earnestly he would not try to kill himself again.

"For anybody who believes in a personal star," pointed out Loftus, "it would be a silly thing to do."

"It wouldn't fit in at all", agreed Hess, "with Haushofer's vision of a return flight." For a moment he reflected in sombre silence. "I am quite certain", he continued, "that if only I could have contacted some influential person in this country we could between us have stopped the war."

"Are you quite sure that Germany would have accepted your proposals?" inquired Loftus.

"Germany is the Führer!" Hess exclaimed, and lectured the disbelieving Guards Lieutenant at some length about Adolf Hitler's love of peace.

"A few days before my flight," he amplified, probably referring to the Reichstag session, "I went to him and asked him whether he still wanted to make it up with England, and the Führer answered that he did."

When Loftus inquired about Russia, Hess admitted that Hitler had meant to attack her all along – ever since writing *Mein Kampf*.

Invade Britain? Hess shrugged. "It depends on him. If he presses the button there will be an invasion. And it will succeed, because whatever the Führer does succeeds."

Lieutenant Loftus rose to leave. As a mark of special favour, Hess showed him the treasured Luftwaffe uniform.

11 A Second Cabinet Visitor

It is plain that Hess had succeeded in winning the admiration of Second-Lieutenant Loftus. The Guards officer, son of a Member of Parliament, left the upstairs room convinced that the Deputy Führer was "fanatically sincere". He was loyal to Hitler, and did not doubt that Hitler could be anything but true to him. True, he was vain and succumbed easily to flattery – about his skilful and heroic flight, for example. But Loftus did not regard him as the subtle, scheming, dishonest man that Major Dicks had found.

> *17 July 1941*   [Lieutenant Loftus's report]
>
> I think he is one of the simplest people you could meet and I very much doubt whether he is at all intelligent, but he has what has lifted the whole mediocre bunch to power – that single-tracked blind and fanatical devotion to an ideal and to the man who is his leader.
>
> But he differs from the rest of Hitler's henchmen in that he is genuinely religious and sincerely humanitarian. He doesn't doubt for a moment that Germany will win the war and he sees himself building a house in Scotland.
>
> His chief interests seem to be skiing and architecture, and like so many Germans he is a great admirer of our style of living.
>
> He has left a wife and small son behind him. The wife doesn't appear to concern him, but he talks of his son and told me how hard it was for him not to give the show away when, the night before his flight, the child asked him where he was going.

Loftus found the man still obsessed with his own "mission", which rendered him incapable of seeing things as they were. He assessed Hess's mind as being as "virginal as Robespierre's", and suspected that given the chance Hess could be as dangerous an idealist, had nature bestowed on him the personality and eloquence.

He left the man after that first meeting with an impression of his courteous manners, his disarming smile and his easy laugh. His features were marred only by the protruding upper teeth and receding chin –

which should not, however, have dismayed a member of the British upper classes – but were redeemed by the remarkable eyes which, Loftus had observed, were astonishingly deep-set and of a striking intensity.

Captain Munro K. Johnston who had just replaced Dicks at Mytchett Place – Camp Z – had considerable institutional experience of psychiatric cases (although in February 1942 he would quite properly declare himself not competent to perform a full medical examination of "Z"). Of *his* first meeting with Hess, on the same day as Loftus, Johnston would write: "His attitude towards me was one of suspicion and correct formality. He appeared to be a sick man – gaunt, hollow-eyed and anxious." Hess expressed satisfaction with Hitler's attack on Communist Russia, since he hoped that the British would now be more sympathetic – he still believed he could restore peace, when he had recovered.

Once, Johnston remarked that the British laughed at Reichsmarschall Göring's plethora of medals and uniforms. "So does Göring!" said Hess, and guffawed loudly. But Johnston deduced that he was jealous of the Reichsmarschall's prestige. "Göring", the prisoner sniffed, "would have been terrified at the thought of making such a flight as I did." (Göring had certainly reassured Hitler, in the twenty-four anxious hours before the BBC announced Hess's parachute arrival, that it was most unlikely that the Me-110 had reached Scotland safely.)

Whereas Scott's diary had earlier shown the prisoner anxious and sleepless because of the air-raid alerts, now he was perplexed by their absence (Albert Kesselring and Wolfram von Richthofen had moved their bomber forces to the eastern front). "They must come soon," he was heard to say.

18 July 1941   [Commandant's diary]

I visited him in the morning and gave him a book on English country houses. . . . Major Dicks R.A.M.C. left and surrendered his pass.

19 July 1941

"Z" continues to improve. . . . He told [Lieutenant T. Jackson] that he now had no intention to commit suicide. He still seems to think that should Hitler & Göring die he would become Führer.

20 July 1941

Took Capt. Ashworth [the new adjutant] up and introduced him to "Z" who was in a very cheerful mood.

He seems to improve every day and one begins to wonder if Col. Rees & Major Dicks were right in their diagnosis that he is "permanently insane".

Three days later Hess regaled his friend Bill Malone with the until then unknown inside story of the Blomberg–Fritsch affair of January 1938, which had resulted in the resignation of the War Minister and

Commander-in-Chief of the army in a sex-and-morals scandal. General Werner von Fritsch had, he revealed, been relieved of his command as he was a member of Berlin's high-society clique, and therefore not loyal enough to the Party. In September 1939 he visited the Polish front as honorary colonel of his regiment, and deliberately walked into enemy machine-gun crossfire to take his own life.

As for Blomberg, he said that both Hitler and Göring had attended the Field Marshal's January 1938 wedding to a young girl, whereupon Berlin's high-society had given out that the bride was, to put it bluntly, no lady. The allegations were found, upon investigation, to be true, and Blomberg had to resign. "But *he* did not go to the front," remarked Hess maliciously.

Malone asked him about Poland – perhaps knowing of the Polish officers who were plotting to kill their prisoner.

"I was never there myself," said Hess. "You know," he continued, "the Polish Ambassador was so sure there was going to be a revolution in Germany in the first fortnight of the war that on his departure he said *Auf Wiedersehen* to the people who saw him off!"

Malone asked if it was true that Hitler had forbidden him to fly. On previous occasions, Hess had rationalized that he had given the promise not to fly for one year, and that the year had just expired. Now the story changed. "Yes," he said, "he did forbid it – but he only forbade me to fly single-engined planes. I came over in a twin-engined machine."

For over a week, the orderlies had seen him writing some document. On 27 July, since Malone had just been withdrawn, Hess took Lieutenant Loftus into his confidence, told him over lunch he was the only person he felt he could trust, and asked him if he would pass a document to his father without divulging it to anybody else at the camp.

27 July 1941   [Commandant's diary]

The duty officer [Loftus] refused to give his parole until he had consulted with his father, who [was] a Member of Parliament and, as the officer impressed on "Z", a "friend of Germany". . . . The officer said this in order to get information, as instructed; he actually had no intention of approaching or informing his father.

Later in the day "Z" began his old requests and demands to see the Duke of Hamilton and seemed excitable again. Warned the doctor that this may be the beginning of another attack and that the medical orderlies must be on their guard.

For several days Hess retained the document. Meanwhile on the 28th the surgeon Major Murray came and X-rayed the fracture: Johnston observed that the prisoner, who had heard that X-rays could sterilize, carefully covered his private parts with a metal lid during the X-ray exposures.

The orderlies' day and night reports show him cheerful and sociable, inquiring about their social lives, drawing and writing and very occasionally lapsing into apparent states of preoccupation, when he would fix his eyes on a corner of the room and seem absorbed in his own thoughts. Sometimes there were episodes which suggest that he had salvaged more of his sense of humour than his custodians.

30 July 1941   [Commandant's diary]

He has been somewhat critical of his food lately so that it was with some surprise that, when the duty officer [Lieutenant Hubbard] jokingly offered him a charcoal dog biscuit, he not only ate it but asked for more.

31 July 1941

Col. Coates [Deputy Director, Prisoners of War] had an interview with "Z".

1 August 1941

"Z" spent the whole day writing out a huge report which was handed to [Lieutenant Loftus] at dinner time . . . only an amplification of his previous statements – demands to be put under the care of H.M. the King; demands for a Court of Inquiry composed of men who had no connection with either the Prime Minister or the War Office, and so on. The old suspicions of attempts to poison him, and accusations against Col. Rees and Major Dicks in particular as being the chief conspirators.

To Colonel Scott, the Commandant, the document seemed only to confirm the unfavourable prognoses of Gibson Graham, Rees, Dicks and Johnston despite their prisoner's "apparent sanity" in recent weeks.

The German original of Hess's fifteen-page handwritten "deposition" passed into the secure archives of the secret service, but a similar text is now in Swiss government files and an English translation dated 30 July is in the Commandant's private papers and Hess was able to hand a copy of this to Lord Beaverbrook five weeks later. If allowances are made for this prisoner's natural state of mind, it is a document that fascinates on several levels – for what it tells us about Hess's powers of memory, for the facts it relates, and for the methodical, legally orientated manner in which Hess presented his case, arranged into paragraphs and sub-paragraphs and adducing "witnesses" who could, if need be, substantiate his more exotic allegations. With the document he enclosed some of the glucose tablets that Major Dicks had administered a few days before his suicide attempt and asked for their independent analysis.

"As I am conscious that my statements in parts sound fantastic," he began, "I have limited myself to cases for which I believe that I am able to submit proof." To start with, he provided an almost clinical description of the "curious development of warmth" he sensed, with its ensuing euphoria and symptoms of withdrawal, after taking the anonymous substances administered to him by Major Dicks – episodes which resulted in an "extraordinary rapid fatigue of the brain". Fearful of losing his sanity completely in consequence, and not wanting to offer this picture to foreigners, and "especially to avoid being displayed to journalists as an insane person", he had decided to put an end to his life if the symptoms should recur. "I wrote the relevant farewell letters in complete calm. When during the night [of 15–16 June] it became abundantly clear that the same consequences as before were recurring, I jumped into the well of the house." After the suicide attempt failed, Hess continued, he felt that the same unknown substance was again being administered to him, and while the feared reaction was much less this time he attributed this to his having concealed a number of the tablets. "There remains a rapid exhaustion of the brain," he said, and added, "It was significant that when Dr Dicks assumed that I had taken the substance he asked me over and over again whether I did not feel that my mind was getting tired."

This was why Hess now requested an independent analysis of the glucose tablets. "I suspect that the substance concerned is in them," he said. "But I cannot say for certain. I assume that the substance would be known of in a hospital for nervous diseases. Its presence in the tablets could be determined in a laboratory."

Trying to reconstruct, through the confusion caused by the medication, the turbulent events of the last weeks, Hess narrowed down the onset of the "warmth" symptoms to the period shortly after he arrived at Camp Z. "After the visit of an officer (from the War Office, I think)," he wrote, perhaps in a reference to the visit made by Colonel Rees on 30 May, "[Dr Gibson Graham] was obviously disturbed. I think that that evening was the first time that I was given a small amount of the substance I have described – please ask him."

His suspicions perhaps naturally aroused by this medication, Hess then turned to the "Veganin" tablets given him after his fall. They certainly had not soothed his pain, but they had, he believed, stopped him passing water. He told Bill Malone of his suspicions, but the Lieutenant "of course . . . would not believe me". After taking one that Hess had squirrelled away, Malone – so he alleged – suffered results that confirmed his suspicions. "He was completely distracted. His features seemed to show that he had suffered badly. . . . I am firmly convinced", continued Hess, "that he reported [to Scott] the effect of the tablets on him and was given an order to deny to me that the tablets had had any such effect." Since that date, Hess continued, he had unfortunately only been given genuine Veganin tablets, so he could not offer samples for analysis.

Since Major Dicks had urged him, Hess testified, to drink as much water as possible, the inference was clear: this, and the painful "catheter incident" – which he described in substantially more convincing terms than the other allegations – suggested to him that the object was to apply to him the "Gestapo methods" of which Atkinson-Clark had spoken. After setting out another episode, in which the surgeon, after conferring with Dicks, had rearranged his splint for twenty-four hours, causing him insufferable pain, Hess suggested that Major Murray be questioned, "As I have the impression that he was not in agreement with such methods."

He then turned to the subtle methods used to lower his self-esteem. It had not escaped him that both Dr Gibson Graham and Major Foley had, within twenty-four hours of each other, asked the identical question: "Has provision been made for your family in the event you do not return to Germany?" And he was well aware why he had been denied access to outside news, even to the official war communiqués. Major Foley and the Companions had told him brutally about the sinking of the *Bismarck* and had added that Admiral Lütjens and the greater part of the crew had lost their lives – "But they omitted to tell me of the sinking of the *Hood*." (The battleship, Britain's biggest, had been blown up by a direct hit from *Bismarck*'s guns.) "I cannot avoid the impression", he wrote, "that my nerves had to be influenced in a negative sense."

The same psychological warfare clearly underlay his isolation: "Since my arrival in England," he complained, "I have not received a single letter or any other mail from Germany. It is out of the question that my family and friends (for instance Professor Haushofer) have not written. It is equally out of the question that the Führer, as a punishment for my flight, has forbidden the forwarding of mail from Germany as Major Foley and other officers are always suggesting. People will not take it amiss if I suspect that the mail embargo, like the news embargo, has been imposed in order to affect my nerves."

The same kind of mental cruelty, Hess suggested, was being used with regard to music. He had asked for gramophone music to be piped from the ground floor into his room, and for permission to listen to the radio. (It will be recalled that Colonel Scott himself had remarked that the MI6 officer Foley had assured him that Hess was not at all interested in music.) Major Foley had promised Hess that he would pass the request on to his authorities in London, then returned and informed the prisoner that "permission had to be obtained from the highest quarters. The Prime Minister had reserved to himself all decisions with regard to my treatment." Hess was surely correct in pointing out that the opportunity of listening occasionally to gramophone and radio could only have a beneficial effect upon him, particularly since Major Murray had now indicated he would have twelve more weeks in bed. "People will understand", accused Hess, "if I draw relevant conclusions."

My requests are:

1. *That an enquiry be instituted on the basis of my statements.* Those entrusted with the enquiry must be given full powers to release witnesses from their pledge of secrecy and to question them under oath; as they are nearly all officers, I presume that only H.M. the King can give such authority. Those entrusted with conducting the enquiry must on no account be placed under, or receive directions from, the War Office, under whose purview I apparently come, or from the Prime Minister.

2. That the Duke of Hamilton be given a translation of this statement. That gentleman promised me when I landed that he would do everything to ensure my safety. I know that in consequence the King of England himself has issued appropriate orders. It is for that reason that Guards officers are charged with my protection. *May the Duke of Hamilton be good enough to ask H.M. the King of England to place me in every respect under his protection.* . . . I request that all those who have been charged with my care be removed.

3. *That the representatives of the British People in the British Parliament be informed in proper manner that I appeal to them.*

Hess listed, in this stubborn document, ten officers whom the Enquiry should question, ranging from the arch-perpetrators Dicks, Foley and "Wallace", through Colonel Scott ("probably initiated") to officers who could give evidence as witnesses who had been "perhaps initiated in part" – the War Office doctors Rees and Gibson Graham, the MI6 Companion known to him as "Barnes", Lieutenants Malone ("Mr Malone", he emphasized, "has always been very chivalrous towards me") and Atkinson-Clark, as well as Corporal Riddle ("I have no complaint against him"). He was confident, he said, that the latter witnesses would speak the truth if properly released from their oath of secrecy and "questioned in the name of the King".

Addressing himself to those whom he identified as the villains – Dicks, Foley and "Wallace" – Hess found himself faced with an enigma:

I have asked myself over and over again how it is possible to reconcile their thoroughly likeable natures with their treatment of me. I am, in fact, faced with a puzzle. I have no real proof, of course, for the suspicion that they are acting under duress, under a powerful suggestive influence or the like. But by their manner, whereby they win and inspire confidence in others, they have succeeded on both occasions when I have tried to complain to visitors, in suggesting to them that I am the victim of an idée fixe. In both cases they invited the visitors to take tea or lunch with them beforehand. . . .

This was the case with the visit of [Lord Simon] who was so convinced that I was the victim of a *Psychose* that he stopped my complaint the moment I started.

It was the same with Col. Rees, who listened very attentively to my statement on the occasion of his first visit. When he visited me for the second time after, as far as I could observe, taking tea with the senior officers, he appeared completely changed and tried to persuade me that I was suffering from a psychosis. . . . Major Dr. Dicks, Major Foley and Colonel Wallace made it a practice to suggest to me that all my sufferings were attributable to a psychosis or to an idée fixe. All my attempts at lodging an official complaint with higher authority through these gentlemen failed, and were dismissed as a psychosis.

He had no complaints whatever against the newcomer, Captain

Johnston, but would not, he announced, be taking his medicines, because Johnston drew these from Major Dicks as well as instructions on a weekly basis.

Asserting that he was too experienced not to know a psychosis when he saw one, Hess now made the startling admission that he had been simulating one, as the only way of getting the army psychiatrists off his back: "If recently I have given the impression that I myself believed in this psychosis, it was only because it appeared to me that I should obtain more peace." It was not a claim likely to endear himself to such a pompous profession.

"The whole business", concluded Hess in this extraordinary deposition, "is obviously the most refined system of cruelty conceivable. To torture a man under the very eyes of those responsible for his protection: perhaps even to ruin his health for life, with almost no possibility of proving it."

Never would I have thought it possible that I should be subjected to mental and physical tortures in England, and that I should be exposed to the cruellest experiences of my life. I came to Britain trusting in the fairness of the British. As a veteran aviator I know that this has been displayed to an opponent time and time again. Since I did not come to Britain as an enemy, there was all the more reason to expect fairness.

I came to Britain completely unarmed, at the risk of my life, with the intention of being useful to both countries.

I still believe in the fairness of the British people. I am convinced that the treatment I have experienced was not according to their voice. I know too that the King of England himself gave orders for my safeguard and comfort.

I have no doubt whatever that only a few persons are responsible for the kind of treatment I have received.

Of course, I shall take care that the German public never hears of my treatment. This would contradict the very meaning of my flight to Britain, which was to improve, not embitter, the relations between our two peoples.

RUDOLF HESS   *July 30, 1941*

The doctors' reactions to Hess's complaint are worth noting. To Captain Johnston, it was the typical effusion of a paranoiac. "He believed", wrote Johnston after the war, "that we were all under the influence of some rare poison." Summarizing his first eighteen days treating the Deputy Führer, Johnston repeated, "He is suffering from paranoia."

1 August 1941   [Captain Munro Johnston's report]
His moody introspection and the recent lengthy written statement he produced with its bizarre ideas of persecution and torture and its quoting of witnesses and proofs are pathognomonic of paranoia.

In my opinion the prognosis is bad, and he requires the care and supervision necessary for a person of unsound mind with suicidal tendencies.

Stamped "Most Secret", the report went into Churchill's files.

Invited to comment when he visited Camp Z on the next day, Major Dicks was even more contemptuous and scathing. The prisoner's attempt to "smuggle [it] past us" showed that his paranoid delusion was still present, despite the superficial improvement. "I am now convinced", wrote Dicks, reverting to his native German syntax, "that no hope of changing this man by any methods whatever is given, and that we must look upon it as any other case of paranoia – i.e., the chances of recovery are less than one percent."

The Commandant quoted this sombre conclusion in his diary without comment. He disagreed, as his earlier entries had hinted: but he was merely the custodian. Major Dicks now recommended that new, suicide-proof surroundings be sought.

The instruction to regard the prisoner as insane baffled the Guards officers at Camp Z. True, he was depressed, often did not want to talk, and stared moodily about his room: what else could he do? "Patient has been cheerful and sociable all the morning," reported Corporal Farr after his shift on the 6th, "and has spent most of his time reading and writing." Everatt, who took over that evening, found Hess still writing: "[He] wrote page after page until dinner time. His interest in writing was so deep that he failed to answer when spoken to at times." And Corporal Riddle stated that before "Z" settled down for the night he had an "interesting conversation" with him.

The writing continued for several days. Speculation mounted about what, precisely, he was committing at such length to paper.

7 August 1941   [Commandant's diary]

"Z" . . . handed [it] to 2nd. Lieut. Loftus at 16.00 hrs. Major Foley started a translation of the manuscript which runs into 45 close-written pages.

A suspicious character was observed taking too much interest in the defences and outer wire. . . . A patrol was sent round to examine the outer perimeter wire and reported back at 22.00 hrs that a portion of the wire by the orchard had been tampered with. . . . It was decided to man No. 6 Post with two men and a Bren Gun through the night.

The new Hess document (which he asked in vain should be given to the Duke of Hamilton) represents a determined attempt by Hess, despite his considerable afflictions and without compromising his country's vital secrets, to set out for Britain her future dilemma – that even if she defeat Germany, she would lose out in the long run to the demands of Soviet imperialism. The manuscript was logical, prophetic, well composed (in immaculate handwriting). MI6 officer Major Foley read it avidly; War Office psychiatrist Colonel Rees found that it confirmed the diagnosis of "a paranoid state".

Starting with the premise that nobody wanted a second "Versailles", he argued that Britain had everything to lose, while the United States could only benefit, if the war dragged on, even to an ultimate British victory. He was, however, sure that Germany would win. Hitler was at that moment disposing of Germany's age-old nightmare, the war on two fronts, by a swift destruction of the Bolshevik armies in Russia. Concealing Germany's very real ammunition shortages in 1939 and 1940, Hess boasted of the Reich's mass production of tanks, guns, bombs and shells and of the stockpiles of oil and raw materials that Germany had captured in France; the output of the new synthetic oil plants made up for the loss of Soviet deliveries. He correctly dismissed Allied claims that the Wehrmacht had already lost one and a half million dead in Russia as "pure fantasy", and he reminded the English that in modern warfare air and motor transport made it much easier to switch reserves about behind the front. Hitler's armies, unlike those of the World War, could not be undermined by starvation at home and by Marxist influences within (notably, Hess omitted "the Jews" from this equation). In short, he expected the Russian front to collapse at any moment.

Britain would then be at Hitler's mercy, he argued, because of her growing shipping crisis (he rightly disbelieved the shipping losses admitted by the Admiralty, but less wisely accepted Berlin's figures as being more accurate). Both David Lloyd George and Admiral Lord Jellicoe had later testified that shipping losses nearly brought about Britain's defeat in 1917. Whereas in that war German submarine warfare had been hampered by the lack of bases, in this war Hitler controlled bases all along the coast from northern Norway to the Spanish frontier. With "early perspicacity" the Führer had ordered increased U-boat production: the boats were being prefabricated and assembled all over occupied Europe, far beyond British bomber range. "I am conscious", Hess interrupted his tract here to admit, "that I am partly betraying military secrets by making these statements, but I think I can justify myself before my conscience and before my people: I believe complete frankness may help to stop a senseless war."

It would not help if Churchill carried out his threat to abandon Britain and fight on from Canada, warned Hess. Hitler would then occupy a few key airbases, and continue the blockade of the island until Churchill surrendered – a policy no less inhuman, he ventured, than Britain's massacre of "26,000 women and children" in Boer War concentration camps.

It was in order to prevent an even more frightful resumption of Luftwaffe air raids that Hess had conceived his own plan to fly to Britain. German aircraft production, he claimed (again grossly inaccurately) was larger than that of Britain and America combined. "If England is hoping to break German morale by increased attacks on the civilian population, she will be disappointed." As Britain herself had found out, morale improved where the air attacks had been heaviest.

Above all Rudolf Hess wanted, with this document, to advise his hosts not to underestimate the Russians. They were turning into the greatest military power on earth. "Only a strong Germany as a counter-weight, supported by the whole of Europe and by the confidence of England, can avert the danger."

He predicted too that if the working classes of Europe suffered as a result of the war, Communism was bound to spread. Britain's overseas empire would be particularly vulnerable to the allures of Marxism–Leninism: "The danger is increased by the attraction which Bolshevism has for natives of lower standards of life, who have come in contact with European civilisation." "I am firmly convinced," added Hess, in words of prophecy that have remained unread in secret archives since he wrote them in that *gulag* Aldershot in the summer of 1941, "that unless her power is broken at the last moment, Bolshevik Russia will be the world power of the future, which will inherit the world position of the British Empire."

Germany's only peace condition of importance, Hess believed, would be the return of her former colonies. Britain must abstain from "meddling in the affairs of the European Continent" – a return, as he put it, to the politics of William Gladstone and Lord Salisbury. "A real understanding with Germany", he wrote, "would mean the realisation of the efforts made by Joseph Chamberlain at the beginning of this century." Thus he appealed to Britain to make at least the attempt to reach an understanding: if it failed, Britain could always resume her "charming Society game" of bombing, crippling, burning, blasting, sinking and bankrupting in the name of war.

After unburdening himself of this tract, Hess lapsed into a quiet and uncommunicative state for several days. When Major Dicks paid his regular Saturday visit on 9 August 1941, "Z" received him with arms folded, to signify that he refused to shake hands with the émigré psychiatrist. That day Colonel "Wallace" came down from MI6, read the document right through, and admitted to the Commandant and Major Foley that it "contained some items of interest".

Talking with duty officer Lieutenant Percival the next day Hess reverted to the Russian war, and predicted that if by any chance Russia did win she would sweep across Germany and France to confront the British Isles. "This", recorded Colonel Scott with an uneasy turn of phrase, "appears to be propaganda on 'Z''s part in favour of his peace plan."

On the 11th the MP's son Lieutenant Loftus picked an argument with Hess over the concentration camps and persecution of the Jews in Nazi

Germany. Hess again brought up the "26,000 women and children" killed by the British in Boer War concentration camps.

A few days later another Guards lieutenant tried to get him to talk about Nazi remote-control aircraft but Hess shut up at once, revealing only a flicker of surprise when told that the British had obtained an undamaged Messerschmitt-109F (a Luftwaffe pilot, who would become a senior Bundeswehr officer after the war, had deserted in it).

The Foreign Office had now given authority for winter quarters to be prepared for Camp Z, so Hess was going to be at Aldershot for some time. Visibly depressed, he was seen writing again. The guards found – probably when he was asleep – that he had written letters to his wife Ilse and his luckless adjutant Pintsch. In each letter Hess again quoted the lines from Goethe that he had used before his previous suicide attempt. He apologized to Pintsch for the "dictates of fortune" that had led to his arrest by the Gestapo, of which he had now heard, and thanked him for his loyalty.

To cheer him up Scott came upstairs one Sunday with a book on the country mansions designed by the master architect, Sir Edwin Lutyens. Hess devoured it at one sitting, and resumed work on the designs for the country house he intended building in Scotland when peace returned. He still found it hard to concentrate, however, and Corporal Farr noticed several times that Hess just stared at the walls, until the banging of downstairs doors jolted him back to his senses.

19 August 1941 [Orderly's report]

[Hess] read the newspaper and appeared quite pleased and stated the news was very satisfying for him. [*The Times* reported German claims that the pursuit of the Russian forces was continuing, and that the enemy was "fleeing in disorder".]

Patient became very quiet after dinner and appeared deep in thought.

20 August 1941

In very good spirits this morning.

15.00 hrs: Soon took up pencil and paper and commenced writing, which he continued with until 18.00. He has been observed to grimace and mumble to himself and smile for no apparent reason. . . .

Disturbed by doors banging and became very annoyed at its continuance and gave ejaculations in German with severe banging of hands on the head and pulling at the bed clothes.

00.10 hrs: . . . Thinks that the banging is done intentionally to keep him disturbed.

20 August 1941 [Commandant's diary]

He talked to [Lieutenant Percival] on the Anglo-American Declaration [the "Atlantic Charter" just agreed between Churchill and Roosevelt] in particular which, he said, was good propaganda for Germany in that it would make her more resolute.

He sent for the doctor after dinner. . . . He went up only to find that "Z" wanted to complain of slamming doors.

The noise from the house door directly beneath his room continued to oppress him, and the orderlies agreed that a sick man should not be put upon like this. On the 21st he "showed great dissatisfaction by his facial expression", when the door banged violently. A week later, the orderly's report shows that each time it banged he asked the attendant to look out of the window to see who was the culprit. By itself, this was hardly the substance of insanity: as he himself pointed out, he was bedridden, with his spine damaged from his parachute jump and his entire leg in a cast, so his nerves were understandably jittery. He asked Colonel Scott to get a vacuum door-retarder fitted, but five weeks would pass before the door was silenced.

At night, his brain furnished him with curious illusions. Several times that August he dreamed that he was still in Germany, that he had never made the flight to Scotland, that he was rushing from Berlin to Munich in some other plane to pick up his Messerschmitt-110 before the Führer could hear about it and stop his departure. In another recurring dream, he saw himself jumping over hurdles – performing acrobatics – with both legs better than ever.

An X-ray showed the fracture had mended, and the last weights were removed. Two days later, Major Murray removed the steel pin. Hess demanded champagne for dinner to celebrate, and got it.

Since there was no reply yet from the Duke, he had painstakingly written out a second copy of his tract and given it to Lieutenant Loftus. The young officer promised (with Scott's knowledge) to show it to his parents.

But there was no intention to let the outside world ever see "Z" again. Preparations began to turn Camp Z into a permanent psychiatric prison for the unwitting Rudolf Hess. On 22 August 1941, after a conference with Scott, Major Foley and Dr Johnston, Colonel Rees submitted this report through MI6 channels to Brigadier Menzies, head of the secret service:

THE FUTURE OF "z"

The documents written recently, which I have seen, confirm the diagnosis that has been made previously of a Paranoid State. In my judgement . . . this condition will continue without any real improvement, although there will be times of remission, some real and some apparent, because, as at present, the patient is masking his symptoms.

"Z" will, therefore, be a constant suicidal risk and precautions must be taken.

I understand that he will be out of his splint in about two months and from that moment he becomes a greater risk even though he may not be down[stairs] and out for another month.

The alternatives appeared to Rees to be to transfer Hess to a prisoner-of-war camp, or to keep him where he was. (The legal requirement that obliged Britain to repatriate Hess to Germany if he had indeed become insane, under the terms of the Geneva Convention, did not occur to the British government until later.) If he stayed at Camp Z armoured glass would have to be fitted throughout his suite and in the sitting room and downstairs mess, and a new lavatory installed – without a dangling chain. "There is hardly any limit to the ingenuity of the man who wishes to die," advised the colonel prophetically, "and it must be accepted that an accident might still occur despite these provisions." The War Office and Foreign Office jointly decided that Hess should stay put, and ordered in particular "that all exercise for 'Z' is to be confined to the upper lawn, which is to be camouflaged from the drive and terrace, leaving enough room for a car to enter and turn if necessary."

For the time being, Hess had no desire to die, and several years would pass before he tried again. His hopes were briefly pinned on Lieutenant Loftus, who was due to see his mother on 29 August. During the day he asked the medical orderlies casually if they knew where Loftus was – just to check if he was being bamboozled again.

The newspaper map of the Russian front could not conceal the Wehrmacht victories, and he chatted cheerfully on the first day of September about how well the war was going – meaning, for the Führer.

Loftus returned, lunched with him, but made no mention of the document. For a day, the prisoner nose-dived.

2 September 1941   [Orderly's report]

At times was noticed to be talking to himself.

[Afternoon:] Solitary and moody in manner, and declines conversation. Little interest in his surroundings . . . when spoken to, has been slightly retarded in answering and often the phrase has had to be repeated as though his thoughts have been occupied elsewhere. Occupied his time vacantly staring at the walls and windows, and has been noticed to mutter silently and grimace with facial expressions of surprise, understanding and disgust.

3 September 1941   [Commandant's diary]

"Z" in a very depressed state. The medical orderlies report that they are very nervous of his present condition which is verging on the suicidal again.

The orderlies, however, were now affected by almost the same prison psychosis as their charge. When Hess sighed loudly on the evening of the 3rd, they ponderously recorded that he "made several sharp agitated movements and [has] blown hard, exhaling a deep breath". More humanly, on the following afternoon, 4 September, they found him "full of complaints", but put this down to the heat.

That day there had in fact been an unexpected intrusion into his solitary life – a letter from a leading Conservative member of Churchill's government: on 1 September, Lord Beaverbrook, now Minister of Supply, had written to the Deputy Führer, recalled that they had met in Hitler's Chancellery a few years before, and suggested that they renew their acquaintance. "So," concluded Beaverbrook's letter, "if this is convenient to you, perhaps you could tell me where and when you would like the meeting to take place." (Over the where and when, of course, the prisoner had little say.)

Beaverbrook's motives are, even now, indeterminate. Had the initiative come from him or Churchill?

One of the liveliest members of Churchill's entourage, he had the streak of anti-Semitism that characterized many high Tories. Three times he had met Hitler and come away with a lasting admiration of him; the transcripts of their talks fell into British hands in 1945, and were probably destroyed along with many another uncomfortable relic of pre-war follies. Born in Canada, Beaverbrook was a profound believer in the empire, and had warned until the very eve of war that Churchill's policies would prosper only its enemies Japan and the Soviet Union. As will shortly be seen, he had met the Duke of Hamilton in Scotland while flying out to Newfoundland for Churchill's conference with Roosevelt in mid-August: they *must* have talked about Hess.

On 1 September, the date of his oddly phrased letter to Hess, Lord Beaverbrook had been appointed to head a Cabinet mission to Moscow to discuss aid for the Soviets. On the following day he telephoned a rather surprised Cadogan and asked him to tell the Foreign Secretary that Churchill wanted the meeting with Hess.

That is all that is known of the background. Hess replied in his copybook handwriting on the 4th.

Dear Lord Beaverbrook,

    Thank you for your friendly note of the 1st. inst., which I received to-day.

    I well remember our meeting in Berlin and shall be happy to be able to see you again.

    I am assuming that the talk will be of an unofficial character and is thus to take place without witnesses. I think my English is adequate for this. Otherwise I should have to ask to be allowed to bring in a German witness.

      Sincerely,

      Rudolf Hess

The meeting was arranged for the 9th. Over the intervening days, Hess went into a bizarre and inexplicable condition which Captain Johnston, the Camp Z doctor, believed was similar to the panic that had preceded the Deputy Führer's interview in June with Lord Simon. It may have had more mundane causes – the racket created by building workmen setting up a Nissen hut next to the house, for Camp Z's inside staff, and the twice-weekly 8 a.m. Guards parades with their shouted commands and stamping feet, to name just two. The orderlies found him cheerful but "distract-able" on the 5th, and detected hallucinatory movements – sharply breaking off conversations to look at the wall, then resuming his talk. Johnston, years later, suggested that the panic lasted until Beaverbrook's arrival, but the contemporary record shows that Hess's malaise was over within one day.

There are signs of "window dressing" by MI6, now that Hess was to receive a powerful visitor. On 6 September Major Foley told Scott that his superiors had decided that Hess was to be allowed to listen to a radio after all – for the first time in four months. Foley rented one in Aldershot, and by that evening it was in full blast in the prisoner's room – tuned in to Berlin's broadcasts, which Hess believed more reliable than the BBC.

6 September 1941 [Orderly's report]

Patient was very disturbed and said he felt very weak. Lay in bed staring at the ceiling for about twenty minutes after lunch and had no interest in his surroundings.

Seems very pleased with having the wireless. Interested in the German commentary of the Leningrad front and became excited translating it into English for attendants.

6 September 1941 [Commandant's diary]

"Z" seems more cheerful. . . . "Z" seemed very agitated over the prospective visit by "B" who has requested to see him. "Z" says it will be impossible in his "present state".

7 September 1941 [Orderly's report]

He then heard a programme from Germany which he appeared to enjoy, and spent a fair part of the morning writing, and read the *Sunday Times* for a short time.

8 September 1941 [Commandant's diary]

The doctor was called at 05.00 hrs to "Z" who complained of great pain in the gall bladder and asked for morphia. The doctor gave him a small injection and he slept most of the morning. He refused all meals and only ate biscuits all day. The anticipation of his coming interview with "B" seems a possible cause of his agitation which takes exactly the same form as his condition previous to [Lord Simon's] visit.

Against this alarming version, rendered no doubt by the doctor to Colonel Scott, must be set that of the orderlies keeping Hess under surveillance on the same day:

> [Hess] enjoyed the radio programmes and was very pleased to hear the German news that Leningrad had been surrounded by the Axis troops. Has been much brighter this afternoon.
>
> Conversed with [the night] attendant on taking over, about the encirclement of Leningrad. Cheerful in conversation, but attitude and facial expression denoted one of depression and solitary [*sic*], with little interest in social life.

Armed with the prescribed Military Permit signed by Cadogan, describing him as "Dr Livingstone", a medical practitioner visiting Camp Z to conduct a medical examination, Beaverbrook was escorted up into the bedroom which had been Hess's private world for three months now, and was left alone with him. Concealed microphones passed every word to the listening MI6 unit.

The transcript later sent to Beaverbrook is marked No. 98, so nearly every conversation since Hess arrived at Mytchett Place must have been transcribed, and we can only surmise what has prevented the release of the transcripts to researchers – it can hardly be their historical content. Possibly they would reveal evidence of the interrogation under narcosis which Lord Beaverbrook later suspected had impaired the prisoner's brain.

"How well your English has improved," opened the Cabinet Minister, flattering the Deputy Führer.

Hess modestly responded, "A little."

"A lot! You remember the last time we talked in the Chancellery in Berlin . . . in your office, and you were understanding everything in English?"

Hess had understood him, yes.

"Well," continued Beaverbrook, "we've come to a bad pass. . . . I was very much against the war."

"Me too!"

"I regretted it greatly. . . . The world is in terrible trouble. Little things beget big consequences and they roll on most majestically, and there's no stopping them at all."

For a while Beaverbrook spoke of his amazement at finding himself, a newspaper magnate, brought into Churchill's Cabinet in May 1940 and put in charge of making warplanes, guns and ammunition. Hess laughed nervously, but did not venture any comments yet. He appears to have felt awkward. Besides, it forced Beaverbrook to do the talking. Hess told him his leg had taken twelve weeks to get better.

"Twelve weeks! That's a long run."

"A long run," agreed the prisoner. "A long run for a man above all who cannot get any visitors. If I were in Germany there'd come my wife, my son and my aunt and my friends." Here he had no friends, he added, and asked Beaverbrook to get permission for the Duke of Hamilton to come, "The only man who is, so to say – so to speak, a friend of mine, even though I don't know him very well."

"I saw him on the airfield the other day up in the north," admitted Beaverbrook. "I flew out to America from one of the Scottish airfields."

This elicited the information that in the early days of aviation, when Kohl and Fitzmaurice had first flown the Atlantic from east to west, Hess had wanted to make the crossing too. "But I didn't get the engine. . . . Today it is much easier."

To Beaverbrook, who had made the crossing to Newfoundland in the bomb-bay of a bomber, the word "easier" must have seemed out of place.

"Is that the radio you have over there?"

"Since two days," said Hess. "A long time, twelve weeks, no radio!"

"They don't give you the conveniences you want?"

"No, surely not," said Hess with a rueful laugh. "For five weeks I didn't get any newspapers. . . . Perhaps you can tell me why." He was sure that if he had not jumped over the bannisters, he would not be getting the newspapers even now. Beaverbrook asked about the food, and Hess assured him, "The food is all right, yes. The serving is very good."

Beaverbrook confided that he liked an occasional glass of German wine, and Hess ventured the hope that in two or three years the British could get German wines again. And so they edged towards the real purpose of his mission.

"I don't know," said the British Minister, "what is going to be the course of events at all. It's not a situation that I can contemplate at all . . . about what's going to happen —"

"— And it is very, very dangerous to play what England plays these days with Bolshevism," interjected Hess, aware from the newspapers that a few days later his visitor would be face to face with Stalin. "Very dangerous. . . . If you have in a short time complications [links] between Bolshevist women and English women, between Bolshevist work organizations and English work organizations, that must have results."

Fishing for things he could say to Stalin, Beaverbrook said, "I can't myself tell why the Germans attacked Russia."

"Because we knew that one day the Russians will attack us. And it will be good not only for Germany and the whole of Europe, it will be good for England too if Russia will be defeated."

Hess interpolated that he knew only what he read about Soviet armaments, but since the Wehrmacht had now destroyed the Dniepr River dam much of the Soviet war industry must be without electric power.

"It's hard", persisted Beaverbrook, "to see why Germany, engaged in such a universal war elsewhere, should turn to fight Russia. . . . I would have thought that Germany would have said, 'First of all we must finish the war with England.'"

"But we had been sure that Russia would attack us before that. It's quite logical." Admittedly, continued Hess, the Soviets had announced several years before that they were abandoning their attempt at staging a Bolshevik world revolution, but "It cannot be true."

Beaverbrook told him he was not looking forward to his trip to Moscow – he would rather be journeying across Europe, or living in his ranch in the south of France. Hess told him of his memorandum about Germany, Britain and the Russian war, and offered him a copy in German.

"I'd like to have it very, very much," said Beaverbrook. "I make no concealment of my views at all. My political opinions are what they *were!*" – and he launched into a speech about how well the British were faring in war. "The war has uplifted them. The war has strengthened them."

Hess responded that the same went for the Germans, and that the heavier the raids on the cities, the stronger the people became.

"You can't tell", observed Beaverbrook, "what will be the outcome of it all."

Bolshevism could only become stronger, persisted Hess. Given Russia's raw materials and manpower reserves, they must end as a world power to rival the British. Hess was sure that the United States would one day formally enter the war.

Beaverbrook asked why the war had broken out, and revealing his own sentiments he reminisced: "The war came so swiftly. . . . I think that Chamberlain, who was Prime Minister, would honestly have liked to escape it." The Canadian paused, and added with the blunt tactlessness that endeared him to his friends, "It's rather beside the point, what made war break out, anyway! It's rather like asking a man, 'What made you fall downstairs?' isn't it!"

Hess had recently been correcting the transcript of his interview with Lord Simon, and invited Beaverbrook to read it now. "It is here in the drawer," he said. "If you would be so kind: the second drawer at the right."

As his visitor browsed through the pages, they talked of the Battle of Britain and the quality of the RAF pilots. "The English airmen are very good," said Beaverbrook, and Hess, who had come up against them in the Great War, agreed. "But I think the German pilots [are air-minded] too."

"You know my views on the Germans," said Beaverbrook.

"You have the best men, and we have the best men: and one kill other, and I think for nothing."

Beaverbrook passed only a few comments on the Simon interview. When the Polish Foreign Minister Beck came to Britain before the war, he told Hess, "he would not deal with Churchill at all." They assumed that Beck was under Hitler's influence.

As for the French: "No spirit left."

"They ran!" cackled the Deputy Führer, explaining, "Communist influence, Marxist influence!"

Turning to Churchill's 1940 plan to invade Norway, Beaverbrook revealed: "[His] nephew who was at Narvik – he was on my newspaper. . . . Giles Romilly, a left-wing socialist. Churchill never took a great view of his politics!"

They both chuckled loudly.

"When you came to England," resumed the Cabinet Minister, "I went down to Churchill's room in Downing Street and he showed me the photograph, and said, 'Who's that?' And I said, 'Hess!'"

Hess laughed delightedly, picturing the scene: "He didn't believe it at first."

"I didn't either!" said Beaverbrook.

"I was the Minister of Information," he said, talking of the World War, and when Hess remarked that the Nazis had learned a lot from Britain's propaganda effort then, Beaverbrook, who had laboured mightily to get Duff Cooper replaced, joked, "I hope you won't take anything from it *this* war."

"One day," Hess said with a smile, "I heard that a bomb had fallen on your Ministry of Propaganda, and I told them, 'That is wrong . . . you have not to bomb our *ally!*'"

Trying to prise out of the prisoner some clue about future Nazi strategy, Beaverbrook touched lightly on Hitler's campaigns in Yugoslavia, Greece and Crete. "I can't understand why he went to Yugoslavia. I can't understand why he went to Greece. Since he went to Greece, I can't understand why he did not go on from Crete to Cyprus – to Syria!"

"Oh, it's not so easy," Hess rebuked him, laughing. "You have a fleet . . ."

"Airborne power was perfect there," his visitor pointed out, and reminded him of the German paratroop assault on Crete – "One of the stories of history." He dipped for a while longer into the Lord Simon transcript. "I was in Berlin the day of Hitler's election," he said after a while. "Of course, you may know, my newspapers always gave him a good hearing."

"I know," said Hess. "I know you had seen, together with Hitler, a film concerning the last war. The Führer told me you had been very impressed, and he himself [saw] a germ of ending by [attaining] an understanding."

"I saw him three times all told," reminisced the Canadian.

"Oh," Hess flattered him, "I know he likes you very much."

Beaverbrook reflected. "The whole thing is bloody," he said quietly.

"Yes, the whole thing is bloody," agreed Hess, picking up that word. "But we can use our blood for better things. You can use your blood in your colonies and for your empire, and we can use our blood for the east."

The Cabinet Minister allowed himself a non-committal grunt.

"I thought", said the Deputy Führer, "I can come here and find here a certain – common sense. I have been wrong. I know it."

"Once you get into the blood and the guns and the sacrifices, then reason goes."

"But nevertheless I thought that some leading men would have common sense enough to say, 'Why continue to fight? . . . It is not necessary.'"

"The difficulty is that when you make such a declaration, you let down the fighting spirit of your own people." Beaverbrook launched into a complicated rationale, lost himself in his own reasoning, and started again: "When two nations fight, it's very difficult to disentangle [them]. . . . There is the morale of the people that you've got to keep at a high pitch . . . all the time. And if you ever disturb the morale of your people, you do something which is really dangerous, don't you?" He did not understand what he was trying to say himself, and Hess fared no better. "I wish," the Canadian continued, "I could see what is going on . . . find some way to penetrate the mists. Everywhere seems to be gloom." Allowing perhaps a glimpse of his own forebodings, Beaverbrook then remarked, "The Russian campaign has gone on much longer than I expected."

"Yes," agreed Hess. The Germans had probably expected victory there before now, but Stalin had been quietly arming all along – "to be ready one day to start the war". He shrewdly added, speaking of the Russians, "They fight well, because the spirit of the people has been uplifted."

Promising to return, Beaverbrook left Hess – whom he never saw again. Hess wished him well for his forthcoming journey to the Kremlin.

12   On Strike

Rudolf Hess would remain at Camp Z, near Aldershot, until the late spring of 1942. The fortress mansion took on a more permanent look; the wire and camouflage within the perimeter fence were thickened, armoured glass was ordered, the padlocks replaced with Yale locks on the outside. To the prisoner's chagrin, only the Military Policeman outside the grille had the key, so even after he was up and about he was confined to an enclosed cage, though with somewhat more liberty than before.

Evidently in a half-hearted attempt to re-educate Hess for future propaganda usage, just as thousands of other more malleable Germans would be re-educated in special centres like Wilton Park during later years, his captors gave him eye-witness reports of German concentration camps to read, and a lurid book by a former Austrian on the same subject. Hess read the book with indignation and remarked that the writer had made no mention of how Kurt von Schuschnigg's regime had thrown thousands of Austrian Nazis into "arrest camps" where they were killed or maltreated. Those languishing in Hitler's concentration camps, the Deputy Führer pointed out, were without exception common criminals or Communists.

"Wherever Communism has been in power," wrote Hess on 18 September, "it has established as a principle the most dreadful terror accompanied by the most bestial tortures." The brutal Communist regimes that had ruled not only in Russia but in Germany, Hungary, Spain and more recently in the Baltic states had treated political opponents, intellectuals and those of higher breeding with methods that made the German camps, in his opinion, look like "convalescent homes". He described the well-documented atrocities committed by Béla Kun's short-lived Soviet republic in Hungary after the World War, particularly against the Catholic clergy, and added, "I am sorry to say Jews were nearly always responsible." Britain, argued Hess, with her record in Ireland, India and Palestine, had no right to accuse. "Germany", he innocently claimed, after referring once more to Britain's measures in the Boer War, "has never sent women and children to concentration camps."

He did, however, promise: "When I return to Germany I shall cause an investigation to be made . . . as to whether subordinates [*Unterführer*] did in fact behave as described, without the knowledge and against the will of the leadership."

Camp Z abandoned any idea of re-educating this stubborn intellect.

Something of the complexity of Hess's case becomes evident from the records of the medical orderlies in daily attendance on him, but only if the scrutiny is dispassionate.

By any standard he was, by the autumn of 1942, an emotionally disturbed man, but much of the distress was in the eye of the beholder: six orderlies kept him under round-the-clock surveillance, but only two or three of them – repeatedly and repetitively – recorded these symptoms, while the others, equally skilled in observation, evidently noticed nothing. The daily reports were written in government-style logbooks, so that each could read the observations of his predecessor if he chose. After a while, a certain similarity in the descriptions settled in.

It was the same when Hess began to complain of severe stomach disorders. The doctor occasionally "humoured him", but more often dismissed them as of hysterical origin, although it is plain from other sources that Hess had suffered from these disorders long before his flight, and they were moreover a predictable consequence for a man who has taken only homeopathic medicines and who has kept to a natural diet of unprocessed and organically grown foods all his life and finds himself obliged to eat the standard diet of a British officers' mess furnished, it turned out, with the most inferior beef and the poorest cook that Aldershot could supply.

Nor, it must be said, was Captain Munro Johnston the kind of doctor who could diagnose a real internal complaint with any certainty: as he had himself pointed out, he was a psychiatrist and not a general practitioner. When the Commandant Colonel Scott fell ill with shingles in mid-October 1941, he did not entrust himself to Camp Z's own "doctor" but called in Colonel D. E. Bedford of the RAMC instead.

Hess tried to get comfortable, but three months in a plaster cast were not conducive to rest or repose. The orderlies adjusted the pulleys and bed, he tried lying flat and at various angles, but none provided the sleep he craved. He avoided the food when he could, allowing himself a milk pudding, or nibbling at biscuits and sipping camomile tea.

He did not look forward to Saturdays because that was when the army psychiatrist Major Dicks usually arrived at the double gates, showed his pass, and was escorted through the grille into the upstairs bedroom. Dicks had now become convinced that Hess was going to inflict violence on him; the feeling was mutual. On 14 September the Commandant noted with amusement that Dicks saw "Z" after lunch "but was not exactly welcomed with open arms". Corporal Riddle observed the prisoner afterwards with a "morbid & miserable expression", staring into a corner of the wall.

On the 15th Hess asked Major Foley to have him moved from Camp Z to a quieter neighbourhood, away from the perpetual noise of machine-gun fire and poorly muffled engines of the adjacent Military Police motorcyclist school.

That evening, the surgeon Major Murray at last removed the splint from Hess's leg – and lectured Hess, who had believed in his innocence that he could get up immediately and sit in a normal chair, that he would be confined to bed for at least four more weeks.

He had now prepared for Beaverbrook an updated list of the violations to which he believed he had been subjected by Dicks and Foley, added the more recent improvements – a door-stop had at last been fixed to the banging front door by the end of September – and included his two-page denial that, so far as he knew, the Gestapo used the methods imputed to it by enemy propaganda. (Atkinson-Clark's sneered remark, "We are treating you the way the Gestapo treats people in Germany!", still rankled.) As in all Camp Z documents, Hess's references to Lord Simon, Lord Beaverbrook and "Cabinet ministers" were blanked out. The document was typed on a little typewriter that the camp officials had now provided for him. Once again he asked for a top-level inquiry into the actions of the three men at Camp Z whom he blamed for disturbing the balance of his mind. "Gradually," he stated in this, "Dr Dicks, Major Foley and Lieutenant-Colonel Wallace made it a practice to try to suggest to me that all my troubles were due to a psychosis." In handwriting he added, "After my arrival in Scotland I appealed to the chivalry of the King of England. I know that he issued orders to secure my safety and to take care of my health."

For the next six weeks, the letters were detained by the secret service; it would be November before Lord Beaverbrook was enabled to see them.

Meanwhile Hess's health went through its now routine crises:

19 September 1941 [Commandant's diary]

"Z" quite cheerful and in a good mood. . . . After dinner "Z" & the D.O. [duty officer] listened to the news together and "Z" commented on the figures of casualties as claimed by the Russian command – saying that the German High Command were most meticulous in reporting the correct figures. [On this date the OKW communiqué had admitted 85,896 dead; the Russians were claiming to have killed one and a half to two million Germans already.]

20 September 1941

"Z" called for the doctor three times during the night, complaining of agonies in gall bladder. The doctor says that his temperature is normal and also his pulse – that in his opinion the pains are entirely imaginary and are an excuse for not receiving visitors, such as Major Dicks who frequently comes down on a Saturday.

During the following days the orderly Lance-Corporal Riddle

perceived him as a patient severely disturbed mentally, as his vivid reports show:

24 September 1941   [Corporal Riddle's afternoon report]

Patient very depressed, does not converse, or take any interest in his surroundings. Content in lying flat in bed & makes no attempt to help himself. Breathing appears easy & normal, but groans at convenient times & expression shows self pitying, with feeble attempts to help his own requirements.

Visited by Major Foley at 16.15 hrs & visited by Capt. Johnston at 17.30 hrs. . . . Still complains of severe pain round the hepatitic region of abdomen. A tepid sponging was suggested to make him feel more cheerful but it was declined & [he] said he did not want to feel more cheerful as the pains may become more acute.

Soup only taken for dinner. Constantly groaning while having it, but at periods stopped & gazed into the corners of the room & lifting his head at times as though looking at something. Often uses phrases in German, & asks questions which are in conjunction with ailment. Asked, had he got a fever because he feels hot & said he can't perspire because the room is stuffy & when answers are given he just says, "Maybe."

25 September 1941   [Corporal Riddle's morning report]

Patient . . . states there is little change in condition & his inside feels red raw & on fire.

26 September 1941   [Corporal Riddle's afternoon report]

Restless & very agitated, depressed & moody. Asked for windows to be opened & a few moments afterwards close them; rubber ring be given, then doesn't require it; sits up & then down. Constantly groaning & gesticulating, but if spoken to or attempted to do something for him, this expression ceases for a few moments. Complained of severe pains again & asked for M.O. ⅓ Atapon injected at 15.55 hrs. States it has no effect. . . .

Continues to gesticulate & groan with facial expression of complete misery. After attendant suggesting the wireless to release his thoughts he listened for a short period but soon became uninterested. . . .

Observes the attendant in a sly manner. At one instance he quietly moved the bed clothes off him & looked conspicuously at the attendant to see if any notice was being taken.

All this was duly reported to the Commandant. " 'Z' still in a difficult mood," wrote Colonel Scott on the 27th. "He kept his doctor on the run last night . . . made himself a perfect nuisance to the orderlies." And on the next day: " 'Z' was quiet, and said he was exhausted after all the pain he had suffered yesterday."

Was he play-acting, and if so why? On the 29th the orderlies found him solitary and moody, "staring at the walls with definite facial expressions".

On this occasion, however, we have a remarkable proof of his logical thought-processes. The orderly reported that Hess "wrote a letter". The text of that letter has survived: whatever happened to it in British Censorship channels – several lines were blacked out before it reached Germany – we know not only what the letter said, but also what it *meant*.

The letter, to Professor Fritz Gerl,* one of Hess's coterie of expert friends, appeared innocent, but within its opening paragraphs was concealed a hidden message.

England, 29 September 1941

Dear Professor,

You can imagine how often, here with "your Englishmen", I think of you. I'm just curious how long I'll keep like this, thinking of you instead of having you before me, with both of us talking about the English again!

I wonder what progress you've made with your various discoveries and inventions in the medical field? I am as hugely interested as ever, as you know, in the thing Dr Gähmann helped you with. Perhaps [Alfred] Leitgen [Hess's adjutant] could give you a hand with it? . . .

As you may have heard from Frau Bread** my stomach has made such welcome progress that it doesn't need a diet any longer. Nevertheless these last few days – despite all my expectations – I had another attack, this time definitely originating in the right kidney. For the first time there were asthma-like symptoms too. As I know that your thyroid [*Schilddrüsen*] treatment has produced positive results especially with asthma I have finally decided, as soon as I return, to start your treatment – of which I hereby give notice. So even though that may be a long time off, reserve a place for me now. . . .

After a few lines blanked out by the censor, the letter concluded, "Please give my folks a ring and tell them I'm getting on all right, apart from a little relapse into the old ailment. I'm looking forward to seeing you, and healthier than ever I hope, whenever that may be! *Heil* Hitler! Your old R.H."

Months would pass before Professor Gerl received the letter at his home in the mountains of Allgäu, southern Germany. He wrote an anxious explanation to the chief of the SS, Heinrich Himmler, providing "marginal comments" to enable him to understand "the true meaning of the letter", and hinting that the letter should be shown to the Führer. The second paragraph had nothing to do, in fact, with "medical progress", but concerned weapons for use against Britain. "The Dr Gähmann that is mentioned is not a doctor at all, but an engineer whom I visited Hess with

* See p. 32.
** In the Hess family code, he was "*Brotherr*", literally "breadwinner"; Frau Bread thus presumably his wife. He had written to her in July 1941 about his "self-imposed dieting" and mentioned that "Reuther of Munich" had enabled him to eat anything without precautions.

to brief him on new means of sinking ships." Gerl explained that the particular weapon that interested Hess was a combined anti-shipping bomb and mine.

If the paragraph had any deeper significance, it was a broad hint by Hess that the Führer should continue with the blockade of Britain's ports and shipping lanes. Annotations on the letter show that Himmler forwarded it to Reinhard Heydrich, chief of the Gestapo, and Martin Bormann, who had replaced Hess as head of the Nazi Party.

For the first time in months he was allowed a dentist. Captain J. M. Barnes of the Army Dental Corps tended him on 30 September, the day after the prisoner wrote his cunning letter, and told Colonel Scott afterwards that there was so much gold in the bridges and crowns of Hess's mouth that his jaw was "worth a small fortune". More clinically, Barnes recorded afterwards, "General condition of the mouth is good," but added, "Exceptional development and size of the mandible is shown, comparable to the 'Heidelberg' man." Commenting on Hess's protruding upper teeth, Barnes noted: "There is marked protrusion of the maxilla, to such an extent that the lower incisors press into the gum behind the upper incisors when the teeth are in centric conclusion."*

A couple of days later, before the dentist returned to complete the job, Hess sent for Captain Johnston and gave him his word that he would not make a further suicide attempt if he could be allowed the use of a proper meat-knife, glass and china tea-cup. Johnston evidently considered him stable enough, and agreed, while reserving the right to withdraw the privilege without notice. It was probably Hess's way of testing his own status. On 7 October, Colonel Scott noticed that he had written another formal protest to Lord Beaverbrook, asking now for the removal of the wire grille and other restrictions to his movement, and – more reasonably – that his German money should be returned to him, exchanged for English currency, to enable him to purchase whatever he liked. (The request was denied: Hess's messing costs continued to be met partly by the Foreign Office and partly by subscription between the Guards officers themselves, who also had to share their food ration cards with him as he had no British ration card of his own.)

Hess practised his studied lack of interest with extraordinary consistency. On 9 October the newspapers announced that his father had died; Major Foley brought him the news. Foley told the Commandant afterwards, "He appeared to be quite unmoved." (In fact we know from other sources that the news upset Hess badly.)

* Hugh Thomas, one of Hess's later prison doctors, would argue ingeniously in *The Murder of Rudolf Hess* (London, 1979) that the Rudolf Hess in Spandau prison was an impostor. I requested the Allied authorities at Spandau in 1987 to compare the 1941 dental chart with the current records of the prisoner. None of them could comply. Colonel William L. Priddy of the US Army's Dental Corps, responsible for Hess's dental care, wrote regretting that he had been unable to obtain permission to release "any dental information regarding Prisoner number seven".

It would be fair to say that Hess had half-won the MI6 officer's affection. The Major wrote that day, 9 October, to his superiors, forwarding the prisoner's latest letter of protest about conditions at Camp Z, and adding that he shared Hess's criticisms. This camp was quite unsuitable for "Z" 's exercise, he said. More importantly, Foley asked for a ruling on the Deputy Führer's precise status: because, if he was a prisoner of war, the Geneva Convention was being contravened by detaining him in a camp surrounded by military objectives. Foley wanted Hess moved to a quieter part of the country so that they could lift the oppressively close confinement on him. Meanwhile, he had arranged for the lightweight typewriter to be supplied for Hess's use, and, because the prisoner found that his eyes tired too easily when using it, Foley arranged for an oculist to come and supply two badly needed pairs of reading glasses for him. It was Foley too who obtained a clothing allowance, because soon Hess would be out of bed and would need new shoes.

Hess in turn developed a soft spot for Foley. "He was an older gentleman and very nice," he recalled after the war. "When he was transferred later and said goodbye to me, tears came to his eyes."

Hess still expected to be returned to Germany, as his private letters showed. "He firmly believes", Desmond Morton had written in a sniggering note to Churchill on 28 July, "that the Government will one day wish to send him back to Germany with an offer of peace terms."

In fact an even more rigorous confinement was about to begin. The entire leadership of the army's Directorate of Prisoners of War had resigned in mid-September and neither the new Director Major-General E. C. Gepp nor his deputy Colonel P. K. Boulnois showed any inclination to render to Hess the courtesies to which he believed himself entitled.

"Bullnose" Boulnois told his fellow officers that he "took a poor view" of Hess – not least because Will Thorne, a left-wing Member of Parliament, had just alleged that Rudolf Hess was living a life of luxury somewhere at the British taxpayers' expense. On the afternoon of 11 October Colonel Boulnois arrived with the psychiatrist Colonel Rees at Camp Z, and after a heads-together conference with Foley and the doctor clumped up the stairs to see Hess. The prisoner was in a state of suppressed excitement over Hitler's great new victories in Russia, and stuck out a happy hand which the Colonel had no option but to accept.

Boulnois disagreed with virtually everything about Camp Z. In particular he frowned on Johnston's having relaxed the restrictions on eating utensils. "I very much resent", he snapped as he marched downstairs, "having had to shake hands with a murderer!" He demanded to be shown Camp Z's defences, since the War Office still anticipated that Polish, French, Canadian or even German assassins might try to take revenge on Hess. To the furtive pleasure of Camp Z's "inside staff", at Post B he fell headlong into a hidden pit. With the help of two soldiers, the adjutant raised the beetroot-faced Colonel to the surface. Wiping the slime from his tunic, the Colonel told Captain Ashworth – standing in that day for Scott – that he considered the camp vulnerable to tank attack. He ordered a snap "alert". A klaxon honked and bells sounded: every defence post was manned within four minutes and twelve seconds. The Colonel drove off, proclaiming himself satisfied.

Oblivious of Colonel Boulnois's displeasure, Hess wrote manuscripts, pecked at the typewriter, tuned the radio to German stations and cheerfully explained the Nazi bulletins to Corporal Everatt. He routinely complained about noise made by contractors erecting more Nissen huts to house the 130 troops now guarding Camp Z, and wondered what the hammering was coming from the next room. "Have they taken the grilles away from outside the windows?" he asked Private Dawkins innocently. (In fact army workmen had begun installing armoured glass.) On the 13th he was surprised to hear a loud voice cutting into the BBC news bulletins – the latest Nazi propaganda ploy. "That is pointless," he told the medical orderly. "That will have no effect on the British people."

At other times he resumed what is best called his performance:

17 October 1941   [Commandant's diary]

Capt. Johnston went on 10 days' leave and his place was taken by Lieut. McGlade R.A.M.C.

"Z" started the day by complaining of the noise caused by the "wind tunnel" at Farnborough Aerodrome [where the Royal Aeronautical Establishment was housed]. Major Foley assured him that this had not been ordered as a form of persecution but was equally disturbing to all the officers. "Z" then said that he was still further convinced that this camp had been specially chosen by H.M. G[overnment] because it *was* adjacent to permanent noises of this nature in order to add to his distress.

17 October 1941   [Orderly's night report]

Reading until 00.30 hrs, but during this time he was attracted to the walls and was noticed to have a complete smile on face several times, but as soon as observed by attendant expression would turn to very stern, and become as though confused in finding what next to do.

He was now able to sit in a chair for two hours at a time. On 19 October he received the first letter from abroad since his flight to Scotland – from an aunt in Switzerland. Two days later, a second letter arrived, this time from his four-year-old son Wolf Rüdiger. He seemed very depressed after reading these childish lines. The orderlies saw him stop reading that afternoon, lay the book aside and become very quiet. "He appeared to be deep in thought, and was muttering to himself – but later he began to read again." Two nights later, the orderly thought that his grimacing and articulations were becoming more prominent – "actions appear to be as though trying to ignore or disbelieve imaginary voices."

But then the prisoner heard on his little radio the Wehrmacht fanfares and victorious communiqués from the eastern front, as two million more Russian troops went into captivity. The fighting in the east was over, he was sure. Hitler announced that he was going to turn against Britain.

On 23 October, Hess picked up his pen and wrote this letter to the one man in Britain whom he could trust to halt this madness:

Dear Lord Beaverbrook,
   The event I have been foreboding all along his now come about. As I heard on the German news service, the Führer – most certainly acting in conformity with his Axis partner – has publicly announced that the war will be fought out to a clear victory.
   I know the Führer too well not to know what that signifies. As tenaciously as he adhered earlier – year after year, despite all his negative experiences – to the idea of reconciliation, he will now adhere to his new resolve. That means a fight to the death!
   I set out in my paper of September 6, 1941 why I am convinced of the outcome of such a fight. You will understand that my confidence in victory has not diminished since the decisive defeats suffered by the Bolsheviks.
   I am nevertheless not happy about this turn of events. I admit quite frankly that to this day I have not given up hope that sound common sense will return to Britain and that ultimately a reconciliation will take place between our two nations.
   But the Führer could not do more than he has already done – again and again stretching out his hand. For my own part, I have staked everything! Evidently it was not to be.
         Sincerely,
         Rudolf Hess

It was 1 November before the Foreign Office forwarded this letter with the earlier Hess documents of "evidence and protest" to Beaverbrook. "I need hardly say", wrote Sir Alexander Cadogan, the Permanent Under-Secretary, "that Hess's accusations that we have been deliberately maltreating him are without the slightest foundation. Though his condition varies considerably from day to day, he is suffering from a marked form of paranoia and some of his delusions have become a complete obsession."

The secret service had met the psychiatrists Rees and Johnston in a room at the Foreign Office on 29 October 1941, to discuss what to do with Hess.

The installation of armoured glass throughout his quarters was nearly complete, and he had been moved into the former sitting room which was more cheerful and bright. But sooner or later he would have to be allowed downstairs, where he would be permitted to walk in the outer kitchen garden, and Colonel Scott was directed to observe the effect on him when he saw the additional security measures introduced everywhere. The question of his long-term status was as indeterminate when the meeting ended as when it began, although Major-General Gepp had been called in as Director of Prisoners of War. He was asked to find a new location, where Hess could get more exercise, and there was some discussion on obtaining "a companion for Z" – meaning a genuine German, rather than the stool-pigeons that MI6 had provided.

There was a brief discussion of the prisoner's medical treatment. Colonel Rees was eager to try electro-convulsive therapy, but when he explained to "C" and the others present what it involved, they were appalled at the political risks involved if anything went wrong. "Higher Authority", they decided, "[is] to be asked as to advisability of drastic electrical treatment as suggested by Col. Rees."

Aerial photographs were taken of Camp Z to test its camouflage. The old slit trench on the lower lawn was still clearly visible.

The trees had lost all their leaves now, opening up fresh vistas to the imprisoned Hess. But his sense of loneliness increased. His father was dead, and he had sensed how the officers attempted to use the news to cause his nerves to collapse – even the sensitive young Captain Percival, whose own father, a former royal chaplain, had just died. But he kept a stiff upper lip: he could not betray any undue emotions. A few days later Foley, Percival and the doctor went to Aldershot to buy him shoes; they came back with a fine pair that had cost thirty-seven shillings and sixpence. Forgetting himself for a moment, Hess climbed out of bed, half dressed and, as the orderly wrote, "gave a display of his walking with them on and his supports".

The orderlies kept him under continued observation, noting down every time he moved his lips, appeared to be muttering or laughing to himself. On the day after the Foreign Office conference, one corporal wrote, "Smiles appeared on his face, and lips were moving as though talking to someone." Hess tried to walk on crutches, but he soon tired and slumped into a chair.

To his orderlies he may have appeared to spend his days staring into the corner, but when it came to his rights as a prisoner he had all his faculties about him. The new room looked out over the road, where motorbikes roared up and down all day long. He had observed the new defences and the very restricted exercise area – reduced even more, now that the autumn trees were bare, because of the ease with which the house and lawn could be observed from the road.

Until now, Hess had suffered his real and imaginary humiliations in silence. "I did not choose the official channels for my protest", he later explained, "because . . . I wished to spare the Führer the knowledge of my plight. After coming to England on my own initiative and thus being responsible for my own position, I wished to get out of it on my own." But since no reply had come from Lord Beaverbrook, on 3 November he wrote formally to the Swiss Consul asking him as representative of the Protecting Power – Switzerland – to visit.

England, 3 November 1941

Your Excellency, I should be grateful if you would visit me in your capacity as representative of the Protecting Power of nationals of the German Reich in Britain.

 Yours, etc.,
  Rudolf Hess

Three days later, Hess wrote a second letter asking the consul to bring a rubber stamp and official seal for a legal document. These two letters, like all the others, were forwarded by Foley through "C" – head of the Secret Service – to the Foreign Office (the two letters that Hess had so far been allowed to receive had followed the same route in reverse). For some weeks he received no reply. On 20 November Hess typed a letter in identical terms to the Swiss Consul, and on this occasion he made Major Foley sign a receipt for it, and secured Captain Percival's signature as a witness. When this too produced no reply, Hess five days later wrote demanding either a formal receipt from the "competent authority", confirming that they had forwarded his letters to the Swiss, or an explanation for why they were being withheld.

In Germany, he had become a non-person. While accepting, in confidential circulars, that he had undertaken his mission from the highest possible motives, the Party authorities had ordered his name removed from all history books, calendars and other publications. On 13 June Goebbels had decreed that Hess's photograph be removed from the walls of office buildings and schools. Streets named after him were renamed.

Despite this Hess remained stable for most of November 1941. He sent for Major Foley and spent the greater part of the afternoon of the 10th with him. Colonel Scott recorded on the 11th that "Z" was improving physically as well as, apparently, mentally.

12 November 1941   [Orderly's report)

. . . was very amused at the news item on the radio concerning him [Churchill had mentioned him maliciously in a speech] and just passed it off as so much propaganda.

13 November 1941   [Commandant's diary]

"Z" asked to see Capt. Percival . . . to say that he had read of the hospital named after him being re-christened which proved that Hitler was very angry with him and would not receive him.

He then said there was not *enough* wire for his protection . . . and that there should be some in the laurel bushes in front of his window which might be used as cover for a sniper. It appears that the combination of the P.M.'s speech referring to "Z" as the author of "useful information" plus the renaming of his hospital has shaken him and opened his eyes as to his personal safety.

Civilian clothes would be the best camouflage if Camp Z were attacked. When Hess asked his captors to obtain a Luftwaffe officer's overcoat, the War Office at first undertook to make inquiries, then ruled that he would have to wear a civilian coat or shiver.

Chemo-therapy, as Colonel Rees had proposed, had now probably been instituted. This would explain why Hess would later associate the return of the same symptoms as before with this period, the days immediately after he wrote to the Swiss Protecting Power. "In November 1941," Hess would write, "I got in touch with the Swiss Minister. . . . I had hardly mailed the letter when, again, huge quantities of brain poison were put in my food." He believed that the motive was to destroy his memory, and added proudly, "I deceived them into believing that I had lost my memory."

17 *November 1941*   [Commandant's diary]

Major Foley had an hour and a half's talk with "Z" in the evening which, he said, was very interesting but that "Z"'s views had in no way changed.

19 *November 1941*

Capt. Percival at "Z"'s request dined with him upstairs. "Z" on being questioned about Germany's "secret weapons" said that he knew there was one [this was bluff] but he had no idea what it was, but that Hitler would not use it except as a last recourse.

"Z" still in a very good humour.

This good humour did not last long. The next day saw Hess begin his now familiar (whether real or fake) performance. After sitting in a chair gazing moodily out of the window, grimacing and muttering in what the orderly found "a very discomforting manner", he began staring at the two corporals on duty, apparently in an acute depression.

When they asked, "How are you feeling?", he snapped the reply, "How would you feel after six months in the same surroundings!"

20 *November 1941*   [Commandant's diary]

"Z" has had a sudden relapse to his persecution mania. He said he knew that the reason why he had been moved to another room for twenty-four hours (whilst the windows were fitted with armoured glass) was really because it was an opportunity to examine his papers, and even suggested that the carpenter, poor old Mr Moxham, was a Secret Service agent in disguise.

22 *November 1941*

"Z" was given a sleeping draught last night and slept heavily all night. This produced the curious accusation that the draught had been given to him so that it would give us the opportunity to go through his private papers. . . .

Later in the day he sent for Major Foley and proudly exhibited his ingenious method of protecting his papers – a method of which he was childishly proud: he had wrapped them in about six layers of tissue paper, each layer stuck down & carrying about thirty of his signatures in indelible pencil. He said that he expected that this would be put down by us to a psychosis.

22 November 1941   [Orderly's afternoon report]

At 18.50 hrs he was lay [*sic*] in bed dozing when he suddenly looked round towards the wall and began waving his hands as though winding something up and was whispering audibly and sternly, but when he noticed the attendant watching his actions he stopped straight away.

Reviewing the records of these two significant weeks before the Swiss Minister finally did appear, it is possible to speculate that Hess, realizing that a *hunger* strike would merely result in forced feeding, devised the *sanity* strike as a remarkable alternative. Foley and the psychiatrists may themselves have unwittingly given him the idea by their talk of a psychosis: he began acting convincingly loopy, dropping broad hints of suicidal depression whenever he wanted to panic the officers into meeting his demands. Four years later, in 1945, he was able to recall the precise sequence of symptoms like "loss of memory" which he faked in these two weeks – but that 1945 recollection was probably itself being used as a super-tactic to baffle the new set of opponents who confronted him at Nuremberg.

The historical picture is complicated by Hess's pronounced fear that he was being poisoned by mind-bending drugs that were causing hallucinations and damaging his ability to read and see. In those two weeks Hess invented a "loss of memory" in order to persuade whoever was poisoning him that the drug had taken effect. So Hess later said.

It is a complicated scenario, but accepting it enables the verbatim records kept by Colonel Scott and the heroic orderlies to be read in a new light.

29 November 1941   [Commandant's diary]

"Z" in one of his worse moods, complaining of everything, and that every noise has been especially "laid on" for his discomfiture – even the sergeant of the Guard had been specially chosen for his loud word of command.

30 November 1941

Col. Rees visited the camp and went up to see "Z" who, with him, was in quite a cheerful mood.

30 November 1941   [Private McGowan's report]

Visited by Col. Rees at 12.00 hrs who stayed until 12.30 hrs. This visit
seemed to have had worsening effect on the Patient, who appeared more
depressed.

30 November 1941   [Corporal Everatt's afternoon report]

. . . very sullen most of the afternoon and not too eager to converse, and
complains that his eyes are giving him trouble again.

30 November 1941   [Corporal Riddle's night report]

Appeared depressed on taking over. Complained of pains in the eyes &
headache & said he was feeling bad in general.

1 December 1941   [Commandant's diary]

"Z" in a very difficult mood and is convinced again that he is being
poisoned and demands that either Capt. Percival, Major Foley or Capt.
Johnston should have all meals with him. His feeling that he is being
poisoned is not altogether to be wondered at, as the food that Pirbright
have been providing for us lately has as near as touch poisoned us all.

  "Z" states that nothing will induce him ever to come downstairs
whilst he is in this camp and only be allowed to take exercise in such a
restricted space. He asks that he may be transferred to Scotland where he
could roam over the moors and indulge in his favourite pastime of
cycling.

On the 2nd the orderlies wrote that he would not talk except about his
ailments: his head throbbed, his eyes were sore, he could not see. "He
states these conditions are brought on by the drugs given to him in his
food and medicine."

Shortly after midnight, the dozing orderly heard a floorboard creak and
saw Hess out of bed standing near a side wall. "I'm looking for my
handkerchief," he said. Hess knew that it was in his bed.

He was suspicious about his breakfast, lunch and dinner. Scott heard he
was "morose, peevish and full of inhibitions". On 3 December he wrote
that Hess was "still in a very bad state", and the next day "if anything
worse than ever". Hess did not bother to dress for dinner, and later paced
the room moaning about not being able to read, write or draw, as his eyes
were failing him. On the 5th he "would only make his cocoa with the
water out of the tap". The orderlies that afternoon saw him as a "picture
of complete misery".

But *picture* it was: a performance. Still campaigning to see the Swiss
Minister, Hess played his "loss of memory" card. He mentioned to
Captain Munro Johnston that he could not converse because he could not
remember words, or even what had happened one hour before. On 4
December the surgeon Major Murray told the Commandant, "This is the
first occasion that 'Z' has complained to me that he's losing his memory."

On the 6th, he asked young Captain Percival to lunch with him, then refused to speak, saying he had lost his memory.

"He really seems ill," said Percival, and declared that he would not return for dinner while Hess was in that condition.

"I have my reasons", said Hess darkly, "for asking officers to take meals with me."

Besides honing the "loss of memory" to a convincing pitch (on the 6th, he had lost his ear plugs, forgotten to listen to the 11 p.m. German news, and even asked Private Smedley to remind him if he had yet been to the lavatory), Hess also played on their fear that he might try to kill himself again. The barber who cut his hair on the 3rd found his scissors missing; the upstairs room was searched without result. On the 6th an orderly found him drifting into what looked like a state of acute anxiety. "When in bed, he puts his hands to his head and he has a facial expression of complete misery." The news of Pearl Harbor made no detectable impression upon him: Hess was fighting a far more personal campaign of his own. On 8 December, Hess asked one of the corporals to enter in the report book that he had asked the doctor to remove anything from his room with which he might harm himself.

These tactics worked.

That day, 8 December, Scott concluded that Hess was indeed in a very bad state. "He called for the doctor and asked that he might withdraw his parole not to commit suicide. The reasons being that he was in great pain, that deliberate attempts were being made to poison him before the Swiss Minister arrived to see him and that he was being driven insane by all the noises." Scott reported this to Colonel Boulnois at the War Office, while Major Foley telephoned MI6 headquarters. Later that day the Foreign Office telephoned Camp Z: the Swiss Minister – who had resumed work only that afternoon, after five weeks leave in Switzerland – would visit the prisoner.

Hess staged a noteworthy recovery. " 'Z' seems a little better," wrote Scott, "and is now in an exhausted state and rather tearful."

On the following day, 12 December 1941, knowing that the Swiss Minister was to call, Hess carefully left his breakfast uneaten – just in case – and reassured Dr Johnston that he still felt confused and had no memory. These symptoms, wrote Johnston reporting the episode later, "disappeared" on the arrival of the Minister.

The visit that morning by His Excellency the Swiss Minister at the Court of St James, Herr Walther Thurnheer, was, however, a disappoint-ment to the prisoner. The War Office took care that the envoy was accompanied by the appropriate specialists. Colonel Rees did not come himself, but half an hour before the diplomat arrived Major Foley's car drove through the double gates bringing Major Dicks and a Lieutenant Reade-Jahn.

Thurnheer himself arrived at 10 a.m., conferred briefly with Dicks and

Johnston, then went upstairs, past the heavy new netting and grille, into Hess's quarters. He stayed talking in private with Hess for over two hours.

The Swiss Government has placed copies of all Thurnheer's reports at this author's disposal.

I set out [Thurnheer wrote on 12 December 1941] at 9 a.m., equipped with the necessary special passes, and was driven by the military authorities to Hess's location about ninety minutes from London. Before I got there Major Foley joined my car to ease my access into the house. Mr Hess is accommodated in a very large and pretty country house surrounded by gardens. From the house there is a rewarding view across the countryside and a small lake, but the rustic surroundings are in part spoiled by the security measures. The garden is encircled by barbed wire and permanently patrolled by special sentries. This outside guard seems to be six men strong, at least I saw that number marching off when the guard was changed. Inside the building there are also certain cordons and security measures and I was astounded at those in the stairwell. . . .

Major Scott received me very cordially. . . . Both the military doctors were in uniform. They declared to me that Mr Hess is not quite normal, he feels persecuted, a feeling manifested by a pronounced mistrust of everybody around him and even of the food offered him. I request a report for my files on Mr Hess's medical condition, which they will give me. . . .

I found Mr Hess lying in bed. His room is large and airy. What astonished me was a heavy iron grille built in front of the central window while those to the left and right had no such protection. This central window was open. Along the left-hand wall facing the bed stands a big table with German and English books, including, I noticed, a set of Springer's history of art. The bed stands by itself to the right of the door with a radio next to it freely available to him.

Mr Hess greets me very correctly, though with some reserve. He was visibly excited. He is pale, even haggard; what I particularly noticed were the deep-set, penetrating eyes and the grave, somewhat melancholy expression. He apologises for not receiving me better but he is up against an old and tedious malady, he says; since he points to his abdomen I assume it is some kind of gastric complaint. . . .

Mr Hess then explains why he has asked for my visit. He has learned through the radio . . . of the death of his father. The old man was already advanced in years and fighting cancer, but he would be grateful if I could find out for certain if the radio item is true. . . . I say that I shall be glad to try and may be able to find out more about the circumstances of his father's death, at which Mr Hess comments that he has already come to terms with the sad news and would prefer not to hear more detail. . . . In connection with his father's death Mr Hess would like to change his will and asks if I will witness his signature. . . .

Mr Hess then states that he has just used the will as a pretext to establish contact with me. He has important statements to make to the

King of England. He came to Britain, he says, in the hope of making a peace; unfortunately, he says, he met with no understanding nor was he given the right opportunities. . . . He is convinced that his peace plans could still achieve something today. He has written out his thoughts on these and asks me to hand this document personally to the King. He asks me to express to the King in handing the letter to him his desire that the King himself be the first to read it. . . .

In addition to his remarks on peace, the document contains his complaints about his treatment so far. He declares that they are systematically doing everything they can to ruin his nerves completely. He does not, he says, want to bother me with the details. . . . He is convinced that if the King hears of this he will immediately see to it that they desist and improve his conditions because the King had assured him that he, Mr Hess, is under his special protection. . . .

Mr Hess then speaks briefly about the war. . . . Regarding his remarkable flight to Scotland he is convinced that his peace attempt was well founded and only failed the first time round because he did not establish contact with the right people; he is still convinced that the Germans will win the war. In this respect he expresses himself very definitely but there is an unspoken question in his eyes – he seems to hope that I will reinforce his view; I cannot, and avoid direct answer, expressing my scepticism only with a shrug of the shoulders.

Hess asked for time to amplify and improve his message for the King. "I withdrew to the window bay," reported the Swiss diplomat, "and passed the time reading." After an hour and a quarter the five-page document was ready. The Royal Archives have declined to release the text of the "peace" letter, but the draft, written on 13 November, was among Hess's papers when he finally left Britain; it shows that he also requested the King to set up an independent commission of officers answerable only to the King to inquire into his maltreatment.*

I came to England banking on the *fairness* of the English people. As a former aviator I know that fairness has often been shown to an enemy. Might I not expect all the more to be met with fairness, having come not as an enemy, particularly since I came to Britain unarmed, at the risk of my life, to try to end the hostility between our two peoples?

Today I still believe in the fairness of the British people. Therefore I feel sure that the treatment meted out to me is not in accordance with their wishes. I have no doubt that only a few people are responsible for it.

I am counting on fairness, Your Majesty,

Rudolf Hess

* After prolonged haggling with the Foreign Office, the obstinate and conscientious Swiss Minister was allowed to hand the two sealed documents – Hess's letter and formal complaint – directly to the King's Private Secretary, Sir Alexander Hardinge, at Buckingham Palace on 9 January 1942. The codicil to Hess's will, in favour of his mother, is still in the Swiss files.

He enclosed a copy of the lengthy protest document that he had handed two months before to Lord Beaverbrook, and recommended the surprise seizure and testing of the medication being used by Dicks and Johnston. He had not, he emphasized in this letter to the King, told the Swiss envoy any of this, in order that Berlin should not come to hear of how he had been treated. These papers were placed into an envelope bearing the seals of the Swiss Legation and the British government.

All this was of a gravity which Thurnheer had obviously not anticipated. Evidently not realizing that Major Foley was the MI6 agent at Camp Z, Thurnheer asked him to come upstairs, to check the documents and help seal them, since Hess was insisting on six or seven official seals – suspecting that any number of hands would otherwise open the envelope before it reached His Majesty. Foley showed a lack of interest (having eavesdropped on their conversation all along). "I'll have to discuss this matter with Sir Alexander Cadogan," the diplomat apologized to him. "I am not an ambassador and so I have no right of access to His Majesty."

Asked if he had any specific cause of complaint, Hess shook his head but requested facilities to communicate with him if need arose. "Please do not tell my government about the codicil," he asked, "in case they think I'm contemplating suicide." Before Thurnheer left, Hess handed to him several documents, and a bottle of liquid and some tablets which he asked him to test independently.

Afterwards, sitting down to lunch in the ground-floor officers' mess, Thurnheer mentioned that his legation had not received any inquiries about Hess from Germany. He expressed curiosity about the major structural alterations in the house – the netting, grille and armoured glass – and why Hess was in bed, and Major Foley told him. It was the first that the Swiss had heard of the suicide attempt. Taken aback, he asked Dicks and Johnston for an immediate written report on the prisoner's medical and mental history since his arrival at Camp Z.

The report, which is given here in full, was remarkable in that it made no mention of any treatment being applied to the prisoner.

1. We are both specialists in psychological medicine.

2. The services of a psychiatrist were asked for by Lt. Col. Gibson Graham R.A.M.C. who was originally in medical charge and who early appreciated the fact that the patient was suffering from a disorder of mind. Col. Graham, in his early reports, has stated that he found the patient subject to fears of being poisoned, to a degree which made the patient insist on his food being sampled by the officers in attendance. In addition the patient showed other abnormal suspicions, such as [that] noises occurring in or near the house were deliberately arranged to frighten him, break his nerve or prevent his sleep.

3. Since taking over, we have had ample evidence to prove the correctness of Lt. Col. Graham's early observations. The patient has been predominantly suspicious and depressed to an abnormal degree.

He has from time to time expressed both verbally and in lengthy documents, the conviction that a secret enemy has been administering subtle poison to him – the effect of this poison being to produce elation and then depression, interference with his bodily functions, and destruction of his power of sleep and reason. He has been subject to fits of great agitation and excitement during which his conduct has been very irrational: he prepares "secret documents" and "depositions" of evidence of persecution on the part of, e.g., Major Dicks, Major Foley, or the Commandant. At the same time he has got one of the accused to help him in the preparation or translation of these documents.

4. At times he appreciates that these feelings of persecution are unreasonable, but that he cannot help them. He has repeatedly stated that he does not accuse the officers of bad faith, but that he believed them to be themselves drugged or hypnotised so as to be the unconscious instruments of the unspecified secret enemy.

5. We believe the mental disorder to be paranoia (systematised delusional insanity), and the prognosis as to recovery to be bad. He requires constant care and supervision, on account of a risk of suicide. For that reason, certain precautions have been taken, and a psychiatrist and six trained mental nursing orderlies of the R.A.M.C. are in constant attendance.

(sgd.) H. V. Dicks, MD, MRCP, Major R.A.M.C.
Specialist in Psychological Medicine, London District
(sgd.) Munro K. Johnston, MB, DPM, Capt. R.A.M.C.

12 December 1941

Foley allowed Herr Thurnheer to read this document, but declined to let him take it away – the Foreign Office would have to rule on that.

Hess, confined in his upstairs room, heard the car drive off, as Thurnheer set off back to London at 2 p.m.

Generally pleased with the morning's work, Major Foley telephoned his report to secret service headquarters an hour later, referring to Hess by the code-name used for him within MI6 and the Foreign Office, and revealing incidentally that the whole conversation had been monitored by the hidden microphones. "I think I may say", the MI6 officer dictated, "that the Minister gained the impression that 'Jonathan' was suffering from delusions. . . . I think that no useful purpose would be served by transcribing the records verbatim."

13 First Loss of Memory

Throughout the winter of 1941–2 Rudolf Hess made himself as difficult a prisoner as he could. He withdrew his promise not to commit suicide; since he could no longer be given a knife and fork, the officers found eating with him an ordeal to be avoided as they had to cut up every morsel for him like a child. The guards also withdrew his pen and pencil – not that he could write easily in the dim light and with the hazy Utility eye-glasses that had been tardily provided for him. He refused to go downstairs into the open air even now that his leg had healed, saying that the yard was too restricted.

He confessed without remorse to the doctor on the day after Thurnheer's visit that he had faked the loss of memory because he was sure that otherwise the British would drug him to prevent his telling his story to the diplomat. Over the following weeks he invented, feigned and portrayed other symptoms of mental and physical illnesses which again completely deceived the doctors: a portion of them may even have been real – who can now tell? All we know is that later he would boast again that the entire Oscar-winning performance had been put on for his captors' benefit. In effect, this chicanery enabled him to reverse the roles: the Guards officers had to dance to his tune. He became rude and overbearing towards them, ordering them to perform petty and demeaning tasks on his behalf, and complaining at the slightest sound.

Christmas 1941 for the prisoner was nonexistent, as every officer refused to share meals with this miserable and solitary man. "He cannot be said to have got the Christmas spirit," recorded the Commandant without sympathy.

Rubbing his eyes Hess bleakly told Everatt on the 27th that he had twice tried to read a book. "But", he added, laying the book aside in disgust, "I can't remember what I read on the page before."

On 29 December, Major Johnston brought to him a letter from the Swiss Minister, which had come through War Office channels. (Major Foley was away on leave.) We do not know what Thurnheer wrote, but a few minutes later Hess told the doctor that he would again give his word not to attempt suicide, if he could be allowed to have back his knife and fork for meals. "He also asked", Johnston told the Commandant that afternoon, "if he might have the key of the grille, as he considers it his right to have it."

When Foley returned the next day, Hess again insisted that an officer share meals with him. Colonel Scott decided that the duty officer would have to perform "this unpleasant task", as the mental strain that Hess imposed on the elderly Major Foley and the doctor had become "too much".

"Later on," dictated Hess imperiously, "I'd like to be taken for drives in a car." He wanted to see more of English country houses, evidently. On New Year's Day he showed to the duty officer Lieutenant Merriam the plans he had been drawing of the lodge he was going to build for himself in the Bavarian Alps when the war was over.

Some of the Camp Z staff had lost friends or relatives in the air raids, and none had even a sneaking sympathy for the Nazis. While the officers and gentlemen found it easier to control their public tempers, others will not have resisted the temptation to bang doors, stomp up the stairs, spice or over-salt the caged Deputy Führer's food, or worse. Even the officers occasionally goaded him. In February 1942 the Brigade of Guards was withdrawn from guarding Camp Z and young Captain Douglas Percival came in to take leave of him. Hess asked who would be relieving the Scots and Coldstream Guards. "The Pioneer Corps?" he said, puzzled, when Percival told him. "What do they do?"

"Their usual duties are digging latrines," said the Captain with malicious satisfaction. (In fact an Army Council Instruction had ruled that only Pioneer Corps officers would take guard duties on prison camps.)

Meanwhile, the staff observed the same helter-skelter pattern in their prisoner, alternately bright-and-cheerful, then depressed-and-morose. After the Thurnheer visit he told Corporal Everatt, unabashed, "My memory is recovering." The officers were baffled. On 21 December Major Foley told Colonel Scott, "I think that the apparent loss of memory is genuine."

Hess's chronic fear of being poisoned was growing stronger. On the 22nd Hess asked for his bottle of whisky to help him sleep – then he leaped out of bed to see where the orderly was getting it from. When the second orderly tried to restrain him, Hess shouted, "Take your hands off me! Don't touch me!", and strode around the room forgetting his crutches.

He still listened to the 11 p.m. news from Berlin each evening, but the news was unremittingly grim for the Germans as their onslaught on Moscow was mired in the torrential rains, then froze to a halt, then turned into a rout under Stalin's unexpected counteroffensive.

In England there was annoyance in the War Office at the need to retain a dozen Guards officers, a lieutenant-colonel and well over a hundred troops to guard this one-man prison camp, this Deputy Führer headquarters, and the search began for an alternative safe location.

12 January 1942   [Commandant's diary]

Second-Lieutenant Bowker had dinner with the patient who again showed signs of his poison mania by replacing his piece of apple tart and helping himself to another.

14 January 1942   [Orderly's afternoon report]

Observing how many times different doors have been banging & marking them down. At one instance, he gave an exclamation and seized the room door and pushed it heavily closed & began laughing in a hysterical manner. . . . Showed annoyance at dinner time and asked to see Major Foley.

14 January 1942   [Commandant's diary]

"Z" complained bitterly of slamming doors in the house, and made his point by slamming his own door several times with such force that it woke the doctor.

15 January 1942

Major Foley reported to me that "Z" had to-day signified his intention of trying to combat his fear of poison and that he would now have occasional meals alone and also consent to have his cocoa made in the kitchen instead of, as in the past, making it himself.

17 January 1942

"Z"'s good resolutions . . . have had a short innings. He now complains that since taking the cocoa made for him for the first time in the kitchen yesterday, he has had a return of his headaches and other pains. He is, of course, convinced it was poisoned and the doctor had the unpleasant experience of having to drink lukewarm and sickly cocoa made by "Z" himself at 11.00 in the morning and again in the afternoon.

The next day Hess expressed to Colonel Scott his disappointment that his experiment of trying to combat this fear had failed.

He spent the following days in acute agitation, abandoned every attempt at drawing, reading or writing with vexed outbursts in German, then paced the room in a miserable and "stereotyped" manner, or complained about noises which the orderlies could not hear themselves.

After taking lunch with MI6 officer Foley on the 20th, Hess furtively opened a box to show him what he had been collecting – biscuits, Ryvita, cocoa, sugar and an assortment of pills. "I suspect that these may contain poison," he told the Major. "I intend taking them back to Germany for analysis after the war."

Foley stuffed a handful of the pills into his mouth, and swallowed them down with a glass of water. He munched the Ryvita, and put on the kettle to make a pot of cocoa – which he insisted that Hess share with him. At 5 p.m. he put his head round the door to show Hess that he had suffered no ill effects.

The effect of Foley's little *coup de théâtre* on the prisoner was devastating. Over dinner with Captain Johnston that evening he wanly admitted that he must have been mistaken. Seeming utterly depressed, he gave his hoard to the medical orderly to throw away. "He now realises", recorded Colonel Scott, "that all this poisoning mania must be psychosis, and consequently is in a dreadful state over it."

On the 22nd, Hess asked for pen and paper to write to the King to admit that he was mistaken in the accusations he had levelled in the letter handed to the Swiss Minister. He was clearly rattled. Corporal Everatt found him in a "nasty mood" that day: he thumped his crutches on the floor, jumped around erratically from one spot to another, and never let the attendant out of his sight for a moment.

23 January 1942   Mytchett Place
RUDOLF HESS TO THE KING OF ENGLAND   2nd Letter

Your Majesty,

On December 12, 1941 I handed to the Swiss Minister a sealed letter to your Majesty, written in German and dated 3 [*sic*] November 1941. As an appendix, I enclosed the English translation of a Protest of September 5, 1941 addressed to the British Government.

I take it that the letter has reached your hands in the meantime.

Today Major Foley, whom I mentioned in the letter, ate before my eyes some of the food and tablets which I had assumed to contain noxious substances. The incident has forced me to conclude that my complaints were the result of auto-suggestion brought on by my captivity. . . .

        Rudolf Hess

The Pioneer troops who arrived were clad in what Scots Guards colonel Scott described as rags – they were "quite filthy". He sent twenty-three of the 130 men straight back to their camps, declaring them unusable.

Very shortly after the new Guard took over, problems of discipline and security cropped up. The gate-lodge telephoned. "There's a Mr R. R. Foster here, claiming to be a reporter on the *Daily Herald*, and asking to enter the camp." The *Herald* was the Labour Party's newspaper. "He says he's been sent down by his London office to get news about an incident that happened here five weeks ago." (Rumours had several times seized London to the effect that Hess had killed himself.) Denied entry, the reporter asked a shrewd question. "Should I apply to the War Office or the Foreign Office for permission?" He was told brusquely that the camp had nothing to do with the Foreign Office, but he was obviously on the right track. All guard personnel were now warned to look out for further attempts to pump them, particularly in the pubs around Aldershot. A few days later a car was seen cruising the lanes around Camp Z, and another *Daily Herald* reporter, E. L. Calcraft, was found to be the driver.

Hess was still fighting his own brand of psychological warfare. On 23 January 1942 the orderlies asked him why he was stamping his feet and flailing his arms. "It's my nerves," he replied, "and the pains in the head!"

The least noise goaded him into an outburst: the planes flying overhead unleashed a torrent of German incantations. On the 26th the noises started coming at him from out of the radio; the Corporal told him it was atmospherics, but he was sure the radio had been tampered with. Foley took it away to check. The next afternoon Hess could not rest, but stomped up and down on his crutches, shouting. "Oh, my head!" Foley brought back the radio, and said there was nothing wrong with it. Hess asked him mournfully to remove his knife and fork again. Holding his head in his hands, apparently the picture of misery, he spent the afternoon of the 30th listening to Hitler's Party Anniversary speech broadcast from Berlin.

30 January 1942   [Commandant's diary]

Major Foley reported to me that "Z" had sent for him and the doctor this morning and made a formal request that he may be provided with a revolver for self-defence. He later stated he intended to commit suicide and was willing that the Swiss Minister should come down, to whom he would signify this intention and the reason for it, so that the British Government should be covered.

This was the baffling picture presented by Rudolf Hess at Camp Z as the officers and men of the Brigade of Guards held their last parade and the Pioneers took over: the orderlies' thrice-daily reports show him complaining of pains in his head and eyes, miserable, often (but not always) unable to remember, persecuted by noise, beset by poison phobias, and lying in bed in the semi-darkness yawning and muttering.

5 February 1942   [Orderly's night report]

Was very miserable & occupied in his own thoughts until 23.30 hrs.

01.50 hrs he awoke & began groaning with exclamations of "Ah-ah, Oh-oh, it is terrible," [complaining] of pains in the low region of abdomen, and it apparently became very acute in about five minutes. Tossing & turning in bed, rubbing the affected part with constant groans. Was persuaded to try the [hot-water] bottle but with no result.

At 02.15 hrs he leapt out of bed & began frantically pacing up & down the room making a terrific noise with his feet and groaning. Kept curling up with the supposed pain, then asked for the Medical Officer.

Immediately the M.O. was sent for he said the pains ceased & then returned to bed and appeared much quieter on the arrival of the M.O.

On 18 February Colonel Rees, the army's consultant psychiatrist, telephoned Major Johnston to inquire if he had made a thorough medical examination of Hess. Johnston had to remind him that he was not competent to do this – he was purely a psychiatrist.

Rees came down a few days later and found Hess unduly pallid and gaunt because of his "abnormal" ideas and his refusal to go out of doors. "Hess's mental condition", he wrote in his report, "has deteriorated since I was last there. The delusional, persecutory ideas have evidently fallen into the background for the moment but, as often happens, he has swung into a depression and with it a distinct loss of memory."

So the loss of memory simulated by Hess had completely deceived Rees, although some of the mental lacunae were of staggering proportion – Hess did not recall having received any letters from his wife (he had received two), nor even having been visited by the Swiss Minister. "This may be due to the increasing mental deterioration," assessed Rees, "or it may be just a phase from which he will emerge." And he emphasized: "His memory was very much at fault."

With Foreign Office approval, Rees asked Lieutenant-Colonel Evan Bedford, a distinguished consultant physician in civilian life, to examine "Z". Bedford found nothing fundamentally wrong.

Colonel Scott left to take command of the alien internment camp on the Isle of Man. He brought his successor, Lieutenant-Colonel Wilson, up to see "Z" on 20 February. Hess put on a good low-key performance for the newcomer. Corporal Everatt noted, "[He] appears to have a vacant air and is unable to remember things very clearly."

On 2 March the Deputy Führer asked Corporal Riddle whether he could give him anything to sleep.

"How about a Luminal?" suggested the orderly, referring to a standard mild sedative.

"Luminal?" said Hess, looking blank. "What's that? Have I ever had one?"

With Scott gone, on the 3rd Hess suddenly relented and agreed to go out into the grounds. The next evening he invited Colonel Wilson to dine with him, and appeared to enjoy it, although he lapsed into moodiness afterwards, and on the 5th put on his confused and suspicious act, blaming the cocoa (and the next day, the curry) for his allegedly painful condition. The orderlies strained to understand his often unintelligible muttering, but usually it was just "Once more!" or "Mein Gott, why does this have to be!"

On 21 March, he spent some time trying to conceal a glucose tablet beneath a floorboard, having evidently first made sure that the Corporal saw him do so. "It's poisoned," he declared, "and I'm going to give it to the Swiss Minister."

Dr Johnston was told, and he reported that both glucose and Luminal tablets were found hidden in the lining of the famous flying boots and under the carpet. Hess gave him the same eccentric explanation.

"As more than a quarter of a year had passed," Hess would write four years later, "since I had given my letter to the King of England to the

Swiss envoy without result, I again asked him to come and see me." On 28 March he received a reply, written on the 20th; Thurnheer agreed to come within fourteen days, but for some weeks there was no sign of him. Hess concluded that the British would prevent the envoy coming to Camp Z until such time as he finally exhibited all the symptoms of lunacy – or, at the very least, of such instability [*Nervösität*] that people would regard him as not worthy of belief. "I pretended", wrote Hess, "to become more nervous from day to day; after I had reached the climax, the envoy came."

The orderlies' daily reports certainly reflected this description. To Corporal Riddle (on 2 April) Hess had merely seemed "childish in ways", while appearing to believe himself "intelligent & a master of all concerned". The real or imaginary stomach pains persisted, with Hess jumping out of bed and dashing wildly up and down grunting and groaning. To Corporal Everatt on the 6th, Hess also seemed "very childish" but he added the perhaps more perceptive conclusion: "Appears to [be] trying the tempers of the staff, while he himself is in a very nasty temper. . . ."

6 *April 1942*   [Private Dawkins's report]

He states the Jews are trying to kill him, and if he stays here much longer he will finish up in the madhouse.

7 *April 1942*   [Corporal Everatt's report]

Took some milk after demanding that I drank some of the milk first. When asked the reason, he told me someone in the kitchen was tampering with his food and drink . . . someone of Jewish faith is trying to bring about his end, in spite of the fact that the staff take great care of him.

8 *April 1942*   [Corporal Everatt's report]

Took a light tea only after I had tasted it to try and convince him it was not tampered with. In a very nasty temper and states we are here with the sole intention of driving him into a madhouse. Says that people in the house bang the doors and cough loudly to affect his nerves.

On the same day the prisoner wrote to the Swiss Minister again: "I would very much like you to accelerate your visit," he concluded. Thurnheer was however himself ill, and it was not until the 18th that his doctor would permit him to return to Camp Z.

In anticipation of the previous visit, Hess had feigned amnesia until the last moment; prior to this second occasion his apparent derangement certainly seems to have peaked. On the 17th Everatt described him as depressed and miserable, attacked by "cramps" and obsessed with delusions about poisoned food, and finally "irritable and in a vile temper". Corporal Riddle reported "several outbursts in German at the least noise", and hinted at a craving for enemas. He suffered a headache all night before Thurnheer's arrival; this was probably genuine. But he solemnly asked Riddle to swear on his honour as a "true British soldier" that nothing had been added to the Luminal tablet he had taken; and this was probably pure posturing.

He lay in bed late that Saturday, rose shortly before lunchtime and went for a brief walk in the grounds. Private Dawkins thought him depressed and moody. The prisoner would not allow anybody to clean his room, and refused to touch either breakfast or lunch.

The War Office had again decided to have the Swiss diplomat briefed by a top psychiatrist, and sent Rees – now a brigadier – down in person. Rees went up to Hess's quarters some time before Thurnheer. If Hess seemed significantly brighter, it was not because of Rees.

[Brigadier Dr Rees's report]

Hess was in bed but very talkative and quite different to his state at my last visit when he was very depressed and shut away. No doubt his condition . . . was due to the fact that he was expecting a visit from the Protecting Power in the immediate future.

He complained of a violent headache: "The worst I have ever had in my life," but he refused to take some aspirin I gave him out of my pocket even though I gave him his choice of tablets and took the others myself. He told me that he was quite certain that he was being poisoned, and he was very emphatic in his criticism of the authorities for leaving him where he now is when he had asked for removal six months ago!

The International Red Cross had forwarded German parcels to the prisoner through Switzerland, but Hess told the Brigadier that on balance he had decided not to open them (even though they had the Berlin postmark and unbroken seals). "I have many enemies in Switzerland," he remarked, silently recalling the fate of German official Wilhelm Gustloff, murdered by Jewish extremists in Switzerland before the war.

Thurnheer spent nearly four hours, from 3.20 p.m. to 7 p.m., with the Deputy Führer. Handing some German-language books to Hess from his own library, he apologized that he had not been permitted to give the Hess letter to the King in person, and the Duke of Hamilton had flatly declined to have anything to do with Hess. So he had given the letter and enclosures to the King's Private Secretary Sir Alexander Hardinge. Unfortunately the Palace had not yet replied. (According to Hess, the Palace never did reply.)

[Swiss Minister's report]

I was received by the Commandant, Wilson, who has replaced his predecessor Major Fox [*sic*, Scott]. The former permanent doctor has also been succeeded by Brigadier [*sic*], a specialist for H.'s illness. . . . On the drive over Captain Foyle [*sic*, Foley] prepared me by saying that my task this time would be difficult. The patient is very agitated, even refuses to eat biscuits from home although an officer ate one in front of him. . . . Hess said it probably contained poison, he has enemies in Switzerland.

I asked the Commandant to take me straight up to Hess as I feared he might become suspicious if I saw the other gentlemen first. He must have heard us drive up and the sound of the car's horn at the gate and I knew he was waiting for me with great impatience. . . .

I was astonished to find him in bed. . . . Mr Hess told me he has stomach cramps. . . . He had to tell me that everybody was trying either to poison him or rob him of his memory. He had positive proof of this.

Hess embarked on the familiar litany, embellished by such details as doors being banged 123 times in half an hour, "accidental" fits of coughing by the attendants, and things being dropped; he had pretended to sleep – the noise began – "as soon as I awoke it abated", and it stopped completely the moment he agreed to take "their" alleged Luminal tablets or eat "their" food, all of which contained, he said, substances to cause headaches, undermine his nerves, destroy his memory. He handed to the diplomat samples of the wine and glucose which seemed to contain the mysterious substance – "Whether it is the well-known Mexican herbal poison or not I cannot say."

The prisoner [reported Thurnheer] then asked me to send this report to the German Government at once so that they can inflict reprisals on the British generals, in return for which he promises to ensure that Switzerland is treated in the New Europe in accordance with whatever desires she may put forward.

I tell Mr Hess that I regret I cannot meet his requests. My mission here is one of trust: I had been allowed in to him without any checks. . . . Taking his hand to create an impression of utter reliability and decency, I add that while I deeply value the promise of special treatment for Switzerland I can assure him that such promises can have no bearing on my attitudes. . . .

Rudolf Hess responds that he did go a bit too far . . . and I should put it down to his desperate plight. But in the present case a crime is being committed and, that being so, he would go further if he were me. . . .

I tell him it is his duty to keep fit, because if Germany wins the war then he must be there to share in her reconstruction. None of these remarks seems to impress him as he is obsessed with the one idea that they are trying to destroy him by noise outside and indoors and by medication. He asks whether I cannot at least send his report direct to the highest judges in Britain? I remind him that the legislature and executive are separate, and I can only forward the report through the Foreign Office, which Rudolf Hess refuses.

Corporal Everatt, who had to attend on him that evening, found him brighter than for some time, but the glow soon dimmed and by bedtime he had relapsed into his usual moody depression, "very tired after the hard work of the afternoon". (The diplomat and Hess had devoted much of their afternoon to carefully wrapping and labelling the samples of glucose, Luminal, aspirin and even claret that the prisoner thought might hold the clue to his malaise.)

"There was", reported Rees to the War Office after escorting Thurnheer out of Camp Z, "no question whatever in his mind, of course, of the mental derangement."

The trend was unaltered in the following weeks. Hess built a model plane, drew architectural sketches, listened nostalgically to the Berlin radio commentary on Hitler's birthday; but he also stamped up and down in vile tempers, and acted like a child. On 6 May he received several letters but showed only meagre interest in them. A few days later, however, he remembered clearly that precisely a year had passed since his flight.

He settled down to wait. The war was going well for Germany, and the British government might decide to speak with him yet. On 13 May his little radio picked up the fanfares from Berlin announcing fresh German victories – Hitler's colossal Operation Fridericus at Kharkov. Good news undoubtedly buoyed him, and on the night of 19 May he "appeared in a rather cheerful mood, conversing about the Russian losses". Corporal Riddle was the only orderly who still believed Hess was a victim of hallucinations, but there were occasional episodes that the others could not explain, like when he asked that the night guard outside make less noise or when he complained a few days later of somebody coughing – sounds that nobody else had heard. "The house staff", he challenged one night, 26 May, "is under orders to make as much noise as possible."

His stay at Camp Z was coming to an end anyway.

"We have for some time felt", the Foreign Secretary had written to Churchill a few days before, "that the present arrangements for housing our prisoner 'Jonathan' are unsatisfactory." Camp Z needed too many men to guard it, and the War Office had found new accommodation, a hospital which they had taken over in Wales and which the Foreign Office agreed was suitable. "Arrangements", Anthony Eden assured the Prime Minister, "can be made to provide quarters for 'Jonathan' completely secluded from the rest of the place and giving satisfactory security."

There was, he admitted, one snag. The place had been a mental hospital before the War Office took it over. He himself hoped that this would not have any embarrassing consequences. "If 'Jonathan' were admittedly certifiable," he advised the Prime Minister, "we could be called on to repatriate him under the Hague Convention."*

It is evident that the prisoner was in command of his faculties at this time. On the same day as Eden wrote these furtive lines, afraid that adherence to an unfeeling, impartial international law might rob them of

---

* The Convention was in fact signed at Geneva.

their State Prisoner, Rudolf Hess was writing to his friend and mentor in Germany:

TO PROF. KARL HAUSHOFER   *England, 20 May 1942*

My dear and honoured friend,

As it turns out that my letters take months to get anywhere I'm sending you these birthday greetings now. With them go all my good wishes for you and yours.

You mustn't feel any concern for me! You have least reason of all for that!

Obviously my plight isn't all that pleasant, but they say that in wartime people often do end up in not very pleasant situations. That is not the point: what the point is, in the long term, you know best of all.

I often have to ponder on the seminar with the late [Professor] Bitterauf and my own contribution to it on Gneisenau. You shared my view, just as you believed so much in me.

> Let the waves crash and thunder,
>   Life and death denote your realm –
> Whether soar aloft or fall asunder,
>   Never take your hand off helm!

It can't be denied that I have failed. Nor can anybody deny that I was my own pilot. So in that respect I've no cause for self-recrimination. At any rate, I was at the helm. But you know as well as I do that the compass that we set our course by is influenced by forces that are of unerring effect even though we know nothing of them.

May these forces be with you in your coming year of life!

The way the war was shaping had not escaped him. While Hitler's armies were thrusting deep into the Soviet Union and across North Africa, Churchill was relying on bombing raids to restore the strategic balance. Since early 1942 he had ordered several heavy raids on German towns, often of only marginal war importance like Lübeck; the target was German civilian morale. Hitler had responded with his "Baedeker" attacks on historic towns like Bath and Canterbury.

Rudolf Hess heard the air-raid sirens and the rival bomber forces passing overhead. This was the development that he had feared, and it was compassion for Europe's civilians that had inspired his winged mission one year before. He blamed Churchill unreservedly for the carnage; when the Prime Minister had broadcast on 10 May, repeating the old lie about how the Luftwaffe "massacred 20,000 Dutch folk in defenceless Rotterdam", and gloating over the damage done to Lübeck, Rostock and a dozen other towns, the orderlies saw Hess hobble across his room in Aldershot and switch off the radio in disgust.

No, he was not too confused or absent-minded to weigh the news crackling out of that loudspeaker from the BBC and Berlin. After listening to the 11 p.m. German news on 30 May 1942 he "eagerly" repeated to Corporal Everatt details of the German claims against the Russians. He made no comment on that night's RAF "thousand-bomber" raid on Cologne, but conversed freely with Everatt on the morning after the 1 June raid on Essen, capital of Alfred Krupp's arms empire. "Essen", he remarked almost approvingly, "is a military target: unlike the other towns you have been bombing of late."

Out of the earshot of the psychiatrists like Rees and Dicks, his brain was functioning normally. When the radio announced on 4 June that SS General Reinhard Heydrich had died of the wounds inflicted by Czech assassins, Hess pointed out that they had been sent by Britain, and he subjected the attendant corporal to a propaganda lecture on Britain and the shooting of innocents in India a century before. Reading in *The Times* on the 11th that the Germans had wiped out the Czech village of Lidice as a reprisal for harbouring the assassins, the prisoner harangued his indignant listeners about how Britain had done the same in Palestine in peacetime – perhaps confusing the British mandate there with the RAF's tactics in policing outlying areas of the Arab Emirates between the wars. "At the end of the discussion," recorded the orderly, "he became more settled and passed it off laughing."

He had thus evidently staged a convincing recovery by mid-June 1942. On 15 June the medical records show him listening to the radio, delighted at a *Sondermeldung* from Berlin announcing the sinking of Allied ships. He conversed "freely and interestingly" with the attendants; and three days later they noted him down as cheerfully occupied with drawing architectural plans and talking about the war. In Libya, Rommel was on the point of taking Tobruk. In southern Russia, Hitler's lunge for the oilfields beyond the Caucasus had begun.

"I wonder what is going to happen in the next few weeks," Hess said.

14 Lies to Stalin and Roosevelt

On 26 June 1942 an army car carried the pale and haggard Rudolf Hess two hundred miles westwards across England from Aldershot to South Wales. Dr Dicks had described it as characteristic of psychotics that they could not bear being passively driven as passengers – they had to drive themselves. Perhaps Hess did not know of this: at any rate Dr Johnston observed him taking an almost childish pleasure in the journey, his first outing for over a year. Through the car's windows he saw the entrance lodge of a typical large hospital; the car halted outside a wing, somewhat to one side, and he was shown into two rooms overlooking a garden. This little suite, and the small caged garden itself, were to be his prison for the next years.

Johnston stayed only briefly with him. His concluding impression of Hess, based on the year at Camp Z, was a picture familiar to the mental hospital doctor – "The anxious, gloomy paranoiac, with a mind strangled and warped by the ever-encroaching tentacles of his own persecutory delusions, until every thought and action minister only to delusional ends." He described in confidence to Major Ellis Jones, the doctor who would take on Hess now, the prisoner's occasional "wild look"; but dining with the Deputy Führer Ellis Jones found him alert and pleasant, and even eager to be liberated from his "fixed ideas". Hess, for his part, liked the doctor: he seemed to have broad interests, and even claimed to have read and enjoyed *Mein Kampf*.

David Ellis Jones was at that time the elderly medical superintendent of the Pen-y-Fal hospital, the County Mental Hospital at Abergavenny, about one and a half miles away. While not itself a mental clinic, Maindiff Court had been its admission clinic in peacetime and now came under the War Office's Emergency Medical Service Scheme. To legitimize its use for Hess it formally became "P.O.W. Reception Station, Maindiff Court", which meant little more than that a rubber stamp was manufactured in that name, and two officers and thirty-one other ranks provided for guard and medical duties.

The choice of this site for Hess's incarceration was no accident. The War Office had insisted that he be accommodated in surroundings suitable for a "psychopathic personality". The Foreign Office, however, had insisted that Hess must not be placed in a mental hospital, to thwart demands for his repatriation. To maintain his status as a prisoner of war, his new residence had to be an institution where British officers were actually undergoing regular medical treatment; and a villa had indeed been reserved for the treatment of officer-patients.

Five RAMC orderlies (Corporals Everatt and Riddle, and Privates McGowan, Dawkins and Smedley) had accompanied "Z" from Aldershot, and their handwritten records of Hess's torment have survived.

26 June 1942 [Orderly's report]

Patient arrived at 15.45 hrs.

Seems quite cheerful & pleased with the new building & has had plenty of exercise. Constantly complaining in his usual manner of doors banging & noises made in the kitchen during preparing for meals. Used toilet room.

27 June 1942

Patient asked for hot-water bottle. Has only slept short periods (approx 1½ hrs) until 04.15 hrs & patient asked for Luminal & said the noise of trains disturbed his sleep.

10.15 hrs he awoke & washed & dressed & took a light breakfast. Then occupied himself for a time reading & walking round his compound. Was visited by Major Ellis Jones who walked & talked with him for some time. . . . He is well impressed by the place.

To Hess, the noise of the trains was an ugly omen that the torment was to continue. As he lay in bed on those first nights, he realized that the clinic was only a few hundred yards from a rail marshalling yard. All night long the engines shunted, the wagons crashed, the steam-whistles hooted.

"There was no thought of sleep," he recalled, setting down his impressions later in the war. "If I needed to catch up on my sleep during the day, this would be prevented by slamming doors and hammering just like in my former quarters." One of the orderlies assured him – "smugly", as it seemed to Hess – that the trains stopped him sleeping too but he took long walks to cure his insomnia; and Dr Johnston assured him before returning to Aldershot that "had he known" he would never have approved the move.

On his second night he lay in bed and told Private Smedley, "I'll try and get to sleep when the noise of the trains stops." But sleep was impossible, so he paced the corridor for an hour, muttering and laughing grimly each time the whistles sounded. Awakened at 11.30 the next morning after taking sleeping tablets Hess snapped at Corporal Riddle, "Why did you wake me up?"

When Major Ellis Jones came at 1.30 to take him for a walk, Hess dashed ahead through the attendants' room and reached the outer door before the Major.

The door was locked.

Hess wheeled round angrily. "I knew it!" he shouted, and dashed up to his bedroom. He slammed the door, banged tables and chairs around, whistled loudly and tried to show his contempt. After a while, he pulled out his papers and began writing. That afternoon, as each train approached he stood up and waited grimacing for the inevitable whistle, then waved his arms and burst out laughing.

When Everatt brought in the afternoon tea, Hess made him taste it first.

His nerves were on a razor's edge. That night Private Smedley solemnly entered in the report book: "At 00.15 hrs patient expressed annoyance at the ticking of the clock in the orderlies' room."

This low point was almost immediately left behind. While the summary written by Major Ellis Jones is chronologically imprecise, the overall picture is clear. After these two or three erratic days – a hangover from the Camp Z nightmare – a remarkable change overcame Hess in these tranquil Welsh surroundings. Major Ellis Jones, who had read the earlier case file compiled by his colleagues Rees, Dicks and Johnston, found their reports "almost incredible".

Suddenly Hess began sleeping proper hours, eating food without complaint, taking exercise; he was sunny and cheerful, and no more sarcastic towards his captors than was proper. He delved into Lloyd George's *History of the World War* or sat on the verandah deep in thought. He worked on his sketches and wrote letters to his friends and family – although the doctors who read them gained the impression that particularly the patriotic and pompous lines he addressed to his four-year-old son were written rather with an eye to posterity.

The records show that Ellis Jones visited the patient only rarely, perhaps once a week. Rather than eat alone, Hess preferred to dine with the army officers like Captain Crabtree, the new Guard Commander who had come with him from Camp Z, or with Lieutenants Fox and Lander. At Maindiff Court there were no hidden microphones, but the lieutenants afterwards wrote reports, and these, like Hess's letters, were read by the secret service, as Anthony Eden made plain in a "Most Secret" report to the Prime Minister:

In a letter written in June [perhaps Hess's letter to Haushofer on 20 May – see p. 214] the prisoner openly admitted the failure of his mission, but from a conversation with the medical officer it was apparent that "Jonathan" felt that the episode of his flight to this country was understood by his Führer. . . . The setback in this policy [of bringing about an era of friendship and co-operation between Britain and Germany], indicated by the detention of "Jonathan" himself, does not appear to have shaken the latter's belief in the ultimate victory of

Germany which he affirmed categorically in a statement which he wrote last year, and which he recently resurrected to show to the Guard Commander [Captain Crabtree].

In his correspondence [conversations?] the prisoner avoids reference to politics and the war, though on one occasion when he was discussing with the Medical Officer where the final battle of the war would be fought, he unhesitatingly ringed the eastern shores of the Mediterranean.

"His certainty of the success of Germany", concluded Eden, "is part of his belief in the predestined course of events, and his faith in the influence of the stars as revealed in horoscopes, is as great as ever."

The dramatic improvement in Hess's condition had two reasons.

No casual listener to the war news could deny that Hitler was doing well in the summer of 1942. Every week Hess could hear fanfares from Berlin as the U-boats inflicted fresh disasters on the Anglo-American convoys, as the Panzer divisions rolled southwards through Voronezh, and as the starvation ring around Leningrad was drawn tighter.

No less important (and perhaps not entirely by coincidence) mysterious alleviations were suddenly perceptible in Hess's prison conditions – alleviations that only the Prime Minister could have allowed. Suddenly, a *car* was provided for the prisoner's pleasure. At Camp Z, Colonel Scott had been obliged to make do with one small car to run a camp with ten officers and 135 men; here, a car and petrol coupons were made available to enable Hess to go for chauffeur-driven rides into the beautiful surrounding countryside literally whenever he pleased.

Equally bafflingly, his headaches cleared and he momentarily lost his fears of being poisoned, although he began a protracted charade of "stomach pains" whose main purpose was evidently little more than to curry sympathy with his medical attendants. (It is worth mentioning that Hitler, Himmler and Ribbentrop all suffered from these acute stomach cramps.)

The attendants rendered a faithful minute-by-minute picture of Hess that summer in their daily reports: occasionally drawing attention to himself by banging doors or scraping chairs and tables; complaining about trivial noises and interruptions; seated in the sun on the verandah, or pacing the compound deep in thought; but reading, writing and improving all the time. He remained glued to the loudspeaker of his radio throughout July. On the 6th Corporal Riddle wrote, "Has been much interested in the news all day," and on the 7th, "Seems to be an improvement in his general health since living in the new quarters." That night Hess cheerfully regaled Private Smedley with the war news from Russia.

It was on 9 July 1942 that Riddle escorted the prisoner out on the first car jaunt. "[Hess] enjoyed the car ride & the short walks," he wrote later that day, "but states the climbing of the hills is rather too strenuous for him." Sometimes it was he who suggested going for a spin; sometimes it was he who declined, finding exercise still genuinely tiring.

Occasionally the officers invited him round to dinner with them, and asked him to stay behind and join in their games. Initially he made shy excuses or feigned "stomach pains"; later he joined in wholeheartedly. On 19 July after a two-hour drive up into the mountains he "took dinner with the officers and played games with them". The next day he was evidently chirpy: "Patient has been soliloquizing quite a lot since lunch in German." But it was natural – he was excited. He told Sergeant Everatt on the 22nd, after listening to the radio all evening, "I think the Germans are very lucky. . . . They're doing better than I thought they would."

Rudolf Hess was now forty-seven. He was in his prime. But the knowledge that he had failed – the transition from frenetic acclaim in Berlin and Nuremberg, from mountain freedom in Bavaria, to this small cage, surrounded by a kaleidoscope of changing faces and petty minds, can only have eroded his spirit, however hard he tried to maintain sanity. He began translating a book into German, but the dictionary mysteriously fell to pieces in his hands; he continued his meticulous architectural sketches; and began to study Johann Wolfgang Goethe's *Dichtung und Wahrheit*, but his eyes hurt, his head ached, and he found it ever harder to concentrate.

Sometimes he was boisterous and demanding, others sullen and morose. Immersed in his thoughts of Germany and family, he often seemed depressed and moody to his attendants, who found him wearing "an expression of complete misery".

Occasional visitors broke the monotonous routine.

Brigadier Rees came on 4 August, learned – apparently without seeing him – that Hess was "considerably better in superficial ways", and returned to London. "Mentally," the psychiatrist summarized in his report to his superiors, "he is markedly better for the moment. He has even got to the point of talking about his delusional ideas, and saying that he hopes they will not recur and that he is practically convinced they were delusions." Hess's improvement, the Brigadier remarked, was coinciding with an upturn in the war for Germany.

But delusions did persist. When, eight days after Rees's visit, the Swiss Minister Walther Thurnheer called, Hess believed he noticed an increased nervousness in the staff at Maindiff Court. Thurnheer had now had the liquids and tablets handed to him by Hess in April analysed. A week after seeing Hess he had discussed with Sir Alexander Cadogan ways of having the samples reliably analysed. He had suggested the German Hospital in London, run by the Swiss Dr Hugo Rast, and so arranged that the hospital would not know Hess's identity; Hess had asked him to use a Swiss laboratory and Thurnheer had originally proposed to use the Institute of Forensic Medicine at Zürich but the Foreign Office raised objections. Cadogan had found the case "too delicate" to decide without consulting

Anthony Eden; and Eden had asked for time to get the Cabinet's decision. On 1 May, Cadogan had notified Thurnheer that Eden preferred the analysis to be carried out in a London laboratory "under the supervision of your own Doctor". The laboratory selected was Harrison & Self, of Bloomsbury Square, and on 25 June they had reported that the liquids and tablets were free of any commonly known inorganic poisons.

Told by Thurnheer now that he had used a London laboratory instead of a Swiss one, Hess sniffed and said nothing. ("Of course," he wrote afterwards, "it was an easy matter for the secret service to observe where they were taken and to give orders that nothing should be found. . . . The envoy however was convinced that everything was in best order and believed more than ever that I suffered from mental fixations.") Thurnheer, who had arrived at 7 p.m., gave some German books, a cigar and a water-colour painting kit to the prisoner; he dined with him and stayed the night. ("The night", wrote Hess furiously later, "was absolutely quiet; whereas otherwise the locomotives would whistle every few minutes, now there were hours between. The envoy had hardly departed when the racket started all over again." In fact the orderly reports show that he had not complained about the trains for weeks.)

I visited Mr H. on 12 August 1942 [reported Thurnheer to the Swiss Government]. . . . Mr H. is located near [word blanked out by Censor] about four hours by rail from London, not a pleasant journey in the jam-packed trains of today.

I was met by Captain Crabtree, a six-foot-tall, strong and good-natured officer who took me over to Mr H.'s new quarters. He is housed in a special ground-floor wing of a hospital. A bedroom and living room are set aside for him at the end of the wing, leading out on to a little meadow completely cut off from the rest of the building on the left by a tall wooden fence while there is an ordinary shoulder-high hedge around the rest, with no barbed wire etc. There is a sentry in the garden on the other side of the hedge. Between the bedroom and living room and the lawn there is a wide glass veranda where Mr H. can sit outside even in poor weather. They are going to spread a tarpaulin across part of the glass roof at my suggestion so that there is some shade when the sun shines. Adjacent to Mr H.'s quarters are rooms for the orderlies and sentries, and a large room for the officers. All these rooms are connected by a long corridor separated from the entrance of Mr H.'s quarters by a plush curtain evidently to keep the noise out.

Immediately I arrived I saw the hospital's senior physician, who is also Mr H.'s doctor. He is a fine old gentleman of good breeding and he briefed me in a friendly and objective manner about Mr H.'s health. . . .
As it was already late I immediately visited Mr H. who was obviously delighted to see me and apologised for having put me to this long journey. I could see at once from his entire manner that Mr H. is considerably better. He is no longer in bed, he moved rapidly and without difficulty, and his facial expression is normal – no longer

inquisitive and suspicious. . . . He has become more active again, wants books, paint box, writing and drawing paper, he is working on plans for a house that are already far advanced; he eats with a hearty appetite, and has obviously completely abandoned his fears of being poisoned. . . .

I mention that the German Consulate in Geneva has asked about his health, and inquire whether I should answer and what. His opinion is that if possible we should not reply at all, because the ones who are interested in him, his relatives and friends, are kept up to date by his letters. If need be I should answer he is in good health.

Hess seemed more cheerful after Thurnheer's visit, but later he became irritable and slammed a few doors in discontent. A non-smoker, he wrapped the cigar in clean paper and gave it to Dr Ellis Jones.

The delusions came and went. The Welsh farmers burned their stubble, and he believed it had been done to annoy him. On 19 August, he stalked into the room where the two attendants were quietly reading: "What's the matter, gentlemen! Why can't you make *more* noise! You don't have to rest, what do you get paid for!"

That day, annoyed by the radio news – the BBC was still maintaining that the Dieppe raid had been a disaster for the *Germans* – he stamped up and down the verandah loudly whistling, he slammed some more doors, and he snarled at Sergeant Everatt, "It's a shame it's raining to-day. It stops them burning even more stubble!" On the 20th, as the truth about the Dieppe disaster emerged, he livened up and began conversing freely again.

Coupled with this childish sarcasm were sporadic flights of elation, morbid introspective thoughts and more delusions. They left an electric stove switched on and a hot bath running; he could only assume that the consumption rates would later be used to prove how well treated he had been.

21 August 1942   [Orderly's report]

Condition remains the same as the past several days. Constantly banging the furniture and visiting the [bathroom] annexe leaving the water running for some time. . . . Signs of agitation, depression, and suspicion.

He has shown a great interest in the pulse rate of the body, asking the attendants what the normal rate is, and how to take it. When asked why he wished to know this, he just said it did not matter.

He has not occupied himself very well and has been continually pacing in and out of his room.

During the afternoon the patient has occupied himself reading and listening to the radio. He remains depressed, irritable, and suspicious. Several times during the afternoon he has been noticed to be talking to himself. He sits for periods staring into space and then for no apparent reason begins to laugh.

This typical day's report, with its echoes of inexplicable laughter, shows further clear symptoms of what doctors recognize as Inappropriate Emotional Response, so perhaps there was some fundamental deterioration in this prisoner.

He showed little interest in extraneous phenomena. Asked by Corporal Riddle if he wanted to see an eclipse, he retorted sharply, "No!" In September 1942, however, Hess resumed his car outings, which had lapsed, he walked around the "airing yard", he picked blackberries in the little garden, and occasionally he chatted through the wire with Ellis Jones's little girl who exercised her pony in the field next door. He did not mind leaving Maindiff Court, but driving back in through the "prison gate" upset him badly.

Sometimes the outings took him to White Castle (Castell Gwyn), an eleventh-century military ruin on the summit of a commanding hill six miles from the hospital; other wartime tourists saw him wandering alone among the Elsinore-like battlements, or sitting in the sun making architectural sketches of the hornwork. The custodian, Mrs Emily Jones, guided him around the ruins, and told a newspaper two years later, "He was very interested in everything. He commented on the architecture." The disclosure, in the Liberal–leftist *News Chronicle*, that Hitler's deputy – "this blood-soaked swine", as the left-wing *Daily Mirror* called him – was being driven around local beauty spots angered readers who had relatives in German prison camps or whose own cars had been laid up for years without tyres or petrol. The War Office acted swiftly, in December 1944, to place the Castle out of bounds to Hess.

But this was still 1942. Hess had begun to try his hand at painting with water-colours brought to him by Thurnheer, and he found that it was not as easy as he had imagined. "You probably need a little instruction to start with," he confessed later.

> I lacked even really basic knowledge. I couldn't find any White in the paintbox, a grievous deficiency in my eyes: how was I to mix Grey? When a tube of White was forthcoming my Grey turned out a ghastly body-colour! Finally they got me a booklet, *Painting with Water Colours*, and this explained that Sky-Blue and Vermilion (of all things!) produce a Grey with every nuance, warm and beautiful, light and transparent. Now I could understand why Goethe was so happy about the artist friend who journeyed with him to Sicily and betrayed secrets like these to him. I've an intense admiration for the really great water-colour artists: it all seemed so simple to me before to dash off delightful evening settings with delicate Greys and pink cloudlets – but Oh Boy, it ain't.

The fresh air and exercise seemed to benefit him, although he again suspected that his food was being tampered with and he remarked on 7 September that everything was being done to annoy and distress him.

In vivid contrast to the word-pictures by the orderlies, the letters that

Hess wrote show a keen intellect, a precise recollection across the whole span of his life, and a long-sustained, subtle attempt to convey to his wife sufficient information to enable her to identify his location (*mountain* scenery, local *dialect*), and even to pass on his advice that mine warfare ("combating crabs") would subdue perfidious Albion. With each letter he enclosed a carbon copy of its predecessor, rightly guessing that the censors would not always excise the same words.

"I often think of my medical discussions with Professor G.," he wrote to Ilse on 9 September 1942, referring to Fritz Gerl, to whom he had written one year earlier (p. 189). "And I ponder particularly upon his ideas on combating *Krebs*" – the word's other meaning is cancer – "ideas that were so close to my heart and which he had hoped, together with a colleague [Dr Gähmann?], to propel forwards just before my flight. At that time I was – alas! – too preoccupied with my flight to devote enough time to this important idea with all its immense blessings for mankind."

After revealing to Ilse how Ernst Udet had tried to discourage him from piloting the difficult Messerschmitt-110 around Berlin, Hess casually remarked, "How closely my life is bound up with mountains. Isn't it a marvel? I worked out that I have lived roughly half my life near mountains."

He continued, referring to Wolf Rüdiger, his son: "I'm really pleased the little lad will soon be a proper mini-mountaineer thanks to his move to Ostrach valley. There certainly won't be any language problems for him, I can see him picking up the 'local dialect' double quick. Just think, him already on a school bench next year and facing up to life in earnest – I can hardly believe it! To me he's still the tiny, wide-eyed fellow sitting on the little white potty in his nursery at Harlaching, just as I last saw him. . . ."

A week later Churchill sent a handwritten request to the Foreign Office asking for a report on his prisoner. The upshot was that at 10.30 a.m. on 28 September 1942 Brigadier J. R. Rees arrived at Maindiff Court to see Hess. He found him tense, rather dramatic and depressed – the doctors told him that Hess was usually like this in the mornings.

Hess informed him of the Swiss Minister's visit, and of the innocent results of the laboratory analysis. "Has that", asked Rees, "really satisfied you that there was no attempt at poisoning you?"

"Yes," replied Hess with a hollow, humourless smile. "But I still feel from time to time that there is this risk."

The local doctors told the War Office expert that Hess had previously been obsessed with the train noises, but during the last three weeks, "since the fighting at Stalingrad got difficult for the Germans", he had begun having his "abdominal cramps" again and was less worried by the noises.

Rees saw no reason to alter his diagnosis that the man was now a psychopathic paranoid type of person with definite hysterical and hypochondriacal tendencies. The possible suicide risk might be lessened if Hess were to be provided with a sufficiently important companion. Although it was now common knowledge in the town that Hess was at

Rudolf Hess's handwriting showed no significant change between his imprisonment at Landsberg (above) and at Nuremberg (below)

67

Maindiff Court, he added, nobody seemed to spy or pry on him. As a human touch, Rees recommended humouring Hess's aversion to entering and leaving through the gate in the compound – he should be allowed to come and go through the main hospital building, he said.

Eden sent Rees's report round to 10 Downing Street.

Almost at once the quiet, haunted figure shuffling through the grass in the hospital grounds in Wales, or muttering "English swine!" beneath his breath as he snapped off the BBC news bulletin, became the object of an unseemly slanging match between Moscow and London.

Ever since May 1941 Moscow had speculated on the Hess episode. The Soviets believed that Hess had indeed been in touch with sympathetic and influential Englishmen and that these had given him to understand that, if he came over with certain proposals from Berlin, Britain would join in Hitler's assault on Russia; alternatively, Moscow suspected that Churchill was keeping Hess "up his sleeve" for the day when it might suit him to "compound with Hitler". It did not elude the Kremlin that literally since the day of Hess's dramatic flight, serious air raids on England had halted.

Not until September 1941 had Britain partially lifted the veil of secrecy, allowing Lord Beaverbrook to describe to Stalin his visit to Camp Z; the Soviet dictator had seemed "satisfied and amused". During 1942 the amusement had worn thin in the Kremlin as Britain failed to produce a Second Front offensive to take the weight off the Russians. Visiting Moscow in August, Churchill had promised the saturation bombardment of Berlin, but this promise had not been honoured, and the Soviet armies were in crisis at Stalingrad.

Out of the blue, on 19 October, breaking the tacit understanding that neither country should criticize the other, the Soviet Communist Party organ *Pravda* suggested that Britain was now a haven for Nazi gangsters, and demanded a clarification of Hess's status in particular. "Who is Hess after all?" asked the Soviet newspaper. "Is he a criminal deserving trial and punishment, or a plenipotentiary representative of Hitler's government in Britain, and hence enjoying immunity?" The British Ambassador in Moscow, Sir Archibald Clark Kerr, choked as he read the words. Moscow Radio repeated them that night, Tass issued the article free to British newspapers, and the *Soviet War News* published it in London.

The monitoring reports were immediately shown to Churchill. With his own victorious desert offensive about to begin at El Alamein, he saw no need to swallow Soviet insults. The Foreign Office agreed. "I don't see", scrawled Frank Roberts, head of the Central Department, in an ironic minute, "how the Soviet Govt. can bring evidence against Hess, with whom they were officially at least on the best of terms when he flew here!" But his colleagues feared that Stalin might even be toying with making a separate peace with Hitler. They suggested that Eden ask Soviet Ambassador Ivan Maisky point-blank whether Moscow's purpose was "to raise a public grievance for the purpose of breaking their undertakings with us".

British left-wingers picked up the jackal's howl, however. Tom Driberg put down a Parliamentary Question asking Eden whether he would comply with Moscow's suggestion that Hess be brought to trial immediately. And the Ambassador cabled from Moscow that he did not think Britain could afford to ignore the article. "We should make it clear beyond all doubt that we regard Hess as one of the leading criminals, and that we are holding him prisoner against the day when he will be put on trial with others."

The midday Cabinet meeting on 20 October in Churchill's room at the House of Commons agreed that Eden should reply to Driberg's Question by stating flatly that there was no reason to apply to Hess any other treatment than prescribed already for war criminals in general. In particular Eden was to point out robustly that Hess could hardly be held responsible for the Nazi misdeeds during their invasion of Russia, "since at the time he had come to this country Germany and Soviet Russia had still been in diplomatic relations".

Churchill sent him this note: "No concession to this [Soviet] behaviour. I liked yr. answer as proposed. WSC., 21.x."

Rudolf Hess, Deputy Führer of the Greater German Reich and Churchill's Prisoner of State, was not at first aware that he had become the object of international vituperation. A few days earlier, the orderlies had cleaned his room and found beneath the armchair which he used a folded sheet of newspaper in which he had carefully concealed a part of the previous night's dinner – fish and chips, potatoes, bread and rice. "This", they solemnly recorded, "is apparently the small portion which Patient removed from plate."

21 October 1942   [Corporal Riddle's report]
Complained sarcastically about razor blades. Took light breakfast after attendant sampling it. Has been writing again throughout the morning.

21 October 1942   [Sergeant Everatt's evening report]
Patient was writing on [my] taking over and has occupied himself thus most of the afternoon. Took light lunch which he asked to be tasted by the nurse on duty. Has been rather depressed this evening, but seemed very interested in the recorded speech of [South African Prime Minister] General [Jan] Smuts, also in Mr Eden's remarks on the patient in the House [of Commons, replying to Driberg's Question] to-day.

Took a good dinner with Mr May.

22 October 1942
Occupied himself most of the time writing, very sarcastic with reference to razor blades not being the type he likes, states it gives him great

pleasure to know the U-boat commanders are doing their job well and making the British go short of things that are necessary to life. . . .

Later that night, at 4.40 a.m., he asked Private Smedley for a pencil and paper: "Do you know how many times the whistles have blown during the night – how noisy it has been?"

Despite Eden's remarks in the House, Clark Kerr warned the government from Moscow that they must publish as full an account as possible of the Hess mission and his proposals, and stress Britain's intention to put him on trial eventually. Eden, recognizing the shaky legal basis of their continued imprisonment of Hess, was strongly against any public document. The Cabinet directed the former Ambassador to Moscow Sir Stafford Cripps to compile a full dossier for possible communication to Stalin.

Meanwhile, on 29 October the Cabinet decided that the British Ambassador should reassure Stalin that there had been no change in Britain's attitude to Hess since Lord Beaverbrook's visit to the Kremlin: "We have never had any intention of making any political use of him either now or at any future date."

Cripps, now Lord Privy Seal, studied all the documents that the government made available to him, and on 4 November submitted his report to the Cabinet. The Cabinet agreed with Eden that it should not be made public, but sent a summary of it with an added note about Hess's medical condition to Clark Kerr in Moscow.

FOREIGN OFFICE TO BRITISH AMBASSADOR IN MOSCOW
Telegram No. 332   *4 November 1942*

Hess landed in Scotland by parachute on May 10, 1941, wearing the uniform of a captain in the German air force. He claimed to be on a special mission to see Wing-Commander the Duke of Hamilton.

2. The Duke of Hamilton had been to Berlin in 1936 in connexion with the Olympic Games but had no recollection of having seen or met Hess. The Duke had previously received a letter dated September 23, 1940 from Dr Haushofer, a German friend of Hess, suggesting a meeting in Lisbon, without referring to Hess. The Duke had shown this letter to H.M.G. at the time. It was completely ignored and no reply was sent.★

3. On May 11 the Duke was ordered by his superior officers in the R.A.F. to see Hess, then under confinement in Maryhill Barracks, Glasgow. Hess claimed that Germany was bound to defeat England but that this was not Hitler's wish. Hess had therefore come to stop unnecessary slaughter and to make peace proposals. He claimed to know Hitler's mind but did not claim to have come with his authority. He was evidently under the impression that a party existed in England ready to

★ This was a blatant untruth. The SIS had intercepted Haushofer's letter, and had replied for Hamilton (see pp. 72–3).

discuss peace proposals. The Duke replied that there was now only one party in Great Britain.

4. Hess was interviewed on May 13, 14, and 15 by Mr Kirkpatrick, formerly of H.M. Embassy in Berlin, to identify him and discover his ideas in greater detail. Hess informed Mr Kirkpatrick that he had come without repeat, without [last two words handwritten] the knowledge of Hitler. He elaborated his views on the certainty of Germany's victory and repeated that Hitler had no designs against the British Empire. Hess proposed a peace settlement on the following basis: (i) Germany to have a free hand in Europe and to receive her colonies back; (ii) England to have a free hand in the British Empire; (iii) Russia to be included in Asia, but Germany intended to satisfy certain demands upon Russia either by negotiation or by war. Hess denied that Hitler contemplated an early attack on Russia.

5. Hess insisted, however, that Germany could only negotiate with an alternative British Government, which did not include Mr Churchill and his colleagues. If [the words "Hess peace offer" deleted] this opportunity were rejected Great Britain would be destroyed utterly and kept in a state of permanent subjection.

6. Hess was interviewed twice by then members of H.M. G[overn-ment], on June 9 1941 by the Lord Chancellor, Ld. Simon ["1941" and next six words handwritten] and September 9 by Ld. Beaverbrook [last three words handwritten]. The object of these interviews was to ascertain any further information of value, more particularly as regards the state of affairs in Germany. It has throughout been [last three words changed from "was"] made clear to Hess that there was no question whatever of any talks or negotiations of any kind taking place with Hitler or his Government.★

7. The conclusion drawn by H.M.G. from these interviews was as follows:

(a) Hess came on his own initiative.
(b) He thought his mission had a considerable prospect of success.
(c) He thought that he would find a strong anti-war opposition party here.
(d) His "terms" attempted to reproduce Hitler's mind as known to Hess.
(e) Hess had contemplated this mission ever since the collapse of France.

8. As has been publicly stated, Hess has been dealt with as a prisoner of war since his arrival and will so continue to be treated till the end of the war. Apart from the above-mentioned persons, his guard and those attending to his health, Hess has seen no visitors.★

9. Shortly after Hess' arrival here his mental state appeared peculiar.

★ Evidently guilt-stricken, Sir Alexander Cadogan's deputy Sir Orme Sargent ("Moley") recommended omitting this whole paragraph, for obvious reasons.
★ This was also untrue. The Protecting Power (Switzerland) had visited Hess three times already, as Cripps wrote in his report. A Foreign Office hand deleted this before his report was circulated to the War Cabinet.

Eminent psychiatrists diagnosed mental instability with signs of persecution mania. There is no doubt that Hess is mentally completely unbalanced, though his condition varies considerably from time to time.

Britain had something to conceal about Hess: not only that he had actually met two Cabinet ministers, but that his health was in a questionable state. Therefore, directing Sir Archibald Clark Kerr to take the statement round to Marshal Stalin, the Foreign Office warned that the Soviet government must on no account make it public. To state now that Hess was mentally unstable would show that Berlin had told the truth and that Britain had lied in May 1941. "If Hess's mental instability becomes known to the German Government," the Foreign Office explained, "they might make out a good case under the Prisoners of War Convention for his repatriation." Justifying this act of criminal concealment the Foreign Office telegram continued: "We naturally do not intend to let Hess return to Germany and so possibly escape answering for his share in German war crimes." ("Nor do we desire", Sir Alexander Cadogan had continued in his original draft of this telegram, "to give the Germans a propaganda weapon by refusing to hand back a man who, as we have publicly stated, is being treated as a Prisoner of War, and whose mental instability would have been publicly admitted by us.")

If Hess had achieved anything by his flight, therefore, it was this: he exposed the shallow ethics of the victors who would later denounce him as a war criminal.

Principal among these were the Soviet government, who had in the thirties cruelly massacred five million Ukrainians, and whose own catalogue of crimes was by no means complete in 1942. On the evening of 5 November the British Ambassador read out the Foreign Office statement on Hess to Marshal Stalin and Vyacheslav Molotov, his foreign minister. Two hours of straight talking followed, with Stalin restive, impatient, but by no means on the defensive. His own victims, tens of thousands of Polish intellectuals and officers, were still resting, their hands tied with barbed wire, their corpses as yet undiscovered beneath the young roots of pine groves freshly planted in the forests of Katyn and Starobielsk. He could still afford a sanctimonious tone about the Germans.

Initially defending *Pravda*'s line, he demanded, "Why is Hess left alone? Is he not a criminal?" But then Molotov showed him the actual article, and Stalin dropped it like a hot potato.

The British Ambassador read out London's statement on the Hess affair.

"All of that", rasped the surly dictator, "has appeared in the press already." He poured out three vodkas, and pushed one towards the Englishman. "I have two questions to ask," he continued. "After a war, it is customary to repatriate prisoners of war: do you intend to send Hess home?" He tipped the fiery liquid down his throat and wiped his moustache. "If Goebbels landed in the UK tomorrow, would you send him back as a P.o.W. too?"

The Englishman set his mind at rest on this. Stalin then showed that he was worried by the plan to set up a United Nations commission to try the criminals. "I would not like to see Hitler, Mussolini and the rest of them escaping like the Kaiser to some neutral country."

Clark Kerr reassured him on this too: Churchill's government proposed a "political decision" – liquidating the enemy leaders upon capture.

Stalin – both on this and on later occasions when Churchill proposed this lynch law in person – was shocked. "Whatever happens, there must be some kind of court decision," he growled. "Otherwise people will say that Churchill, Roosevelt and Stalin were wreaking vengeance on their political enemies!"

"I am sure", replied the Ambassador with a thin smile, "that the political decision that Mr Churchill has in mind will be accompanied by all the necessary formalities."

Hess had sent his little boy a fond birthday letter, but now remembered that it would pass through the hands of countless censors, and regretted the private family intimacies that he had thus allowed enemy eyes to see. "That's dreadful," he wrote to Ilse a few days after the birthday in question. "I used to get the same feeling sometimes after delivering a speech: there was some sentence that you blurted out, and you'd like to be able to haul it right back in again – but an Eternity cannot retrieve what it took only a second to say!"

Later in this pensive letter the prisoner added, "It must be odd for you to get a letter from me commenting on something you wrote nine months ago. It's an odd world whichever way you look at it. But the day will come when it will be put together again – and then we'll be put together again too!"

Frau Hess, perturbed by hints in letters such as these, requested the International Red Cross to find out the true state of his health. This perfectly legal request set the cat among the pigeons at the Foreign Office. Refusal to allow the IRC to visit Hess might hamper the task of its delegates dealing with British prisoners of war in Germany.

The request was nevertheless refused. Instead, the War Office sent their most senior physician, Major-General Arnold Stott, to Maindiff Court with Brigadier Rees on 26 October. Stott found Hess in good health, and stated this in his report (co-signed by Rees).

This certainly pleased Hess. The corporals found him more cheerful on the following evening. He talked freely of the war, and expressed glee at Japanese claims to have sunk several American warships without loss.

"The war is turning in favour of the Axis," Hess said.

But it was not. Rommel's army in Africa had begun a retreat that would end in Tunisia six months later. The Red Army was about to

counterattack at Stalingrad, and the RAF were inflicting gaping wounds
on German cities. After the Russians encircled the German Sixth Army at
Stalingrad, his mood changed again.

29 November 1942   [Orderly's report]

Miserable and solitary condition. . . . Seems to be annoyed at the claims
in the paper, and passed sarcastic remarks. Banging the doors and chairs
each time he moves.

The "Most Secret" psychiatric report which Brigadier Rees, evidently
under political guidance from the War Office, submitted to Sir Stafford
Cripps to append to his report read as follows:

Hess is a man of good intelligence but of poor character and personality.
He had certainly been over-anxious and "neurotic" earlier in life. Whilst
under observation here he has shown definite delusions and for more
than half his time has been unable to control them and has in fact been
suffering from a "paranoid" psychosis. This unsoundness of mind might
very well be hidden if he had to take the lead in a "party" once more,
but his personal relationships and his judgment would, however, be
disturbed by it. The fluctuations in the severity of his symptoms will
recur and there is a perpetual risk of another suicide attempt without
much warning. For that reason he must be under constant psychiatric
and nursing supervision.

Were he an ordinary civilian patient it would have been difficult to
justify certification, save just after his attempt at suicide. He could
moreover be living at home and doing his work, although his difficult
personality and eccentricities would probably lead to trouble.

From the angle of "responsibility" it is in my opinion doubtful
whether at any time he has been prevented by his mental difficulties from
knowing the nature and quality of his acts.

The last sentence revealed the schizophrenic trend in the British official
argument on Hess: Hess was mentally ill, but not enough to allow his
repatriation or to mitigate his putative "crimes" in a future trial. The
convolutions would become even more apparent as the war progressed.

The Foreign Office had sent to Washington the same mixture of truths
and half-truths about Hess as had been shown to Stalin. Lord Halifax,
who showed the document to President Roosevelt over lunch on 8
December 1942, was given the same obfuscating reasons to impress the
Americans with the importance of not revealing them.

The appeal by Ilse Hess to the International Red Cross had put
Churchill is something of a quandary, as Lord Halifax explained to
President Roosevelt on 9 March 1943. Allowing IRC access would have
revealed the truth about Hess's indifferent mental health. So the report by
General Stott and Brigadier Rees had been concocted instead – doctored
to conceal their War Office ranks (they were well-known specialists in

civilian life). It was given to the International Red Cross with a letter emphasizing that it was for the personal information of Frau Hess alone: "There must be no publicity whatever."

Ingenuous though these British precautions were, it is hard to understand the anxiety, given that even this report had been still further doctored. "You will see", the Foreign Office elaborated in messages to both Stalin and Roosevelt explaining the omissions, "that this report makes no explicit reference to Hess' mental state. . . . This was done deliberately to avoid the danger that the medical certificate might be used publicly by the Germans to expose our original propaganda. . . . They might even be able, on grounds of insanity, to claim Hess' repatriation."

The Red Cross refused to go along with this deceit. In June 1943 they lectured the Foreign Office that it was impossible to convey even this document to Frau Hess without taking the German government into their confidence. The Foreign Office therefore decided not to make any communication at all to her. "His Majesty's Government", Lord Halifax was instructed to tell Roosevelt, in what was perhaps one of the Washington Embassy's most fatuous remarks, "are not prepared to trust the German Government to refrain from undesirable publicity."

15   Red Earth

Separated from his son and Ilse by the width of England and Germany, the breadth of a sea that all of Hitler's armies had not dared to cross, Rudolf Hess felt the tide of insanity lapping around his feet throughout the winter of 1942–3. If he was distantly aware from the pages of *The Times* that he read each morning, and the BBC broadcasts that he tuned into each afternoon, that he and his former colleagues might be tried for their lives when the war ended, he did not show it in his letters home.

For weeks, as the battle for Stalingrad dragged on, he hardly read at all – except for Commander Grenfell's great work on naval strategy which he devoured, and then read through again. Telling Ellis Jones that he thought he might have a heart ailment, he refused to leave the grounds at all, restricting his exercise to morning and evening walks with the doctor in the airing yard.

He remained depressed and mildly deluded, believing that his radio, his clothing, his socks, his food were being interfered with. His real or imaginary stomach cramps persisted – the orderlies paid as little attention to these gripes as, if truth be told, Hess did himself. They became as much a part of his daily ritual as Private Clifford massaging his damaged leg, the walk to the bathroom annexe, the shared meals in the officers' mess and the games of darts with the young officers. Ellis Jones provided all types of medicine against these "pains", including belladonna, but was sure that the prisoner never took any of them – that Hess squirrelled them away for later examination by some honest Superior Power.

Occasionally there were breaks in the routine. When the regular stomach pains occurred on 22 December, Hess decided that he wanted to die: he refused the soap-and-water enema ordered by Ellis Jones, and invited him to attend his post-mortem instead. "An enema's no use," he groaned. "I want to let whatever poison is in my bowels stay there – where the International Commission can find it."

A remorseless nature duly thwarted his intention, and he survived. He remained quiet and totally uninterested in his surroundings: on Christmas Eve in Wales, of course, this could hardly be held against him. He barely talked with his captors, and threw suspicious looks at them. "[I] had to have part of his tea," wrote Corporal Riddle that afternoon, with only a report book to hear his complaint.

After Christmas 1942, Hess was eased out of his self-imposed solitude by the need to install a new power point in his room. One of the new guards, Lieutenant May – a likeable, heavy, fair-haired officer who took to wearing shorts and tropical kit in the summer, but recognized that sunshine was a rarity because he organized the men's tomato and cucumber crops in a covered solarium at the end of the dining room – found the right way to coax him out of doors. It just needed the right stimulus. If he said outright, "Come and see the lovely sunset," Hess would not budge; but when May remarked in his hearing, "There's a lovely sunset tonight!", that would lure Hess to his window, and then outside to see it. Eventually Lieutenant May persuaded him to go for country walks again, and his health improved. On 30 December, Everatt marvelled that Hess had left at 3 p.m. with the Guard Commander Captain Crabtree for a car ride, taken a long walk up a local hill and then walked back home again, feeling very tired but pleased with himself.

Major Ellis Jones remarked upon the change in his mood from depression to mild elation: Hess took a renewed interest in his personal appearance, asked for hair cream, re-entered into friendly conversation, and rediscovered his shelf of German and English books.

8 January 1943 [Orderly's report]

Patient awoke 09.00 hrs rather cheerful and delighted with the morning news [about Arnim's local victory in Tunisia]. . . . Was visited by Dr Phillips [Superintendent, Monmouth County Mental Hospital] at 11.45 hrs, and Major Ellis Jones at 12.00 hrs, and walked in the grounds for a time. Took lunch with Capt. Crabtree, M.C., went for a car ride & a country walk at 14.15 hrs.

10 January 1943

Patient went for a walk with Capt. Crabtree . . . took a light tea, visited by Brigadier Rees who was very impressed by the improvement. . . .

Despite these encouraging signs, Major Ellis Jones was ever-conscious of the residual possibility that Hess might still be moved to kill himself. "I feel", the doctor wrote to the War Office on 14 January 1943, "that stringent and adequate precautions would make his life unbearable, increase the prominence of his delusions, and accelerate his deterioration, and that if he was determined to commit suicide, he is so intelligent and secretive that he would outwit us all."

Over ensuing weeks, some of the orderlies' entries deserved an award for nonchalance:

23 January 1943

Occupied himself writing for some time. Took his meals alone. Sat out in the evening sunshine dressed in his flying suit. Had an attack of "pains" 18.00 hrs. Nothing unusual to report.

It had all become a commonplace for them. On 4 February, their prisoner had as usual complained about how disturbing the sound of doors banging was; but, walking past doors later that day, he banged each and every one as hard as he was able.

The six orderlies stood the ordeal better than the guard commanders or their officers. The turnover was high. On the 16th, yet another commanding officer was introduced to Hess, Captain Nelson-Smith. He started with the best intentions, and scarcely a day passed without him taking the prisoner out on extended motor journeys or rambles in the countryside. "Whenever Hess went for a walk," recalls medical orderly J. Clifford, who still lives in Abergavenny, "he would be accompanied by an officer and, about thirty or forty yards behind, two RAMC personnel. In the summer Hess would wear a blue sports coat, grey flannel trousers and brown sandals. In the winter he would wear a long blue overcoat." But the curiosity value palled. Even the games of darts were a trial of nerves. Hess hurled the projectiles at the board so hard it was difficult to extract them. His aim was deadly, but his fears showed themselves here too – he would duck instinctively if he collected his darts and turned round to find his opponent poised and ready to throw.

He declined the drinks offered to him in the mess. "Wine or beer or whisky," this puritan figure lectured the young officers in guttural tones, "They cloud the judgement." "My job", he explained to Lieutenant May, "was to assess public opinion for the Führer: you needed a clear head for that." It was the same with tobacco. "Tobacco ruins the palate," he explained to Lieutenant May. "And it prevents you from smelling the countryside." May could not help but notice how much this simple man liked the Welsh countryside. Out for a stroll, Hess liked nothing better than to watch children playing and listen to their laughter. He threw a passing glance at the older girls too, but disdained those with rouge and heavy lipstick. "I like things and people clean," said the Deputy Führer after passing one group of giggling Welsh women. "Clean – but neat."

In those first months of 1943 little changed. He drew the £6 a month allowed him as a Luftwaffe captain by the German Red Cross. He still had the "pains", the complaints about slamming doors and barking dogs and stamping sentries. He still suffered the alternating moods.

It all became such a routine that one night Private Clifford would enter in the report book, "He did *not* make any remark about the noise made by the sentry." For the most part, the entries show little pattern or progression during those months. On 15 March, he "sat down, relapsed into the depressed & thoughtful attitude". On the 22nd, apropos of nothing at all, he told Riddle, "Many people in England are annoyed this morning because the Führer spoke yesterday." He still had his faith in victory. "Eleven U-boats a week," he boasted to Lieutenant May. "Eleven U-boats a week we are launching. How can an island stand up to that!"

And then he would retire to his room, sink to the carpet and roll over in contrived agony – gripped by sudden abdominal spasms which, the doctors knew, were not organic spasms at all because he never drew up his knees in the normal reaction to such pain. They were pains produced by the mind alone, no less intense for it, but incapable of treatment by any mortal remedies.

Lieutenant May found it hard not to like this man. "You could spend forty-eight hours with him," he later said, "and not realize anything was radically wrong with him." He found the captive "painfully conscientious" – the man was that rarest of animals, a genuine idealist who unashamedly extolled the pure National Socialist doctrine, and idolized its Führer. Hess had, said May, "some of the virtues and all the lack of balance of that furious creed". He was a physically brave man too, said May. Once, their ramble took them across a field, at the far end of which emerged a bull, snorting and bellowing at the intrusion. The two soldiers, the officer and the medical orderly all turned and ran, but not the Deputy Führer of Nazi Germany.

Hess read deeper into Goethe, developed a "completely new" picture of the poet's stubborn old father, and penned literate and well-organized letters that betrayed none of the bizarre traits that his captors saw in him. "I am so happy", he wrote to Ilse on 14 February

that the boy still remembers his Papa! That he still knows where to find all the splendid rolling, rattling, rumbling and puffing toys that we secretly played with in my little study in the last few days before my flight. All the time, I'm figuring out what I'm going to tell him and show him to make a "technical, geographic and scientific" boy out of Buz [Wolf Rüdiger].

I never dreamed how important my own technical and mathematical ability were going to be one day for me: without them I'd never have managed the "flight of my life". I wouldn't have mastered either the Me-110's complex controls or the navigation. In our human existence, everybody has his purpose, even if some people take half a century to realize theirs. And some don't perceive it at all.

In another letter that he wrote to Ilse five weeks later his thoughts were still on their little boy. "*Ach ja,*" he reflected,

it was a long-nurtured dream of ours to grant a great musician or poet to the human race! But: "man fears and Another steers" – and from what I hear of the little fellow's pet subjects I too no longer doubt that his talents are on the technical side. And now, unfettered by my paternal prerogatives, he'll be able to develop this gift – which I was never able to, aside from my little ocean flights~. All those years ago when my aim was to be the first one to do a Lindbergh in reverse, we never guessed how much I was one day going to need all the expert knowledge I picked up during the year-long preparations.

Major Ellis Jones told Rees that at times their prisoner still talked as though he expected to return to Germany and resume his functions as Deputy Führer. He often talked of the heyday of his career. He had inaugurated a wartime system of marriage by proxy, enabling a pregnant girl to be "married" to the father of her unborn child even though he was fighting in Poland or France, or commanding a U-boat thousands of miles away. Once he had conducted an agricultural experiment, he told Lieutenant May: bulldozing a plot of land, covering it with a special top-dressing and planting it; then they had had to replace the hedges, he found, because the ecology could not do without the birds of the hedgerows.

That seemed to be his message: that Providence had made each creature for a purpose, and he believed he had not exhausted his usefulness. Passing his hands wearily across his temples, he retired to his room to listen to the BBC news, the volume turned low as was the custom in Nazi Germany. He still believed that Hitler would win.

He was aware that his intense, dramatic manner often did not make him good company. On 6 April he asked to dine alone, saying, "I think it would not be pleasant for the officer this time."

Sometimes his remarks were disjointed, betokening far-distant thoughts, closer to the dark and fir-clad mountains of Bavaria than to the purple slopes of a mellow Welsh spring evening. After breaking two tumblers on 12 April, he remarked to the Commander, Captain Nelson-Smith, "In Germany that is said to bring good luck."

One evening – it was midnight of the vernal solstice – Private Smedley had given Hess a hot-water bottle for his "stomach pains" when both men saw a black cat ambling with a proprietorial air out of Hess's sitting room. Hess smiled a knowing smile. "That must be the devil!" he said. Smedley assured him that black cats were a sign of good luck, where he came from. Hess preferred his own beliefs; with the devil temporarily departed, he returned to bed and fell into a fast and pain-free sleep.

In mid-May 1943 Hitler's army in North Africa went into captivity in Tunisia with its commander, General von Arnim. No German could pretend that this was anything but another major defeat, though not as tragic in human terms as Stalingrad.

Hess's attitude hardened. On the 21st Brigadier Rees visited Maindiff Court. For the first time that he could recall the prisoner refused to shake hands with him; he did not even rise from his chair. "I have decided", announced Hess, "not to shake hands with anyone until after the war."

To the psychiatrist this was a clear reaction to the worsening news, although Hess still maintained that Dr Goebbels's propaganda broadcasts were more accurate than the BBC's.

As Rees would have expected, the abdominal "pains" were noticeably more pronounced when the war news was unfavourable.

Hess asked the Brigadier on this occasion whether he had yet met Colonel-General von Arnim or General von Thoma (the Afrika Korps commander captured at El Alamein in November).

"Why do you ask?" inquired Rees. "Do you miss companionship?"

"No – it is better that I am here by myself," was the lonely reply.

He was very much conscious of his status as Deputy Führer, and to some extent the British pandered to it – allowing him to believe that the standard "G.R." (Georgius Rex) crest embossed on the government tableware meant that he was His Majesty's personal guest, and that the guards and orderlies were his own establishment.

Occasionally, to get his way, he raised his voice. "That is what I wish," he would pronounce. "Those are my orders." And once Lieutenant May heard Hess end one argument with a medical attendant: "In future I will *write* my orders!"

As July 1943 – an ill-starred month for the Axis cause – progressed, the symptoms of apparent delusions became more marked in Hess. Hitler's offensive in the east was stalled; the Allies invaded Sicily; the Italian regime collapsed. The fanfares heralding an inevitable victory were coming now from London, Moscow and Washington, not Berlin.

5 July 1943   [Orderly's report]

Patient . . . had an attack of pains at 07.50 hrs . . . settled down to reading until 11.50 hrs, had a further attack of pains. Hot-water bottle given. . . .

Lunch was served. Patient called on Major Ellis Jones to taste his lunch, also asked him to give a signed statement that food and medicine were not tampered with. Request was carried out.

Went for country walk at 15.00 hrs with Mr May. . . .

Took a good dinner with Mr May, was given massage by Private Clifford. . . . Settled down to reading until 21.00 hrs, when he again had an attack of pains. . . . Has been very depressed, deluded & hallucinated at times.

10 July 1943

Slept until 04.45 hrs when he had a violent attack of "pains" which caused him to lie on the carpet in the dining room for ten minutes groaning and waving his arms about. (Hot-water bottle given.)

16 July 1943

At 04.55 hrs an attack of "abdominal pains". Hot-water bottle given, also a drink of hot water. Patient spent twenty minutes on the dayroom floor moaning and rolling about, and then returned to bed.

19 July 1943

He awoke with abdominal pains at 05.20 hrs. This lasted twenty-three minutes. During this attack he rolled about the dayroom floor, and made an unusual amount of noise. Hot-water bottle given.

Such was the picture seen by the doctors and their staff.

At the same time, the prisoner was capable of writing beautiful prose to his wife, incidentally dropping further hints to help her locate the mountains among which he was being held:

16 July 1943

For some months, between breakfast and luncheon here I have been translating a book from English into German. I also occasionally spend time setting down on paper anecdotes about my son's life so far, or writing down such episodes of my own life and the like as seem worth preserving for you and what I hope will be a multitude of grandchildren; or writing letters home – tho' that's really rather less of an everyday occurrence!ᨆ.

I've given up taking an after-lunch nap. Instead, I often get the opportunity to go for a stroll in the unquestionably beautiful country around about, pausing for little rests if the weather's good: of course I choose these breaks where I can enjoy the most pleasant view.

Particularly attractive and unusual are the colours of this countryside – of which the bright red earth is the most striking feature, between green meadows and fields ripening to yellow hues like trees in the autumn. The shadow of each passing cloud changes the colour schemes and thus the whole effect.

It sometimes happens that in the changing light a mountain dominating the distant scenery changes colour within a few minutes from violet-black, dark blue, olive and emerald green, to reddish-brown and yellow or blue-grey. I think the colours of late autumn and winter are far more beautiful than those of the other seasons, which probably has something to do with the softer light and, again, the way that the freshly ploughed fields splash their even redder hues among meadows that stay green even in winter.

When people tell me painters adore this countryside, I can believe it.

He hoped that Haushofer would know that this red earth was found only around Abergavenny. The words "red earth" were routinely excised by the British censor from this letter but they slipped through in the carbon copy enclosed with the next.

He concluded with a quotation from Goethe, remarking pathetically that the more beautiful the setting, the more these lines held true:

> When the Nightingale sings to lovers
>   Its song with love caress'd,
> It sounds like aches and sighs
>   To the captive and oppressed.

As the clouds gathered over the Reich his symptoms became more acute. For a while he refused to have the radio in his room, and declined the loan of Lieutenant May's either. Its effusions were only bad – Mussolini overthrown, Sicily evacuated, firestorms sweeping Hamburg. The fear of poison did not leave him. On the night of the first fire raid on Hamburg he asked Private Clifford for a Soneryl tablet, then challenged him: "Will you take half?"

Clifford smiled, and agreed,

"It's not necessary," Hess blurted out helplessly, and took the tablet whole.

In the autumn of 1942, the Nazi Party had quietly deleted Rudolf Hess's name from the membership lists. He himself was beyond the Party's reach, but his entire staff had been arrested and imprisoned after his flight. Since that time his secretary Laura Schrödl, his adjutants Alfred Leitgen and Karlheinz Pintsch, his manservant Josef Platzer, his private detective Kriminal-Kommissar Franz Lutz and the other staff members Rudi Lippert, Günther Sorof and Ernst Schulte-Strathaus (who was over sixty) had languished in prison camps; more ominously, the Party had refused to accept their membership dues. Bormann was behind all this, and even Himmler was powerless to intervene.

By the spring of 1943 all except one had been released. But Bormann now took steps to ensure that their livelihoods were permanently ruined. After discussing the case with Hitler on the evening of 10 April, he wrote to the Party Treasurer, Franz Xaver Schwarz: "The Führer has decided that the accomplices in the Rudolf Hess affair are to be evicted from the Party with effect from 12 May 1941. . . . Only Alfred Leitgen is still in custody, and the Führer is not disposed to release him yet. The other males involved are to be posted to punishment battalions."

At the end of August Hess received a disturbing letter from Ilse: it opened his eyes for the first time to the draconic steps taken against all of his personal staff for their presumed complicity in his flight to Scotland. The corporals saw him open this letter after breakfast on the 30th. "During the morning," they reported, "he became rather agitated – apparently after reading his mail."

In fact such an impotent fury gripped him that several days passed before he felt able to respond. He then wrote her these cool, dispassionate lines, designed evidently to protect her from worse:

England, 4 September 1943

I am so glad to see again and again from all your letters that nothing has changed in your innermost feelings towards the man with whose fate we have been so closely bound up, for better or for worse, for over twenty years: nor has anything changed in me in this respect.

One must never forget what an immense burden these hard times place upon his nerves – a burden that can result in angry decisions that he would not have taken under other circumstances. I'm not thinking of myself at all in saying this, but of my men: for my own part, I had already taken all this into account.

Taking his anger into account did not, I admit, prevent a great rage from overwhelming me over the fate of the "lads": your latest letter shows things in a light totally different from how I in my innocence saw them before.

The upshot has been that for several days in a row I stamped up and down my room for hours on end literally foaming with rage and in the course of a regrettably somewhat one-sided dialogue I stated my opinions in very down-to-earth language and stated a few basic truths as well.

It is clear from his closing remarks, full of sarcasm about the real culprit and his "executive decrees" (*Ausführungsbestimmungen*) that Hess ascribed the blame to his successor Martin Bormann for the persecution of his staff.

Despite heavy censorship, bubbles of interest did surface in newspapers about Hess. Questions were asked in the House, and invariably stonewalled. An MP – it was the incorrigible Will Thorne again – asked about the "£15,000 of securities" that Hess had brought with him. And in August 1943 the loose-tongued Minister of Information Brendan Bracken aired some painful indiscretions about Hess while visiting the United States. Little or nothing of this outside curiosity penetrated to Hess himself. He was hermetically excluded from the outside world, or so the Foreign Office thought.

On the agitated, irritable day that the letter about Bormann's machinations had come from Ilse, Lieutenant May had lunched with the prisoner – then he virtually vanished from Maindiff Court. A few days later he was arrested by Military Police and court-martialled for having talked to the press.

Under the headline "THE STORY ALL BRITAIN HAS AWAITED" journalist Guy Ramsey published May's revelations – without of course naming him – on the front page of the London *Daily Mail* on 1 September. It sent a shockwave through the government. "The most public account that I have yet seen of Herr Hess's present conditions of confinement and state of mind", was how one Foreign Office official described it. General Gepp demanded a report from Captain Nelson-Smith, Commander of the Guard, because if one thing was plain it was that the information came from inside the hospital.

The article revealed how many officers and men were guarding Hess, and described the hospital set among beautiful western slopes; it disclosed his daily routine, and his phobias and habits. It stated that he was suffering a persecution mania, "fearing poison in his meals", and added that he had refused to listen to the radio since the fall of Sicily.

"He is old-maidish in his tidiness," the article stated, "and if anything is moved while he is out at exercise, he objects. . . . His papers are filed as they were when he was Deputy Führer. His notes, his occasional verses, his many drawings – the bulk of them architectural designs constructed with considerable skill and delicacy – are all tabulated."

Lieutenant May had told Ramsey that the casual witness might spend two days with Hess and not see anything wrong with him. "Only those who know him can spot it: the sudden jerk of the head, the inclination of the ear to catch the non-existent voice; the careful moving of a piece of meat on his plate to one side, and the cunning concealment of it behind a piece of potato or cabbage leaf."

Foreign Office official William Strang read this front-page article and minuted to Anthony Eden: "It will certainly give some of us a lot of trouble." "Yes," Eden agreed, and demanded an immediate War Office search for the culprit.

Hess has said [the *Daily Mail* article reported] that Hitler's whole plan was not aimed at world-domination but merely to gain her rightful place for a Germany unbearably humiliated by the Treaty of Versailles; that no war against England was ever intended.

"Only to two things", concluded the article, "can [Hess] look forward, say his physicians: a lunacy which will obliterate the world – or death."

The War Cabinet, whose ministers had agreed never to reveal what they knew about Hess, fumed at the article. "It was somewhat embarrassing", the minutes of their next morning's meeting concluded, "that these disclosures should now have been made." They were likely to lead to awkward questions when Parliament returned from the summer recess. On 13 September, *The Times* published a leading article on Hess, and several Questions were indeed put down.

On the 20th the Cabinet asked Eden to give to the House a statement closely following the memorandum drafted by Sir Stafford Cripps in 1942 for Stalin and Roosevelt. Roosevelt was at once informed that Eden proposed to reply to a Question on the lines of that memorandum, "but with certain important omissions and additions". Once more, there would be no reference to Hess's mental state to prevent the Germans "expos[ing] our original propaganda that Hess was sane", and claiming his repatriation.

At Maindiff Court the days were sunny, and Hess improved. A new officer, Lieutenant Fenton, had replaced the hapless May, who was now like Hess a prisoner. Dining with Fenton on the 17th Hess appeared "in good humour with usual appetite". The Deputy Führer read copiously, wrote prolifically and listened to music broadcast from Germany. He sunbathed and exercised, often stark naked, on the verandah. He had started slimming, eschewing fats and eating only dry toast for breakfast. ("He still asks the orderlies to taste his breakfast and tea," they remarked, amused at his lack of consistency. "Never lunch and dinner.") The improvement was obvious to Brigadier Rees, visiting him for an hour on 5 October. Hess was talkative and amiable.

He liked Lieutenant Fenton, who was slimmer than his predecessor, May, and more mild-mannered – less of an extrovert, and trusted him closely: he asked to be taken for country walks again, and ambled round the little compound, engaged in conversation with the newcomer. For a time even the "pains" subsided. He also shed his poison phobia – evidently literally, because two days after the Rees visit a plumber found the lavatory basin obstructed, blocked by "a fair quantity of food".

But then a change overcame him, like a dark shadow cast across a landscape. Almost certainly he had read in *The Times* on 21 October 1943 the Parliamentary discussion on the trial of war criminals. One MP (Captain Cunningham-Reid) asked whether Hess would be tried forthwith, "and the sentence carried out immediately afterwards" as a deterrent to war criminals at large. The government replied, "No, Sir."

During the ensuing weeks, the orderlies' diaries show the subtle lowering of Hess's mood, although it would be hard to pinpoint precisely when the relapse began. As November began he had still been amiable and content; as the month ended, all of the old phobias had returned.

Had he still been there, Lieutenant May would have recognized the first stray signs: on the 8th, the prisoner complained that his radio was not working properly – always a first hint of impending trouble. Five days later, he sliced a finger accidentally on a broken tumbler, and "adopted an attitude of extreme pain" as a sergeant gave first aid; that evening, depressed and still unshaven, Hess brooded over the cut finger and began complaining about noises again. On the 15th he wrote to the government, asking to be moved elsewhere (the War Office had him notified that he had no right to claim confinement in any particular type of camp). By the end of the month all the old complaints were there.

Of greater importance, seen in retrospect, was that he claimed to have lost his memory. Breakfasting on 14 November, he asked the orderlies why they casually helped themselves to samples off his plates. They reminded him that he had asked them to. "Really?" asked the prisoner, his eyes wide with astonishment. "I don't remember that!"

The onset of Hess's amnesia startled Brigadier Rees and the medical specialists although such cases were not entirely unexpected. They had no reason to doubt that it was genuine. True, he used this new ailment several times as a handle upon which he hung a request to be transferred to a proper PoW camp, and this was one of the main topics in his discussion with the Swiss Minister on 27 November.

Walther Thurnheer had arrived without advance warning and was able to spend ninety minutes with him. He found Hess thinner and paler than before. As usual he avoided politics: during his last visit, Hess had been convinced Germany was about to conquer all of North Africa. Now the boot was on the other foot.

I inquired [reported Thurnheer] whether Mr Hess had any wishes. . . . He is suffering from loneliness and from the isolation from his fellow countrymen and he would like to be transferred to a German prisoner-of-war camp as this would give him a change. . . . What he does not want is to be transferred to a camp where only German generals are held. . . . He cannot perceive any reason why this request should be turned down. . . . I myself am of the opinion that – quite apart from his state of health which I am not competent to judge – Mr Hess would do well to stay put, particularly now that the really hard fighting is about to begin. . . . Mr Hess insists however on being told of the legal reasons if his request is turned down.

Hess assured him he was being treated well, he had complete trust in the staff, and no longer feared poison attempts. The Commandant told Thurnheer afterwards that they had had to limit the outside exercise because of problems from spectators.

Remarkably, there was no trace of amnesia during the visit by the Swiss diplomat. It was also a very unusual feature in a paranoiac. But to Rees, it seemed clear that the condition was "psychogenic, and not organic". Reviewing the symptoms on 3 February 1944 he would conclude that although an *organic* loss of memory – a brain disease – could not be ruled out it would be rare indeed and usually not brought on in such a short time. "His condition", reported the psychiatrist, "is therefore an hysterical amnesia, very comparable to the state which is developed by many soldiers in war-time, and by not a few civilians in peace-time when confronted by situations which they feel it is impossible to face. A loss of memory is in these cases a self-protective mechanism."

From November 1943 until February 1945 the prisoner Rudolf Hess apparently submerged into a cloud – a cloud so opaque that no matter how hard he furrowed his dark brows and peered into his past he could not see even a glimpse of it. He had forgotten his childhood in Egypt, his schooldays in Germany, his leading role in the early years of the Nazi Party; he could not recall the visitors and sometimes even the orderlies. And yet, when these devoted and long-suffering NCOs and privates caught him unawares, it was occasionally as though he did remember something after all.

16   Laughter Line

Before continuing with the narrative of the apparent mental decline of Rudolf Hess, it would be fair to consider an extraordinary letter that he composed three years later when – mortal judges having disposed how he was to spend the rest of his natural life – he no longer had anything to gain from a deceit.

"That my letters from England were for a while few and far between", he wrote with a chuckle in March 1947,

> was connected with the fake amnesia. Because it is *very* hard to write letters if you're claiming you've lost your memory. At very least you run the risk of making mistakes that will lead to your unmasking. For a while I just barely allowed that I knew I had a family – and no more than that! Their address had also "slipped my memory". Of course it was on this or that letter from you, but I had "forgotten" that I had them.∿ [the Hess family laughter line].
>
> Only fresh letters from home jogged my memory to hunt for the earlier ones with the address. Each letter from you then mentioned something or other that apparently stimulated me to write, without having to flex my memory to a suspicious degree. In short: I always had to wait for letters from you until I could write one back. However there were intervals of four and even six months between deliveries of your letters, thanks to the imponderable decisions of faceless authorities, and there you have the explanation for my own prolonged silences.
>
> Somewhere, the mail for me piled up, so that I used to receive heaps of letters all at once but at long intervals.

(The British blamed the German authorities for the delays, but he noticed that letters from his aunt in Zürich, Switzerland, also took nine weeks to reach him; he asked the International Red Cross and the Swiss Minister to investigate.)

For a time Hess's symptoms had remained unchanged: easily thrown into apparently uncontrollable rages by the banging of doors, showing a "jumpiness" manifested in sudden, nervous movements, and taking only very occasional motor rides into the country or walks in the Welsh mountains. The "pains" had logically vanished for a while – loss of memory entailed forgetting how to stage hysterical symptoms. He read books and wrote letters – letters composed in the fullest expectation that the wartime Censor would report them to military Intelligence; he had lulled the Censor by an earlier letter into believing that he had forgotten about the censoring of mail.

England, 15 January 1944

Dear little Mummy

Now I've been sitting here literally for hours thinking what to write to you all, and getting nowhere. Unfortunately there's a real reason for it.

As you're going to hear of it or find out about it sooner or later, I'm writing to tell you: I've completely lost my memory, the entire past has floated off into a grey fog; I can't recall even the most obvious things any more. I don't know what it comes from. The doctor gave me a long explanation, but meantime that has vanished from my memory too. He assures me it'll all turn out all right again one day. Hope he's right!

But this is why I really can't write you a coherent letter, because you need your memory for that – more than you'd think.

It's different when you've got letters to answer which supply talking points and hints; but I got the last letter from you on 13 September last year!

He asked Ilse to send more books, explaining, "In the monotony of my solitary confinement they are of the greatest value to me."

The letter slowly filtered through Intelligence channels: the copy that reached Brigadier Rees was dated 21 January. Rees believed that the amnesia was genuine, and pondered on the proper treatment. If Hess were an ordinary civilian and willing to co-operate, he believed that a doctor could almost certainly retrieve the missing memory either by hypnosis – which Rees anticipated the Deputy Führer would resist – or by "narco-analysis", for which they would, however, have to inject an intravenous anaesthetic. "Unfortunately," wrote Rees on 3 February, "some objection has previously been raised by the Foreign Office to the use of drugs which I suppose still holds."

Rees asked Dr Henry Dicks – the psychiatrist who had been Hess's *bête noire* at Camp Z – to travel to Wales and persuade him to allow them to use narco-analysis. Dicks, who now held the rank of lieutenant-colonel, would be able to understand any German phrases that the prisoner uttered once he had been drugged; and from his previous knowledge of "Z", Dicks could better assess his clinical state and any drug-provoked reactions.

It was a borderline experiment. Even if Hess agreed, Dicks was not anxious to carry the can if anything went wrong. He did not want to figure as the prime mover in suggesting the drug treatment. "I decided",

he wrote in his report a few days later, "to subordinate myself to Major
Ellis Jones, in clinical charge of the patient."

On the day that unknown to him the hated Dr Dicks arrived at Maindiff
Court, Hess wrote to Ilse, still not having heard any news from home:

> *England, 26 February 1944*
>
> Do write to me again. I haven't had a letter from you since September.
>   If *you* don't write I can't write either, because I need something to
> write about. Without a letter from you I really don't know what to write
> or tell you about. I've completely lost my memory, as I told you in my
> last letter – even if it's only temporary, as the doctor has promised me.
>   At least write about how the lad's liking school.

Colonel Dicks, author of the brand-new textbook *Analysis Under
Hypnotics*,★ had arrived at 9 p.m. that evening, but kept out of sight while
he discussed with Ellis Jones a plan of action. They decided that the
Welshman should introduce Dicks as a doctor who had looked after him
before and had come down from London to help him remember the past.
Ellis Jones would suggest possible remedies – their aim was to get Hess to
consent to an injection of the narcotic, Evipan.★★

They came into Hess's sitting room the next day. Dicks's impression
was that the Deputy Führer's physical condition was good, but that his
facial expression had become more fixed and unhappy. Hess's self-
control was astounding: he deeply detested Dicks, whom he had
associated with the "drugging attempts" at Camp Z three years before.
Yet now he showed not a flicker of recognition. He seemed pleased to
find somebody who could talk German with him; he shortly uttered
a convincingly spontaneous expression of despair at being unable to
remember familiar names and things that had happened a few days ago.

With Dicks hovering in the background, Ellis Jones introduced the idea
that such amnesia was not incurable and mentioned casually that the best
treatment was an injection. Having planted that idea in Hess's brain – or
so they thought – they began a long, congenial chat during which the
Estonian-born doctor Dicks reminded the Deputy Führer, in German
and as affably as he could, about the salient features of his life and career.
"He opened up with evident pleasure to me," wrote Dicks in his report a
week later, "and liked hearing about his past. . . . He laughed with
amused incredulity at the idea that he could ever have been close to Hitler,
jumped with a parachute, or lived in Egypt."

Dicks flattered him mercilessly, and Hess must have enjoyed every
second of the charade: the roles were reversed with a vengeance, and he
performed his with Oscar-winning ability. Dicks concluded that the

★ Individual Psychology Pamphlets, No. 23, 1944.
★★ Evipan was a proprietary brand of the intravenous "truth drug" Pentothal (Sodium
Thiopental, or $C_{11}H_{17}N_2NaO_2S$).

amnesia was entirely genuine. "From time to time," noted the doctor – and we can readily picture the scene – "he asks one to define a simple notion like 'skiing', or who Shakespeare was." (He noticed, however, that Hess did accept other definitions and terms which should have been no less opaque.) Hess lyrically described his mental state as being like a fog, into which past events and ideas gradually vanished: "I can only remember the most recent twenty-four hours of my life." Dicks solemnly noted, "It is a construction of the field of consciousness in so far as it depends on past relationships, associations and references."

Summarizing the staff's views, the psychiatrist found general agreement that the prisoner had become easier to manage since this amnesia phase had begun. For his benefit, however, Hess staged a neat display of "pains" – heavily dramatized – and replied, when Ellis Jones suggested a tablet, that he was opposed to any form of medicines. "And that, of course, includes injections," he added. "Have I always been against medicines?" he went on to ask innocently.

The doctors exchanged glances. Here, noted Dicks, was an obvious first reaction by Hess to the proposed Evipan injection. Hess must have been apprehensive about any injection: under a narcotic, he might not remain in control. Dicks, for his part, was determined to administer the test. Such were his instructions from Brigadier Rees.

On the following morning, Dicks ordered a trolley prepared with the necessary apparatus and came in to see Hess just before lunch. He detected at once a certain frostiness – "cold shouldering" was how he described it in his report.

After lunch, Ellis Jones asked Hess outright if he would agree to the injection.

"I should prefer mental training," pleaded Hess, without being more specific.

Ellis Jones persisted: "That would not be effective in your case."

"My present condition", replied Hess, speaking German with a voice rooted some miles behind those inkpot eyes, "is good enough while I am a prisoner. I have had it for some time now. It doesn't really matter whether I can remember what I have done before. So long as I can read, draw and amuse myself somehow to kill time, I am satisfied. I do not suffer unless I am reminded of my disability."

He wearily stroked his forehead, and suppressed the glint of humour in his voice. "When I get back to Germany," he continued – Dicks wrote these words down verbatim too – "perhaps it will pass, or I can find some treatment. Perhaps it is even a merciful dispensation of fate which makes me forget. If I got back my full memory I might suffer more. So I prefer to wait and see" – and he burst out in peals of laughter.

He remained in good spirits throughout the day, knowing that he had spiked Dicks's little project and brought him out to Wales for nothing.

Dicks made one last attempt to persuade Hess before telephoning to report his failure to Brigadier Rees. "That letter to Ilse," he lisped. "It will scare your family stiff. It's your duty to accept treatment."

Hess remained adamant. "I shall wait for a natural cure," he said. He handed his latest letter to Ilse to the officers to mail, and this time they noticed that he had stuck down the envelope.

That last afternoon Dicks joined Hess and Lieutenant Fenton on a country walk. Fenton, who enjoyed these friendly rambles, was astonished at the change that came over the prisoner. After a few minutes Hess turned on his heel and asked to return to the hospital.

Before returning to London, Dr Dicks called in to say goodbye.

"Oh," said Rudolf Hess blandly. "Leaving? I'm sorry you can't stay."

3 March 1944   [Colonel Dicks's report]

It is unlikely that this patient, with his long-established persecutory system about poisoning, will consent to what must seem to him a "chemical assault" on his body. Should he do so, in the absence of the suspicious stranger (myself), I suggest that someone with knowledge of German, not necessarily myself, be despatched to Maindiff, by fast car if need be.

This interpreter should only be present in the room during the stage of narcosis and not enter into the patient's ken at all. Any notes made should be worked through by Dr Ellis Jones, whom the patient trusts. The suggestion for treatment might most suitably be revived by a non-medical confidant, e.g., Lieutenant Fenton.

Some form of suggestion therapy, as by the use of an electrical or light apparatus, might be tried. I regard the patient as too intelligent to be amenable to this. . . .

Two months passed. Hess complained about the meat, the beans, the salt; sat on the verandah reading in the sunshine; complained of the slightest noise, like distant radios, lawn mowers, even the creaking of any chair (except of course his own). The orderlies continued to log every unusual detail. "At 22.30 hrs," they noted on 16 March, "he went outside on the verandah making hissing noises as he walked up and down at irregular speed and with much stamping of feet." Three days later, after dinner with the new Commander Major King and Lieutenant Fenton, the attendant wrote: "He had to be prompted to converse and appeared to lack concentration." On 1 April – All Fools' Day – he sent Private Reygate to get the doctor, then could not remember what he wanted the doctor for.

On the 26th he was driven out to White Castle again – Hess told the officer he could not recall ever having been there before. He asked Ellis Jones the next morning about it, visibly distressed, "Can't something be done about this?" The doctor told him they might be able to recover his memory by using an injection. To everybody's surprise, Hess asked to see the Major that afternoon. "I am willing to submit to the treatment," he said. Ellis Jones wrote at once to Brigadier Rees:

> This afternoon he asked to see me and stated that he was willing to submit to the treatment. Owing to the probability of his native language being used during treatment I feel it would be advisable for Col. Dicks to be present during the treatment. Of course he may again refuse to co-operate, but the above is the present position.

Rees, who after the war refused to accept that Hess could have fooled experienced doctors, felt it significant that the prisoner had himself been so worried by his failure to remember details like White Castle that he had asked for the treatment which he had in February flatly rejected. He telephoned Dicks to travel back to Wales, and take his hypodermic with him.

2 May 1944 [Sergeant Everatt's report]

Patient sat on the verandah most of the afternoon. He appeared agitated & was clapping his hands, etc. At 16.30 hrs he had an attack of "pains". . . . Again at 18.30 hrs.

3 May 1944

Lunch . . . he again complained about the beans not being properly cooked, threw himself into a temper and stamped about his room demanding to see Medical Officer, officers, or anyone who could explain why this had happened two days together.

4 May 1944 [Corporal Cooper's report]

In the evening he was agitated & went pacing around the compound although it was raining sharply & very windy. He wore his overcoat & appeared to be enjoying himself.

6 May 1944

He went out to sit on the verandah but about 21.00 hrs came in & rang his bell. He said he wanted to "see the officer" & seemed depressed. Mr Fenton was fetched & the patient requested that the guard be moved away because he (the guard) made him nervous. Afterwards the patient strode round the compound in an agitated manner. . . .

Why had he now agreed to the narcotic experiment? Writing a statement to read out at the end of his trial two years later he recalled being asked strange questions about his past. When they explained that they could recover his memory with an injection, he was faced with a dilemma. "Since I had to remain consistent in my 'loss of memory'," he wrote, "I could show no distrust." It was clear to him that they wanted to test if his amnesia was real.

Once again the "real" Hess should be allowed to speak first. "Ultimately," he wrote on 10 March 1947,

> the play-acting went so far that I even allowed them to give me injections against my amnesia. I had no real choice, after having initially declined; otherwise I would have reinforced the hardy suspicions of my attendants that I was at least exaggerating. Fortunately I was told in advance that they could not be sure my memory would return if they gave me the shots. But the worst of it was that the procedure was coupled with a period of narcosis during which I would be asked questions designed to "reunite the upper and lower levels of consciousness".
>
> Thus I faced the danger not only that I might blurt out things that were "secret" from my standpoint as a German – which was probably what the inventor of these injections had had in mind! – but that my whole swindle might come to light while I was in this state.
>
> As I said, however, I had in the long run no choice but to conform. I managed however by summoning up every ounce of willpower to remain conscious – although they pumped more of the stuff into me than normal – while all the time miming unconsciousness.
>
> Of course I answered each and every question. "I don't know," I said, with long pauses between each word, and speaking in a low, toneless, distant voice.ᴹ.
>
> I finally recalled my own name, and I murmured it in the same voice.

Colonel Dicks arrived secretly at Maindiff Court on Saturday 6 May at 6.30 p.m. He conferred behind closed doors with the other doctors. They agreed that he should stay out of sight until Hess had been put under narcosis the next evening.

Corporal Everatt's report for 7 May 1944 gives the bare outline of the macabre experiment. After an afternoon car ride with Lieutenant White and a stroll in the airing court, Hess was visited after dinner by Major Ellis Jones at 7.30 p.m. and then again with Dr Phillips at a quarter to nine, "to be given treatment which the patient accepted".

> [Patient] was given an injection of Evipan in solution 5½ c.c. Colonel Dicks then joined the party and they remained with the patient until 22.30 hrs.
>
> The patient recovered somewhat and asked for some bread & butter & some milk. . . .
>
> The patient was asleep at 23.00 hrs and was visited by Major [Ellis] Jones at 23.35 hrs who conversed with him. Lieutenant-Colonel Dicks was called in at 23.45 hours by Major Jones and they stayed with the patient until 00.05 hrs.

Dicks had waited outside until 9 p.m., as planned. By that time the Sodium Evipan solution injected by Ellis Jones appeared to have taken effect, because Hess had ceased to count, his muscles were relaxed, and snores could be heard. Dicks tiptoed into the room and checked that Coramine had been prepared in case of an emergency. Hess's pulse was steady. Dicks noted the fact down, and started to take a verbatim record.

Struggling to remain awake, Hess stirred and heard the familiar voice of Dicks speaking to him in German. "You will now be able to recall all the names and faces of your dear ones. Your memory will return. We are all here to help you. Dr Jones is here. He is healing you . . ." Hess made no response, and Dicks repeated the words. The Deputy Führer groaned convincingly. "What troubles you?" Dicks asked softly.

"Pains! In my belly!" groaned Hess. "Oh, if only I were well. Belly ache." He groaned again. "Water! Water! Thirst!"

"You will soon have water," Dicks assured him, adding somewhat inscrutably, "Tell us now what you have forgotten."

"Oh, I don't know. Pain! Thirst!"

Dicks tried another angle. "You will tell us now what you have forgotten," he intoned.

"Water! Pain in my body! A fog . . ."

"Remember your little son's name?"

The reply was a whisper – "I don't know."

"Your wife's? Ilse, it is."

"I don't know."

"You remember your good friends, Haushofer . . ."

"No."

"Willi Messerschmitt."

"No," groaned the prisoner. "Belly ache! Oh, God!"

"Why this pain?" Hess only groaned. Dicks delved further into the past. "And how you lived in Alexandria as a little boy . . ."

"No."

". . . and all the stirring times with Adolf Hitler in Munich."

"No."

"You were with him in the fortress at Landsberg."

"No."

"Come, it will help you to tell us everything that hurts you!"

"Pains, pains, pains," repeated Hess. "I don't know, I don't know, I don't know."

"But Ilse you know!"

"I don't know."

Dr Ellis Jones now interpolated, in English, "Speak and answer, it will help –"

"– Speak and answer," echoed Hess. "*Leibschmerzen!* Stomach pains!"

"You have had these for years –"

"– For years. *Leibschmerzen!*"

"You will recall all the other parts of your past," ordered Dicks.

"– Recall all the other parts."

"All the great events of your life –"

"– All the great events," echoed Hess, uttering more groans and asking again for water.

"Your boy's name?" persisted Dicks.

"The boy – his name?" echoed Hess, with more groans rising to a crescendo. "Oh, belly ache."

Ellis Jones asked in English, "Why do you groan?"

Hess replied in German: "*Leibschmerzen, Leibschmerzen.*"

"Why this self-torment," Dicks pressed, "why give yourself so much pain?"

By way of answer Hess uttered a piercing scream.

"How did the bad pain get inside you?"

"Water, water!"

"You speak," urged Ellis Jones in his kindly, lilting Welsh accent. "It will do you good."

The answer was more groans.

"Why do you torture yourself?"

"Water!"

"Who has done you wrong?"

"I don't know."

"Come, come," Ellis Jones coached him. "Tell us why you are in pain. Speak – we want to help."

"Pain," groaned Hess. "Water!"

"Now tell us what was your wife's name," cooed the Welsh doctor seductively, "and your boy's –"

"– Wife's name," echoed Hess in the same Welsh lilt. "And your boy's."

Ellis Jones urged him: "You were in Alexandria as a little boy – remember? And how you told me that your father took you to school, your trips to Sicily . . . to the circus –"

Hess distantly echoed the last words of each sentence the doctor spoke.

"And your army service in Rumania –"

"I don't know," said Hess in English.

"Haushofer," whispered Ellis Jones. "He was your dear friend. And Sauerbruch, the great surgeon who operated on your wound?"

Hess remained silent, but both Phillips and Jones noted a quick scintilla of recollection at the two names.

"But at least – who are you?" asked Ellis Jones. "And your wife?"

"RUDOLF HESS," said the prisoner, then echoed: "– And your wife?"

His listeners chorused several times that they were his old doctors, all eager to help him.

At this Hess sat up on his bed and announced: "Water please – and some food."

Colonel Dicks quietly withdrew.

Proud of having defeated the truth drug, the Deputy Führer received doctors Dicks, Ellis Jones and Phillips an hour later. "He looked cheerful," recorded Colonel Dicks, without suspecting the real reason why. Ellis Jones bluffed to the prisoner, "We have now been able to satisfy ourselves that your memory is intact – you were able to remember quite a number of things – but there has not been the full restoration of memory sometimes achieved in a single session."

Hess thanked them courteously for their efforts, and declared himself reassured by their finding that no irremediable defect existed. "Unfortunately," he said, before settling down for the night, "my mind is just as blank now as before."

During the next twenty-four hours he led the medical staff a merry song-and-dance with his "pains".

8 May 1944 [Orderlies' reports]

At 00.20 hrs patient . . . retired, shortly afterwards having a mild attack of abdominal pains. . . . He slept until 04.05 hrs when a further attack of "pains" developed. . . . Had a further attack of pains at 08.30 hrs. . . . 11.15 hrs had a further attack of pains.

Took a good lunch alone, was visited by Major Ellis Jones and later by Colonel Dicks, who stayed with him for some time in conversation. Patient states he feels rather unwell after last night's treatment. . . .

Later Dicks sat on the verandah for an hour talking with the "friendly but very fidgety" prisoner. Both he and Ellis Jones pleaded with Hess to allow further injections of the drug. Hess flatly refused – he had allowed too much "foreign substance" to be introduced into his system already. The Welshman appealed to his conscience – the sorrow he would cause his family. Colonel Dicks appealed to his vanity – a man of Hess's importance should keep abreast of the historical events now taking place. Hess gave no hint of having recognized the Colonel. His reply was simple: "I do not want to go through that ordeal again."

Dicks reported his conclusion to Brigadier Rees on 10 May: "The patient's mental state after Evipan treatment was the same as before this procedure. . . . He has maintained his amnesia."

The virtuoso performance did not avail Hess. Unaware that the Churchill government was deliberately withholding details of his medical condition from the world in order to thwart any claim for his repatriation, he had hoped to find himself collected one magnificent day unexpectedly from Maindiff Court by a sealed ambulance and taken to a southern port where he would be escorted aboard one of the Swedish hospital ships that had repatriated so many hundreds of other incurably ill prisoners of war. "They did drop hints", he would recall in the letter of March 1947, "that I was going to be sent home with the *Drottningholm* on its next crossing. You can imagine what that did to me! But then it sailed without me, and the next time and the time after that too."

He found some slim consolation in how he had fooled all the experts. "It's plain my doctors were convinced by their drugs experiment that my amnesia was genuine," he wrote, "because when I decided it would be good tactics to reveal the deception – as I had already done in Britain on one occasion! – the gentlemen doctors simply refused to believe it at first: and they only admitted that I had their '*legs gepullt*' when I recited to them all the questions they had asked while I was 'unconscious', and repeated my 'awakening' performance, and adopted the same faint and faltering tones of voice as then.〰. Altogether," reflected Hess grimly, "I did everything humanly possible to 'summon the gods to arms' for my return to Germany. But the gods had otherwise disposed – and no doubt better."

17 The Eight-Inch Blade

For the remainder of his period in Britain the medical records on Rudolf Hess confront the historian with a dilemma: because even if the amnesia symptoms were counterfeit – and the psychiatrists stoutly insisted in later years that they were not deceived – there remain unexplained the profoundly disturbing recurring signs of persecution mania. The residual picture is either of a tragic and helpless paranoiac, or of a cunning captive, brilliantly and randomly miming the essential symptoms of a growing madness for motives that he has himself never satisfactorily explained.

After the experimental narcosis in May 1944, Hess began to affix messages to the window facing his table. The first was a note, remarkable for its clumsy handwriting, spelling and grammar, reminding himself not "under any circumstances" to allow another injection experiment. "The doctors are convinced memory will come back in Germany so not to worry or get worked up if at moment its bad and you don't even recognize people you seen before."

Worry, he did not.

On 15 May Dr Phillips, the elderly mental hospital consultant, visited him as usual. Hess asked the RAMC Corporal afterwards who the doctor was. "He asked again at lunch," recorded Corporal Cooper, "but said he could not remember him when I tried to explain." Hess spent the afternoon looking confused on the verandah.

He began complaining even more irritably about everything: the pudding was underdone, the custard-powder was bad, the milk tasted of carbolic; the guards' clock ticked too loudly; rifles were firing on a distant rifle range ("the mad English!" he screamed, when told that the men had to be trained); a shirt collar that he had worn for ten months was now suddenly "too large"; armadas of warplanes flew overhead; the fish was foul, the fowl was flawed, the meat was salty, over-seasoned or otherwise inedible. Hospital food is never a gourmet paradise, of course; and several times the attendants had to agree his complaints were justified. Few Welshmen on the kitchen staff loved the Nazi cause.

Frequently Hess railed at the loudness of the guards' radio, but this was invariably when the bulletins were bad for Germany and good for Britain – like news of a particular success in Italy on 23 May.

The bombing war, which he had hoped by his flight to halt, hurt the most. "At 21.45 hrs," wrote Cooper on the 27th, "when the English news was on re: bombing of Germany, patient suddenly stamped down the verandah & impatiently asked for it to be turned down. . . ." A few days later Major Ellis Jones brought him the news of the Normandy invasion: "The patient did not seem perturbed, and showed little interest in any news items." The Allied penetration of the Nazis' vaunted Atlantic Wall succeeded. On 10 June, depressed and irritable, he asked the soldiers to turn off their BBC news altogether.

The orderlies were suspicious of him. After one of his regular attacks of "pains" on the 15th, a corporal recorded: "It is possible patient had this 19.00 hrs attack as a cover to listen to the German news: I found him listening to the wireless (turned very low) and apparently quite alright when he is supposed to be in the middle of his 'pain' period." On the following evening the orderlies again faintly heard the atmospherics as the prisoner softly tuned his wireless to Berlin. "Later," they wrote, "he sat on the verandah. Rather agitated to-day."

The Allied beachhead at Normandy was about to burst into France.

Perhaps realizing that the atmospherics had been overheard, on 3 July the prisoner staged a subtle new performance. "Throughout the afternoon . . . he has been excitable and has shown signs of mental deterioration, banging about his chair, unable to keep still, hissing and making peculiar noises and at one time he was imitating the atmospherical noises of wireless."

Four days later it was back to the amnesia: he again "appeared not to recognise" Dr Phillips; and when the new Guard Commander himself, Major Cross, came in after dinner on the 10th Hess blandly inquired, "Have we met before?"

As Britain came under intensive flying-bomb attack, and the BBC bulletins voiced the anger and alarm that Churchill felt about this manner of reprisal, Hess's spirits revived, as the orderlies' reports show:

15 July 1944
Dinner was delayed (patient listened to German news) and then he had a good meal with Mr Fenton. . . . Two fresh notices in German have been gummed on his windows by patient.

17 July 1944
He listened to the wireless and was banging and stamping in his room to the music in noisy enjoyment. Later he complained of the noise of the civil wireless . . . demanded it turned right down or window closed, in spite of extreme heat.

21 July 1944
Dinner was delayed whilst he listened to German news. Then he had a good meal with Mr Fenton. Patient was extremely talkative with much

gesticulating in a very exhilarated manner. He appeared very pleased that the Führer had escaped assassination.

His amnesia became quite outrageous. Attendants saw him carefully wrap and save food to show to the doctor: he then forgot all about it. Sergeant Everatt, who had tended him since the first days at Camp Z in June 1941, noted on 22 August 1944: "At 18.30 hrs the patient looked at me with wide open eyes and asked me, was I a new nurse, and claimed he did not remember me."

That summer a letter came from Ilse Hess. She calmed him with word that doctors in Germany had assured her that he would recover his memory when the war was over. He gummed it on to the window next to the other jottings of things that he must try not to forget. Brigadier Rees, visiting Maindiff Court on the first day of September, saw it there, and regarded it as further confirmation of the amnesia. The Brigadier also noticed that the nightly "pains" usually coincided with the German radio news bulletins, and took this as further evidence that they were of hysterical, not physical, origin.

As the remains of the German armies fled before the Allies liberating France, the Deputy Führer can hardly have found the bulletins palatable. Two days before, he had "spent some time listening to the radio with German news [and] paced up and down the room shouting and raging about something that was being told . . .".

Brigadier Rees was convinced anew that, unlike the pains, Hess's amnesia was genuine. "He is quite clear", he reported to the War Office, "that to recover his memory would mean facing many unpleasant and unhappy memories of failure." In a long conversation he pointed out the moral aspect of this attitude of mind to Hess, but doubted that this would have any effect.

As for the symptoms of hallucinations, if they were simulated they were often very inventive. At 7 a.m. on 13 September, he told the attendant who brought him a hot-water bottle: "There is a wounded man out there and in great pain, because I can hear him."

A bizarre scenario, repeated every Sunday from now on, involved the clean under-garments brought to him: he claimed to find unrinsed soap-powder in them, and thrashed them for as long as ten minutes against a cupboard door so that the attendant could see the (invisible) clouds of powder. These violent Sunday linen-flagellations became as regular a feature of the orderlies' reports as the "pains" and other complaints.

The "pains" ritual itself became more complicated. He would utter the requisite number of groans; the attendant would bring a hot-water bottle and retire; Hess would at once surreptitiously slide the bottle on to the floor. The attendants caught him at it, remonstrated, tried to find explanations, gave up, and finally went along with the infuriating ritual because those were their orders from London.

He took to pacing round the compound in the dark, whatever the weather and particularly in the rain. Meanwhile the authoritative placards in his room multiplied. On 16 October a German notice appeared attached to his room door: MIDDAY MEAL 12.30 HRS.

Perhaps there was some justification in this lonely prisoner's sense of grievance. On 9 October, when he returned from his walk in the dark, the Guard Commander Major Cross brought him a bundle of mail – eleven letters that his captors had callously stockpiled. Sulking, he no longer went on country outings – his last had been when he and a lieutenant went gathering blackberries on 2 October.

3 November 1944   [Orderly's report]

Still makes complaints of noise made in the corridors, spent much of his time reading and writing. Had a further attack of pains at 18.30 hrs and went into a terrible rage when given an earthenware hot-water bottle. Wanted to know what kind of hospital is this, and if all British hospitals were the same, would not have his dinner until 20.20 hrs . . . then settled down to reading. Took a stroll in the compound after dark.

4 November 1944

Apparently has developed a new technique of rolling about in his chair during a "pain". He said he had jaw ache & was holding his jaw – doing two movements, up & down, of his head & then finishing with a circular movement. The whole process was continually repeated.

He perfected the "jaw-ache" charade over the following six weeks. He walked around room and compound with a scarf tightly wrapped around his neck and looked miserable. He held his jaw constantly (but only when he thought he could be seen) – and there were other reasons to doubt if he was really hurting. "Although he complains of pain with his teeth," triumphed Private Graver one day, "he consumed two large rounds of very hard toast."

On 20 November Major Ellis Jones invited him on a car-ride. Agitated and restless, Hess declined. Two days later he told the doctor, "The kitchen staff spoil my food deliberately, to upset me." After lunch on 28 November – still wearing his scarf – he repeated this allegation, and flew into what Sergeant Everatt described as a terrible rage. "They have made the food salty to torment me!" he shouted. Told that more vegetables were not available, he moaned, "Then I must starve!"

10 December 1944   [Orderly's report]

During the afternoon he was agitated and restless, banging & stamping about & occasionally making sybillant [*sic*] & guttural noises as if swearing in his own language.

Dinner was served at 19.10 hrs . . . after which he was pacing up & and down holding his jaw.

16 December 1944

When he came in he appeared to be troubled with a pain in his face for he was walking around the room holding it.

17 December 1944

He rose at 12.30 hrs & was apparently in a bad humour. He was banging about in his room while dressing.

Lunch was served & he immediately got up & staggered out of the room holding his stomach. Hot-water bottle was given. . . . Patient was eating hard, dry toast. He banged on the chair arm, kicked his hot-water bottle, threw open the verandah door & commenced [to] rush up & down the room in very agitated manner.

The convincing array of symptoms was a product of his campaign to be evacuated to Switzerland. On 26 November he had written to the Swiss Minister as the Protecting Power explaining that his health had deteriorated badly (although there is no trace of this in the handwriting), that he was suffering agonies from abdominal pains and that he had lost his memory six or seven months ago. "I have long forgotten a large part of the facts in this letter," he cautiously explained, "and I could not have written it at all if I had not been keeping a diary these last few weeks recording everything the doctor here, Dr Jones, told me when I asked him." Fortunately, he added, Ellis Jones was convinced that a shock might suddenly restore his memory: "Seeing my family again might, for example, be one such shock." Another would be to return to a more familiar landscape. In short, Hess requested leave to travel to Switzerland, and offered his word of honour to return to Britain any time it was desired. He attached a medical certificate from Ellis Jones to support his request. On 19 December however Brigadier Rees advised the War Office against it. "I am strongly of the opinion", he wrote, "that such a visit would not produce any result beneficial to his present condition."

The new Swiss Minister, Dr Paul Rügger, brought this bad news to Maindiff Court the next day.

As they parted, the orderly saw him in an "alert good humour". He had picked up enough information from the radio to know that Hitler's V-missiles were raining down on Antwerp, General Dwight D. Eisenhower's main supply port; and that Hitler had launched his totally unexpected Ardennes counteroffensive in a desperate gamble to win the war. Berlin began claiming that the Allies were on the run – as indeed several American divisions were – in the bulge that Field Marshal von Rundstedt had hammered into their front line.

Once again Hess crouched by the wireless in his little room, his belief in Hitler undimmed. Echoes of his "pains" persisted, but lapses of memory dwindled to an occasional whispered request (on 3 January 1945) to an attendant to switch on the wireless ("I have forgotten which is the switch"), or a faint bleat (on the 7th) that the dinner was "very poor for a sick man".

But even the trumpets that William Joyce sounded from Berlin were soon blowing an uncertain note again. While Hess took dinner alone on the 8th Corporal Cooper, outside the door, could hear the German news bulletin, turned very low. On the 9th, Private Clifford heard the prisoner making "peculiar noises" in German, softly turning on the German news during dinner, then "crowing & whistling & talking to the set when it oscillated".

Beginning on 12 January, the long-awaited Soviet winter offensive lunged across central Poland and the last barriers before Berlin. For a day or two Hess remained jubilant, believing Berlin's claims that the Russians had been halted. On the 14th, Cooper saw him leave dinner untouched to listen to the radio. He sat beside it, beating time with his feet as the bands played at the end.

A letter that Rudolf Hess wrote to Ilse on the next day shows no signs of abnormality. He expressed pleasure that she was not trying to awake a slumbering genius in their plodding schoolboy son, consoling her: "Those who cram their way to the top of their class get there by swotting and not through any intellectual gifts; and they are usually the ones who disappoint most in later life." Rather sadly, he continued: "I wish my son only one thing in life: that some idea shall 'fire' him – an engineering design, or a new concept in medicine, or a drama – even if nobody is willing to build his engine or to stage or even read his drama and the doctors of every faculty come down on him in rare unanimity to tear his ideas to shreds."

The last half of January showed Hess increasingly affected by the disheartening news from Germany. He walked round the snow-mantled compound swinging his arms and stamping his feet; he listened to the radio; he was heard muttering to himself; he banged his chair; he complained about the food; he again feigned a loss of memory. "He asked", recorded an orderly on the 23rd, "that the Officer of the Day should visit him occasionally although Lieutenant Fenton had only been in at lunch time to see him."

His agitation at the war news bulletins increased as the Allied leaders departed to meet with Stalin at Yalta.

25 January 1945   [Orderly's report]

He chose the deepest parts of the snow to walk through & was kicking it about. . . .

26 January 1945

Dinner was delayed until 19.30 hrs. When it was served he soon left the table to switch on the wireless. He ceased eating until the end of the news about half an hour later.

30 January 1945

Went out into the compound where he walked through all the deepest snow he could find. . . . [19.30 hrs Hess] did seem bothered by the news [Warsaw had fallen, the Russians had reached the Oder river]. . . . The patient was listening to the radio until 01.20 hrs.

He was on the brink of a serious emotional crisis. On 2 February the orderlies heard him fiddling with the radio in a seemingly random way, clicking it on and off for the last fifteen minutes of the 7 p.m. news broadcast. On 3 February Corporal Cooper saw he had hardly touched his supper, and heard him again clicking the radio at the same time (it is not impossible that Hess hoped in this way to send a signal to somewhere).

"Is the set all right?" asked Cooper.

The prisoner said it was, but he looked agitated. After midnight he complained again of intense jaw pain: "Can I have two of the white tablets?" Clifford gave him two Phenacetins.

It was now 4 February 1945. Waking unusually early, soon after 6 a.m., Hess called out to Private Clifford, "I want to see the doctor first thing this morning. I have something very important to tell him." But fifteen minutes later, he spoke again. "It can wait until I have finished my sleep. I don't want to be disturbed."

Sergeant Everatt, who had looked after Hess for nearly four years now, found him in his sitting room that morning looking confused and agitated. He asked again for Ellis Jones and the doctor, summoned by house telephone, had a long talk with him.

"My memory has returned," announced Hess, "and I have something important to tell the world." He produced a sheet of paper with a list of names. "I want you to forward this information to Mr Churchill," he said.

As the doctor ran his eye down the list – the names were of monarchs, generals and the German officers who had tried to blow up the Führer – the prisoner declaimed (according to the doctor's notes) that he had realized that all these people must have been unwittingly hypnotized by the Jews to act in certain ways. To Hess the notion of being hypnotized by a Jew was entirely plausible. Had not Colonel Dicks attempted precisely this when they believed him under narcosis in May 1944?

Ellis Jones patiently listened while his patient enlarged upon this bizarre thesis: the King of Italy and Marshal Pietro Badoglio must have been "hypnotized" to break their word to Hitler and conclude the secret armistice with Eisenhower; the would-be assassin Baron Schenk von Stauffenberg had been hypnotized to kill Hitler; Mr Churchill had been hypnotized to change from being anti-Bolshevik to pro-Soviet; Field Marshal Friedrich Paulus had been hypnotized into broadcasting from Moscow; he himself, Hess, had once been hypnotized into a display of rudeness at a state banquet in Italy; likewise Mr Eden had been rude to

Reichsmarschall Hermann Göring at a state banquet – "obviously he too had been affected by this hypnosis," Ellis Jones wrote down.* Then there was "General J." (probably General Gepp). He had been "rude" to Hess at Mytchett. Less than tactfully, Hess even suggested that Ellis Jones himself had been hypnotized into placing poisons in his food. The Hess list concluded with Brigadier Rees and the Bulgarian regency council – all of them had been manipulated by the Jews in a display of mind-bending. "In an agitated state," recorded Ellis Jones finally, "he maintained that his amnesia had been simulated."

Was this craziness simulated too? Given the superior, rational intellect displayed by Hess's private letters, it is a hypothesis that cannot be ignored. Ellis Jones refused to believe that he had been duped, but Sergeant Everatt afterwards made a puzzled note of the evidence that Hess's memory was indeed unimpaired – the prisoner "talked to me of many officers and other men that has [*sic*] been with us at different times."

After eating some of the Sergeant's bread and butter and drinking a glass of milk, the prisoner settled down. He tried to sleep in bed after lunch, but found it impossible and shortly after 5 p.m. Sergeant Everatt could see that he was restless again. At 5.20 Everatt heard him ask a private for the bread-knife saying, "I'd like to make myself some more toast." Hess was given the knife with an eight-inch blade – he had had the use of normal cutlery for months.

Back in his bedroom, Hess changed into his air force captain's uniform – the one he had flown to Scotland in – and walked into the sitting room, leaving the tunic open. Firmly gripping the handle of the knife in both hands, he plunged it into his left chest. But stabbing takes more force than most men think, even with the sharpest of blades. The blade did not penetrate. Hess repeated the blow with twice the strength, and this time the knife sank in – "up to the hilt", he said.

He jabbed the bell push and screamed out loud.

Everatt ran in, and found him slumped on the floor "in a very distressed condition", bleeding profusely.

Was his head once again filled with shrieking voices, urging him to kill the devil within, or was this a sane man's demonstration of despair – a final, frantic attempt to force his repatriation? Why the uniform? To die like a hero, or to authenticate his suicidal intent? He had taken the trouble to study the precise position of the human heart, and the blade penetrated the sixth intercostal space (though "up to the hilt" was, the doctors found, not true). Whatever had triggered the impulse, it was an act tinged with lunacy.

Hess was carried into bed and kept under strict observation; the room was searched for other suicide instruments, and at 7.30 p.m. the doctor injected Sodium Luminal intramuscularly to force him to sleep.

---

* At the banquet on 26 March 1935 Göring had sat just to Eden's right, facing Hess, according to the table seating plan.

The next morning he told Private Clifford – and later Sergeant Everatt too – that he had tried to kill himself: "I sat in the chair half an hour and the intention came to me to stick the knife into my heart – the first time I did not succeed, but the second time the knife went in up to the hilt. I got the position of the heart from a book I had read the day before."

He was quiet and tractable. At first it did not worry the doctors that he was now refusing to eat and had begun drinking only hot water. "In the interests of health," he told Everatt cheerfully, "it is good to starve."

For the next months he would be confined to a room measuring twenty-four feet by sixteen, under constant supervision. For the eight days after the bread-knife incident he refused to wash, shave or eat. Visited by Ellis Jones on the 5th he gave two reasons for the "attempted suicide": he feared that he was never going to be allowed to leave Britain, and that he could see Germany was done for – the Bolsheviks would now overrun the Fatherland, reach the English Channel and proceed to subjugate Britain too.

On the following day the signs of his (real or simulated) persecution mania were very pronounced during a long talk with Ellis Jones. "The Jews placed the knife there to tempt me to commit suicide," he declared, "because I am the only person who knows of their secret power of hypnosis." To prevent them from drugging his water he covered his glass with paper tied down with string after each drink. He made sure both water jugs were empty, and watched Corporal Cooper with intense, dark eyes through the open door as he filled them from the tap.

Shortly before midday on the 8th he asked Sergeant Everatt for a pen and paper, saying, "I want to write statements to various people." He added that he had decided to fast to the death – in Germany, he added, any person who believed himself "incurable" could put an end to his own life.

He laboriously wrote out declarations addressed to the German and British governments attesting to his desire to die, since he considered his abdominal illness to be beyond cure. In the letter to Berlin – addressed through Switzerland as Protecting Power – he left to them the decision whether he should continue his self-starvation. He signed these documents, and handed to Sergeant Everatt a further paper stating that in the event of his death he wished to be dressed as he arrived in Scotland – in complete Luftwaffe uniform and flying kit – and to be returned to Germany with his two overcoats, Commander Grenfell's book *Sea Power* and his translation of it. "If you are away for more than a day," urged Hess, pressing this document into Everatt's hand, "you must hand it to your relief or whoever is in charge."

To Everatt the increasingly haggard and unshaven prisoner looked agitated and deluded. He seemed restless and unable to concentrate. Undeterred by his own mental turmoil, on 9 February the Deputy Führer began writing an immense document which would occupy him for several weeks.

Meanwhile his hunger strike continued. "As usual drew his water which is the only thing taken by him," recorded Private Graver. "Refused food, and appeared annoyed when asked if he required any."

On the 10th, Ellis Jones hinted at force-feeding.

"I will resist and fight against it," said Hess.

He spent all afternoon writing, evidently a work with historical connotation because occasionally he shuffled through his papers or checked a reference in *Sea Power*. Ellis Jones suspected that he was preparing a defence for the trial which he now knew from the newspapers to be inevitable.

Early on the 11th his pulse was weaker. Signs of mental disorder multiplied. He left both water taps running in the bathroom annexe for fifteen minutes, and when Graver remarked upon it Hess caustically replied, "That's in lieu of the water I should have used for baths which I have not taken since being here."

The orderlies noticed that he was silent, weakening and not even drinking as much water as before.

After visiting him on the 12th, Phillips and Ellis Jones decided to force-feed the prisoner. The orderlies brought into Hess's room a tray with the tubes and other paraphernalia. With memories of the catheter episode of June 1941 he protested vigorously. The doctors yielded, but persuaded him to take the juice of two oranges in water – thus penetrating the weakening walls of his suicidal resolve. The hunger-strike collapsed. It had not, incidentally, escaped the attention of either doctors or prisoner that during it there had been no "pains" at all – which confirmed to the former that they were of hysterical origin, but hardened Hess in his belief that his food had been poisoned.

The War Office ordered Colonel Dicks to see Hess (since Brigadier Rees was out of the country). In lengthy conversations with the émigré, Hess now cheerfully claimed to have been faking his amnesia all along and to have fooled all the experts.

12 February 1945   (Corporal Cooper's report]

He sat for long periods in bed just doing nothing except apparently being deep in thought. . . . When I took his temperature at 18.00 hrs he asked what it was & entered it on his papers. He took concentrated orange juice again at 19.30 hrs.

At 20.50 hrs Major Ellis Jones brought Lieutenant-Colonel Dicks to visit him. He seemed to become exhilarated & spoke voluble German in apparent good humour. Major Ellis Jones then left them on their own together.

13 February 1945

Patient slept in restless manner until 11.50 hrs when he was visited by Major Ellis Jones [and] Dr Phillips. They brought Lieutenant-Colonel Dicks with them. Patient drank a glass of egg & milk while they were in the room.

13 February 1945 [Sergeant Everatt's afternoon report]

Reading for a time, then he spent some time talking to me about things in general. Was visited by Lieutenant-Colonel Dicks at 21.30 hrs, had a long conversation together. Has since sat in bed staring about the room, does not seem able to concentrate on reading and writing.

Dicks reported at length to the War Office on the "very dramatic recovery" that Hess had made. His memory was now functioning "very fully and accurately". "I cannot", the psychiatrist however continued, "accept his own statement that the memory loss never existed. There was at that time a true partial dissociation of the personality, which permitted the patient to 'take in' what was going on around him, but caused difficulty of recall." His opinion was that Hess, unwilling to admit having displayed a momentary debility, preferred to believe that he had duped the specialists. Be that as it may, Hess had now entered a much calmer phase, and even discussed his "suspicions" rationally as a symptom.

Dicks was disinclined to accept the recent suicide attempt as evidence of a personality disorder: the Deputy Führer, he reminded his superiors, was a German, and in the German ethical code suicide was "almost the normal way out of indignity and loss of face".

15 February 1945 [Colonel Dicks's report]

Thus I find the patient at much the same level of mental and physical health as when I left him three and a half years ago: i.e., intellectually vigorous and alert; somewhat grandiose and indeed overbearing when acting "officially"; simple and rational, indeed sociable, in private; rather egocentric, fussy and suspicious.

For a few days the orderlies found this too. "Patient has been quite sociable this afternoon," wrote Corporal Cooper on the 16th. "His manner has been very nice when he has asked for anything. He had a dinner of vegetable stew, he ate a lot." The two weeks' growth of beard was shaved off. Ten days later, however, he was again seen locking away little parcels of food, and the "pains" started to return.

This extraordinary prisoner wrote to his wife on 9 March 1945 an erudite critique of literature that he had been reading:

Some time back I was reading the novelettes collected in *A Reader of German Storytellers*. To my surprise, Jean Paul was the one who delighted me the most – although I once wrote you not to send me anything by him or his ilk. But like so many others I probably took him up at too tender an age, when one's lack of patience with fine detail makes breadth seem tedious. When I'm back home I shall certainly read *Little Schoolmaster Wuz*, and [Adalbert] Stifter too, whose *Brigitta* has been no less of a delight for me. What an immense range of form and style, of characterization and narrative, our poets and authors encompass! A range like our major – and minor! – composers in the field of music.

In the same letter he crowed to Ilse that his memory had returned – "better than ever before".

His memory was indeed now good again – he asked Corporal Cooper casually on 13 March if he had passed on to his son some chocolate which he had given him four months earlier. But a week later Cooper saw again all the old, familiar signs of delusions – "At times [Hess] has laughed & behaved in an almost maniacal manner."

As the defeat of Nazi Germany became inevitable, Hess grew more distraught. Keeping him under surveillance around the clock, his attendants could see his agitation. He made jerky, involuntary hand movements and delivered soliloquies to unseen listeners.

When the strategically important bridge across the Rhine at Remagen fell into American hands he stated that the Jews had hypnotized the German soldiers guarding the bridge. A corporal saw him walk out on to the verandah after a meal at this time laughing and apparently talking to himself. A few days later when the doctors came with a radiator-key to release air trapped in the system (because Hess had complained of the hissing radiators) Private Clifford noticed how he "stood in their rear & laughed in a silent, maniacal manner abruptly changing to an erect sternness".

Expressing the now familiar signs of persecution he remarked at the end of March that the hot-pot and soup were too salty. "It is only to be expected," he added, "knowing that I am in a British hospital." Later, the attendants saw him sprinkle more salt on the food that he had just rejected as too salty.

3 April 1945   [Sergeant Everatt's report]

Dinner was served at 19.00 hrs about which he complained and passed a lot of sarcastic remarks about the doctors Phillips & Ellis Jones being "doctors of lunatic medicine", and that he had asked to have meat every other day. He asked me to write a statement which he dictated to me, that he had meat twice to-day and no fish, and that the meat was too salty and that the milk was sour. But he ate some of the meat and drank most of the milk.

Has done a lot of writing this evening. . . .

6 April 1945

Still remains very sarcastic, remarks passed by him about slight noise, that he knows we can't help it and that we are under orders just to annoy him.

8 April 1945

Asked for his hot-water bottle to be filled at 07.00 hrs but put it on the floor when he thought I was not looking.

It all seemed sadly familiar to Brigadier Rees, visiting late on 19 April. During dinner, Hess thought it prudent to ask Private Reygate to sample his fish, so the poison mania still prevailed. By Hess's own account, written a few days later, Rees urged him to accept that he was the victim only of his own mental fixations.

"There is no purpose saying anything more," Hess interrupted. "I know what I know!"

He saw Rees ponder this cryptic response with a gloomy face.

"Oh well," the Brigadier said, hurrying out. "I wish you good luck."

He reported to the War Office that although the prisoner's "hysterical amnesia" had disappeared he had now reverted to a mental condition even more obviously unbalanced than at Camp Z – he was rude, arrogant and difficult to manage. "His delusional state", the report concluded, "is a good deal more marked than it ever has been."

After Rees departed, Hess began writing as though he had only a few days to live. Barely pausing for meals he covered sheet after sheet of foolscap paper. "Patient has been writing the whole afternoon," Corporal Cooper jotted down on 28 April, "only breaking off to take a hot-water bottle at 18.30 hrs for an attack of pains. He then had dinner, eating a good meal, after which he resumed his writing of which he is doing a tremendous amount just now."

Aware that the war was nearly over, the prisoner became more erratic and frenzied in his behaviour.

29 April 1945   [Corporal Cooper's report]

Before putting on his under-pants he smashed them violently against the wardrobe for a full minute. He started to write, then he put on his overcoat, went outside to sit down & came in again within five minutes to pick up the newspaper he had been reading.

He was laughing maniacally at the news of the German offer to surrender & the photographs of the present leaders of that country. He then became serious, stopped me sweeping out the room, made me alter the carpets on the floor several times.

Then he started to write & hardly had time to eat his lunch before he was back at the table again to carry on.

30 April 1945

Patient was out on the verandah when I took over. He was busy writing in spite of the low temperature.

Lunch was served at 15.00 hrs. He took a good meal. Resumed his writing, during which time I saw him dropping a small key on to the paper at intervals. . . . Dinner was served at 19.00 hrs and he consumed a hearty meal. He returned straight away to his writing. He seems to be working against time. . . .

The ritual with the tiny key – observed for the first time at the precise moment that Hitler was killing himself in Berlin, although the world did not yet know it – was repeated over the ensuing days. He brooked no interruption to his writing, although he sometimes rose to open all the doors and windows, or paced up and down in an agitated way. Often he was too busy to talk with the doctor; but sometimes he wanted to write and found he could not concentrate. On some days he delayed meals by an hour or more, or placed his plate on the radiator, while he continued his writing, like the mad Captain Nemo in his cabin in the closing chapters of Jules Verne's *Twenty Thousand Leagues Under the Sea.*

Imbeciles! Like a madman driving the wrong way down an autobahn, Hess encountered lunatics on every side. He entered this thought in his manuscript: "I had been imprisoned for four years now with lunatics; I had been at the mercy of their torture without being able to inform anybody of this, and without being able to convince the Swiss Minister that this was so; nor of course was I able to enlighten the lunatics about their own condition." It was worse than being in the hands of common criminals, he reasoned, because there was always a little common sense "in some obscure corner of their brain" – a grain of conscience within them.

"With my lunatics," wrote Hess, in this extraordinary, sarcastic document, "this was 100 per cent out of the question. Worst of all were the doctors, who put their scientific knowledge to work devising the most refined tortures. The fact is that I have been without a doctor these last four years, because those who call themselves doctors in my entourage have had the task of adding to my suffering." Lunatics, everywhere around him.

> Outside my garden lunatics walked up and down with loaded rifles! Lunatics surrounded me in the house! When I went for a walk, lunatics walked in front of and behind me – all in the uniform of the British Army.
>
> We met columns of inmates from a nearby lunatic asylum who were led to work. My companions expressed pity for them, and did not sense that they belonged in the same column: that the doctor in charge of the hospital [Dr Phillips] who was at the same time in charge of the lunatic asylum, should have been his own patient for a long time. They did not sense that they themselves needed pity.

"I pitied them honestly," emphasized Hess. "Here, decent people were made into criminals."

The newspapers filled with sickening photographs and descriptions of the atrocious conditions found by the advancing Allied troops. Hess wrote to his captors an undated note:

> I gather from the press that films are available of concentration camps in Germany, now occupied by British and American troops in which atrocities have occurred. I should greatly value a chance of seeing these films.

His request was disallowed.

Although he did not show it, much less discuss it with his captors, the death of Adolf Hitler – whose obituary took a whole page in *The Times* – did not leave him unmoved. He found consolation in two pasages in a book by Konrad Guenther, *Natural Life*. "The work of great men", Guenther had written, "does not attain its full effect until its creator has passed on – the present day cannot comprehend it. . . . Can there exist any being more heroic than the one who treads an undeviating path in pursuit of a preordained mission, however entangled that path seems to become, and even if it turn into a path of martyrdom?" And Guenther had quoted these lines from Schopenhauer too: "The supreme goal to which man can aspire is a life of heroism. That is the life led by a man who in some affair or deed fights superhuman difficulties for the common weal, and goes on to final victory, even though he draw little or no reward therefore."

8 May 1945, VE-Day [Orderlies' reports]

He had an attack of "pains" at 01.10 hrs, hot-water bottle provided. He has been whispering to himself in German. He repeatedly used the number "94" however.

Spent most of his time reading and writing. . . . Did not appear to be interested that it is V.E.-Day. . . . Writing again. . . .

That evening he began burning some of his papers, evidently drafts of the manuscript. It seemed to be reaching an end. Cooper remarked on the 9th, "He is not writing quite so much now."

VE-Day raised complicated issues for the British government. Technically, Rudolf Hess was still a "high-ranking Prisoner of War", as Orme Sargent of the Foreign Office wrote to Churchill on 12 May 1945, informing him that General Gepp, the Director of Prisoners of War – "who is responsible under your personal authority for the custody of Hess" – was proposing to refuse all media access even though the war was over.

Churchill agreed. In fairness, he had little option: the revelation that the Deputy Führer had seemingly gone mad in British custody was one that, for political reasons, he wished postponed as long as possible.

Gepp was in no doubt about Hess's condition. On 11 May his deputy Brigadier Boulnois had visited Maindiff Court and been humiliated by Hess, who evidently recalled their earlier meeting at Camp Z. Waiting for the Brigadier, he nervously laughed, he grimaced, he jumped to his feet, he shook with silent laughter although averting his face so that Corporal Cooper could not see it. In a state of exaltation when the new Guard Commander Lieutenant-Colonel Hermelin brought Boulnois in, Hess refused to speak to him. The Brigadier angrily turned on his heel and left. Hess stalked restlessly out on to the verandah, then snarled at Private

Graver: "Go and make a noise with the door. Rattle the key! Slam the door – it hasn't been done for ten minutes!" Cooper did as told, while Hess clapped his hands and shouted, "Bravo!"

Irritated to find the blinds still drawn each evening – to protect him from an assassin's bullet – he mocked the guards with heavy sarcasm on 12 May: "Do you think a Japanese plane might come over and bomb this place?" Seeing the Corporal's blank look, he explained: "Blackout!", and laughed. Midnight found Hess sitting at his open bedroom door with the light full on and no blackout screen. This time Lieutenant Fenton had to come explain to him that in his own interests the blind must remain drawn.

On the following day, 13 May, the Sunday newspapers were full of the story of the capture of several Nazi leaders. Hess read the front pages and began chuckling wildly and looking exhilarated when he saw the familiar faces. It was as though he did not associate his own plight with them at all. He asked Sergeant Everatt a few days later if the men were looking forward to demobilization. "I feel sorry for them," he explained. "They will soon be called up again to fight the Russians."

The manuscript that the Deputy Führer had written was a rambling, bizarre but often self-critical account of events since his parachute arrival in Scotland.★ Too long to reproduce here, it was nonetheless significant for two features: it established that he had a precise recollection of events, and of the names and ranks of the many men he had met over the four years in Britain; and it displayed symptoms of a persecution mania so gross that the suspicion arises that the final document was purposefully concocted (and its less adroit earlier drafts burned) to establish the basis for some kind of defence plea.

It added little to the allegations that he had handed to Lord Beaverbrook and others in 1941. He related how the SIS officer Major Frank Foley (coyly identified only as "Major F." in the English translation) was "horrified and confused" when Hess admitted faking amnesia just before Lord Simon came. He accused the émigré Dr Dicks of injecting what he called "brain poison" after the first suicide attempt, and the Guards officers of unwittingly planting the same substance in his meals. He again charged that he had been victimized by motorcycle, rifle, door, hammering and aircraft noises.

In this inventive document Hess also claimed, however, to have observed in Lieutenant Malone, Brigadier Rees and others a "peculiar change in the eyes". It might, he admitted disarmingly, have been due to alcohol: but he was now sure that they had been mesmerized. He recalled having seen the same "glassy-eyed" look in his new doctor, Ellis Jones, on the first morning at Maindiff Court, and the doctor had yawned

★ An English translation produced at Nuremburg is published as the chapter entitled "Hess's Version of Events" by J. Bernard Hutton, *Hess: The Man and His Mission* (New York, 1970).

continuously too. Hess dismissed the idea of alcohol completely – surely a Welsh doctor would not drink before midday? So Hess piously reasoned in his manuscript.

His captors had found other ways of tormenting him too. When he had begun drawing architectural sketches, the "poison" had caused his eyes to malfunction; mysteriously the radio had also failed when he began to listen to it. Each time a new misfortune befell him Major F. had "appeared and expressed his regrets in a most moving manner", giving his word of honour that Hess's allegations were not true.

Goaded often to the very brink of insanity, he had managed to restrain himself from violence – "I knew that then I would only be doing what the criminals were hoping for in the back of their minds. I imagined myself already in an asylum, clad in a straitjacket." Therefore he had hit upon the device of feigning mental illness and amnesia in order to enforce his repatriation, the only way that he could escape the clutches of the British secret service – so Hess now claimed in this document, which layered insanity upon amnesia in a manner now virtually impossible to disentangle. He convincingly described how he had perfected his amnesia techniques, passing even the severest tests like the sudden appearance of people he had not seen for years (a reference to the hated Dr Dicks). "My hope that in consequence of being ill I would go home", he observed, "proved illusory."

Symptoms of paranoia still bubbled to the surface. The writing finished, he took the file with him everywhere, even when he went to the bathroom annexe, lest the staff interfere with it. He secreted small samples of his meals in locked drawers. Once in June Cooper observed him on the verandah hissing, talking to himself and making guttural sounds, and he saw him pulling faces; but later that day he was whistling and singing, and commenting cheerfully on "this lousy English summer", and the puzzling ritual with the tiny key began.

10 June 1945   [Corporal Cooper's report]

He smashed his clean underpants against the wardrobe, apparently to knock out the deposit of soap. Later he went onto the verandah & appeared exhilarated, drawing lots of enjoyment from the news in the paper.

Periodically he extracted a tiny key from his pocket & dropped it on some selected portion of the ground, afterwards retrieving it & putting it back in his pocket. He then carried on reading.

During all these weeks his letters home remained reasonable and urbane. "I want", he wrote to Ilse on 18 June 1945,

to send you a few lines even if I can't write you what I'd really like to – and given all the Censorship hands it passes through, I wouldn't want to. You can imagine how often these last few weeks my thoughts have drifted back over the years – over this quarter-century of a history that is linked for us with just one Name: but also a quarter-century lived really to the full. The story is not over: with its sense of unremitting logical consistency history shall one day gather up the threads which may today seem sundered for all eternity, and weave them into a new fabric. The mortal part is over and lives on only in our memories.

Thus, in a private euphoria, defiantly quoting Nietzsche in letters to his wife, Rudolf Hess awaited his own uncertain future – his admiration undimmed for the leader who had died by his own hand in the ruins of his Carthage.

"How few people", he wrote on 21 June 1945, "can claim the privilege that we can – to have shared right from the start with a unique personage all his joys and sufferings, his hopes and fears, his hatreds and loves: to have witnessed every expression of his greatness, as well as all the petty signs of human weakness which go to make a man worthy of affection."

Part Three

Nuremberg

18 Return to Germany

At Church House, Westminster, the legal eagles freshly arrived by air from Washington DC met with the British War Crimes Executive on the morning of 21 June 1945 to discuss which Nazis to put on trial. Sir Hartley Shawcross, British Attorney-General, read out a short list. When he came to the name of Rudolf Hess the chief American prosecutor, the bespectacled idealist Justice Robert H. Jackson, objected. "The list should not be over-loaded," he argued.

"I hope", Shawcross intimated delicately, "to be able to supply information about Hess shortly. I suspect that his case may have to be investigated internationally."

After dinner that same day Brigadier Rees examined Hess at Maindiff Court. Both Ellis Jones and Dr Phillips – who was, as Hess had said, in charge of the Monmouthshire County Mental Hospital – told the War Office psychiatrist that the prisoner was in fact looking forward to a trial and had prepared an extremely lengthy statement to that end.

Clearly charged with investigating Hess's fitness to stand trial, Rees reported to London that he was technically a "constitutional psychopath", but added the helpful opinion: "He has, I think, at all relevant times . . . been responsible for his actions. He certainly is . . . able to plead in a court of law." "Physically he is well," summarized Rees; "mentally he is as well as he has been at any time in this country."

Justice Jackson only now became aware of the Hess problem. Anticipating the need to have Hess and the other defendants examined by top-flight American specialists, on 23 June he wrote to Dr Millet, who had approached him on behalf of a group of US psychiatrists, agreeing that what he called "the defective mentalities and abnormalities and perversions" of the German leaders should be ascertained for posterity to prevent future generations of Germans from creating a myth. "As to your suggestion", Jackson concluded in this confidential letter, "that a victim be shot in the chest and not in the head, I would say that the general attitude of the [US] Army is that those who are subjected to death sentence as criminals should be hanged rather than shot. . . ."

Over in Wales Hess wrote another balanced, reflective letter and gave it to Lieutenant Fenton to post. "How often", he remarked to Ilse, "have I seen *The History of the Popes* in the shelves back home and taken fright, never guessing how dramatic Ranke's narrative could be – how lively in style – and what superb general commentaries I should find scattered about its pages. Unfortunately, I'm now coming to the end of vol. ii. But I'm sure I'll read it through again and again. Schopenhauer once advised that good books ought to be read at least twice. . . ."

At first Hess had continued his erratic (and often dramatic) routines. On the 25th, the perceptive Private Cooper saw him look up from the books that the Swiss Minister had brought for him, and again take out the tiny key when he thought he was unobserved and drop it on "some place of importance to himself". As July began Hess asked for his food to be tasted, and he flushed bits down the toilet. He asked a new private to taste some bread and milk; the man refused, thinking that the prisoner was taking a rise out of him.

Perhaps he was. On the morning of 4 July, "The patient made a mixture of soup, veg. & toast which in my opinion was not fit to offer to a pig [and] called upon Private Reygate to eat it (he also refused). It appears the patient is doing this for sheer devilment." On the 5th he asked for the drug that the kitchen staff used on his food so he could use it his own way instead. Scenes like these alternated with the usual "pains" and often culminated in bursts of wild laughter. On 11 July he took up writing again but "threw himself into a towering rage when the men were having a knock at cricket".

Then he revived the device that had worked so convincingly before. After seeing Major Ellis Jones on the 12th he told Sergeant Everatt, "My memory is failing me again."

This time the doctors could not agree that the loss of memory was genuine. After visiting him with Phillips on 13 July, Ellis Jones reported most emphatically to Brigadier Rees at the War Office that Hess was faking:

> On July 13, 1945 he again reverted to the condition that you have previously seen him in, best described I think as a *pseudo*-dementia.
>
> The loss of memory is again grotesque, e.g., loss of memory for prominent places in Berlin, that he was Deputy Führer, failing to recognise one nurse who has been here for two years, etc.

The orderlies were divided in their opinions, although he seemed emotionally very distressed. They saw him restless, agitated, suspicious, confused and depressed; on the 14th Cooper again caught sight of the "tiny key" routine. He was seen to renew the German notices on the wall over his writing table, and post a new one on the door leading from his room to the bathroom annexe. On the 28th the long-suffering Sergeant Everatt wrote dubiously: "[Hess] claims he has lost his memory and is unable to remember from day to day." When Private Graver came on duty the next evening, Hess inquired: "Are you a new nurse?" He appeared confused when Graver said he had been with him for years. "Still claims," recorded Everatt on 1 August, "his memory is failing him and pins up notes to remind him what to do. . . ."

Opinions at Maindiff Court discreetly differed. Lieutenant Fenton and Ellis Jones were in agreement that the close observations had shown that this time Hess was consciously simulating; but the other officers disagreed. Ellis Jones warned the prisoner several times over the next weeks that if called upon to testify in court he would attest that Hess's memory was normal – a statement which did not elicit even the mildest protest from the prisoner.

Everatt too was not easily duped. After Hess sat on the verandah on 6 August reading *The Times* and laughing and talking to himself, the Sergeant took over the evening shift, and wrote: "[Hess] still plays on the fact that his memory is bad, but [he] betrays himself with his actions." He added, puzzled, "He then settled down to reading, during which time he kept taking a small key from his pocket and dropping it on the mat, trying to do this without being observed."

In keeping with the amnesia the Deputy Führer had "forgotten" the war completely. Shortly after midnight on 15 August the local air-raid siren wailed one unwavering note – the All Clear. Hess sat up and asked, "What was that for?"

"I think it's to announce the cessation of hostilities with Japan," volunteered Private Clifford. Hess shrugged and seemed quite uninterested. On the following day the church bells pealed for the same reason. He seemed merely amused. Later that night, Clifford found him sorting through sheafs of foolscap manuscript. Hess asked for permission to burn them in the compound. Looking into the flames, he burst out laughing and told the Private, "This is *my* Victory bonfire!"

His defence manuscript was complete. Now he began clipping news items from *The Times* and sealing them away – no doubt to embellish his defence. When William Joyce came to be put on trial at the Old Bailey he closely followed the defence arguments in the newspaper's Law Report, obviously believing the judges would dismiss the case.

"You remember all about Joyce, then?" asked Ellis Jones.

"Oh, yes," said Hess quite simply, adding, "His name over here was Lord Haw-Haw, wasn't it?"

Over the next five months the experts remained deeply divided over his true mental condition. It was disturbingly inconsistent in its pattern.

He sat up late on 17 August sorting out papers and burning those he deemed useless. "[Hess] expressed surprise at some of the things he discovered," observed Sergeant Everatt. On the 24th he was seen to cut out and mark the picture of Josef Kramer, whom the daily newspapers labelled "the beast of Belsen", and stow it away in a drawer. On the 27th, RAMC Private S. H. Jordan noticed as he brought in the lunch that Hess was carefully clipping an article headlined "QUISLING PROVED SANE" from the previous day's newspaper (he seemed to be laughing to himself as he did so). On the 30th he was seen sitting in a state of amusement out on the verandah, and again he was clipping articles from *The Times*.

But Ellis Jones, who came in for several long conversations during September, was still not fooled. Later that summer he mentioned that his daughter was leaving for boarding school. "What are you going to do with her pony?" asked the prisoner.

The orderlies also had massive doubts. "He never forgets", observed Sergeant Reygate on 9 September, "to give the underpants the usual beating against the wardrobe each Sunday, despite the fact that he says that he can't remember anything."

Over the next week there were two articles in *The Times* about the Me-110 plane in which he had flown to Scotland (it was now on public view). The news stories evinced no comment from Hess. During this phase the now familiar signs of eccentric behaviour were also manifest – particularly the spasms of silent laughter and grimaces. RAMC Sergeant David Barnett wrote on 2 October 1945, "Patient's condition continues to deteriorate mentally & he seems to be becoming more agitated & depressed."

If he guessed that these were his last few days in Britain he did not show it. He clipped newspaper on the verandah, he had his usual "pains", he complained about the meals and slight noises. Above all, he continued to display a sporadic loss of memory. At 2.10 p.m. on the 3rd, he demanded, "Where is my lunch? I've been waiting for it for half an hour."

"You've only been dressed for ten minutes," he was reminded.

More papers were burned on the evening of the 5th, as he sorted through the remaining documents in his despatch box and resealed them. On the following day the War Office ordered Maindiff Court to have the prisoner ready to fly to Nuremberg on the 8th.

Although in deference to the prisoner's stubbornness the doctors left him unaware of his impending departure until the last moment, for the last few days he refused to eat. On the eve of departure Sergeant Barnett found him mentally unchanged – depressed and agitated – but with his physical condition also deteriorating.

The exit from Wales was thus rather an inglorious one for Hess. Sergeant Reygate woke him at 5.40 a.m. on 8 October: he had slept badly and showed it. Looking drawn and haggard he learned that within a few hours he was to be flown back to Germany. It took considerable persuasion to make him pack his cases.

Ellis Jones looked in, anxious that Hess take nothing belonging to Maindiff Court. He singled out one particular grey dressing-gown, but Hess said simply, "I brought it with me to this hospital." So his memory evidently reached back to June 1942 – and beyond that, because while he carefully removed the pictures of his wife and son from the wall he left that of the Führer. No doubt he reflected that the latter might not advance his cause in the courthouse of his enemies.

He lost his haughty manner. He was loaded aboard a plane with his manuscripts, Dr Ellis Jones and a package containing the RAMC orderlies' diaries, at Madley airfield not far from Hereford. They refuelled on the airfield at Brussels.

Once again Hess did not eat. "What's the matter, old chap?" asked Ellis Jones. "Not hungry?"

"I'm too excited," replied the former Deputy Führer with a shrug.

He had no fears of the coming trial. As the plane circled bomb-devastated Nuremberg, his own conscience was clear: he had tried to stop all this. As the plane landed, he raised his voice and turned to the doctor with this prophecy: "Time will prove me right. Within ten years Britain will agree with everything I've said against Communism. It will then be the world's biggest enemy!"

As they stretched their legs on Fürth airfield, Lieutenant-Colonel A. J. B. Larcombe of the 5th Royal Inniskilling Dragoon Guards, who had taken charge of Hess the day before, asked him casually which way Nuremberg lay. Hess cannily replied that he did not know.

Awaiting their transport into town a little later, Ellis Jones put the same question. Hess pointed out the direction without demur.

19 "Do You Remember 'Heil Hitler'?"

Nuremberg, home of the massed drum-beating Nazi Party rallies of the thirties, was dead: gutted, blasted, flattened, dehumanized – 51 per cent of its built-up area destroyed by the 14,000 tons of bombs rained on it by British air raids. The rambling, ugly, over-ornate Palace of Justice was one of the few big buildings left standing, which was why the Americans had chosen to stage the "international military tribunal" in this city.

Hess had brought with him cases full of the most diverse documents which he had compiled over the four years in Britain – three envelopes of newspaper clippings, two pages of architectural drawings, a description of his flight to Scotland, a motley collection of manuscripts on socialism, his health, the political situation, history, the atom bomb, economics, reconstruction, Conrad Hetzendorf, the war, Hitler, dreams, politicians, Lange; the texts of his interviews with Lords Simon and Beaverbrook, four letters to the King of England, fifty-nine pages of extracts copied out of Farrer's book on Edwardian England, and a large number of mysterious sealed and numbered packages. All these items were now taken away from him, despite his loud protests.

Manoeuvring to establish position, Hess demanded to see the Commandant. Here at Nuremberg that man was Colonel Burton C. Andrus, a fierce, moustachioed US cavalry colonel with wire-framed spectacles and a bright-red lacquered helmet. "I wanted to keep the parcels," exclaimed Hess. "It is one of the efforts that the British made to poison me. I want the packets for my defence." Andrus struggled to keep his temper. Within these prison confines he was all-powerful, and he saw no reason to humour Hess. He made it plain to the troublesome newcomer that from now on American – not British – interrogators and doctors would take over. The Welsh doctor who had brought him here would return to Abergavenny.

Hess did not like the new regime at all. Accustomed to being treated properly, as a high-ranking prisoner of war, he now found himself shown into a small, sparsely furnished stone cell on an upper floor of the adjacent prison block. His name was already painted on the door. The door was locked behind him.

Shortly, Andrus sent Dr Douglas McG. Kelley to examine the former Deputy Führer. Kelley, a US Army major, was the prison psychiatrist. Hess played his amnesia act for all it was worth; Kelley even found himself telling the prisoner when and where he was born in Egypt, and informing him that he had lost his memory back in July. All these disclosures evinced only a polite but faintly disbelieving interest from Rudolf Hess.

The table was too flimsy to lean on; his spectacles were taken away each night; the windows were out and the nights were cold; and the sentries had orders to shine a floodlight into his face all night long.

Sleepless and unwell, but still mustering enough presence of mind to put on his Luftwaffe captain's uniform for what he deduced was to be another historic day, Hess was taken out at 10.30 the next morning, 9 October, manacled by his right wrist to a GI, and marched along a wire-walled catwalk into a well-furnished office where he was curtly instructed to sit down.

He was in the office of Colonel John H. Amen, Chief of the Interrogation Division. On Amen's left sat an interpreter, on his right a court reporter, Clair Van Vleck. A Signals Corps photograph shows him lolling in a hard-backed chair, his legs crossed casually despite the black fur-lined flying boots with knee-length zippers.

The questioning began – a kind of Mastermind contest in reverse, in which Hess's aim was to know as few answers as possible without destroying his credibility entirely.★

"Do you prefer", asked Amen, "to testify in English or in German?"

"In German." (Any delay would blunt the edge of tricky questions.)

"What is your full name?"

"Rudolf Hess."

Amen grunted. "What was your last official position?"

"Unfortunately," said Hess politely – he remained excruciatingly courteous throughout these weeks – "this already comes into a period which I cannot remember any more. . . . There are many cases where I cannot even remember what happened ten or fourteen days ago."

Amen asked him what was the *period* that he could not remember.

"Anything longer ago than, say, fourteen days. It has frequently happened that I met gentlemen and I could not even remember their faces when I saw them again. It is terrible! Yesterday I was told by a doctor – or maybe," Hess interrupted himself, anxious not to seem too precise, "it was a clerk over there – that it sometimes happened that people don't even know their own names any more, and he said that perhaps a shock would suddenly bring it all back to me." He repeated: "This is terrible – everything depends on it for me, because I shall have to defend myself in the coming trial. . . ."

★ The transcripts are reproduced at length, as they have never been published before.

"You mean", Amen coaxed him incredulously, "that you cannot even remember what your last official position was in Germany!"

"No, I have no idea. It is just like a fog." This was Hess's favourite analogy: it had worked before.

"Do you remember that you used to be in Germany?"

"Well," reflected the ex-Deputy Führer amiably, "I think that is self-evident: because I have been told so repeatedly. But I don't remember just where I was – or even what house I was in. It has all disappeared. Gone!"

"How do you know that any kind of proceeding is coming up, as you say?"

Hess batted that one straight back at the Colonel. "This trial has been talked about all the time. I have seen it in the newspapers . . . and only yesterday I was told about it. And then when I was brought over here I was told that it was for the trial in Nuremberg. Such a big event has naturally made an impression on me, and I can remember it: I am thinking of it all the time at night."

"But you don't know what the proceeding is for?"

"I have no idea," said Hess – and allowed himself the gentlest of digs at his inquisitors: "I know that it is a *political* trial. . . . Perhaps I have even been told what I am accused of. But I don't remember."

"Do you remember how long you have been in England?"

"No . . . when we left there, I was told that I had been at that place for a long time."

Amen now handed across the table a book of Reich laws and ordinances, and asked if he had seen it before.*

"That there", said Hess, pointing to his printed signature, "is me."

Amen indicated the first few pages. "Will you read this portion."

"This is good," said Hess after studying the text, "and there's no question about it." But he could not recall ever having written it. At Amen's invitation, he read on. "My name appears below all these things," Hess informed him. "There is no question about that."

"Don't you know what they are?"

Hess shook his head – he would have to look at the book first. His patience strained, Amen asked him if he knew what *laws* were, and when Hess replied that that was obvious, he pressed him, "Don't you remember having anything to do with the enactment of various laws in Germany?"

"Do you mean I myself?"

"Yes."

"Enacted laws?"

"Yes."

"No trace of it," said Hess. "According to this," he continued, pointing to the book, "I must have – uh, how shall I say – I must have had a very

---

* *Anordnungen des Stellvertreters des Führers* (Franz Eher Verlag, Munich, 1937).

prominent position!" The pages showed that he had once been a "Deputy Führer". It meant nothing to him, he said.

Colonel Amen took a more aggressive line. "Do you know who *Jews* are?"

"Yes. They are a people – a race."

"You didn't like them very well, did you?"

"The Jews? No."

"So you had some laws passed about the Jews, didn't you!"

"If you say so, I have to believe it," agreed Hess. "But I don't know it. It is terrible."

Amen invited him to look at the relevant part of the book's index, but Hess again denied any memory of this at all.

"Isn't this whole book full of laws for which you were responsible?" asked Amen. "And isn't that why your name appears on the front?"

"If my name did not appear below this Introduction," the prisoner said flatly, "I should believe without reservation that somebody else was the author."

"Do you remember the Führer?" prodded Amen.

"Yes. During all that time," replied Hess, referring to his imprisonment in Wales, "I had a picture of him hanging in my room in front of me." However, he had no recollection of being a member of the Führer's secret Cabinet Council or even of attending meetings with him: merely that the man had been head of state: "The Führer was the leader." He allowed himself to add, "He was a personality who outshone everybody in every German's mind." He admitted knowing that Hitler was dead, but could not explain how he knew.

"Do you think you have ever talked to him?"

"According to this," said Hess, pointing to the book, "I must have. If somebody constantly issues laws as Deputy to the Führer, then he must have talked to him."

Amen seized on that. "You *remember* that you were Deputy Führer!"

"No," rejoined Hess. "I see it from this book."

Asked whether he recalled having discussed with Karl Hermann Frank what to do with the Jews in the Sudetenland, Hess replied that he could not even recall Frank, let alone what he had talked about.

"Why don't you like the Jews?"

"If I had to explain that to you in detail, I am again facing nothing. I only know that this is deeply within me."

Abandoning that topic, the Colonel threw the names of fellow defendants at him and watched the reaction. Ribbentrop meant nothing. Göring?

"Göring, yes . . . He means something to me." Amen grinned expectantly. "I read his name on a door," explained Hess. "I merely know the fact that he is here, and that he is some personality." He would not admit to knowing anything else about the Reichsmarschall – not even whether he was fat or thin. "If somebody were to come into this room right now," said the prisoner, in a deadpan voice, "and you told me, 'Here is Göring,' I'd just say 'Good day, Göring.'"

Whatever feelings Amen had, he choked them down. "Do you remember the Luftwaffe?"

"That is the organization of the aviators in Germany."

"Did Göring have anything to do with that?"

"You could kill me on the spot but I still wouldn't know."

Goebbels, Lammers, Brauchitsch, Keitel, Jodl, the OKW – the names meant nothing to him.

He said that he recalled nothing about having tried to commit suicide, but he knew that there had been a war, with Germany and Japan against America and Britain – and perhaps the French, and the Belgians too. "Yesterday," he explained, "we travelled through Brussels and there we saw the air forces and the armed forces, and also the damage that had been done to the buildings." He could not recall who had started the war or when, but he knew that it was finished: "I have read the newspapers during the last day, and it is quite evident from that."

"Do the newspapers make sense to you when you read them?"

"Partly yes," said Hess, sizing up the question. "And partly no."

Amen picked up the Nazi book of ordinances again. "Suppose", he challenged Hess, "that I tell you that this is a book of laws for which you were responsible as the Führer's Deputy!"

Hess looked him in the eye. "I have to believe it," he said. "I do not suppose that you are not telling the truth."

To Amen's questions about how and why he went to England he knew no answer.

"Did you have a family?"

"Yes."

"How do you happen to remember that?"

Hess stared back at the enemy Colonel: the separation from his little family had been the cruellest torment after the British declined to allow his return.

"I have had the photos of my wife and my little boy hanging in front of my eyes, alongside that of the Führer, all the time."

"Do you remember '*Heil* Hitler'?"

"That must have been a greeting," Hess suggested helpfully; he could not recall ever having used it himself.

Amen tried a little trick – showing him a fake Hess signature. Hess spotted the forgery. "I did not write that," he said, and explained that his H was different, and that he always used the German characters – Heß, not Hess. Asked how he could write letters to his wife if he knew neither her name nor her address, he gave his standard reply. "What probably happens is . . . I check in the papers what the address looks like."

"When did you last see your wife?" the Colonel's inquisition continued.

"It is logical to assume", replied Hess with practised ease, "that I saw her before I departed."

Exasperated but contriving to conceal it, Amen asked whether Hess had ever seen an aeroplane – before yesterday, he added hurriedly.

"Yes of course, they constantly flew over the house in Britain," said Hess, and volunteered the information: "That was where I was, before my departure."

"They dropped bombs, didn't they?" probed the Colonel.

"Not on our house, at any rate."

"Do you know that aeroplanes drop bombs?"

"Yes of course."

"They dropped them on Jews?"

"No. . . . Especially on Jews? I wouldn't know where."

"Do you remember having orders issued to burn up the Jews' places of worship?"

"You mean I, myself?" asked Hess, suppressing his indignation. "No, I know nothing at all about that."

Asked when he last saw the Führer, Hess obligingly offered what he called a logical reconstruction. "It appears in the book", he said, motioning with his manacled hands towards *Anordnungen des Stellvertreters des Führers*, "that I was his Deputy; thus I must have been with him very often; thus I must have seen him before my departure."

Beyond that, his mind was blank. He denied knowing when he left Germany; whether he had been in Munich; even what a *putsch* was – "To my mind," said Hess, "a *putsch* is an expression for an impact on water – hitting water."

Amen brandished at him a telegram of congratulations from him to Rosenberg. "Did you order a lot of Germans to be shot?"

"No, I have no idea. . . . If it says so here – and this appears to be an original – then it must be so."

"How do you happen to know the difference between an original and a copy?"

Hess pondered, admitted he could not give a precise definition, then brightened. "This", he said, nodding eagerly to another document, "is a *copy*. And this is an *original*. It's obvious from looking at the document."

Once or twice Hess slipped, like when he recognized an indecipherable wavy-line signature as Martin Bormann's, but he always managed to gloss over it. He knew too that the coming trial was of war criminals and, asked whether he was one himself, he assured Colonel Amen, "Evidently – otherwise I should have to be a murderer to have these manacles on."

"How do you know you aren't?"

"I have been told all along", said Hess, ignoring the question, "that I was going to be present with the so-called war criminals."

"What is a war criminal?"

"I would far prefer", said Hess, straight-faced as ever, "to ask *you* this question."

This first session on 9 October 1945 had lasted nearly two hours. After lunch Hess was escorted back before Colonel Amen at 2.30 p.m.; again a sound recording was made.

"Will you look over here to the right," instructed the Colonel, "to this gentleman here."

Hess had already seen the very familiar figure of the Reichsmarschall, Hermann Göring, clad in a pearl-grey uniform that was oddly empty of medals and now hung shapelessly from his once ample figure.

"At him?"

Göring beamed encouragingly at him: this was one contestant whose vanity demanded that Hess recognize him. "Don't you know me?" he coaxed.

"Who are you?" intoned the prisoner without a flicker of emotion.

"We have been together for years," protested Göring.

Hess lifted his manacled hands in a helpless gesture. "That must have been at the same time as that book they were showing me this morning."

Was he trying to drop a hint to Göring as he now added, "I have lost my memory for some time – especially now, before the trial."?

"You don't recognize me?" gasped Göring.

"Not personally, but I remember your name."

Nobody had spoken Göring's name, but the slip passed unnoticed. Everybody was enjoying Göring's punctured ego. For a few minutes Hess had some fun at Göring's expense, imperceptible to those unaware of the rivalry between them as Hitler's heirs apparent.

"If I was all the time in the position of Deputy Führer," mused Hess out loud, "then I must have met the other high personalities like you, but I can't remember anyone however hard I try."

"Listen, Hess," said the Reichsmarschall, his hackles rising. "I was the Supreme Commander of the Luftwaffe: you flew to Britain in one of *my* planes. . . . Don't you remember that I was made a Reichsmarschall at a meeting of the Reichstag at which you were present!" Since Hess shook his head, he continued: "Do you recall that the Führer, at another Reichstag session, announced that if anything happened to him I would be his successor, and that if anything happened to me, you were to be my successor? . . . We two discussed it for a long time afterwards."

"This is terrible," sighed Hess. "If the doctors hadn't assured me time after time that my memory will return some day, I should be driven to desperation."

Göring tried to prod his memory about visits that their families had made to each other – the times that Hess had come out to Carinhall, Göring's luxurious forest mansion outside Berlin, or the times they had both visited the Führer at his Obersalzberg mountain home.

"That means nothing to me."

"Hess! Think back to 1923, when I was Commander of the SA. You had led one of my SA troops in Munich since before 1923. Don't you remember how we both attempted a *putsch* in Munich?"

"The *putsch* in Munich," said Hess in a voice that he might have used describing a Tibetan religious festival, "was already referred to this morning."

"Do you remember how you arrested the Minister?"

"I 'arrested the Minister'?" gaped the prisoner. "I seem to have had a pretty complicated past –"

"Do you remember early 1933 – how we took over the government and you got the central political office from the Führer, and you and I discussed it for a long time?"

"I have been told that everything will come back all of a sudden – by shock," said Hess.

Göring asked if the name Messerschmitt meant anything to him. "You were well acquainted with him. He designed all our fighter planes. And he also gave you the plane that I refused to give you – the plane you flew to Britain in. Mr Messerschmitt gave that to you behind my back."

Hess explained that anything over fourteen days ago had vanished into darkness. Göring nevertheless persisted with a string of questions while Hess shook his head. "Do you remember that you flew to Britain. You used a Messerschmitt plane. Do you remember that you wrote a long letter to the Führer?"

"About what?" asked Hess, perhaps to give Göring a chance to say what he now did.

"About what you were going to do in Britain – that you were going to bring about peace."

Hess denied all knowledge of it, and Göring threw up his hands. "I cannot ask him anything else."

"All right," instructed Colonel Amen. "You move over here." He signalled to the psychiatrist, standing discreetly behind Hess, to have the next surprise witness brought in.

Determined to break down this prisoner's mental defences – to *prove* that he was malingering – Amen confronted Hess with the one man he should certainly recognize, Professor Karl Haushofer. Haushofer had been the intimate friend of Hess; their lives had been fatefully entwined ever since 1919.

The famous geopolitician was now seventy-six, and he had not had a good war. His wife of fifty years, Martha, was half Jewish, and he and his family had been protected from Nazi wrath only while Hess was there to extend a shielding hand, as he had in countless other cases. After Hess's flight Haushofer had been tossed into Dachau concentration camp; the Gestapo had arrested his younger son Heinz and shot the older, Albrecht, in Berlin on 23 April 1945, after he had tried to end the war through secret talks in Switzerland. A few weeks later the US Third Army had arrested and interrogated Professor Haushofer, but had formally released him; and now he was faced with the pseudo-legal chicanery of the American army all over again.

His arrival at Nuremberg jail had come about after Justice Robert H. Jackson, the chief US prosecutor, had caved in to the demands of a colonel on his team, Father Edmund A. Walsh, to have the aged professor brought in. Walsh was campaigning to have Haushofer included among the war crimes defendants even at this late stage. In civilian life Walsh was himself a professor of geopolitics at the Catholic university of Georgetown, and a lifelong, poisonous critic of Haushofer's academic theories: getting Haushofer hanged would be a neat ending to their academic rivalry. He visited the Professor at his mountain home near Lake Ammersee on 25 September, ingratiated himself with the elderly German, eventually revealed his name (but not his true intent) and lured him back to Nuremberg on 2 October – only to find that Colonel Amen would not hear of arraigning Haushofer at this late stage. As DeWitt C. Poole of the State Department pointed out, admonishing the crestfallen Walsh, prosecuting academics would be a dubious innovation for the American forces. "We are liable to be accused of witch-hunting," he said. Walsh's angry expostulations that Haushofer had been the mentor of Hess and other high Nazis fell on deaf ears.

The Nuremberg authorities subjected Karl Haushofer to remorseless interrogation, and he collapsed with a heart attack on the 4th. The US Army doctor warned that the old man might die at any moment. Queasy at the prospect of contributing to the death of a noble and innocent academic, Jackson allowed Walsh one final interrogation to persuade Haushofer to atone for his "evil teachings". Walsh conducted it rigorously, in fact to the verge of another heart attack: the Professor went red, his lips trembled and he collapsed. After sending out the stenographer, Walsh bent over to hear his words.

"Since Hess, who protected us, left for England," said the Professor, "I have lived with the fear that she [Martha] would be whisked away to Theresienstadt or Auschwitz. I have lived under a Sword of Damocles," he said, taking off his spectacles and dangling them over his head.

After a further interrogation on the 6th, Walsh informed him that he was free to return to his home, the Hartschimmelhof estate in Bavaria. Haushofer clutched at him in tears of gratitude; unaware of Walsh's intentions, he later christened the finest oak at Hartschimmelhof after him, not far from the oak "Rudolf Hess". He was still Jackson's "guest" a few days later, however, when Colonel Amen directed that he be retained for one final task. "We want Haushofer to confront Hess unexpectedly," the Colonel told Walsh, "in order to test the sincerity of his amnesia."

The shock was all Karl Haushofer's that afternoon, 9 October 1945, as he set eyes on the haggard, emaciated and unshaven Hess.

"*Mein Gott!*" he gasped.

"Do you know this man?" Colonel Amen challenged the prisoner.

"Pardon me," said Hess, looking unwaveringly at the Professor, "but I really don't know who you are!"

"Rudolf – don't you know me any more? . . . I am Haushofer!"

"Are we on first-name terms?"

"We have called each other by our first names for twenty years," wailed the Professor. He added, "I saw your wife and your child, and they are well." He grasped his friend's left hand to shake it (the prisoner's right wrist being manacled to the escort). "May I shake your hand?" the old man said, affectionately. "Your boy is wonderful. He is seven years old now. I have seen him."

For Hess, the pain of this confrontation, of this disavowal of his closest friend, the news about Ilse and Wolf Rüdiger and the burning desire to learn more must have been overwhelming, but he acted his chosen role with ice-cold precision to the end.

"In order to calm down an old friend," he said, selecting his words with exquisite care behind expressionless eyes, "I can only assure you that the doctors tell me that my memory will all come back to me . . . and then I shall recognize an old friend again. I am terribly sorry."

Tears filled the aged professor's eyes. "Your son is very well," he whispered. "I saw him. He is a fine boy, and I said goodbye to him under the oak, the one that bears your name, the one you chose at Hartschimmelhof where you were so many times. Don't you remember – the view of the Zugspitze mountain, the branches of the tree that hung so low? Don't you remember Heimbach, where you lived for so long?" Hess was shaking his head. "I am sure it will all come back," said Haushofer. "We have been friends for twenty-two years now: you were at our university studying to become a doctor."

Clutching Hess's hand, he gazed into his eyes. "You will see – it will all come back. I can even see the light in your eyes, like the old days. . . . Just imagine, your little boy – he has grown so high," he said, indicating with his free hand. "He is seven – he looks half like you and half like your mother."

A glistening came faintly into the prisoner's eyes.

Göring seized upon it. "Do you remember your boy?"

"Of course I do," said Hess, "because I looked at a photograph of my wife and boy all that time. It stays in my memory."

"You wrote me a letter once," continued Haushofer, "by devious routes, which got to me finally; you wrote to me about the long walks you were taking, you told me about the hay and the smell of the flowers; you told me you could take walks of two hours, and you had an honour-guard. That made me and your wife very happy. . . . Your last letter then contained the sad line, 'I am beginning to lose my memory . . . I cannot even imagine my own son any more, and perhaps that is the greatest blessing for me.'"

He reminded Hess of the early years – the flight to Munich from Berlin, when they had flown circles round his mother's hunting lodge in the Fichtelgebirge mountains.

"Do you have any news from her?" Hess asked.

"In her little, fine handwriting she has written letters to me. . . . Don't you remember the time when I was forbidden to write to your wife and to your mother; and I told the Gestapo they could arrest me because I would not give up my old friendships?"

"Why was that supposed to be stopped?"

Haushofer realized that Hess had left Germany, of course, by then. "When you flew to Britain it was believed that your romantic friend was guilty."

Göring intervened again at the mention of the dread police agency which he himself had founded: "Do you remember an institution which we had, called the 'Gestapo' – the secret state police?"

"No."

Haushofer forgave Hess for Dachau, and said so. "I should like to look into your eyes," he said. "Because for twenty-two years I have read in your eyes. And I am glad to see that a little bit of recognition is coming back into them. . . . Don't you remember Albrecht," he added suddenly, "who served you very faithfully? That was my eldest son. He is dead now."

The prisoner's face was once again a mask. "It doesn't mean anything to me."

Thus Haushofer had failed to penetrate the barrier that Hess had erected, as Göring had before him.

Colonel Amen ordered Franz von Papen, the arrogant former Vice-Chancellor, to be brought in.

"Who is that?" asked Hess.

Amen turned to the new contestant: "Do you know this gentle-man?"

Papen bristled. "Yes, I know him."

"I'm sorry," said Hess simply. "I don't recognize him."

"He has changed very much."

"Yes, I have changed," agreed Hess. "I didn't have any chance to shave." (The prison Commandant was trying to break the defendant's self-esteem.)

Invited by Amen to recall to Hess incidents during his vice-chancellorship in 1933, Papen tried hard. "You must remember," he said, "that when we formed Hitler's government on 30 January I was the Vice-Chancellor . . .?"

"I can't remember anything," Hess said pleasantly. "I just explained that to these gentlemen."

Ernest William Bohle, the Gauleiter who had been closest to Hess, was next and fared no better.

"There's another gentleman whom I don't know," said Hess, pre-empting the now familiar routine.

"Mr Hess, you know me of course," the newcomer began confidently. "My name is *Bohle* —"

"That means nothing to me."

Bohle was astonished. "That is most remarkable," he said, speaking English with his native Bradford twang. "He has known me for years," he added helplessly.

Göring too was goggling. "Remind him that it was you who translated his letter."

"Don't you remember that I translated your letter to the Duke of Hamilton for you?"

"No."

"Don't you remember that you took this letter to the Duke of Hamilton — that it was I who translated it?"

"I don't have the least recollection of that."

"That is *flabbergasting!*" said Bohle in English.

"Perhaps he wasn't called Hamilton then," volunteered Haushofer. He turned to his old friend, raising his voice slightly as though deafness was the problem. "Don't you remember [Lord] *Clydesdale*, the young aviator who flew over the Himalayas? Don't you remember that he was your *guest* in Berlin at the Olympic Games? . . . His name became Hamilton later — that was the British way of giving out titles."

"If I don't remember a person I've known for twenty-two years," Hess pointed out doggedly, "how do you expect me to know this Clydesdale?"

"If I brought you his picture," said the Professor, "you'd probably recognize him again because we found him very likeable [*sympathisch*] at the time. Don't you remember: you liked his feat when he flew over Mount Everest — when he dropped two thousand metres and barely got away? . . . Don't you remember that was something like where you used to ski, in the Höllental; but that was two thousand metres that he dropped! Don't you remember that that made a very deep impression on you?"

"Remember the other war," Göring chimed in again, "the *earlier* war, when you were a young Leutnant in the air force as I was. . . . Don't you remember when you flew to France as a fighter pilot? . . . The Fokker plane? Don't you remember the aerial combat that you were in?"

"Don't you remember", asked Haushofer, "when you got wounded so badly, when you were shot in the lungs?"

"Don't you remember Max and me," said Göring, referring to the legendary Immelmann, "who flew together with you?"

Hess denied all these memories — even the vivid picture that Haushofer conjured up of how they had once played hide-and-seek between the oaks at Hartschimmelhof.

"I am sorry", the prisoner said finally, "that I am facing here an *old friend*, and that I cannot share these old memories with him."

Colonel Amen sighed deeply, and asked Colonel Edmund Walsh, who had hovered in the background, to take the Professor into the next room alone with Hess. The resulting dialogue was little different – Hess was sorry, but he could not recall anything before ten or twelve days ago.

> At one point [reported Walsh afterwards] Haushofer produced something from his wallet. . . . I intervened and asked to see what it was before Hess could take it. It was a photograph of a man approximately 35 to 38 years of age, seated in an automobile with a woman by his side.
>   On looking at it Hess instantly replied, "That is myself – and that is my wife."
>   There followed an exchange of intimate conversation. . . . Attempting to coax Hess's memory up to the present time, Haushofer suggested that if he, Hess, could again see the old familiar landscape of Bavaria he might recover his memory.
>   Hess always assented. . . .
>   He was, or pretended to be, under heavy mental strain. Here as in the other room he was extremely nervous, fidgety, crossing and uncrossing his legs, blinking his eyes, fumbling with his coat, etc. At one moment he referred to the manacle with which he was attached to the soldier ". . . wie ein Kannibale" – like a cannibal.

After twenty unproductive minutes Walsh ended their dialogue. The two friends, master and pupil, clasped hands in silence and gazed intently into each other's eyes – Haushofer visibly more moved than Hess.

The Professor was devastated, and told Walsh as he was driven back to his lodgings, "Hess was my favourite pupil, and today I saw the ruin of it all." Hess's fanatical belief in Hitler was entirely sincere, but those around them betrayed him – Ribbentrop and Bormann, suggested the Professor, had both used the man to climb to more exalted positions themselves. "Did you hear the insolent Von Papen only asking if he could not remember the Vice-Chancellor!" Finding his idealism betrayed, Hess, in keeping with his character, had flown to Britain. "That was the only time he violated our friendship – by concealing his plans from me. I suspected that something was up . . . he was extremely nervous for some time. I accused him of hiding something from me, but he only evaded my eyes."

Hess returned to his cell, took a sheet of yellowing paper and began to keep a pencilled diary – aware of course that it was liable to be read by his captors:

> Göring and an old gentleman who is supposed to have been acquainted with me for a long time were brought face to face with me, apparently in order to ascertain whether I would recognize them.
>   I did not recognize them.

"Did you think that Hess was telling the truth?" the interrogator, Colonel Amen, asked Göring later that afternoon.

"Yes, absolutely," replied the Reichsmarschall. "He is completely changed . . . he gives me the impression that he is completely crazy."

"Would you say", Amen inquired, "he seemed to be crazy before he went off on this flight?"

"I wouldn't say outright crazy, but he was not quite normal then, and he was very exalted, so to speak – very exuberant."

Göring volunteered what he took to have been the reason behind Hess's dramatic 1941 flight: "In spite of the high position, he had relatively little to do after the outbreak of the war. . . . It was his wish all the time to *do* something – and do something *decisive* – and this made him very, very nervous. Then he probably felt that his chief of staff, Bormann, was talking to the Führer and not telling him about it; and that may have added to it." Thus, concluded Göring, Hess had decided to compensate for this relative inactivity by doing something decisive: "He had to fly to Britain and bring about peace."

"How is your memory today," opened Colonel Amen pleasantly on the day after these extraordinary conversations.

"It hasn't altered at all," replied Hess through the interpreter.

He was not feeling well, having just suffered one of the old abdominal "cramps". Amen promised not to detain him too long, but asked him nonetheless a series of questions trying, he said, to probe how far back his memory reached. Hess allowed that he could just remember leaving Wales and the hospital quarters there.

Suddenly Colonel Amen abandoned his bedside manner.

"When did you get this idea", he snapped, "of losing your memory?"

"I don't know. It is a fact that I don't have it now."

"I said," repeated Amen, a perceptible edge to his voice, "when did you get the idea that it would be the smart thing to lose it?"

"I don't quite understand that," answered Hess. "You mean to say by that, that I thought it might be a good idea to lose my memory and deceive you like that?"

"Yes. That is just what I mean!" retorted the Colonel, and continued, when Hess denied it, "Well, it might be very helpful in connection with the coming proceedings, might it not?"

Hess tried to be helpful, in the unhelpful manner of which his training in Wales had made him a master.

"Well, take for instance the book you showed me yesterday. I don't see what benefit I could derive from losing my memory there."

"Oh no," agreed Amen. "But for instance when you directed the murder of various people – which you did!"

"I did that?"

"Yes," replied Amen, and bluffed, "so the witnesses say."

"You mean", reflected Hess, "that because *I* can't remember it, *your* witnesses are less creditable?"

"Uh," said Colonel Amen, "somewhat."

"Or," said Hess, "do you mean because I am lying? If I seem to have lost my memory," he pointed out, "then people will not like me and

it might influence the trial in such a way that I will get a worse judgement."

Amen reminded the prisoner that according to Haushofer they had
once read together a Swedish novel about students who had lost their
memory and then regained it with the help of music and poetry. "As a
matter of fact," he triumphed, "that is where you got this idea of losing
your memory, isn't it!"

Hess cackled and said, "No, certainly not."

"What do you think is so funny about that?"

Hess invited "the gentleman", as he addessed him, to put himself in his
shoes, given that a trial was imminent: "I won't be able to defend myself. I
sit in my cell all the time and think about these things. . . . It hurts my
mind very much. Then somebody mockingly asks when did I get the idea
of losing my memory because I read some story, and it leaves a very
ridiculous impression on me – because of the contrast."

The Colonel chided him: "You were the one who was laughing,
not I."

"There is only one thing that I can do at the coming trial," said Hess,
"and that is to fight for my own skin with everything I have: and the only
instrument I have to fight with is my brain and my memory."

The American prosecution was faced with a conundrum.

Hess had challenged Colonel Amen during this further interview to
explain just why he should be faking: "Does he think I am so childish," he
had asked, appealing to the interpreter, "or so naive, that I think I might
improve my position with this?"

Amen had only murmured, "I'm not quite sure why you are" –
meaning, faking.

Hess too was probably unsure: but his instinct had told him to
destabilize the enemy, to present them with an unpredictable target in an
unfamiliar situation.

It produced an awkward predicament for Justice Robert H. Jackson.

"What do *you* think," his assistant prosecutor Thomas J. Dodd asked
Papen three days after the Hess confrontation. "Do you think his mind is
really gone?"

"It seems to be. I found him very changed, and his face too. . . . That he
didn't recognize any of those people, and the way he spoke: it *must* be
insanity."

"Well, you know what naturally occurs to us: is he pretending or not?"

"Why should he?"

"I don't know!"

According to a confidential oral history of the trial dictated by Justice
Jackson in 1953, Göring was among those who considered Hess's loss of
memory a fraud. "Bring the so-and-so in," the Reichsmarschall said,
using an uncomplimentary term, "and *I'll* make him remember."

Göring [Hess recorded in his diary] tried for an hour to refresh my memory – in vain. He told me that when I flew to England I was said to have left a letter behind for the Führer.

"Don't you remember any more?" asked the Reichsmarschall (the conversation, in Room 167, had been secretly recorded). "Can't you remember the noise of an aeroplane engine?"

"Yes of course," replied Hess. "But I don't know whether that is just from the flight I took recently."

"Now I want to ask you if you can remember, do you know how to steer a plane?"

Hess said guardedly that he was not sure, so Göring turned to German history.

"Do you remember Frederick the Great?"

"Well I just know the name – it doesn't mean very much to me."

"Do you remember you had his picture?" (It was a painting that Göring had evidently coveted for himself.)

"Yes."

"Do you *understand*, even if you do not remember, that we were together very much in our lives? . . . Please be convinced that I want to help you in every way."

"Yes, I am convinced of it," said Hess – possibly puzzled by this unaccustomed "Dr Kildare" role that Göring was playing.

"It is extremely important for both of us to try to strengthen your memory." Göring added, "It *is* quite clear to you why you are here, isn't it?"

"Yes."

"You must realize that the fact that somebody doesn't remember anything is a defence."

"Yes," agreed Hess, obscurely, "I discovered that too." He continued, "But that is not why I lost my memory."

Göring found it encouraging that Hess had recalled at least the name of Frederick the Great, and he ventured to explore that avenue of history, trying to prise individual diamonds out of what he took to be the darkened walls of his former colleague's mind.

After a while, however, Hess politely inquired, "Do you think you can bring back my memory like this? The doctor told me it could be done only by shock."

Göring, still acting the part of psychiatrist and counsellor, continued, "You are supposed to relax and try to recall those things."

Hess explained that trying to concentrate placed a terrible strain on his mind. "For two hours afterwards I have to lie down on my bed, and I don't know what's going on."

The Reichsmarschall just was not cut out for this role. Losing patience, he snapped, "Now look here, Hess, it wasn't simple for me to come here and talk to you, because I too have to concentrate."

"Why in hell should the both of us exert ourselves so much in here then?"

"Don't let's argue about it. . . . But if we discuss some points quietly something will come back to you."

He tried to draw Hess out on book reading, but failed to get him to admit that reading produced associations of ideas with real life. Past events were a blur. The name of Reich Youth Leader Baldur von Schirach produced the blank response: "Who is that?"

"Do you remember the Führer?"

"Well, I know what he looked like – I had a picture in my room."

"Do you remember the way he spoke?"

"His picture didn't speak . . ."

When Göring tried to ascertain precisely why Hess had kept a picture of the Führer, Hess could not offer any reason.

"But you kept *looking* at the picture, didn't you?"

"That I do not know," answered Hess – to have admitted otherwise would have betrayed his deceit.

"What do you mean, you don't know! The picture was with you all the time."

For five minutes Göring badgered him about the Hitler photograph in Wales – "with variations in the questions", as the American private monitoring the recording stated, "and none in the answers".

"Frankly," said Hess, tiring of this dialogue, "it was a matter of indifference to me whether the picture was there or not. . . . You know, it is not very good for my brain in its present condition to keep probing into these things."

"You *refuse* to remember," the Reichsmarschall accused him. "You refuse to *want* to remember!"

At this moment Colonel Amen, waiting outside, abandoned discretion and pushed into the room. "Do you still think that you will be better off at the trial if you refuse to remember anything?" he snarled (the microphones were still recording).

"It is all the same," said Hess eventually, "whether I say anything or not."

Amen evidently showed him some of the documents he had written at Abergavenny, which clearly referred to earlier episodes in the war. "You did write it afterwards," the monitor heard the Colonel insist. "You think you wrote it *before* you left Germany?"

Hess evaded making an immediate reply, and asked to read the items in his cell. "I can't imagine", he said self-deprecatingly, "that I was in a position to write a thing like that."

"Is it written in your handwriting?"

"I didn't have any typewriter," replied Hess, rattled, "so I guess it must have been written by me."

Amen pounced triumphantly. "How do you know you didn't have a typewriter?"

"Oh, just by coincidence I can remember that – my memory goes back that far!"

"It reaches just about where you want it to reach," mocked the Colonel. "How about the letter you wrote to the Führer?" he then asked. "Have you got a copy of that in the package with you?"

Hess said that he did not know what was in that package, nor, he said at first, did he remember that Amen had asked him these questions before – but then he blurted out that he did. "I remember them only too well – that's why I am so worked up and angry at you for asking them all over again."

"Why don't you exert some of that energy trying to think back to before you left England?"

"Nobody", replied Hess ironically, "has given me the prescription as to how to do that."

"Well," drawled Colonel Amen, "we'll have to start giving you the 'shocks' then, I guess."

"Oh, yes please – and also the papers that you promised me."

Originally, Justice Jackson had wanted to keep the psychiatrists away from the defendants until sentence had been passed. Hess's performance, however, gave him no option but to bring them in. Nor was Hess the only inmate whose health aroused concern: Labour Front leader Dr Robert Ley was seriously unbalanced, as his writings showed, and a few days later he would confirm it by strangling himself.

Jackson recalled the Park Avenue psychiatrist John Millet who had urged him two months before, on behalf of the Psychiatrists' Associations of the United States, not to have the condemned prisoners shot in the head (so as to preserve their crania for the scrutiny of a prurient posterity). "Circumstances have arisen", Jackson now wrote to Dr Millet, "which may make it advisable for us to have psychiatric examinations of the high Nazi officials in advance of the trial." He invited Millet, in the strictest confidence, to suggest the names of psychiatrists of international repute.

On the same day he despatched his son by air to Washington, with instructions to explain the unexpected problem to the Secretary of War. "What we must have", the chief US prosecutor directed him to say, "is not just a psychiatrist but . . . outstanding men who are fitted to give a judgment that the medical profession will accept." They should not, he felt, be "regular service men" either. (Several army officers had now criticized this "political trial" in the American press.)

Meanwhile he authorized the prison's consultant psychiatrist Major Kelley to carry out tests on Hess. Kelley used a variant of the ingenious "ink blot" test invented twenty-five years earlier by the Swiss psychiatrist Herman Rorschach: the subject was shown ten standard cards overprinted with black-and-white and multi-coloured ink blots and asked what he could see; from the response, an expert could determine what image the subject projected from himself on to the shape. For example, "seeing" humans in action would be indicative of a high intelligence.

Administering the Rorschach test Kelley and an interpreter placed themselves on either side of Hess – they sat on his bunk bed because he was not allowed a chair.

Probably curious about this interesting new challenge, Hess co-operated well. In the second card he saw "two men talking about a crime – blood is on their hands". As he rambled on in this vein, it seemed to Kelley significant that Hess still retained "bloody memories". When he came to the ninth card, his interpretation that the ink-blot was like the "cross section of a fountain" was taken by Kelley as evidence of inner anxieties. Given the subject's situation, this should not have raised many eyebrows at Nuremberg.

Kelley made his report on the 16th. Addressed to Colonel Andrus, the two-page document conceded that on arrival Hess had displayed what Kelley called "a spotty amnesia"; he quoted Ellis Jones as saying that Hess had presented the symptoms of total amnesia from November 1943 to February 1945, and again from 12 July to the present. As for the numerous samples of food, chocolate and medicine that Hess had parcelled up as "evidence", the opinion cited by Kelley was, interestingly, "Such behaviour could be either simulated or a true paranoid reaction."

Kelley clearly believed that Hess had faked the paranoia, since his own examination had revealed only "vague paranoid trends". "There is no evidence of any actual psychosis," he asserted. As for the current amnesia, Kelley was cautious and confused – wrapping up his diagnosis with so many ifs and buts that Andrus and Jackson were left little the wiser.

16 October 1945   [Major Kelley's report]

Internee Rudolf Hess has been carefully studied since his admission to Nuremberg Prison. . . . Present examination reveals a normal mental status with the exception of the amnesia. . . . Special examinations with Rorschach cards indicate some neurotic patterns. They point to a highly schizoid personality with hysterical and obsessive components. Such findings are confirmed in the patient's present reactions. He complains bitterly of "stomach cramps", which are obviously neurotic manifestations.

He is over dramatic in his actions, presenting typical hysterical features, complaints and symptoms.

His amnesia is at present limited to personal events concerning his history after joining the Party. The amnesia however shifts in a highly suspicious fashion. . . . It is quite possible that he has suggested an amnesia to himself for so long that he partially believes in it.

Summing up, Kelley termed Hess "sane and responsible", and attributed the amnesia both to auto-suggestion and to "conscious malingering".

Having said that, he recommended that treatment might overcome it.

Evidently not realizing that Major Dicks had attempted precisely this in May 1944, Kelley advised narco-hypnosis – interrogation after an intravenous injection of the "truth drug" sodium pentothal. This, he explained, ought to show whether Hess was indeed malingering. Kelley added one warning: "It must be borne in mind, however, that occasional accidents happen with any intravenous techniques." Using sodium pentothal or similar drugs of the barbitol series had led to fatalities.

Colonel Andrus passed Kelley's report on to Justice Jackson the next day with his own comment:

> Hess believes or has pretended that the British attempted to poison him. Treatment with drugs might call forth the same suspicion or allegation against us by him. Undue alarm might be injurious to the patient.

Hess was being as unhelpful as he could. After a dental examination, he was asked to sign the form finding his teeth to be defective. He refused, and the dentist had to sign the statement instead. Asked a few days later for a signature on an innocuous library slip, the prisoner said, "I will not sign anything that has not been filled out." Now, despite intensive cajoling by Kelley he refused to sign a consent form to the proposed trial narco-hypnosis. The Americans were loath to take even a 1:1000 risk of accidentally killing him, and on 20 October the executive officer on Jackson's team, Colonel Robert J. Gill, wrote to Colonel Andrus, "Any treatment of this case involving the use of drugs which might cause injury to the subject is disapproved."

Hess continued to write faintly bizarre notes in his prison diary:

17 October 1945

Great excitement because I made a fuss over not getting the things I had asked for from my baggage. Afterwards I was told that I could make a complaint to the Commandant, but that I must not shout at people. . . . Have hung up small notices in the cell saying: QUIET PLEASE. DO NOT SHOUT AT PEOPLE. One of the officers who came in said this was a good idea.

18 October 1945

The American doctor was quite definite in his assurance that my memory would be brought back by one single injection.

19 October 1945

Indictment handed to me. One hundred pages. I thumbed through it in five or ten minutes and read the headings.

The indictment in the case against "Hermann Wilhelm Göring, Rudolf Hess, Joachim von Ribbentrop" *et al.* charged him on all four counts including atrocities and crimes against peace.

"It is expected", Colonel Amen formally notified him as the clock showed 4.46 p.m. that day, "that you will continue to be interrogated from time to time unless you expressly object thereto."

Hess had no real intention of falling into this trap – of incriminating either himself or his colleagues through his own utterances. "I believe", he said, "that in practice there would be no purpose to that."

Amen called upon him to attest whether he considered his interests would be better protected by refusing further interrogation.

"In my opinion," Hess cheekily replied, "there is no difference either way: because nothing will ever come of it. I have read the indictment and it is completely devoid of meaning for me. . . . However, if the gentlemen desire to put questions to me, I shall be glad to listen to them."

The emphasis was on the word *listen*.

20 Triumph of the Will

The four prosecution teams which had been convening in Berlin as a sop to Soviet pride had now arrived in American-controlled Nuremberg for the trial, but the Russians were still asking for several weeks' delay. Although the Americans grumbled, they were by no means unhappy given the snags that their own preparations were running into.

The case against Hess was causing the biggest headaches. The evidence against him was thin. Indeed, teams of Intelligence experts were still scouring the land trying to produce a credible dossier against him. On 29 October 1945 Erich M. Lipman of Third US Army headquarters reported after visiting Ilse Hess that she had willingly shown him some sixty box-folders rich with the correspondence conducted through their *Privatkanzlei* (whose secretary since 1933, Miss Hildegard Fath, was already in American custody). The material was unlikely to advance their case against Hess: on the contrary.

"Frankly," reported Lipman to Lieutenant Blumenstein at Nuremberg, "I am rather impressed with the type of friends he had and the manner in which he frowned upon favoritism, even in the cases of his own family."

Lipman had, however, spotted the intriguing role of the doctor among Frau Hess's neighbours at Hindelang – to whom Hess had written, it will be remembered, cryptic messages from Wales. "Particular attention is invited to the folder of Dr Gerl," advised Lipman, forwarding three selected files to Nuremberg. "[He] was employed by Hess and Hitler personally to undermine high-ranking British statesmen and people 'behind the throne' and to sell Germany to them." Searching for correspondence with "Lord Hamilton", Lipman had found only a Christmas card from him, which he took as an interesting sidelight on British appeasement circles before the war. Ilse Hess had advised Lipman that if they played Mozart to him it might bring his memory back; she wrote a letter for Lipman to forward to Nuremberg, and enclosed with it a snapshot of Wolf Rüdiger in an envelope of the type that Hess's office had used for confidential material to be seen only by him.

Hess had been notified on 20 October that the trial would begin one month later. He saw no reason to co-operate. Asked to complete a long questionnaire on his "future occupation", religion and other personal data, he filled in only his name. He refused to appoint defence counsel, and recorded in his diary on the 21st that he did not care whether the Tribunal did so for him; this he confirmed in writing to the Tribunal's Secretary-General the next day.

He was still denied exercise and allowed to shave only at three- or four-day intervals. He was also losing weight rapidly. His apathy now may even have become real. When Kelley asked on the 23rd why he had not bothered to read the indictment, Hess answered, "There's no point in my doing so, because I would forget the contents anyway – I may take a look at it shortly before the trial."

Kelley tried to persuade him to take an insulin injection to get his weight up before having "the injection to restore his memory". Hess refused, and asked for raw apples instead. Despite the refusal Dr Ludwig Pflücker, the elderly German doctor assigned to the prisoners, appeared in his cell brandishing an insulin syringe. Hess still declined it.

"How's the appetite?" asked Kelley the next day, 24 October.

"I can hardly be expected", said Hess, "to have much appetite in view of the little exercise I get."

A day or two later, when Kelley warned that the weight loss since the photographs of 1941 was quite noticeable, the prisoner replied, "I am sure I'll soon get my old weight back once I am set free." The skies were clear and sunny over Nuremberg that afternoon, but still he was not allowed out into the open.

Alarmed by the rapid deterioration in the mental condition of the prisoners, Kelley wrote to Colonel Andrus, specifically mentioning Hess, Keitel, Ley, Ribbentrop and Sauckel, and demanded that they be allowed adequate outdoor exercise. The prison doctor Colonel Rene H. Juchli backed this up. But the Commandant refused to give his consent.

Thwarted in his intention of administering a truth drug to Hess, Kelley asked for the Tribunal to appoint an international commission to confirm his findings on the prisoner's sanity. He had a powerful ally in this. Major-General William Donovan, chief of the OSS – the Office of Strategic Services, forerunner of the CIA, which was taking a close hand in managing the trial – submitted the same recommendation on 25 October:

> In view of the assertion made by Hess that he has amnesia I suggest . . .
> the appointment of a commission by the Court to inquire into his state of
> mental health as well as his ability to confer with his counsel in the
> preparation of his defense.

Two days later two more American doctors visited the prisoner, urging him to allow some quite harmless injections – "Your weight loss must be a worry to you," they said.

"I prefer to get my weight back by completely natural means," was his reply.

"We only want to make you feel more comfortable."

Dr Pflücker begged him to reconsider insulin. They allowed Hess no outdoor exercise even now, but did offer to let him have a chair during the daytime.

"I don't need any chair," said Hess.

On the 30th they confronted him with the packages he had brought from Wales.

30 October 1945

I was taken to a building next door. Masses of documents in my handwriting were put in front of me & sealed packets which I was told had been brought from Britain with me.

I couldn't remember anything about the documents or packages. The packets – one of which I opened – contained samples of medicines and foods which I assumed to contain harmful substances (poisons).

I was assured that the documents – which appear to be of great importance – would be handed to me after translation, before the trial started.

I have not officially handed the documents over, however, nor have I for instance taken them as the basis for my defence.

He had now been at Nuremberg for over three weeks; over fourteen days had elapsed since his last interview with Colonel Amen – with results that the Colonel clearly had not anticipated.

"When you came up to Nuremberg," Amen challenged, "you brought with you various papers and documents?"

"I don't know that."

"You told me the other day that you had."

Hess pointed in astonishment at the Colonel.

"To this gentleman here?" he asked the interpreter. "I don't even know that I ever saw the gentleman before."

Amen swallowed hard, and asked if he did not recall being questioned at all since arriving here, at Nuremberg's Palace of Justice.

Hess cunningly wove into his reply a renewed statement that he did not want counsel. "Well," he said, "I must have been interrogated before, because among my papers I found the statement, 'I stated that I didn't want a defence counsel.' So I presume I had been asked. . . ."

Challenged again by Amen, "Don't you remember that I have questioned you many times?", the prisoner stated unequivocally that he did not.

"Your memory", snapped the Colonel, "is getting worse instead of better. Is that right?"

With infallible logic, Hess pointed out that he could hardly say.

Amen now proposed to show Hess the items that he had brought from Britain. "Before I do that," he began, "I want to ask you again what you said about somebody telling you that you were not entitled to any counsel?"

"I have a document over there," said Hess, nodding in the direction of the cell block, "and it contains the statement that I am free to name counsel if I want to, but I do not have to."

Amen, not realizing that defending himself would be an important part of Hess's strategy, passed on to the various packages with no further comment.

"Here is one," he intoned formally, "being a package sealed with seven red wax seals. I ask you to look at that and tell me whether you know what it is."

"It says on the back of the envelope", read Hess, "that its contents are medical pills which contain materials in them that are harmful." He did not, he added, recall ever having seen it before, but it was certainly his handwriting.

"Did you bring any poisoned articles with you from England?"

"No. Well, what do you understand by poisoned articles?"

"I don't know what's in the envelope. I'm trying to find out whether you do!"

Hess repeated that he knew only what he read on the envelope.

"How about *this* envelope – indicating", Amen intoned, "an envelope with five wax seals thereon, four of them being purple and one of them being green on the reverse side thereof."

Hess denied being conscious of having seen it before.

The Colonel pompously directed that it be marked for identification as "EXHIBIT 'A' HESS OCTOBER 30, 1945".

Hess pointed to the seal between two of the purple seals on the back. "This is the seal of the Swiss Legation in London," he recognized.

Amen pounced on that. "How do you know that?"

"It says 'Légation de Suisse à Londre'," the Deputy Führer explained.

He did not recall that one either; Amen had it marked as an exhibit too. So, in short order, Exhibits B, C, D, E were disowned by Hess and identified by Amen until they reached an official British envelope from which Amen extracted a manuscript beginning with the words, "I landed in Scotland on 10 May 1941 in the evening." (It was Hess's version of events, written in the closing weeks of the war at Abergavenny.)

"Do you recall having written it?"

"No, not in any way."

They invited him to read it through. After a long while he looked up and said: "This is an incredible story . . . It says here: 'apart from the chemical that caused toothache, there was unmistakably a powerful laxative and a poison which irritated the mucous membrane. . . . This last caused my nose to stop up with congealed blood, my mouth to bleed profusely, and my intestines to burn like fire.'"

Hess admitted that it was his handwriting, but said that he did not recall how or when or even if he had written it. He allowed Amen to have it translated into English, but added, "Could I receive a copy of these documents in my cell so I can look at them? . . . Because apparently they have significance with respect to the trial."

More Hess manuscripts were produced – about the First World War, the atomic bomb and reconstruction – and he commented, "It seems I was very productive."

"Very prolific," grunted Amen.

"Did you tie these up yourself?" he asked, indicating the scores of smaller packages.

"That I do not know. At any rate, if I did it was a good pastime. This", he said, having opened one, "is cocoa, and it says: 'It will cause headache'."

Another packet, of iron tablets, had been marked: "It will cause shutting of the intestines." Others were marked, "Poison for the heart", "Poison for the brain".

Major Kelley, the psychiatrist, intervened: "Why did you carry these poisons around?"

Hess, of course, had forgotten that – or so he said, freely allowing Colonel Amen to continue opening the parcels by himself.

"I attach no further value to that," the prisoner said.

"Now," pressed the Colonel, "do you intend to retain counsel for the trial?"

Hess said he did not care. "I believe counsel could not do very much."

Since Hess continued to show no interest in the preparations for the trial, the court appointed Günther von Rohrscheidt to defend him. He visited Hess on 2 November.

I told him [recorded Hess] that I regard the entire trial as a farce; that the judgement will be a foregone conclusion; and that I do not recognize the Court's authority.

Watching him closely, Rohrscheidt said that the press was hinting he might be unfit to plead.

"I don't want to be separated from my colleagues," insisted Hess. "I want to be tried with them. I want to share their fate."

Speaking perhaps for the benefit of any American eavesdroppers he rebuked the attorney the next day for not believing that he really had lost his memory.

"I only wanted to warn you", Rohrscheidt apologized, "what the Court will assume." He felt bound to add that since his client was refusing to co-operate he was thinking of declining the case.

"Are you aware", he asked the prisoner, "that you are the only one they manacle?"

Hess shook his head, but added, "That too is a matter of indifference to me."

He talked about my flight to England [Hess carefully pencilled into his prison diary afterwards] of which I had, however, no recollection.

Over the next days Dr Douglas Kelley tried various means of reviving Hess's memory. After a convincing display of concentrating, the prisoner allowed himself to recall meagre details – geographic terms and the like.

"What matters", Kelley patiently told him, "is that you gradually become able to recall events which have taken place recently."

Hess expressed profound gratitude – but when Rohrscheidt came later that day, asking him to sign a routine power of attorney, Hess refused and invited him to get his powers from the Court. Lest there be any misunderstanding, he told Rohrscheidt the next day that he would not be entering any pleas, and would not consent to the appointment of neutral medical experts to examine him either.

They allowed Hess some exercise, but under cover in the prison gymnasium where one year later the hanging team would set up their gallows. As in Wales, he stood his water beaker on the central heating pipes to take off the chill: but the cell was frigid, the windows broken, and the radiators stone cold.

On 8 November an old gentleman whom Hess thought to be possibly a Russian – certainly not British or American – tested his reflexes and appeared to find some of his answers to the memory tests amusing. Hess looked at him blankly.

They gave him a private screening of a captured print of *Triumph of the Will*, Leni Riefenstahl's chilling documentary film of the 1934 Nazi Party rally. Forty or fifty American and Russian officers watched with him. "Hess", recalled Jackson afterwards, "was willing to be entertained and we sat expectantly as the film began with German martial music."

At first they thought the film had indeed awakened old memories. As Rudolf Hess, prisoner of his enemies, watched Rudolf Hess, Deputy Führer of Germany, striding down the aisle of the vast, purpose-built arena at Nuremberg, he leaned forward and looked at the screen intently. With the blare of massed bands and the speeches of Hitler, Hess and Julius Streicher in their ears, the psychiatrists, psychologists, lawyers, interrogators and interpreters never took their eyes off the prisoner – his face illuminated by a soft glow from a lamp positioned below. But after a minute he settled back and seemed to be taking no more notice of the film. His face remained a mask; but his hands did clench slightly each time he saw himself on the screen, and he could see the psychiatrist, Major Kelley, staring intently at them.

As the lights came on, Hess avoided talking with the spectators. "I should not have recognized myself", he entered warily in his cell diary, "if my name had not been mentioned."

The cell was now over-heated, and he was both feeling and looking ill.

The American prison surgeon, Captain Ben Hurewitz, came on the 10th to give him a thorough check-up. Ignoring the prisoner's protests, Hurewitz took blood samples, explaining that they wanted to find out why Hess was losing weight. To Hess, the answer was simple. "As soon as I am free," he said, "I shall get enough to eat and enough exercise. Then my weight will go up again."

In his report Hurewitz remarked on the loss of weight, the sunken eyes, the drawn face and the protruding chest bones, but found everything else normal. He also noted and measured the two scars over the heart left by the "suicide attempt" in February: these were each about an inch long and were an eighth of an inch apart.

For the Soviet Union, ever since Hess's flight, Rudolf Hess had always been regarded as the principal war criminal, not just because he was the late Adolf Hitler's deputy, but because of the wartime canard launched by the British government to conceal the real purpose of his mission – the claim that Hess had tried to persuade Britain to join in a crusade against Bolshevism.

Although at the regular secret meetings of the prosecutors the Soviet prosecutor General Rudenko had explicitly agreed to the private film viewing, it caused a scandal in the left-wing press, orchestrated by articles in the Moscow newspapers. Chronically suspicious and paranoid, the Communists saw in the Allied "stunt" a manoeuvre intended to let Hess off the hook with some kind of insanity plea.

Acting in defiance of his client's instructions Dr von Rohrscheidt, Hess's luckless attorney, formally asked the tribunal to appoint a *neutral* medical expert, whom the universities of Zürich or Lausanne in Switzerland should designate, to examine the prisoner's mental fitness to stand trial; Rohrscheidt also moved to have him dismissed from the trial, pleading that since he could get no information from his client it was impossible to prepare a defence.

It testified to the Tribunal's lack of impartiality that it rejected out of hand the idea of having a neutral medical opinion. Before setting a date to hear the attorney's application, it instead ordered an *ad hoc* Four Power medical commission to inquire:

1. Is the defendant able to plead to the indictment?
2. Is the defendant sane or not? And on this last issue the Tribunal wishes to be advised whether the defendant is of sufficient intellect to comprehend the course of the proceedings of the trial so as to make a proper defence, to challenge a witness to whom he might wish to object, and to understand the details of the evidence.

Over the next days a dozen medical experts, major and minor, came jointly and severally from all the victorious powers, eager to try their

skills on this extraordinary case. Hess thus became something of a
fairground attraction. There was a French professor who urged Hess to
accept injections, electro-convulsive therapy and shock treatment by
reunion with his family ("I rejected the last mentioned proposal
particularly," recorded Hess). The British War Crimes Executive in
London of course nominated Brigadier Rees as their delegate; but upon
learning that the Russians had already selected three Moscow professors –
Eugene Krasnuchkin, Eugene Sepp and Nicholas Kuraskov – they added
Churchill's personal physician Lord Moran and the eminent neurologist
Dr George Riddoch to their team before it left for Nuremberg. The
Soviet experts had already arrived, as had Colonel Paul L. Schroeder, a
neuro-psychiatrist from Chicago.

When Hess was marched into a long room on 14 November,
handcuffed as usual to a GI, he found these teams of distinguished
strangers sitting round three sides of a table waiting to question him. He
took his place at the remaining side, and the contest began. Hoping for a
surprise knock-out, they brought in Dr Rees through a door behind him
while the experts studied his face. Rees shook hands with the prisoner he
had come to know so well since 1941 in Britain. The German's face
offered no trace of recognition.

After a few minutes of questioning in English, Hess asked these
gentlemen to address their questions to him only in German through the
interpreter. The British Brigadier suspected that this might well be
significant – a tactical move by Hess to gain time to think while the
interpreter intervened.

Rees felt that Schroeder and the Russians asked particularly astute
questions. Nonetheless, while Hitler's lifelong disciple admitted re-
membering a certain amount about the Führer – fearing perhaps lest "the
cock crow thrice" – the experts totally failed to break down his amnesia.

The untidy outcome was four reports: one signed by a Paris
psychiatrist (Professor Jean Delay) and three Soviet colleagues on 16
November; one signed by the three Soviet doctors alone on the 17th; one
signed by the three English doctors on the 19th; and yet another signed by
Professor Delay and the three American psychiatrists Schroeder, Nolan
D. Lewis and D. Ewen Cameron on the 20th. There was also another
British report by Rees and Riddoch, significantly omitting the name of
Lord Moran who felt, according to Rees, "that Hess's symptoms and
disability were so marked that they made him unfit to stand his trial, since
he could not challenge witnesses".

This was the point that Hess's counsel Dr von Rohrscheidt was trying
to establish. On the 13th he had put a second motion to the Court,
applying for the production of specific British witnesses and documents
to prove that his client was mentally ill.

Obviously, despite the complete lack of assistance from Hess himself,
Rohrscheidt had researched well (perhaps even with the clandestine
assistance of a sympathetic prosecution officer) because he knew enough

to ask the Court to order the British government to produce all the relevant files of the hospitals in Glasgow and the Foreign Office in London, as well as the reports made by the Duke of Hamilton, Dr Dicks, Ivone Kirkpatrick and other interrogating officers, and for the latter to be subpoenaed as material and expert witnesses. Rohrscheidt also asked the Court to produce records of the Gestapo that established that Hess had suffered from mental disorders for some time before his flight.

"The above mentioned records", stated the lawyer in justification, "contain, according to information received by the defence, very important conclusions as to the motive of Hess's flight and his state of health, especially about the mental disturbance and mental disorder when he arrived." Certifying the pertinence of his motion, Rohrscheidt stated that his client was unable to prepare a competent defence because of his loss of memory and the lack of strength evident from his unusually rapid fatigue.

The British government released only the less helpful documents applied for – the first reports made by Hamilton and Kirkpatrick, which revealed no hint of the later "psychotic episodes". The reports of Dicks and the other medical experts were withheld.

Everybody joined in the controversy. The medics were more convinced by his symptoms than the military.

Colonel Burton C. Andrus had little time for either category of professional. The prison Commandant, frustrated at the prospect of losing his prize captive, suggested his own preposterous theory to Dr Kelley. "Memory gone bad (supposedly)," he wrote on the 15th, "yet he remembers his speaking knowledge of English perfectly." Accordingly, Andrus suggested instructing an interpreter to misinterpret Hess deliberately, and watch the result.

The reason that Hess recalled Hitler but apparently could not recall his wife was easy, according to Andrus: Hitler had been having a homosexual affair with his deputy – how could Hess forget that?

> 1. It is known all over the world that he got his start in the Munich beerhall; and we know that he had normal sex relations with his wife and probably many other women.
> 2. We think that the only reason he remembers Hitler is because of abnormal sex relations with him. A homosexual naturally would tend to remember a man with whom he had abnormal sex relations, instead of his wife with whom he had normal sex relations.

The Commandant suggested that Dr Kelley try to win Hess's confidence along these lines: "You have all the other doctors fooled – but you're not fooling me! Since you and I are the only ones wise to the fact that your memory hasn't gone bad, I want to ask you something. If you get out of this trial all right – and I think you have a very good chance if I don't tell you what I know – will you testify against the other prisoners? If you will not do this, then I shall expose you."

Schroeder and Kelley, the two psychiatrists, preferred more conventional methods, since the trial was due to open in only four days' time. With Amen's consent, they tried shock tactics, confronting Hess with the two secretaries who had been close to him for eight years. At 2.30 p.m. on 16 November Hess was escorted to the Interrogation Corridor. Ingeborg, Sperr, now an attractive brunette of thirty-three, had joined him as a secretary on 1 May 1934. At first she did not understand when Colonel John H. Amen asked if she would agree to "help Hess to remember" – the secret of his amnesia had been well kept – but she said, "If I can help him, of course . . ."

Amen decided to confront Hess with Miss Sperr's senior colleague Hildegard Fath first. Now thirty-six, she had joined Hess on 17 October 1933. Amen took a reporter and interpreter into the hearing room where the prisoner was waiting, manacled to a guard. A few minutes later the doctors Kelley and Schroeder and a visiting US senator were brought in, followed by Miss Fath.

She showed unmistakable signs of recognition and began to talk in German to Hess. When the Colonel began questioning him about his memory, she interjected, "Well – I'll show you something that will help you to remember," and started to take out a photograph of his son Wolf Rüdiger. He averted his face, whispered, "No, no, no!" and refused to touch the picture.

After about ten minutes' conversation during which the reporter caught little except a reference to a doctor at Freiburg, Amen fetched in Miss Sperr. Heedless of the American uniforms and hostile voices all around, the two young women embraced tearfully.

Then, while hidden microphones listened, Ingeborg Sperr began speaking softly to Hess in German. The transcript showed that Hess impassively heard the news she brought of his brother, of Ilse and of the little boy who had all been to visit her. She encouraged him, "You'll recover your memory. I also sent you photographs of your wife and your boy," she added. "But I don't know if you received them."

"Yes," he said. "I received photographs in January."

She urged him not to be so agitated.

"I have continuous anxiety," he said. "Everything is so changed. I am very worried. . . . I just cannot remember who this Hess was. . . . I have the impression . . ." His voice tailed away.

"I was very happy to be with you," the girl said. "Before I joined you I was a medical–technical employee in Ulm. . . . I was a prisoner, and have already been interrogated several times." She smiled. "They asked me which I preferred – an honourable enemy, or a false friend." She had told them she preferred the false friend.

"Who asked you?" inquired Hess emptily.

She told him it was an "Ami" – then had to explain that this meant an American. "It has nothing to do with *ami*, the French for friend."

"I've always said", agreed Hess, "the Americans are riff-raff."

After a while he was heard to say, "In my journeys around the world I have lost everything. I am somewhat confused."

She consoled him that she too had been a prisoner, in Dachau camp for six weeks (after his flight). "I suffered a great deal."

"Were you happy, working for me?"

"Yes," she said. "I have been with you since 1934."

"A mad chapter . . ."

She reminded him that they had written many letters to him in England, and that he had written back.

"But everything went through so many checks," he recalled. "Once I even perpetrated a little *Schwindel*."

He hoped they would let him see her again.

Colonel Amen interrupted after a while.

"You remember these young ladies," he told Hess, "don't you?"

"No, no. I do not remember them."

"You never saw either of them before?"

"It has just been stated in the conversation with these two young ladies that I have not seen them before."

"And you don't remember any of the pictures that were shown to you?" echoed the American. He inquired, "Are you glad to see them?"

"I am always glad to see Germans," replied the prisoner. "Germans who tell me about my family."

"What makes you think", asked Amen, ignoring the inhospitable undertone, "those are pictures of your family?"

"The ladies told me that," Hess replied easily. "And besides, I have a picture of my son in my cell."

"You believe what the young ladies say, do you?"

"I have not the least cause to think that Germans do not tell me the truth."

"Do you think all Germans will tell you the truth?"

"Yes," said Hess tonelessly. "All Germans with whom I am closely acquainted."

He admitted there were a few bad characters in every country.

"How do you know they are *German* young ladies?"

"By their language," explained the Deputy Führer with the same expressionless eyes. "I got the impression that they are not Americans."

"Did you [just] tell one of these women that she could work for you again later on?"

"Yes, yes," said Hess. "I told her she could depend on being able to work for me again one day."

Amen asked what on earth he meant by that.

"I have been informed", said the prisoner, "that I formerly held a high position in the National Socialist state, and I consider that one day this will again be the case."

The Americans goggled.

"Uh, you mean you're going to have a high position in the Nazi state again? The same position? You have those plans for after the trial – is that it?"

"Yes," replied Hess – after admitting that he could not know for certain what the future held for him. Pressed to enlarge upon his remark – "But now there isn't any Führer!" Amen exclaimed – the former Deputy Führer elaborated in a matter-of-fact voice: "I merely want to say it will again be a high position in the German Nationalist state."

Amen showed stunned disbelief.

"I do not know how often I should repeat that I have the conviction that Germans tell the truth," Hess shortly declared, his temper rising. "But perhaps these gentlemen might make a note of that fact."

"I could bring a lot of Germans in here that won't tell you the truth!"

"Yes," snapped Hess, "especially out of a prison where criminals are usually kept."

"Such as Göring, for example?" the American challenged.

"Obviously I did not mean that."

"Well, is Göring a criminal?"

"Yes," said Hess and added, his sense of honour displacing his previous prudence, "but an honourable criminal – a 'war criminal'."

"How do you know what kind of a criminal he is?"

It was a lethal question, but Hess sidestepped with a dexterity worthy of a better cause. "Because he is the same type of 'criminal' as I am."

Colonel Amen was shouting, and Hess calmly invited him not to raise his voice.

"I'm asking you," raged the American, "how do you know he's not a pickpocket or a thief?"

"I am convinced that neither pickpockets not thieves or others of that ilk are elevated to high office," retorted the prisoner. "Not in Germany, at least!"

"Take him out!" snapped Amen to the guards. "And leave the girls."

As Hess was dragged out by his handcuffed wrist he whispered to the two ladies in German, "You can be proud of the fact that you are prisoners!" He warned that he would not be writing to them.

"*Heil* to you!" he called out, before the door closed between them; he would never see them again.

Rudolph Hess's cell diary shows that his memory tallied closely with the verbatim transcript:

Two of my former secretaries were sent in to me. I did not recognize them. One of them brought photographs of home. Both are "housed" in the prison, although one of them is no longer under detention but works in an American hospital.

The interrogating officer who was present attempted to use this opportunity to provoke me by asking me three times how I knew the two ladies were not lying to me.

After the third time I said very sharply that he should accept my assurance that Germans of my acquaintance would not lie to me; at which he shouted, how did I know that Göring was not, among other things, a common criminal, a pickpocket or the like? To which I replied that it was not usual, in Germany anyway, to appoint pickpockets as ministers.

21   Will the True Rudolf Hess Please Stand Up

There had been public rumours about Rudolf Hess's amnesia ever since word of his private viewing of *Triumph of the Will* leaked out. At a press conference on the morning after, Andrus had said, "Gentlemen, many of you have made inquiries about some psychiatrist." He explained, "A psychiatrist, Dr Krasnuchkin from the USSR, visited the Russian delegation here and, in conjunction with our Major Kelley, examined Hess. There may be other psychiatrists. . . . The findings, however, have not been reported to me, and the doctors declare it would be unethical for them to give out their findings except to the Court when the trial comes."

The rumours would not go away, however, and on 19 November, the day before the trial opened, a reporter asked again about the health of the prisoners. Andrus answered about Hess first. "Apparently in fair condition," he read out. "Gained slightly in weight and appearance, and complains of abdominal cramps."

Kelley tried hard to get Hess to remember during the final days before the trial opened. He failed. "Though he spoke English well," he reminisced later, "and answered most questions quite readily, I never succeeded in getting him to be friendly. He was almost constantly on guard, aloof, clicking his heels and saluting."

One day, after Kelley had again tried to persuade him to accept an injection, Hess smiled and said: "You are kind, yes. But I do not know if you are a friend. I shall wait until the trial is finished. Then I shall know."

With the exception of Göring, who had cannily refused to sign any of his interrogation records, all of the other prisoners were more or less assisting the prosecution – some wittingly, like the conniving chief architect of Hitler's wartime arms miracle Albert Speer; others out of an abysmal sense of grief, like Poland's Governor-General Hans Frank.

But Hess remained aloof and uncollaborative, offering neither succour to the prosecution nor assistance to his own defence. It is not hard to divine his motive: all others might have deserted and betrayed the Führer; but he, Rudolf Hess, would deputize faithfully for him to the bitter end.

Sure that Adolf Hitler would have acted just this way had he fallen alive into the hands of his foes, Hess kept his lips sealed and defied the authority of the Tribunal to dispose otherwise. "I've learned from his attorney," wrote Ilse to Martha Haushofer, "that R. has strictly forbidden the testimony of any witnesses or the production of any affidavits; he says his reason is he refuses to 'have third parties testifying to his decency'. R. is giving a hard time time to R[ohrscheidt] who's not exactly the type to winkle R. out of his shell: so if he's to plead any kind of defence at all he's going to have to base it all on our few conversations. You'll both have learned by now that R. was only faking on 9 October. . . . He'll have had his reasons," Hess's immensely loyal wife wrote, "reasons that we can neither know nor guess at." Rohrscheidt, she continued, had warned her that the defendants were being "railroaded" into guilty verdicts. "I see no hope whatsoever", she wrote, "that decency or humanity will get anywhere in Nuremberg. . . . The defence hasn't got a chance, all the usual recourses are denied it."

In fairness to his weaker colleagues, it must be said that for Hess the prison existence was easier to bear than for the others. He had been in Landsberg jail for a year with Hitler, and of course he had been in solitary confinement for over four years already. He had shut himself inside a little world of his own, reading voraciously – a list of thirteen books supplied over ten days from 16 November included Rudolf Pechel's study, *Goethe and Goethe's Places*, an Edgar Wallace thriller and several travel stories.

Faced with the former Deputy Führer's obstinate attitude, the prosecution extracted affidavits from his two young secretaries on 20 November.

Hess had treated the first, Miss Fath, like one of the family and she knew a lot about his family's medical history: his mother's brother had committed suicide, his father had been over-severe with his sons; his father's sister had died rather young – Miss Fath believed that she had been in a mental hospital, but as she was born long after the other children and her mental disease had evidently come from her father's being drunk at the time of conception the evidence for any inherited illness was only tenuous.

"The most important quality of R.H.", she testified, "was a fanatical obligation to his duties, and he never forgot his principles at any instant. In all things he did he was really a model to other people. I would put it like this: he was a National Socialist in the best sense of the word." A modest, unassuming young man, he had neither tolerated pictures of his wife appearing in the Party press, not allowed her to accept grace-and-favour positions in the Party's women's organization; the Hesses had lost their only home at Harlaching, Munich, to fire-bombs in a 1943 air raid. The remaining half-burned shell of an outdoor shed where Miss Fath lived was being turned over by US decree to concentration camp prisoners.

The Rudolf Hess that Miss Fath recalled was very polite, even tender-hearted. "I remember on one occasion when we were having tea in the garden some wasps got stuck in the honey pot and couldn't get out. He picked them out with his spoon, washed them off carefully and put them in the sun to dry."

It had been her job to open the thousands of letters that arrived at Harlaching, mostly from strangers asking for his help or thanking him for what he had done on their behalf.

> For anybody who knows him, it is both absurd and grotesque to see him now indicted as a "war criminal". His ambition always was to make peace – both between individuals and between nations.
>
> The whole of Europe knows his speech★ to the veterans of all nations – the veterans who want peace, because they know war. He knew war, because he was a veteran too.
>
> If ever there was a statesman who was ready to make every personal sacrifice to bring about peace, it was Rudolf Hess.
>
> It in no way gainsays this, that some people now think he must have been insane at the time.

Ingeborg Sperr echoed Hildegard's feelings. "If you worked for him", she wrote that day, 20 November, "you very soon had to worship this man: his entire life was dedicated to setting an example to the German people of what our *Weltanschauung* was all about. I was repeatedly fascinated by his deep-down incorruptibility and his eagerness to do good for others. But he just could not make headway against the tough guys."

He fell prey to nervous ailments in consequence, and resorted to wilder and wilder medical practitioners in the search for his lost health. In the last months before his flight, she had sighted him alone and brooding at his desk, tortured by the recognition that he was no longer the strong man – in either sense. "Given his fanatical patriotism, it was characteristic of Rudolf Hess as a human being that he wanted to make the maximum possible sacrifice for Adolf Hitler and the German people, if it would serve to bring about the peace with Britain that everybody yearned for – even if it meant risking his own life, his family, his liberty and his own honourable name."

All this was not of much use to the prosecution, of course; Major Kelley snaffled the two long documents for their autograph value, which did not prosper the defence either. Kelley in fact would shortly leave Nuremberg under a cloud and Captain Gustave M. Gilbert, a German-born psychologist who had arrived on 20 October as a replacement, had interpreted for the American psychiatric commission when they came to examine Hess. In his *Nuremberg Diary* Gilbert would write that Hess sat in

---

★ At Königsberg on 8 July 1934. Widely reported at the time, the speech was described fifty years later in the *International Herald Tribune* as "the most eloquent appeal by a German statesman to France to help restore peace since Chancellor Heinrich Brüning's radio message of June 23, 1931".

his cell all day in a state of apathetic absent-mindedness. "Occasionally he would seem to be deliberately suppressing a recollection that flickered through his clouded mind, but there was little doubt in our minds that he was essentially in a state of complete amnesia."

The trial opened on 20 November 1945 with the prosecutors taking it in turns to read the unwieldy indictment into the record. Through an IBM multi-translation circuit simultaneous interpretations were fed into earphones all around the courtroom; but Hess did not even bother to put his on.

Cadaverous and birdlike, wearing a freshly pressed suit, he sat with a book in his hands in the number-two position next to Hermann Göring at the end of the dock and gazed about the panelled courtroom. He and his fellow defendants literally had their backs to the wall – cramped into two pews along one of the long side walls of the courtroom. Along the facing wall the judges of the Four Powers were arrayed against them; in the no-man's land between, there sat the ranks of defence lawyers and court officials. To Hess's right were the four enemy prosecutors' tables, and behind them the hundreds of newspaper reporters. After a while he opened the book and immersed himself in its pages, oblivious of the droning enemy voices until lunchtime.

As the Court rose at midday the prisoners stood up to stretch their legs – it was the first chance that they had had to meet since their capture. Outside the dock, among the Negro guards fingering their truncheons, Dr Gilbert – a smartly uniformed, bespectacled young officer with boyish features and black slicked-down hair – craned to hear what they were saying. The psychologist's job was to make notes on everything he overheard them say to each other; over supper and in their cells he would continue lending them a sympathetic and professional ear. As Jackson's private papers show, the doctor passed the Intelligence thus gleaned straight to the American prosecution staff. It was a "dirty trick" with which Hess had probably reckoned in advance.

When Gilbert pricked up his ears as he saw Ribbentrop arguing with Hess all that he heard was the Deputy Führer replying that he had no recollection of any of the events related in the indictment.

Ribbentrop mentioned the atomic bomb; Hess feigned interest. "Atomic bomb? What's that," he asked.

"The atomic fission bomb," said the former Nazi Foreign Minister.

Hess's face remained blank and uncomprehending, and he returned to his book.

"You'll see," he hissed to a stunned Hermann Göring in the dock that afternoon, "this apparition will vanish and you will be Führer of Germany within a month."

20 November 1945   [Hess's diary]

Start of the trial, very fatiguing. I spent most of the time reading the Bavarian peasant novel [by Hans Fitz] *Der Loisl*, or relaxing with my eyes closed. None of the proceedings at the hearing remains in my memory. . . .

Chief American prosecuting counsel Robert H. Jackson, who had eyes on White House office, was determined that the Nuremberg tribunal should make legal history. But just as courts try cases – as Jackson himself was fond of saying – so the cases try the courts. It was essential to force the defendants to toe the line: the satisfactory conduct of a trial requires the acceptance, or failing that the imposition, of the court's authority. From their very first words it was plain that neither Göring nor, within the parameters set by his own charade, Rudolf Hess had any plans to help the august enemy judges to establish their sovereignty at Nuremberg.

Asked on Day Two whether he pleaded Guilty or Not Guilty, Reichsmarschall Hermann Göring tried to read a page-long declaration manfully accepting full responsibility for the Reich's activities while denying the enemy tribunal's competence to try him; and to the horror of the orderly, berobed, uniformed and bewigged prosecution Hess merely stood up (in a fit of anger, as he wrote in his cell diary afterwards) and shouted "*Nein!*" ("He stole the show," reminisced Jackson indignantly years later.) The invited spectators packed into the gallery roared with raucous laughter.

Lord Justice Lawrence, the British President of the Tribunal, peered over his reading glassses and declared in clipped tones, "That will be entered as a plea of Not Guilty."

"Charlie", Hess would write to Ilse, referring to Karl Haushofer as the trial neared its end, "once said that when the stakes were high you must be prepared to be branded as a traitor for a while by your people – to which I would add: or as a madman."

Even so, his mental acrobatics having failed to attain their short-term goal he must have begun to ponder whether it was time for the world to witness a miraculous recovery in his sanity. As Hitler's erstwhile Deputy Führer, ever since he had found himself dumped into the dock alongside those who were beyond doubt criminals, Hess had no doubt shrewdly calculated how little shrift he might expect from his enemies, whatever the merits of his own career.

As the prosecution opened, the general prospects of the defence did not seem promising. The idea formed within him to abandon his bizarre amnesia act – which he had first begun in November 1943 – altogether. It had been an extraordinary feat. Even now, with the trial under way, nobody knew whether he was faking or not. Doctors Gilbert and Kelley were satisfied that the amnesia was genuine. Colonels Amen and Andrus were sure that it was not, but could not catch him out. The four commissions of international experts had come up with views that can be called only loosely convergent.

After examining Hess on the 14th Lord Moran had argued strongly that the British should answer all three of the Tribunal's questions in the negative – in short, that Hess was not fit to plead. His colleagues talked him out of it, evidently upon their return to London because their report was not telephoned to Nuremberg until five days later. This agreed text signed subsequently by Moran, Rees and Riddoch determined that Hess was a "psychopathic personality" who had suffered from paranoid delusions while in Britain and had developed a marked hysterical tendency as shown by the bouts of amnesia. The British report cast no doubts on its genuineness but forecast interestingly: "This amnesic symptom will eventually clear when circumstances change." "At the moment," the British report added, "he is not insane in the strict sense." They agreed, however, "His loss of memory will interfere with his ability to make his defence." They recommended that "further evidence" (about his true health) be obtained by drug injections.

The French professor Jean Delay accepted this, and having absorbed the British recommendations he examined Hess in his cell on the 15th, together with the three Russian professors. Hess politely but firmly refused the Soviet and French offers of injections. "In general," he explained, "I shall accept steps to cure my amnesia only when the trial is over."

The Soviet experts, in their separate report of the 17th, deprecated "the behaviour of Mr Hess". After perusing the dossier shown them by Dr Rees, the British War Office specialist, the Russians noted that the prisoner's wartime symptoms of paranoia had *alternated* with those of the amnesia. At present the amnesia was paramount – thus, asked what he felt caused his frequent stomach cramps, Hess did not now mention "poison", but said, "That is for you doctors to find out."

Apart from this, the Russians found him psychologically clear and coherent: "He answers questions rapidly and to the point, his thoughts [are] formed with precision and correctness and accompanied by sufficient emotionally expressive movements." They cited Captain Gilbert's finding that Hess was of above-average intelligence, and concluded in their own report that there were *no* manifestations of paranoid schizophrenia. They suggested that his alleged amnesia since November 1943 was a psychological reaction to "the failure of his mission, arrest and incarceration". He was not, they stated bluntly, and never had been, insane. His amnesia was, they averred, a defensive, conscious, "hysterical" amnesia.

They echoed the British forecast thus:

Such behaviour often terminates when the hysterical person is faced with an unavoidable necessity of conducting himself correctly. The amnesia of Hess may end upon his being brought to trial.

Otherwise, the experts failed to agree. Only the Russians and the Frenchman signed the general report on 17 November.

On the 19th the three American specialists and the French Professor visited Hess in his cell. Subsequently, the Americans would realize that that interview had unmasked the real Hess – he had claimed no mental image of his parents at all, yet answered other questions about his family without resort to his stock phrase, "I don't know." He was also obviously carrying on the various mental and physical activities of daily life "despite the alleged loss of memory for the time when he learned them". The list of a dozen titles that he had recently read showed that he had retained his background education although he claimed to remember neither what studies he had undertaken nor his tutors. Asked whether he had ever studied astrology, Hess snapped, "No!", instead of "I don't remember." Explaining his refusal to permit mind-exploring injections, he said things like: "My memory has nothing to do with my responsibility," and "I can get my memory back by experiments after the trial," and "It is not so important to get cured before the trial." All this, they concluded when they were wiser and sadder, was proof that he "obviously wanted to retain the amnesia".

However, in the report which they submitted before the trial, on 19 November, the Americans (with the French Professor concurring) cautiously accepted the amnesia as a genuine symptom of a hysterical behaviour pattern which the prisoner had developed as a "defense" against the unhappy situation he found himself in while in Britain – a pattern which had now become habitual. They warned that while he could comprehend the proceedings, the amnesia would "interfere with his undertaking his defense". That said, they also warned that he was consciously exaggerating the amnesia and exploiting it to "protect himself against examination". Their recommendation too was that Hess was not insane in the strict sense of the word.

To the anger of the lawyers and judges, Hess scarcely heeded them now that the trial had begun. "Hess", dictated the chief American prosecutor later, "was ostentatious in reading frivolous books during the trial. He would sit, read, and not listen to the testimony."

He spent Day Three browsing through *Youth*, the childhood reminiscences of a Flemish writer – it bored him, he told Captain Gilbert afterwards, but then the court proceedings were even more boring to him. The psychologist asked if he was therefore having difficulty in following the proceedings. "You ought to try," he urged.

"I don't intend to," retorted Hess.

"But what the Führer said to you is important," the psychologist persisted.

"It is important for me personally," retorted Hess, seated uncomfortably on the edge of his cot. "And, one day, for the German people too. But it is of no concern to the rest of the world or to you foreigners present in court."

"These proceedings are a matter of life and death for you," said Gilbert.

"That is true", responded the prisoner, "whether I listen to these foreigners talking or not."

Gilbert was moved by this ice-cold attitude to return that evening with the surgeon. "This trial is a matter of life and death!" they said.

"I know. But I do not regard my life as of such importance."

"Most people do."

"I", said Hess, "differ from 'most people'."

"Well," said the young army Captain. "Your way of looking at things will probably help you to sleep okay."

"I shall certainly not sleep worse than usual," sniffed Hess.

On 24 November the Tribunal ruled that on the last afternoon of the month it would hear legal argument on the medical findings. The time was thus fast approaching when Hess would have to decide whether to continue his present performance or allow himself to be called to account along with his several companions in misfortune.

Within the mask presented by his deliberately starved features there watched a feeling human being that dared not yet to reveal itself, at least to its enemies. He asked the German doctor, Ludwig Pflücker, to give his cigarette ration to Schirach and his cigars to Walter Funk – so he had neither difficulty in recalling those names, nor inhibitions about revealing this to the German doctor. But for a few days more he continued his charade. Invited by the American army chaplain to attend a prison service, Hess declined on principle:

> I therefore asked him [he wrote in his diary] not to visit me – glad though
> I was in normal times occasionally to discuss this problem or that with a
> clergyman. . . .
>   I thought to myself, "I wish you the strength to maintain the same
> inner composure that I do."

It was not that he did not still hold on to his childhood religious beliefs. "Call it what you will," he remarked to Fritz Sauckel, sitting behind his left shoulder in the dock during one recess, "there is a Power that is greater than the power of the Jews."

"That is true," agreed the former Manpower Commissioner, and Papen and Arthur Seyss-Inquart sitting next to him nodded approval.

"Perhaps we shall see a miracle yet," Hess comforted them – "and before our heads roll, at that!"

The next day, 27 November, Rohrscheidt predicted to him that when it heard the legal arguments on Friday – the last day of the month – the Tribunal would probably rule that he was not fit to stand trial. Hess pondered the implications of this. He was already beginning to feel that it would be wrong to abandon his colleagues.

"I am well enough to stand trial myself," he objected to his attorney. "I want to continue to take part."

The prosecution presented, during the darkening afternoon of Thursday 29 November, film footage shot by American troops when they overran Nazi concentration camps like Buchenwald. In the hushed Nuremberg courtroom lamps fastened below the dock threw a ghostly light on the prisoners' features as the scenes of emaciated and diseased convicts and corpses flickered across the cinema screen on the far wall to their left. Kelley and Gilbert, posted at opposite ends of the dock, made a careful scrutiny of how the prisoners were taking it. "Hess glares at screen," jotted Gilbert after a few minutes, "looking like a ghoul with sunken eyes over the footlamp." After half an hour he again looked at the former Deputy Führer: "Hess keeps looking bewildered" – as well he might, since nothing of this had happened while he was still in Germany.

When the courtroom lights came on again, Hess turned to Göring on his right. "I don't believe it," he said loudly. But the cockiness that the Reichsmarschall had shown that morning was gone and he urged Hess to be quiet.

The defendants' discomfiture was compounded on the following afternoon. Lieutenant-General Erwin Lahousen, former chief of Hitler's sabotage and counter-espionage organization Abwehr II, had decided to save his skin by giving evidence for the prosecution. He brassily testified from the witness stand to how the SS and Gestapo had massacred Communists and Jews in Russia, and to Hitler's orders for the extermination of the Polish clergy and intelligentsia, and to other infamous episodes of recent German history. True, neither Admiral Wilhelm Canaris nor his Abwehr had made any protest at the time; now, unjustly, the Nazis' atrocities were being laid at the feet of men like Rudolf Hess.

It was 4 p.m. on the last afternoon of November 1945. The Tribunal announced its intention of going into closed session to hear arguments whether Hess was fit to plead. As the dock was cleared, Gilbert heard Göring seething with fury about the "traitor" Lahousen.

Hess too had been taken aback by the General's disloyalty. He realized that there would be more witnesses like Lahousen, and it probably hit home when Dr Gilbert remarked casually, as he stepped down from the dock, "They'll probably find you incompetent to defend yourself. You may not be coming into this court any more. But I'll come down and see you in your cell – once in a while."

"I am perfectly competent to defend myself," Hess snapped, but he was looking worried.

The dock that afternoon was empty except for him: and the real Rudolf Hess had now resolved to stand up.

Just as his unsuspecting attorney, Günther von Rohrscheidt, was about to open his argument – that his client was unfit to plead – Hess whispered, "I have decided to say that my memory has returned!"

"Do as you wish," said the attorney, turning away, and began his long, untidy speech regardless.

Hess sat silent for an hour, listening with unusual intensity through the earphones. In deference to him, Rohrscheidt remarked after a while dismissively that he was bound to report that his client *did* feel fit to plead and desired to tell the court so himself. Nobody paid any attention. Instead, an hour-long wrangle started in the packed courtroom, during which Rohrscheidt and the Court became hopelessly mired in the differently dated medical reports. Rohrscheidt, of course, dwelt on the experts' unanimous finding that the amnesia would hamper Hess's defence; the prosecution inevitably emphasized the separate finding that Hess was not insane.

As each side quoted from their law-books and cited learned precedents the ex-Deputy Führer became more impatient. Captain Gilbert saw him pass a note to his attorney. (The whole matter could be shortened, it urged, by letting him speak.) The lawyer ignored him. Indeed, Hess heard him now suggest to the Tribunal, "The contrary opinion of the defendant himself, namely that he is fit to plead, is irrelevant!" Perhaps for the first time, Hess also heard from Rohrscheidt's lips that under Article 12 of the Tribunal's charter he might be tried *in absentia* if found unfit to plead; and he heard the lawyer say, "Such terrible crimes are laid at the door of the defendant that even the death penalty is to be expected."

The legal argument droned on. "It has never", intoned Sir David Maxwell Fyfe, the British prosecutor, "in English jurisprudence to my knowledge been held to be a bar either to trial or punishment, that a person who comprehends the charge and the evidence has not got a memory as to what happened at the time."

The Tribunal pondered. Lord Justice Lawrence mused that Hess would surely be able to argue, "I should have been able to make a better defence if I had been able to remember what took place at the time."

Flourishing Dr Kelley's report which stated how often Hess had refused the drug injections, Robert Jackson interjected, "I respectfully suggest that a man cannot stand afar from the Court and assert that his amnesia is a defence to his being tried, and at the same time refuse the simple medical expedients which we all agree might be useful. He is", concluded the prosecutor sardonically, "in the *volunteer* class with his amnesia."

Rohrscheidt countered with the Tribunal's own medical reports that established that Hess had a mental defect and was suffering from amnesia. Hess, he said, had every right to refuse the "forceful" drug injections. "The defendant Hess tells me that he has a deep abhorrence of such means, and always favoured the natural method of healing."

A few seconds later, Hess stood up, at the invitation of the Tribunal. It was time to come clean – time to admit that he had been faking his amnesia ever since July. From his pocket he produced a sheet of paper

and, before reading out the pencilled lines, he bobbed a little curtsey to
Lord Justice Lawrence.

"Mr President," he said,

> I should like to say this:
>
> in order that I may be allowed to continue to attend the trial and receive
> judgement alongside my colleagues as is my wish, and in order not to be
> declared unfit to plead, I submit the following declaration to the court – a
> declaration which I had not intended to make until a later point in the
> proceedings:
>
> From this time on my memory is again at the disposal of the outside
> world.
>
> The reasons why I simulated amnesia are of a tactical nature.
>
> In fact, only my ability to concentrate is slightly impaired. On the
> other hand my ability to follow the trial, to defend myself, to question
> witnesses, and to answer questions myself – these are not impaired.
>
> I emphasize that I assume full responsibility for everything that I have
> done, everything I have signed, and everything that I have co-signed.
>
> My deep-seated conviction that the Tribunal has no competency is not
> affected by the above statement.
>
> I have successfully maintained the illusion of amnesia with my official
> defence counsel; he has acted accordingly in good faith.

He looked at the judges and prosecutors, savouring the delayed
reactions as the translation was fed into their earphones. He saw them
gape, and heard the gales of delighted laughter from the press box beyond
the prosecutors. A hubbub arose and the President rapped his gavel for
silence.

"The trial", he announced briefly, "is adjourned."

Back in his chilly, ill-furnished cell, Hess received a message from the
Tribunal – they urgently wanted a copy of the text that he had just read
out. On a minuscule, personal scale he had restored his own sovereignty
in his own land.

> I took my time [he pencilled into his cell diary] and first had a meal – in
> peace.

Epilogue: A Lifetime to Repent

After a trial in which he barely spoke, Rudolf Hess was sentenced to life imprisonment.

He had repeatedly advised his new attorney Dr Alfred Seidl (he had dismissed Rohrscheidt) that he did not recognize the authority of the Court. Seidl, a wiry lawyer whose puny stature was balanced by his pugnacious spirit, advised him to display his indifference unmistakably in the dock, and to refuse to enter the witness stand. In every other respect a difficult client, Hess read books in the dock, yawned, laughed out loud; occasionally, as the newsreel cameras showed, he grimaced, then doubled up with real or imaginary stomach pains. Chief American prosecutor Jackson heard his subdued remarks about the witnesses as they stepped down – some amusing, others vulgar. But one seasoned British diplomat who watched Hess closely in court dismissed his colleagues' suggestion that Hess was insane. "I do not think him in any strict sense 'mad' or even very near it," he wrote in Foreign Office papers. "He carries on conversation with Göring & can laugh quite naturally at Göring's jokes."

Although broad doubts about his mental stability remained – his state can perhaps best be described as a fluctuating sanity – his recent amnesia had obviously been faked. Rejoining his co-defendants on 1 December 1945 he regaled them with proofs of his clear memory. "The last time I saw you before my flight", he said, turning to Admiral Dönitz in the row behind him, "was at Wilhelmshaven in 1939 when I delivered my Christmas broadcast to the Reich.★ You sat on my right in the mess, and I asked if you had any other U-boat commanders who could have got into Scapa Flow apart from Günther Prien!"

Göring slapped his thigh with delight that Hess – their very own Rudolf Hess – had swindled the Tribunal and its pompous psychiatrists. "Any doubts I had", he confessed to Hess, "left me when you failed to recognize Haushofer at that confrontation."

The months passed; the warring armies of attorneys trudged through the Tribunal's merciless wastes of legal argument, mapping and

★ See p. 49 above.

surveying the mountainous evidence of Axis criminality. Hess paid no heed, although he showed a willingness to assist his comrades with affidavits sworn on their behalf.

The case against him began on 7 February 1946. The British had always known that they were on shaky ground with three of the defendants: the British Admiralty and the Foreign Office had warned that there was no evidence in captured records that Admiral Dönitz was a war criminal; while against the names of both Hess and Papen they had set question marks. British prosecutor Mervyn Griffith-Jones explained that they had originally intended to establish Hess's guilt by captured documents but now, he added lamely, their case was that the crimes were organized on such a vast scale that "everyone in authority must have known of them". Thus disembarrassed of the customary need to produce evidence, he charged that the Deputy Führer was "deeply involved" in the Nazi aggressions against Austria and Czechoslovakia, while the Waffen SS that "he sent" to Poland had destroyed the Warsaw ghetto (two years after Hess left); nor did Griffith-Jones allow the Tribunal to forget that the Auslands-Organisation, which he called the Nazi "Fifth Column" abroad, came under Hess's jurisdiction. As for his flight to Britain, the prosecutor produced the statement rendered by Eden to Parliament in September 1943 (we have already seen how this document was concocted in 1942 for the express purpose of deceiving Roosevelt and Stalin).★ The prosecution claim was that Hess merely wanted Britain out of the war so that Germany could attack Russia (which overlooked the evidence that Hess had planned his historic mission ever since June 1940, a year before the Russian campaign began). The case against Rudolf Hess was weak, and the intimidatory methods used by Griffith-Jones in March, in a secret interrogation of Hess's secretary Laura Schrödl, showed it.

On the second day of the prosecution case, 8 February 1946, Hess was taken ill; the diary kept by the prison Commandant Colonel Andrus recorded that on 21 February, 21 June, 12 and 30 July, and 6, 8 and 12 August the former Deputy Führer had to return to his cell on doctor's orders.

Later in February the Colonel tightened up regulations, forbidding the prisoners to talk to each other. In the solitude of his cell, deprived of newspapers except those which an attorney might let him glimpse, Hess tried to keep sane, but his mind was already entombed – mummified somewhere between 1941 and 1945. The laughter lines still snaked through his letters, but his humour was wearing thin.

Once Ilse wrote, pleading with him to read at least the *Neue Zeitung* published by the American occupation forces. "I think", he chided her in his reply, "that even without the *Neue Zeitung* I enjoy a better view of things than those who 'regularly read up on the world situation.'⌒." In the space marked "MY ADDRESS IS AS FOLLOWS" he entered, "Rudolf Hess,

★ See pp. 228 and 243 above.

Nuremberg, Prison for 'War Criminals'ᴡᴡ". "There's truly no lack of the absurd around here," he wrote, "and I can only advise everybody to see the funny side of this current entr'acte as far as humanly possible."

Over lunch in a second-storey room of this "great amphitheatre" as he called it, he could make out the hills to the north-east of Nuremberg – there were few buildings left to impede his view. He returned to the dock each afternoon with a far-away look in his empty eyes. His soul was climbing in those mountains; his imagination was filled with Mozart, Wagner, with the marching music of past decades, and with voices reciting to him the poetry of Goethe, Shakespeare and Dietrich Eckart.

Back in his cell he maintained his own level of sanity by reading books, writing a diary and composing letters to his family. He urged Ilse in one, on 31 March, to let Wolf Rüdiger dabble with Greek at school for at least a year, but to let him take "acrobatics" as a subsidiary for all he cared: Germany's harsh plight would teach the boy all he needed to know. "Who isn't growing up now!" he exclaimed in another letter a month later. "Even I am, I think!ᴡᴡ".

Seidl had opened for the defence on 22 March 1946. His client, he said, challenged the Tribunal's jurisdiction to try him except for "war crimes proper", on which he had a clean conscience. "He does, however," continued the attorney, "specifically accept full responsibility for all laws or decrees which he has signed."

Over the ensuing days Seidl planted what was to prove a bombshell under the Tribunal. Despite furious protests from the Russian judge and prosecutor, he disclosed that the Soviets had signed a hitherto unknown secret protocol to their famous August 1939 pact with Nazi Germany. In two clauses typed on a single sheet of paper, the document – signed eight days *before* the war began – had drawn a line dividing Poland and five other Eastern European countries between Nazi Germany and the Soviet Union. And these were the people who now appeared, straight-faced, to pronounce sentence upon the criminality of their partners in aggression.

The Russians never forgave Hess for this.

On 31 August the defendants were allowed to make a final statement. Hess had intimated to the others that he proposed to say nothing, but as the GI held the microphone on a pole before him Hess gripped it, asked the Tribunal's permission to remain seated as he was unwell, and delivered a speech that began inchoate and rambling, then pulled itself together with these defiant closing words, broadcast later by British transmitters all over Europe. "To me was granted", declared Hess,

to work for many years of my life under the greatest son my country has brought forth in a thousand years of history. Even if I were able, I should not want to erase this epoch from my past existence. I am happy to know that I have done my duty to my people – my duty as a German, as a National Socialist, and as a true disciple of the Führer.

I regret nothing. Were I to live my life again I should act once more as I have acted now, even though I knew that at the end a funeral pyre was already flickering for my immolation: I care not what mere mortals may do. The time will come when I shall stand before the judgement seat of the Eternal. I shall answer unto Him and I know that He will judge me innocent.

Philosophical, eager almost for martyrdom, Hess expected prison, asylum or the gallows. Led in to hear the Tribunal's findings on 1 October he declined to put on the earphones or to listen. He appeared indifferent as one of the judges began to read out their verdict. In fact the Tribunal acquitted him of any Crimes against Humanity but found him guilty of Conspiracy and of Crimes against Peace. Following the British prosecution's argument they ruled that he had been an informed and willing aggressor against Austria and Czechoslovakia in 1938, and against Poland in 1939. (That it was the *Russian* judge who actually read out the findings against Hess brought out the irony of the proceedings.) "The specific steps", the verdict added, justifying the thinness of its case, "which this defendant took in support of Hitler's plans for aggressive action do not indicate the full extent of his responsibility. Until his flight to England, Hess was Hitler's closest personal confidant. Their relationship was such that Hess must have been informed of Hitler's aggressive plans when they came into existence. And he took action to carry out these plans whenever action was necessary."

That afternoon Hess again declined the earphones as the English judge who had presided over the Tribunal announced sentence. "Defendant Rudolf Hess, on the counts of the indictment on which you have been convicted the Tribunal sentences you to imprisonment for life." (After Hess vanished into the lift behind the dock, the judge added that his Soviet colleague had voted for the death sentence on Hess.)

Hess would remain at Nuremberg prison for nine months. The diary of Field Marshal Erhard Milch, sentenced in the next American trial, affords glimpses of Hess during that spring of 1947 – stand-offish, eccentric, hammering at a typewriter and emerging occasionally to put questions to the six other prisoners. "Speer is afraid", wrote Milch on 10 May 1947, "that Hess wants material from us for a book proving that National Socialism and Hitler were okay while the subordinates were the failures!" Milch tried to prove the stubborn, inflexible Deputy Führer wrong, but gave up. "He's a strange fellow," continued the diary, "not unintelligent, but hopelessly vague and so fanatical and ascetic that one can't talk of sound commonsense. He's the only one of us who still believes in Hitler and his own National Socialist mission."

On 8 June the Field Marshal learned that Hess was groping for a "better name" for the Propaganda Ministry. "I fear he's flipped completely," reflected Milch. "Because he hasn't got a table he lies on the flagstones for his meals and eats off the floor like a dog – to the delight of the sentries.

. . . And all the time he's at his typewriter. What on earth is it?"* Ten days later Hess joined them for a stroll in the sun. In his own cell afterwards Milch recorded: "Hess tells us about his imprisonment with Hitler in Landsberg" – his memory was perfect in every detail. Milch noticed that Hess refused as a matter of principle to give autographs to the guards. As he heard the truck in the prison courtyard bearing away the seven prisoners to Spandau on 18 July 1947, Milch summarized his own inside view of Hess: "Abnormal looks and manner. Totally self-centred, crafty and not at all dumb, but the product of his thinking is warped or downright wrong. Has made a complete martyr of himself, and regards everything that happens as personal spite. . . . The only 'Nazi' of us eight."

Spandau jail was a gloomy red-brick building designed to hold six hundred prisoners. Now there were seven. Hess, known henceforth as Convict No. 7, would be the last to survive there. Although the Tribunal had not ordered hard labour, the prisoners were put to work during the day and held in solitary confinement at other times. Conditions were so grim that US newspaper columnist Constantine Brown raised an outcry: "Their small cells have blackened windows, their food is just little more than a bread-and-water ration. They are theoretically allowed to see one member of their families each month for fifteen minutes" – Hess in fact refused to see his wife or son for the next twenty-three years. "Their guards", continued the journalist, "make regular half-hourly inspections throughout the night, flashing electric torches in their faces, thus preventing a continuous night's rest." Brown pointed out that the Tribunal had not provided that these men should be confined in solitary, nor "be subjected to treatment approaching physical torture".

Constantine Brown's report, which called the Spandau routine "this Gestapo treatment of individuals", appeared in 1948.

One by one the prisoners were released. Constantin von Neurath, sentenced to ten years, and Grand Admiral Erich Raeder, also sentenced to life, were released prematurely when their health collapsed. Speer and Baldur von Schirach served their twenty-year terms in full and were released in September 1966, leaving Rudolf Hess to spend the next twenty-one years in solitary confinement – alone with the flying suit, boots and helmet that he had worn in May 1941, carefully hung on a peg, awaiting perhaps the moment when he would don them and emerge to his liberty when his mission was finally over.

The West German government subsidized the cost of Spandau with 2.5 million Deutschmarks every year, but joined every other western government in calling for his release. For four decades Alfred Seidl maintained his plucky campaign to the same purpose, protesting to the international community and to the German constitutional courts that the

---

* This author has seen all these Nuremberg and Spandau writings of Rudolf Hess. Hess was hammering out the Reichstag speech he proposed to deliver upon being called in by the Allies as regent to govern Germany.

continued imprisonment of Hess violated every United Nations convention on human rights – specifically those of 10 December 1948, 4 November 1950 and 19 December 1966.

Hess's prison cell was enriched by a television set in 1969, but by then he was going blind. Each week he was allowed to write one heavily censored letter of 1300 words; those that have been published display a philosophical outlook innocent of any trace of mental disturbance. He last spoke with Ilse in 1981 – she was unable later to make the strenuous trip to Berlin. When Wolf Rüdiger briefly hugged his father once in the following year, it was the British who lodged a formal complaint.

On his ninetieth birthday, 26 April 1984, *The Times* commented: "It is unclear whether Hess is sane or not." Hess, of course, had decided as long ago as 1945, in Wales, that the whole world had gone lunatic.

Alone but not forgotten, Rudolf Hess gave up the struggle to survive on 17 August 1987. He was found by his warder, strangled by a length of electric flex. The blind man's flying suit had a few months earlier been pilfered from his cell; within days of his death bulldozers began the demolition of Spandau prison – this decaying red-brick monument to man's inhumanity. The British Army had kept the demolition gear standing by for years.

His ashes were to be buried in the family plot at Wunsiedel in Bavaria.

Altogether it was, as Schopenhauer had predicted, a poor reward for a brave enterprise. But then, when Germany government officials had arrived earlier in 1987 at the prison gate, bent on including the twentieth century's most famous prisoner in the Official Census, the Allied guards had turned them away empty handed. No longer "Z", the lowest letter in the alphabet; no longer No. 7, the last of the seven prisoners – it was as though Rudolf Hess had never existed.

Acknowledgements

Any investigation of the Rudolf Hess affair of 1941–5 is still inhibited by restrictions imposed by the British government on certain files, presumably because they contain Intelligence information, personal medical details, court-martial proceedings and the like. With the exception of the rather one-sided account published in 1948 by the War Office's chief psychiatric consultant John Rees, *The Case of Rudolf Hess*, virtually nothing is known about the Missing Years – the period 1941–5 during which Hess was incarcerated as Churchill's Prisoner of State. In 1981, however, a wartime file of Hess's papers turned up in the United States bearing the name of the British Lieutenant-Colonel A. J. B. Larcombe; extracts were published in the *Sunday Telegraph* (London) on 13 December of that year.

This material is identical with the missing file of evidence carried by Hess to Nuremberg in October 1945 and labelled "Hess-15" (cf. *The Trial of the Major War Criminals Before the International Military Tribunal*, Nuremberg, 1948, vol. xxxx, pp. 279ff.). That original file has vanished: my inquiries at the Nuremberg Staatsarchiv (for which I am indebted to Archivrat Dr G. Rechter) and at the National Archives (John Taylor) drew a blank, as did those at the Imperial War Museum, where the Nuremberg Documents and other foreign collections were kindly placed at my disposal by Philip Reed. This missing file Hess-15, a yellow spring binder stamped "Most Secret", originally contained such items as "Minutes of a Conference which took place on 9.6.1941 somewhere in England" ("amended minutes dated 17.xi.1941"), a seventy-one-page transcript of Hess's talk with the Lord Chancellor, Lord Simon; pasted between pages 5 and 6 a page of British newspaper clippings from October 1942 to January 1943 with pictures of the funerals of children killed in air raids. More importantly, the missing file also contained sixty-five carbon copies of memoranda and letters written by the prisoner Hess to the King, Lord Beaverbrook (with two replies) and others; a note by Hess on his September 1941 talk with Beaverbrook); Hess's memorandum on "Germany, Britain, from the point of view of the War against the Soviet Union"; studies by Hess on the 1941 Atlantic

Charter and scraps of paper with names, addresses and historical dates.

According to papers in the National Archives, these were handed to US Colonel John H. Amen of the Interrogation Division at Nuremberg (Larcombe was the British Colonel who had escorted Hess from Wales). I located other copies of the Beaverbrook–Hess correspondence in the House of Lords Records Office. Amen's listing of the Larcombe file referred to fifteen (*sic*) medical notebooks. Researching in May 1986 in the Federal Records Center in Maryland (under the useful guidance of archivists Amy Schmidt and Richard Olsen) I chanced upon *eighteen* RAMC record books, detailing minute by minute the behaviour of a patient never identified by name. That it was Hess was clearly established by the diary of the Commandant of Camp Z, Lieutenant-Colonel A. Malcolm Scott – quoted extensively in these pages by kind permission of the Imperial War Museum and the Scott family. In my search for the surviving doctors, medical staff and their papers I was aided by Desmond Kelly of the Priory Hospital, London; Susan Floate of the Royal College of Psychiatrists; Linda Beecham of the *British Medical Journal*; Geoffrey Davenport, librarian of the Royal College of Physicians; Maurice Caplan of the Tavistock Centre; Brigadier (ret'd) P. D. Wickenden, Professor Emeritus of Military Psychiatry; and D. Dale, administrator of Pen-y-Fal Hospital, Maindiff Court, who enabled me locate Joe Clifford, a former guard soldier there, who in turn kindly provided the information which located Stan Jordan and the other surviving RAMC orderlies who cared for the prisoner and filled the 2000 pages of the eighteen record books with their reports on Hess. I had useful talks with Lord Fortescue, who had guarded Camp Z in 1941; Agnes Petersen, at the Hoover Library, who helped me to identify Foley; and Duff Hart-Davis, who passed on reliable hints about the Hess materials. Stuart Welham offered his original photograph of Hess & Son; P. Welti of the Swiss Embassy provided information on Swiss archives; Frances Seeber extracted Halifax's reports from Roosevelt's archives.

In Wales, I drew upon the kind efforts of Lizbeth Barrett and Rob Lewis of the Welsh Historic Monuments office, of Gwynn Jenkins of the National Library of Wales, and of S. M. Hodges of White Castle, for details of the Deputy Führer's visits to this beauty spot. From Fort Meade, Maryland, Robert J. Walsh Jr sent me a copy of the Hess materials held by the US Security and Intelligence Command; in West Berlin, Dr Daniel P. Simon provided me with personnel files from the Berlin Document Center; from Boston, Massachusetts, Dr Howard B. Gotlieb, director of the university's Special Collection, notified me that they held the original of Albrecht Haushofer's letter of September 1940; in New York, William E. Jackson allowed me to study the private files of his late father Justice Robert H. Jackson; in Colorado Springs, the family of the late Colonel Burton C. Andrus Jr made his private Nuremberg trial papers available to my assistant Susanna Scott-Gall, whose own proficient endeavours have helped to enlarge the compass of this book's research considerably. Would that one could say the same about Oliver Everett, the librarian in whose custody the Royal Archives at Windsor are vested: their exclusive sympathies towards Court-favoured historians wear poorly in the twentieth century – or is it because the files on Rudolf Hess held at Windsor contain materials which, even now, it would be undesirable for His Late Majesty's subjects to see? Finally, I am indebted to Ilse Hess and her son Wolf Rüdiger for their kindness in allowing me to quote Rudolf Hess's letters from England, which are the copyright of Drüffel Verlag, Leoni am Starnberger See.

David Irving
London, August 1987

Abbreviations used in Notes

AA	Auswärtiges Amt (German Foreign Ministry)
ACAD	Sir Alexander Cadogan file at Churchill College, Cambridge
ADAP	*Akten der deutschen auswärtigen Politik*
AIR	Air Ministry file at PRO
BA	Bundesarchiv (West German Civil Archives, Koblenz)
BA–MA	Bundesarchiv–Militärarchiv (West German Military Archives, Freiburg)
BBC	British Broadcasting Corporation
BDC	Berlin Document Center, US Mission, Berlin
BL	British Library, Manuscript Division
CAB	Cabinet Office file in PRO
CIOS	Combined Intelligence Objectives Survey
CSDIC	Combined Services Detailed Interrogation Centre
DI	Microfilm made for this author, available from Microform Ltd, East Ardsley, Wakefield, Yorkshire
DIC	Detailed Interrogation Centre
EAP	Einheitsaktenplan (German archival system initially adopted by Americans)
FD	Foreign Document at IWM
FDR	Franklin D. Roosevelt
FDRL	Roosevelt Library, Hyde Park, New York
FO	Foreign Office; also, Foreign Office file at PRO
HL	Hoover Library Archives, Stanford, California
HLRO	House of Lords Record Office, London
IfZ	Institut für Zeitgeschichte (Institute of Contemporary History), Munich
IMT	International Military Tribunal, Nuremberg
INF	Ministry of Information file at PRO
IWM	Imperial War Museum
J[onathan]	British codename for Rudolf Hess
KTB WFST	Kriegstagebuch Wehrmacht Führungsstab (War Diary, German High Command operations staff)
LC	Library of Congress, Washington DC
LCO	Lord Chancellor's Office file in PRO
LKEN	File in A. L. Kennedy papers, Churchill College, Cambridge

MI5	Security Service
MI6	Secret Intelligence Service
NA	National Archives, Washington DC
ND	Nuremberg Document
OMGUS	Office of Military Government of the United States in Germany
ORB	Operations Record Book (i.e. war diary)
OSS	Office of Strategic Services (wartime forerunner of CIA)
OUSCC	Office of US Chief of Counsel at IMT
PM	Prime Minister
PREM	Prime Minister's file at PRO
PRO	Public Record Office, London
RAMC	Royal Army Medical Corps
RG	Record Group in NA
RGBI	*Reichsgesetzblatt* (Reich Law Gazette)
SIS	Secret Intelligence Service
T253/46/9958	NA microcopy T253, roll 46, frame 9958
USFET	US Forces, European Theater
USSBS	US Strategic Bombing Survey, file at NA
VfZ	*Vierteljahrsheft für Zeitgeschichte*, IfZ quarterly
WO	War Office file at PRO
WSC	Winston Spencer Churchill
Z	British codename for Rudolf Hess

Notes

Chapter 1

p. 3 Article by Clive Freeman, "Hess's War Relics are Stolen from Spandau", in *Sunday Times*, London, 12.4.1987.

p. 4 Family tree of Rudolf Hess, published both in "Die Ahnentafel von Rudolf Heß", in *Heimat-Blätter*, Nr 5/6, Gera, 22. Jahrg., 1935, and in the series *Ahnentafeln großer Deutscher*: "Die Ahnentafel von Rudolf Heß (BA, Slg Schumacher, /236); I also rely on answers given to Capt. Richard V. Worthington, MC, 31.12.45 at Nuremberg (in LC, R. H. Jackson papers, box 107, file: "Psychiatric and Personality Studies of Nazi Leaders"); and on the "Memorandum about Rudolf Hess", by his later secretary Hildegard Fath, affidavit, Nuremberg, 20.11.45 (HL, Ms. DD247 H3F22).

p. 4 More biographical material: Office of Strategic Services, Research and Analysis Branch, Biographical Report: Hess, Rudolf, 7.9.45 (based largely on printed reference works); and British Foreign Office Research Department, confidential report on Rudolf Hess, 7.7.45, in LC, R. H. Jackson papers, box 100.

p. 5 Letters Rudolf Hess to Ilse Hess, 23.1.49 (192); and his mother, Klara, 3.7.49 (ibid., 202ff.). Published in Ilse Hess, *Ein Schicksal in Briefen* (Leoni am Starnberger See, 1984).

p. 6 For Hess's war record, see Zentralnachweiseamt für Kriegeverluste u. Kriegergräber, Zweigstelle München: Kriegs-Rangliste der bayer. Flieger-Ersatz Abteilung I für Ltd.d.Res (1.F.K.) Rudolf Heß 1914–1920 (BA, Slg Schumacher, /236).

p. 6 Cf. also *Das Deutsche Führerlexikon 1934/35* (Berlin, 1935), 25.

p. 7 Max (Eduard) Hofweber, b.1891 in Regensburg, had been the Brigade-general Karl Haushofer's Ordonnanzoffizier 1914–17.

p. 7 Münchner Wohnungskunst GmbH, designing furniture units, operated unsuccessfully from 1919 to 1921.

p. 7 Haushofer Ms.: Erinnerungen, written 1945/46, cited in Hans-Adolf Jacobsen, *Karl Haushofer, Leben und Werk*, vol. i; (Boppard am Rhein), 226ff.; also the Taschenkalender and Martha Haushofer diaries quoted there, now in Haushofer Archiv.

p. 7 Haushofer said (5.10.45, see below) that Fritz Hess lived in a palatial house at "Ramleh"; there is no trace of this in *The Times Atlas* so I have ignored it. Probably shorthand error.

p. 7 Testimony of Karl Haushofer taken at Nuremberg, Germany 5.10.45, 1445–1600, by Col. Howard A. Brundage, JAGD, OUSCC. Also present: Dr Edmund A. Walsh, expert consultant to Justice Jackson; Siegfried Ramler, interpreter; and S./Sgt William A. Weigel, court report (LC, R. H. Jackson papers, box 104, "Individual Responsibility: Karl Haushofer").

p. 8 Rudolf Hess, "Wie wird der Mann beschaffen sein, der Deutschland wieder zur Höhe führt?" Published in the Nazi press in 1933; Willi Schlamm, former editor of *Weltbühne*, brought it to the *American Mercury*, a Communist-orientated American monthly, which published it July 1944, vol. liii, No. 211. It was also published in Konrad Heiden, *Hitler*. Cf. ND, 3787-PS, in NA, RG238, Jackson papers, box 180, "Hess".

p. 8 Family-album advice: Jacobsen, op. cit., 233.

p. 9 The SA began as NS-Studentenhundertschaft later NS Studentenbattaillon. Hans Volz, *Daten der Geschichte der NSDAP* (9th edn, Berlin, 1939), 93.

p. 10 Letter Ilse Hess to her lawyer, 13.7.45, describing how she met Hess.

p. 11 Karl Haushofer, Ms.: "R.H., ein Kämpfer geht in die Zeit", September 1933, Privatarchiv Haushofer.

p. 11 Karl Haushofer, testimony, Nuremberg, 5.10.45.

p. 11 Karl Haushofer, Ms.: "R.H., ein Kämpfer geht in die Zeit", September 1933, Privatarchiv Haushofer.

p. 11 Letter Rudolf Hess to Ilse Hess, in post-war captivity.

p. 12 Karl Haushofer, testimony, Nuremberg, 5.10.45.

p. 13 Letters Rudolf Hess to Herr Heim, Festung Landsberg/Lech 16.7.1924; 15.9.24; and dedication, 28.9.24 (BDC Akte Rudolf Hess).

p. 14 Letters Walther Hewel to his mother, 9.11. and 14.12.24, from the collection of his widow, Frau Blanda Benteler (DI, film 75b). He described his cell and prison environs in a letter dated 3.10.24. Hewel followed Hitler to the end, committing suicide in the Berlin bunker on 1.5.45.

Chapter 2

p. 15 Tischgespräch Wolfsschanze 3/4.2.42 abends (Henry Picker edition, 262).

p. 15 Walter Stubbe, "In Memoriam Albrecht Haushofer", in *VfZ*, 1960, 236ff. And "Angaben über die Personalien von Dr Albrecht Haushofer und Familie", in Haushofer papers, NA, film T253/46/0096.

p. 16 Albert Krebs, *Tendenzen und Gestalten der NSDAP. Erinnerungen an die Frühzeit der Partei* (Stuttgart, 1959), 170ff.

p. 17 Police documents in BA, Slg Schumacher, /236.

p. 17 Letter Rudolf Hess to "Lieber Herr Doktor", 18.10.30, in Haushofer papers, NA, film T253/46/0094f. The "Doktor" is addressed as *Sie*, so cannot be Karl Haushofer, whom Rudolf Hess addressed as *Du*.

p. 18 Tischgespräch, Wolfsschanze 5.2.42 mittags (Henry Picker edition, 265).

p. 19 Hess as the "conscience of the Party": *National Zeitung*, Essen, 27.4.41.

p. 19 Letter Rudolf Hess to Gregor Strasser, 9.9.32, in BA, Slg Schumacher, /236.

p. 19 Hitler's decree of 21.4.33: "Der Führer. Verfügung. Den Leiter der Politischen Zentralkommission Pg. Rudolf Hess, ernenne ich zu meinem Stellvertreter und erteile ihm Vollmacht, in allen Fragen der Parteiführung in meinem Namen zu entscheiden. ADOLF HITLER. 21.April 1933" (BA, Slg Schumacher, /236).

p. 19 Hermann Göring, testimony, Nuremberg 14.10.45 (NA, film M1270, roll 6).

p. 19 Law of 1.12.33: Gesetz zur Sicherung der Einheit von Partei und Staat, 1.12.33: published in *RGBl.*, 1933, I, 1016: ND,1395-PS; exhibit GB-252.

p. 20 BDC Akte Alfred Leitgen, b. 1.9.02. And IfZ, ZS-262 of Leitgen, 1.4 and 19.12.52 and 3.12.65.

p. 20 Hochschulkommission der NSDAP.

p. 20 NS Deutscher Studentenbund, -Altherrnbund, -Dozentenbund.

p. 20 Prüfungskommission zum Schutze des NS Schrifttums (later Parteiamtliche Prüfungskommission). (BA, Bestand NS 16.)

p. 20 Martha Haushofer diary, "Arierangelegenheiten". Cf. Jacobsen, op. cit., 473.

p. 20 Letter Albrecht Haushofer to Dr Goebbels, Herrn Reichsminister für Volksaufklärung und Propaganda, 9.8.33 (NA, film T253/46/0098).

p. 21 Cf. James Douglas-Hamilton, *Motive for a Mission* (London, 1972), 43f.

p. 21 Letter Albrecht Haushofer to Rudolf Hess, 24.8.33 (NA, film T253/46).

p. 21 Letter Albrecht Haushofer to Rudolf Hess, 7.9.33 (ibid.).

p. 21 Heinz Höhne, *Mordsache Röhm. Hitlers Durchbruch zur Alleinherrschaft 1933–1934* (Hamburg, 1984) 42, 47, 172 etc.

p. 22 On Mecklenburg meeting, cf. Martin Bormann diary, 25–27.5.34: "Gauleiter Tagung, Zipperndorf b Schwerin/Meckl. Redner: Pietzsch, Staatssekretär Backe, Staatssekr. Reinhardt, Reichsjugendführer v Schirach, Gauleiter Adolf Wagner über Reichsreform, Reichsschatzmeister Schwarz und Reichsleiter Amann" (HL, roll 1, NSDAP Hauptarchiv).

p. 22 Alfred Leitgen, IfZ, ZS-262. J. R. Rees, *The Case of Rudolf Hess* (London), 11, states, "In 1934 it is said that Hess played an important part in the Röhm purge and he was probably personally one of the main executioners." This was rubbish. Rees adds: "When in [Britain] when he talked about Röhm his manner and feeling seemed to indicate such a degree of hatred that it suggested the repression of homosexual trends."

p. 22 footnote Julius Schaub, IfZ, ZS; the K. Heiden manuscripts are at IfZ now.

p. 22 footnote Compare the IMT indictment and the OSS R&D reports on Hess *et al.*, and the Foreign Office Research Department reports on Hess *et al.* (LC, R. H. Jackson papers, box 100). The Nuremberg prosecutors openly cite Heiden and Rauschning.

p. 23 Letter Marianne Adler to Heß, 12.7.34, Archiv Fritz Tobias, cited in Höhne, op. cit., 301f.

p. 23 Lämmermann case: Letter Stellvertreter des Führers iA gez Winkler, to Fritz Wiedemann, Führeradjutant, 13.5.35 (BA, NS 10/219).

p. 23 Letter SA-Standartenführer Gottlieb Rösner to Heß, 1.8.34, Archiv Fritz Tobias, cited in Höhne, op. cit., 302.

p. 23 Letter Karl Haushofer to Rudolf Hess, 1.7.34, cited in Jacobsen, op. cit., vol. I, 377f.

p. 23 Nuremberg Laws; Gesetze zum Schutz des deutschen Blutes und der deutschen Ehre, 15.9.35.

p. 23 As is emphasized in legal opinions by Alfred Seidl.

p. 24 Hildegard Fath, affidavit, Nuremberg, 20.11.45 (HL, Ms. DD247 H3F22).

p. 25 Geoffrey H. Shakespeare, memo, secret, to Secretary of State, 14.5.41 (IWM, GHS2 (Shakespeare papers)).

p. 25 Schmitt revelations: News story in the *New York Times*, 21.5.45: "HESS' DOCTOR GIVES 'INSIDE' NAZI STORY: CALLS DEPUTY LEADER WHO FLEW TO SCOTLAND A PSYCHOPATH WITH A GUILTY CONSCIENCE". The late Rudolf Hess's lawyers have enforced the excision of this Schmitt material from the German edition of this book, claiming that its publication violated his rights to privacy.

Ernst "Putzi" Hanfstängl who fled Germany in February 1937 wrote that Hess's "weirdness" reached the point where "he would not go to bed without testing with a divining rod [*Pendeln*] whether there there were any subterranean water courses which conflicted with the direction of his couch."

p. 26 Alfred Leitgen, IfZ, zs–262, 1.4.52.

p. 26 American doctor: Dr Douglas McG. Kelley, *Twenty-two Cells in Nuremberg* (New York), 21f.

However, one might point out that in the mid-West and southern United States chiropractors are rich and plentifully abound; while in South Africa, the leading Black newspaper, *City Press*, in Johannesburg has a back page devoted almost entirely to advertising by "witch doctors".

p. 26 Ingeborg Sperr, affidavit, Nuremberg, 20.11.45. (HL, Ms. DD247 H3S75).

p. 26 Wolfgang Bechtold, of Bormann's staff, stated on 30.4.46: "Hess had gathered a small group of personal associates and friends with whom he would discuss strange matters such as astrology, cures through herbs, etc." (NA, R. H. Jackson papers, RG238, box 180, "Hess").

p. 26 Hess's medicine cabinet: report cited in Rees, op. cit., 16.

p. 27 Dr Morell's tablets: interview by Ottmar Katz of Frau Johanna Morell. She even claimed that her husband knew that Hess needed the vitamins etc. for this flight.

p. 27 Report by British Medical Research Council, 29.5.41, cited Rees, op. cit., 16 footnote.

p. 27 On Schmitt arrest see *New York Times*, 21.5.45, op. cit.

p. 27 Hitler's remarks to the Reichs- und Gauleiter on 13.5.41. Gedächtnisprotokoll über Ausführungen des [dort anwesenden] Generalgouverneurs Hans Frank am 19.5.41 (Hans Frank diary, Anl., IWM, AL 2525). cf. Bormann diary, 13.5.41: "16–18 Uhr 30, Rücksprache des Führers mit allen Reichs- und Gauleitern".

Chapter 3

p. 28 Article by Albrecht Haushofer in *Zeitschrift für Geopolitik*, 1935, Heft 4 (April 1935), 232f.

p. 29 Hitler's meetings with British visitors: Paul Schmidt's Niederschriften of these talks, "Aufzeichnung über die Unterredung zwischen dem Führer und . . .", were in American hands; now only a list, EAP 2-m/4, survives in BA, Kl.Erw. 501. One Hitler meeting with Lord Beaverbrook was on 22.11.35 (and, according to what Beaverbrook told Hess, two other occasions too).

p. 29 Albrecht Haushofer, "Englische Beziehungen und die Möglichkeit ihres Einsatzes", 12.5.41; sent with covering letter to Hitler, 12.5.41 ("weisungsgemäß") (NA, film T253/46/9958ff.).

p. 29 After first visiting London and Paris in 1928, Albrecht Haushofer had journeyed to Britain every year, often several times. In May 1932 he spoke with Lord Lothian (Lloyd George's former Private Secretary) and with Foreign Office officials; in 1934 he went to Britain three times on Ribbentrop's behalf, meeting Lord Halifax, Ralph Wigram and William Strang at the Foreign Office on 16 November; he was in Britain six times in 1935 and three times in 1936. By 1937 Haushofer had decided that if Britain was in danger the United States would join in out of common interest. (cf. Jacobsen, op. cit., 348f.)

p. 30 Swedish speech: Rede des Herr Reichsministers Hess in der deutsch–schwedischen Gesellschaft in Stockholm am 14.5.35 (LC, R. H. Jackson papers, box 104, file: "Individual Responsibility: Karl Haushofer", ND, 3674-PS).

p. 31 Hildegard Fath, affidavit, Nuremberg, 20.11.45 (HL, Ms. DD247 H3F22).

p. 31 Geburtstagsbrief Rudolf Heß an s. Vater Fritz Heß (z.Zt. Berlin), 24.10.35 (his father's birthday was on 31.10.35). PRO, FO371/26566; these letters were sent to the Foreign Office in London in June 1941. Some of them have *French* translations attached.

p. 33 Stellvertreter des Führers Anordnung Nr 184/35 v. 3.9.35. Published in *Anordnungen des Stellvertreters des Führers* (Franz Eher Verlag, Munich, 1937); also ND, 2639–PS and 2787-PS.

p. 33 Stellvertreter des Führers Anordnung Nr 160/35, Verhinderung von Ausschreitungen, Einzelaktionen gegen Juden (BDC Akte Ordner 240/I).

p. 33 Secret orders of February 1936: Stellvertreter des Führers Anordnung Nr 17/36, München den 5.2.36: Verhütung von Ausschreitungen aus Anlaß der Ermordung des Landesgruppenleiters der Schweiz der NSDAP, Pg Gustloff. gez. R. Heß (BDC Akte Ordner 240/I).

p. 33 Confidential speech of September 1937: Rede des Stellvertreters des Führers vor den Gau- und Kreisleitern am 13.9.37 (BDC Akte Rudolf Heß).

p. 34 *Organisationsbuch der NSDAP* 1937 (Eher Verlag, München), 151.

p. 34 Nuremberg speech: Rede des Stellvertreters des Führers vor den Gau- und Kreisleitern am 13.9.37 (BDC Akte Rudolf Heß).

p. 34 On Hof speech, see article in *Frankfurter Zeitung*, 13.10.36: "KEIN ZWANGSSYSTEM, KEIN MARKENSYSTEM. RUDOLF HESS ÜBER DIE LEBENSMITTELVERSORGUNG – EIN APPELL AN DIE HAUSFRAUEN".

p. 35 Olympic Games engagements: Bormann diary, 1.8.36: Eröffnung d. Olymp. Spiele; Essen m. Olymp. Ausschuß in der Führerwohnung. 12.8: Einladung b. Führer aus Anlaß des Besuches von Vansittart. 16.8: Schluß. Also Jacobsen, op. cit.

p. 36 Douglas-Hamilton, op. cit., 69ff. Based on the Hamilton family papers.

p. 36 Letter Albrecht Haushofer to Karl Haushofer, 16.3.37 (NA, film T253/46/9835f.).

p. 36 Letter Ilse Hess to Klara Hess, 20.10.37, in PRO, FO371/26566.

p. 37 Letter Ilse Hess to Klara Hess, 3.11.37.

p. 37 Letter Ilse Hess to Klara Hess, 15.12.37 (ibid.).

Chapter 4

p. 39 IMT Sentence, 1.10.46.

p. 39 Secret Cabinet Council: Erlaß des Führers und Reichskanzlers über die Errichtung eines Geheimen Kabinettrates vom 4.2.38, *RGBl.*, 1938, I, S.112: ND, exhibit GB-249, quoted from *Dokumente der deutschen Politik*, 1939, vii/1, 4f.

p. 39 For sources of these speeches see David Irving, *The War Path* (London, 1978), 273ff.

p. 39 Letter Rudolf Hess to Klara Hess, 15.1.38, copy in PRO, FO371/26566.

p. 42 Letter Ilse Hess to Klara Hess, 28.1.38, in PRO, FO371/26566.

p. 42 Regulation extending Nuremberg Laws to Austria: Verordnung über die

Einführung der Nürnberger Rassengesetze im Land Österreich v. 20.5.38, gez. Frick, Heß, Schlegelberger (i.V), ND, 2124-PS. *RGBl.*, 1938, I, 594; exhibit GB-259.

p. 42 Jacobsen, op. cit.

p. 42 Letter Prof. Dr Karl Haushofer to Martha Haushofer, 10.9.38, in Hartschimmel-hof Archiv. Cf. Jacobsen, op. cit., 369.

p. 42 Wolfgang Bechtold, Former Government Adviser to Bormann's General Staff, "Communication concerning the time of my activities in Bormann's office in Munich", 30.4.46, in NA, R. H. Jackson papers, RG 238, box 180, "Hess". Bechtold was an editor 1936–7, and 1939–43 was in the economics, then cultural branch of Hess's staff, later on "Parteikanzlei".

p. 43 Secret decree: Stellvertreter des Führers Anordnung Nr174/38, Wiederholung des Fernschreibens vom 10.11.38, München den 10.11.38 (BDC Ordner 240/I).

p. 43 Ingeborg Sperr, affidavit, Nuremberg, 5.3.46.

p. 43 Schutzbrief von R. Heß für Haushofers, 14.11.38 (BA, Nachlaß Karl Haushofer/912e. Cited in Jacobsen, op. cit., 384f).

p. 43 Regulation mitigating Berlin decrees: Stellvertreter des Führers Anordnung Nr194/38 v. 1.12.38 (BDC Akte Ordner 240/I).

p. 44 Row on 10.11.38: Karl Haushofer, testimony, Nuremberg, 5.10.45 (LC, R. H. Jackson papers, box 104, file: "Individual Responsibility: Karl Haushofer").

p. 44 Martha Haushofer diary, 8.7.39.

p. 44 Letter Albrecht Haushofer to Martha Haushofer, cited in Jacobsen, op. cit.

p. 44 Letter (in English) Dr Albrecht Haushofer to Lord Clydesdale, 16.7.39; published in full in Douglas-Hamilton, op. cit., 91ff.

p. 45 Letter Rudolf Hess to Heinz Haushofer, 21.7.39, in Ilse Hess archives, cited in Jacobsen, op. cit., 385ff.

p. 45 Martin Bormann, [later] Der Sekretär des Führers, "Daten aus alten Notiz-büchern", 30.1.34–30.6.43. Two versions, one on roll 1 of NSDAP Hauptarchiv, micro-film (DI film 23) and one in LC, appendix 5 472E, Ac9705 (DI film 19).

p. 46 Graz speech: article, "RUDOLF HESS ANTWORTET CHAMBERLAIN, 'WIR STEHEN ZUR FAHNE DES FÜHRERS, KOMME WAS DA WOLLE!'" 7. Reichstagung der Auslandsdeutschen . . . am Freitagabend (25.8.). – Bericht in *Völkischer Beobachter*, Berliner Ausgabe, 28.8.39 (IMT exhibit GB-266).

p. 46 Ministerial Council for Reich Defence: Erlaß des Führers über die Bildung eines Ministerrats für die Reichsverteidigung v. 30.8.39: ND, 2018-PS; those appointed included Göring, Hess, Funk, Lammers, Keitel. *RGBl.*, 1939, I, 1539 (IMT exhibit GB-250).

p. 46 "that nincompoop": Kelley, op. cit., 35f.

Chapter 5

p. 48 For Hitler's lamentations, see Albert Zoller. *Hitler privat. Erlebnisbericht einer Geheimsekretärin* (Düsseldorf, 1949).

p. 48 For Fritsch's funeral, see report in *Völkischer Beobachter*, 27.9.39.

p. 48 Decree of 8.10.39, published in *RGBl.*, I, 1939, 2042f.

p. 48 Hildegard Fath, affidavit, Nuremberg, 20.11.45 (HL, Ms. DD247 H3F22).

p. 48 Open Letter: *Völkischer Beobachter*, 26.12.39, "BRIEF RUDOLF HESS AN EINE UNVERHEIRATETE MUTTER". Commentary: Prof. Helmut Krausnick, Dr Hildegard von Kotze *Tagebuch eines Abwehr-Offiziers* (Stuttgart), appendix I, p. 470: "Die SS-Männer würden danach – so mißverstehen das manche – aufgefordert, sich den Frauen der im Felde stehenden Soldaten zu nähern."

p. 49 Cf. Bormann diary, February 1940.

p. 49 Hildegard Fath, affidavit, Nuremberg, 20.11.45 (HL, Ms. DD247 H3F22).

p. 49 Bormann diary, ibid.

p. 49 Akten der Seekriegsleitung.

p. 50 Reich Chancellery lunch: Bormann's adjutant Heinrich Heim was present too. Irving interview of Heim, 25.6.71 (IfZ, Slg Irving).

p. 50 General von Weichs, Ms. (Bundesarchiv-Militärarchiv).

p. 50 Letter Christa Schroeder to her friend "Johanning" in Switzerland, 25.6.40 (IfZ, Slg Irving).

p. 50 Hitler–Hess conversation: related by Hess in conversation with Lord Simon 9.6.41, and on other occasions. He states this was "during the French campaign".

p. 50 Relevant files on WSC's private talk with Air Chief Marshal Charles Portal on 20.7.40 are in PRO, AIR14/1930, PREM3/14/2, PREM3/4/4. Portal replied that conditions would not be favourable until 1.9.40.

p. 50 Letter Albrecht Haushofer to Karl Haushofer, 2.8.40 (Jacobsen, op. cit., 402).

p. 51 Kriegstagebuch der Seekriegsleitung, 1. Abtlg, 14.8.40.

p. 51 Field Marshal Wilhelm Ritter von Leeb diary. 14.8.40 (Militärgeschichtliches Forschungsamt).

p. 51 Secret talk at Langenbeck referred to in Jacobsen, op. cit., chronology ("15.8.40: Albrecht H. wird zu R Hess zur Besprechung in Langenbeck gebeten Beginn der Sondierungsvorbereitungen").

p. 51 25–6 August raid on Berlin: Churchill, 'phone call to Sir Norman Bottomley at RAF Bomber Command, High Wycombe, 25.8.40, 9.10 a.m.; transcript in Bomber Command directives file, PRO, AIR14/775.

p. 51 28–9 August raid on Berlin: ibid.

p. 51 For Hitler's return to Berlin, see Bormann diary, 29.8.40; the KTB OKW WFSt makes plain that Hitler returned to Berlin because of the air raids.

p. 51 Wehrwirtschaftsamt: Aktennotiz, Besprechung beim Amtschef [Thomas] 30.8.40 (ND, 1456-PS).

p. 52 The president of the Swedish Hofgericht Ekeberg approached Mallet on 5.9 to ask if he would receive Weissauer. The Foreign Office (Halifax) replied on 6.9 refusing permission. Bernd Martin, *Friedensinitiativen und Machtpolitik im Zweiten Weltkrieg* (Düsseldorf, 1976), 342f.

p. 52 Letter from Karl Haushofer, Munich, to Albrecht Haushofer, 3.9.40 (BA, HX832; cf. *ADAP*, Serie D (1937–1945), ix, 1, p. 13, No. 12; U. Laack-Michel, *Albrecht Haushofer und der Nationalsozialismus* (Stuttgart, 1974), 214ff.; and Martin, op. cit., 430ff. Albrecht Haushofer in his notes called it "ein heikles Problem".

p. 53 Coffins: from stenographic record of Hess's conversation with Lord Simon, 9.6.41; he made the same remark on later occasions. Cf. Rees, op. cit., 20.

p. 53 On volunteering for Luftwaffe, see Ilse Hess, op. cit., 63. Hess referred to the "one-year promise" on several occasions in British custody.

p. 53 Affidavits by Ingeborg Sperr and Hildegard Fath (Exhibit Hess-13, in IWM, FO645 box 31, 3).

p. 53 Cramps: because Albrecht ends his next letter to Hess on 19.9, "Mit . . . guten Wünschen für Ihre Gesundheit".

p. 53 Albrecht Haushofer, memorandum (dated 15.9.40): Gibt es noch Möglichkeiten eines deutsch–englischen Friedens? Typescript, Streng Geheim. BA, HC832; *ADAP* D, ix, 1, No. 61; cf. Walter Stubbe, "In Memoriam Albrecht Haushofer", *VfZ*, 1960, 246ff.

p. 55 Letter Rudolf Hess to Professor Karl Haushofer, 10.9.40, cited in Jacobsen, op. cit., 353f. (No. 81). BA, HC832; *ADAP* D, xi, No. 81.

p. 55 Letter Albrecht Haushofer to his parents, 18.9.40, published by Michel, op. cit., No. 82, p. 354, and by Jacobsen, op. cit., I (BA, HC832). In his letter Albrecht Haushofer writes to Hess on 19.9.40, "Mit einer – durch die altertümlichen Postverhältnisse der Partnach-Alm bedingten – Verzögerung ist ihr Brief vom 10. gestern in meine Hand gelangt" (NA, film T253/46/9976ff.).

p. 55 Letter Albrecht Haushofer to Rudolf Hess, Berlin, 19.9.40; in BA, HC832; *ADAP* D, xi, No. 76; Stubbe, op. cit., 249f.; ND, 1670-PS (NA film T253/46/9976ff.).

p. 56 Draft typescript letter Albrecht Haushofer to the Duke of Hamilton, undated, in BA, HC832; Michel, op. cit., No. 84.

p. 56 Letter Albrecht Haushofer to parents, 19.9.40, in BA, HC832, and Michel, op. cit., No. 83.

p. 56 For bombs dropped, see Basil Collier, *The Defence of the United Kingdom* (London, 1957), app. xxvi.

p. 56 Letter Albrecht Haushofer to Rudolf Hess, from Berlin, 23.9.40, BA, HC832; *ADAP* D, xi, No. 13; Michel, op. cit., No. 86, p. 357.

p. 57 Letter Albrecht Haushofer to father, from Berlin, 23.9.40, BA, HC832; *ADAP* D, xi, No. 14; Michel, op. cit., No. 85, p. 356.

p. 57 On the German Section of the SIS: author's interview with Dr (William) Kurt S. Wallersteiner, in Vancouver, BC, 22.10.86. Wallersteiner, now deputy chief of British Columbia's Board of Deputies of Jews, was from 1938 to the 1960s a member of the SIS. Frankenstein became "Sir George" F.

p. 57 Statements by Ernest William Hans Bohle, b. 28.7.03; G2 Historical Interrogation Commission, Ashcan, July 1945; USFET FIR No. 10, 26.7.45; interrog. by Harold Deutsch, 5.8.45; and statement for Robert Kempner in German, published in *Das Dritte Reich im Kreuzverhör* (Munich, 1969), 103ff.

p. 58 The Duke of Hamilton reported on 11.5.41: "He [Hess] requested me to ask The King to give him 'parole', as he had come unarmed and of his own free will" (PRO, PREM3/219/7). He flew down to London. There, on 15.5 Cadogan wrote in his private diary, "Duke of H. turned up. Wanted to see King. I advised him to see P.M. first." Churchill's desk diary shows that the Duke did not; but he *did* see His Majesty the next morning, because Duff Cooper so notified Churchill later that day: "I saw the Duke of Hamilton last night. . . . He saw the King this morning, and reported to me this afternoon that His Majesty thought the latter" – that Churchill make a reply to a Parliamentary Question – "would be the preferable of the two alternatives" (PRO, INF1/912). On 17.5 Cadogan wrote somewhat cryptically, "Hamilton called, looking more and more like a golden spaniel." On 30.5, "A. Hardinge at 3.30. Told him – for H.M. – all news about Hess, and Simon" (Churchill College, Cadogan papers, ACAD1/10). Every reference linking the Duke with the King was excised from David Dilks (ed.), *The Diaries of Sir Alexander Cadogan, O.M., 1938–1945* (London, 1971).

p. 58 Re Beneš: Beneš' secretary Edvard Táborsky diary, 12.5–1.6.41 ("Rudolf Hess přiletěl jednat o mír") (HL, Táborsky collection, box 4, Accession 82087 8M02); his own account, Přisna duvěrna zpráva z briského ředního prameno [vojenského], ibid., box 6; and cf. Beneš' conversation with Compton Mackenzie, shorthand record, 13.12.44, box 4.

p. 59 German investigation: Hitler reported to his generals, etc., on 15.5.41 (cf. General Franz Halder diary).

p. 59 Ibid.

p. 59 Hildegard Fath, affidavit, Nuremberg, 20.11.45 (HL, Ms. DD247 H3F22). Insert added by (?) Dr Douglas Kelley.

p. 59 The ban on flying: cf. Halder diary, 15.5.41, and the wording of the Parteiamtliche Mitteilung, 12.5.41: "Pg.Heß, dem es auf Grund einer seit Jahren fortschreitenden Krankheit vom Führer strengstens verboten war, sich noch weiter fliegerisch zu betätigen . . . [usw]" (BA, Slg Schumacher, /236).

p. 59 Führer's permission: letter Rudolf to Ilse Hess, 9.9.42 (Ilse Hess, op. cit.).

p. 59 Hess at Augsburg: cf. Halder diary, 15.5.41; USSBS interrogation of Prof. W. Messerschmitt, 11–12.5.45; and Messerschmitt's version in *Frankfurter Neue Presse*, 12.5.47: "Wie Hess nach England [*sic*] flog" (Ilse Hess, op. cit., 65 n.).

p. 60 Messerschmitt docket: Aktennotiz, Messerschmitt für Piel, Hentzen und Bringewald, 7.1.41: "Me-110 des H.Heß", Nachlaß Messerschmitt, IWM, Handakten Messerschmitt, FD4355/45, vol. 4 (Box S206).

p. 60 Obersalzberg briefing: Halder diary, 15.1.41; Bormann diary, 7–8.1.41; KTB WFSt, 7–9.1.41.

p. 60 Hess himself stated to Lord Simon on 9.6.41 that he made his first flight attempt on 10.1.41.

p. 61 Letter Max Hofweber to Heinz Haushofer, 18.10.61, quoted by Jacobsen, op. cit., 404 footnote.

p. 61 Conversation Ribbentrop–Duce, 13.5.41 (ND, 1866–PS); Goebbels Minister-besprechung, 15.5.41.

p. 61 Laura Schrödl, British interrogation at Nuremberg, 4.3.46, in IWM, FO645, box 161, Interrogations Sa–Sk. She herself had only become aware of the planned invasion of Poland in the last days of August 1939, said he planned his 1941 flight because "he was anxious about Russia, and that we must form a western bloc so as to be prepared to meet the possible attack of an eastern bloc." She had heard nothing about "Barbarossa". Hildegard Fath, affidavit, Nuremberg, n.d., ND exhibit Hess-13, IWM, FO645, box 31, no. 3.

p. 61 Hess in conversation with the Duke of Hamilton, 11.5.41 (ND, M116).

p. 61 Hans Baur, *Hitler's Pilot* (London, 1958).

p. 61 Kalundborg: Ilse Hess, op. cit.; Halder diary, 15.6.41; and Nachlaß Julius Schaub, Slg Irving, IfZ.

p. 61 Leitstrahl: Bodenschatz ascertained this: CSDIC (UK) report SRGG1236(C), 20.5.45.

p. 61 Hess explained this reason for delay in conversation with Hamilton on 11.5.41 (ND, M166). Printed also in *The Trial of the Major War Criminals Before the International Military Tribunal, Documents in Evidence* (Nuremberg, 1948), vol. 38, 174ff. (Hereafter referred to as *IMT*.)

p. 61 Stays with Professor Haushofer: Jacobsen, op. cit., chronology.

p. 62 Ulrich von Hassell, *Vom anderen Deutschland*, diary, 10.3.41.

p. 62 BBC Research Unit (Overseas), Confidential, Studies in Broadcast Propaganda, No. 29, "Rudolf Hess: Broadcast References to his Activities during the Period April 20–May 14, 1941". Dated 15.5.41, in PRO, INF1/912.

p. 62 Burckhardt meeting: Jacobsen, op. cit.

p. 62 Albrecht Haushofer, report, 12.5.41, in NA, film T253/46/9958ff.

p. 63 In his Augsburg speech, Hess said, "The German soldier knows that he has only the years of effort of the Führer and his collaborators to thank for the unique quality and the abundance of the arms which he now possesses. . . . I can remember, for instance, when this entire factory consisted of a few buildings that could only be picked out with a magnifying glass among these gigantic workshops." *Völkischer Beobachter*, Berliner Ausgabe, 2.5.41.

p. 63 Unpublished Aktenvermerk Prof. W. Messerschmitt an Herrn Caroli, Nr 92/41, v. 2.5.41, in Handakten Messerschmitt, IWM, FD4355/45, vol. 4, box S206.

p. 63 BBC Research Unit (Overseas), Confidential, Studies in Broadcast Propaganda, No. 29, "Rudolf Hess: Broadcast References to his Activities during the period April 20–May 14, 1941", loc. cit.

p. 63 Bodenschatz, in CSDIC (UK) report SRGG1236(C), 20.5.45.

p. 63 Hewel diary, 12.5.41.

p. 63 Ibid.

p. 63 Letter Rudolf Hess to Ilse Hess, 8.5.47 (probably based on conversation with Albert Speer, who was present at the Berghof: cf. Speer office chronicle, May 1941 (DI)).

p. 63 Text of Reichstag speech in *Völkischer Beobachter*.

p. 63 footnote: Milch in CSDIC (UK) report SRGG1236(C), 20.5.45.

p. 64 Hitler–Hess conversation: stated by Hitler at Berghof on 13.5.41 (Hans Frank Gedächtnisprotokoll, loc. cit.).

p. 64 Bormann diary, 4.5.41. Hitler's speech was two hours long, so any talk with Hess cannot have been long.

p. 64 Hess conversation with Kirkpatrick, 13.5.41 (ND, M117).

p. 64 Laura Schrödl interrogation, 4.3.46, loc. cit.

p. 64 Hitler's movements: Bormann diary, 8–9.5.41.

p. 64 Statement of Wolfgang Bechtold, one of Klopfer's staff, 30.4.46, in NA, RG238, Jackson papers, box 180, "Hess".

p. 64 Forschungsamt: On 12.5 Darré was instructed to report to Tempelhof airport at 11 a.m. for the flight down to Berchtesgaden. Frick told him at this time, "You were on the 'phone to Hess three times the day before yesterday evening." Darré: "It wasn't I who 'phoned – he tried to 'phone me, but my compliments all the same on the way we are kept under surveillance!" (Interrogation report 824DIC X-P/5, 16.5.45).

p. 64 Letter Rudolf Hess to Reichsleiter R. W. Darré, 9.5.41, in BDC, Ordner 236.

p. 65 Karl Haushofer, testimony, Nuremberg, 5.10.45 (NA, film M1270), 15.

p. 65 Episodes like Albrecht Haushofer's journey to Switzerland make it particularly tragic that his diaries were looted by the Americans in 1945.

p. 65 According to Bernd Martin, citing Michel, op. cit., 262, Botschafter Stahmer sent his telegram from Madrid on the night of 10–11.5.41 to Walter Stubbe, Haushofer's confidant in Inf. Abtlg of AA (Martin, op. cit., 435).

p. 66 Letter Rudolf Hess to Ilse Hess, Spandau, 12.2.50 (Ilse Hess, op. cit., 211f.).

p. 66 Weather: Wettermeldung, 10 Mai 1941, published by Leasor as illustration.

p. 66 Ilse Hess refers to the new uniform (and the subsequent tailor's bills that came).

The British officers noted that it was of unusually expensive quality for a Hauptmann.

p. 66 Compass: letter Rudolf Hess to Ilse Hess, Spandau 9.5.48 (Ilse Hess, op. cit., 180).

p. 66 Flashlamp and Bengal matches are referred to in the War Office file, as is the envelope.

p. 67 Alfred Rosenberg, interrogation by Lt-Col. T. S. Hinkel, 16.11.45 a.m. (in IWM, FO645, box 160); and referred to in NA, Jackson papers, RG238, box 180, "Hess". I do not know the source for Leasor's belief that Hess discussed the coming flight with Rosenberg. I don't believe it either.

p. 67 Ilse Hess, op. cit.

p. 67 Potty: letter, Rudolf Hess to Ilse Hess, 9.9.42 (ibid., 94).

p. 67 Beams: reports by DAC [Duty Air Commodore] in Fighter Command War Room Log, 10.5.41, 1907 and 1945 hrs, PRO, AIR16/698.

p. 67 The cheap metal watch was commented on sarcastically by the British doctors. Leasor is wrong therefore in writing of an "expensive gold watch" at one stage.

Chapter 6

p. 71 W. Churchill, BBC Broadcast, 11.9.40, "Every Man to His Post", HMV Recording ALP1436. Cf. Martin Gilbert, *Winston S. Churchill*, vol. vi: *Finest Hour, 1939–1941* (London, 1984), 778f.

p. 72 It is now clear (and Prof. F. Hinsley and Prof. M. R. D. Foot the official historians agree with the author) that Eden and the rest of the Cabinet were not aware, at least in 1940/1, of the Ultra secret (and not even in 1943).

p. 72 Memorandum from E. S. Herbert [chief of Postal Censorship] to the Director-General, 26.5.41, setting out the history of the interception of Albrecht Haushofer's letter of 23.9.40 (PRO, INF1/912).

p. 72 Analysis Sheet by Terminal Mails Branch (Private Branch), No. 10782, on letter dated 23.9.40, to Mrs V. Roberts, Lisbon, sent on to MI12 for MI5 (PRO, INF1/912).

p. 72 The Censorship Examiner's report quotes only part of the letter. A photostat of the whole original letter was clearly given to the Duke because it is in his family papers. Douglas-Hamilton, op. cit., 146f.

p. 73 Wallersteiner interview in Vancouver, BC, with author.

p. 73 Beneš papers and Táborsky papers in HL. Beneš' appointment diary shows several visits from Robert Bruce-Lockhart, the SIS liaison to the Czechs, in the days after the arrival of Hess. He may have been the source.

p. 74 Anonymous, unsigned "Report on Interview with Herr Hess by Wing Commander the Duke of Hamilton, Sunday, 11th May 1941", prefacing "Personal Report by Wing Commander the Duke of Hamilton" (PRO, PREM3/219/7); and typed certified copy in ND, M116 (printed in *IMT*, xxxvii, 174ff.). The author of the preface was perhaps F/Lt Benson, the Duke's Intelligence Officer.

The ORB (Operations Record Book) of RAF Station Ayr, 10.5.41, is the only one to refer specifically to the arrival of Hess (PRO, AIR28/40).

On 10.5.41 the ORB of No. 13 Gp recorded only, "1 Me-110 crash-landed near Glasgow at 23.06 hrs not due to fighter action" (PRO, AIR25/233); it shows that A Flight of 603 Sqdn arrived at Turnhouse that day. The ORB of No. 603 sqdn (PRO, AIR27/2079) shows no activity that night. There is no direct reference to the Hess incident in the ORB of RAF Station Turnhouse (PRO, AIR28/861), apart from S/Ldr G. F. Chater DFC assuming command temporarily from the Duke on 12.5 (when the latter flew down to London), and again on 14.5, and a circular on 15.5 (in appendices, PRO, AIR28/864), forbidding personnel to communicate "any service information" to unauthorized persons. Wolf Rüdiger Hess refers (op. cit.) in a note to the operations of two Hurricanes of No. 245 Sqdn; this unit was based in Belfast, N. Ireland, and the two Hurricanes concerned, which took off at 21.35 and landed at 22.40, are specifically shown with six others as escorting a shipping convoy out of Belfast (PRO, AIR27/1481).

p. 75 ORB 141 Sqdn, 10–11.5.41 (PRO, AIR27/969).

p. 75 Fuselage marking: some sources, e.g. the *Sunday Telegraph*, 13.12.81, say NJ+OQ. On the front of Sinclair's folder AIR19/564 is written the line: "3869 VJOQ Me 110 Hess aircraft" (without explanation).

p. 75 Leasor, op. cit., 16ff. And *New Yorker*, 16.2.57, "The Aging Parachutist".

p. 75 Home Guard company commander: Leasor says "Clark". But Scottish Command records identify him as Clarke, cdr of "C" Company, 3 Bn.

p. 76 Duke's report, M116 (11.5.41); in a second report, written in 1945, "Additional Notes on the Hess Incident by Group Captain the Duke of Hamilton" (evidently written in connection with his proposed USA tour), he said, "I was informed very late at night by telephone that the German pilot . . . wished to see me" (PRO, INF1/912).

p. 77 Rudolf Hess, chapter: "Der Flug", written May–June 1947, publ. in Ilse Hess, op. cit., 82ff.

p. 77 Report by Commander, Glasgow Area, 6.6.41, to HQ Scottish Command, in PRO, WO199/3288A.

p. 77 Abbotsinch: "Extract from Duty officer's report for night of 10–11.5.41, 14th (H.D.) Bn A. & S. H. Headquarters, Paisley", in PRO, WO199/3288A.

p. 77 Report by OC, 3 Bn, loc. cit.

p. 77 footnote I suspect that the lists include the letter that Hess brought for the Duke (or even one for the King). However, files on court-martial proceedings are routinely kept closed; not that 3288A makes any reference at all to any such disciplinary actions.

p. 78 The Hess–Donald exchanges are described in a letter from Graham Donald, of Craig & Donald Ltd, Machine Tool Makers, Glasgow, to "Sir Harry" (his superior), 19.5.41, 2 pp. manuscript, in IWM, Misc. papers collection. And in "Report by O.C. 3rd Bn Renfrewshire Home Guard of the Incidents of the Nights 10–11.5.41" (PRO, WO199/3288A). The Donald episode was also recounted often by Hess (in Scott diary, Camp Z, and in Ilse Hess, op. cit., 89: "Ein Major . . . sagte dann in tadellosem Deutsch, ich sähe genau wie Rudolf Heß aus. Er sei . . . oft im Zirkus Krone gewesen").

p. 78 Map found: Eden cited by *Times* journalist A. L. Kennedy, diary, 11.6.41 (Churchill College archives, LKEN24).

p. 78 Capt. Anthony C. White, Staff Captain A, Night Duty Officer, report re: German POW captured night 10–11.5.41 (PRO, WO199/3288A, dated 15.5.41).

p. 78 Report by Col. R. Firebrace in Scottish Command files PRO, WO199/3288A. Col. J. P. Duke of Glasgow Area stated on 18.5.41: "The R.A.F. Intelligence at Turnhouse appeared to be in no hurry to interview the prisoner but two other RAF officers from Ayr turned up promptly at the scene of the crash" (ibid.).

p. 79 Evidently disciplinary proceedings were contemplated against Lt Fulton. The file contains letters on this episode. Letter Major James Barrie to OC 3 Bn HG Renfrewshire, 11.5.41; Second Lt B. Fulton, "Report on the arrival of Hauftmann [*sic*] Alfred Horn to Maryhill Bks", 11.5.41; report by Lt F. E. Whitby to OC 11 Bn The Cameronians (Scottish Rifles), 11.5.41 ("At no time did the Duty Officer [Fulton] pay Major Barrie the usual compliments") (PRO, WO199/3288A).

p. 80 Major C. W. Greenhill, RAMC OC Reception Station, Maryhill Barracks, Glasgow NW, "Report on Prisoner Hess", 15.5.41 (PRO, WO199/3288A).

p. 81 Cadogan recorded this episode in this diary thus, 11.5.41: "5.30 Addis rang me up with this story: a German pilot landed near Glasgow, asked for the Duke of Hamilton. Latter so impressed that he is flying to London & wants to see me at No. 10 tonight. . . . Half hour later heard P.M. was sending to meet His Grace at airfield and wd bring him to Chequers [*sic*]."

p. 81 The quotations are from the Duke's second report, "Additional Notes", loc. cit.

p. 82 General Karl Bodenschatz in conversation with Milch *et al.*, 20.5.45 CSDIC (UK) report SRGG1236(C), in PRO, WO208/4170; and in interview with author, 30.11.70.

p. 82 Hildegard Fath, affidavits Hess-13. loc. cit.

p. 82 Prof. Messerschmitt, USSBS interrogation, 11–12.5.45.

p. 82 Note that Hewel diary refers to letters, 13.5.41.

p. 82 Cf. Halder diary, 15.5.41.

p. 82 Ilse Hess, op. cit., 78.

p. 82 Hans Frank addressing his staff, 19.5.41, Gedächtnisprotokoll 21.5.41 CO, IWM, AL2525.

p. 82 Letter G. Schäfer to Pg. Wagner [Gauleiter Wagner?], 7.6.41; SHAEF PWD report DE404/DIS202, in HL.

p. 82 Walter Darré, interrogation X-P/5, of 16.5.45.

p. 83 Drive to Dytchley Park: diary of John Martin, 9.5.41, WSC's private secretary (copy in author's possession).

p. 83 Luftwaffe extract: Fighter Command War Room Log, entry for 10–11.5.41, reports by DAC at 1907 and 1945 hrs (PRO, AIR16/698).

p. 83 Sir Joseph Ball, Chamberlain's chief accomplice, was the main villain who ordered these wiretaps.

p. 83 Anthony Eden, *The Reckoning* (London), 255. quoting Eden's diary, 12.5.41.

p. 84 Medical Quarterly Report, Military Hospital Drymen, 22.7.41 (PRO, WO222/885).

p. 84 Undated memo, "Security – at Drymen Hospital" (PRO, PREM3/219/7).

p. 84 Letter of "Doctor at Military Hosp.", Drymen, 15.5., Postal Censorship Reports, 27.5.41: "Report on the Arrival of Hess (Cont'd)" "No. 2" (No. 1 is not in file at PRO) (PRO, INF1/912).

p. 84 Brendan Bracken described the scene in a US speech, *The Times*, 28.8.43, and fourth leader article, 13.9.43. John Hamilton, WSC's secretary, kept a diary , and refers to the episode on 11.5.41.

p. 85 Hamilton, "Additional Notes", loc. cit.

p. 85 Eden on photographs: Eden, op. cit., 255, diary.

p. 85 Churchill appointment diary, 12.5.41, in possession of the author.

p. 85 Hamilton, "Additional Notes", loc. cit.

p. 85 Beaverbrook on photographs: described by Beaverbrook to Hess, in their conversation on 9.9.41.

p. 85 Ivone Kirkpatrick, *The Inner Circle* (London, 1959), ch. vii: "Hess 1941".

p. 86 Hamilton, "Additional Notes", loc. cit.

p. 86 Prime Minister's timings from Churchill appointment card, in author's possession.

p. 86 Private Secretary's handwritten note in PM's files (PRO, PREM3/219/4, undated).

p. 86 Handwritten summaries of Deutschlandsender and D., 20.00 [hrs] in PM's files (PRO, PREM 3/219/4). German texts are in the papers of Gen. d. Polizei Kurt Daluege, marked in handwriting, "Herrn Gen. d. Pol. Daluege", entitled "Uberwachung ausländischer Rundfunksender" (i.e. German monitoring of BBC etc. broadcasts), in BA, Slg Schumacher, /236.

p. 86 Diaries of Eden and Cadogan, 12–13.5.41, op. cit.

p. 86 Churchill's draft statement, PRO, PREM3/219/4. It clearly assumed in advance that Kirkpatrick would identify the aviator as Hess as the closing sentence (omitted from published version) said: "Accordingly an officer of the Foreign Office who was closely acquainted with Hess before the war was sent up by aeroplane to see him in hospital. He reports that the German officer in question is undoubtedly Rudolf Hess. As soon as he is recovered from his injury his statement will be carefully examined." First statement as issued is in PRO, FO371/26565.

p. 87 Hamilton, "Additional Notes", loc. cit.

p. 87 A. C[adogan] memo on 'phone call from Kirkpatrick, 13.5.41, 10.50 a.m. (PRO, PREM3/219/7).

p. 87 footnote Report by Lt-Col. J. Gibson Graham to Glasgow Area, 13.5.41 (PRO, PREM3/219/7); and telegram Maj.-Gen. i/c Administration, Scottish Command, 14.5.41 (PRO, WO199/3288A).

p. 88 Gibson Graham report, 13.5.41.

p. 88 Special mission: Gibson Graham report, quoted in Rees, op. cit., 15.

p. 88 A. C[adogan] account of 'phone call from Kirkpatrick, 13.5.41, 10.50 a.m. (3 pp.) (PRO, PREM3/219/7).

p. 89 Churchill, personal minute No. M540/1, to Eden, 13.5.41, in PRO, PREM3/219/7.

p. 90 "D"-notice is mentioned in unpublished private diary of Cecil King, editor of *Daily Mirror*, 13.5.41 (Univ. of Boston, Mass.).

p. 90 Berlin announcement: see e.g. Transocean in English 14.5 in PRO, PREM3/219/4 and other BBC Monitor Report intercepts. And Press Flash to Brit. United Press from NY, 14.5: "German authorised documents left behind [by] Hess revealed wanted meet Duke Hamilton attempt effect GermEnglish peace" (PRO, INF1/912).

p. 90 Telegram J. G. Winant to State Dept, #1907, 9 p.m. 13.5 (NA, US St. Dept, conf. file 862.00/4016).

p. 90 New York telegrams in PRO and INF1/912.

p. 90 Memoranda by James H. Rowe Jr of White House Staff to FDR and to Missy LeHand, FDR's secretary, 14.5.41, on FDRL microfilm of messages WSC–FDR, Film #1, pp.00242f. Unfortunately, very few transcripts of these conversations survive in the archives.

p. 90 Well-wishers: Memo E. S. H[erbert] to Duff Cooper, 15.4.41, enclosing first telegrams for Hess intercepted by Censors. Rosen cabled: "Kindest Regards of Good Wishes". "Courage"-text was telegram from Hugh Latham, New Haven, Conn. (PRO, INF1/912).

p. 91 Maria Theresia Medal: he had discussed this with Ilse a few days before (Ilse Hess, op. cit.).

p. 91 Lord Provost speech: cf. A. L. Kennedy diary, Churchill College, Cambridge (LKEN24), 11.6.41.

p. 91 Hess's requests: Letter Col. J. P. Duke, for Maj.-Gen. i/c Administration Scottish Command, to Under Secretary of State, PW1, 15.5.41, in PRO, WO199/3288A.

p. 91 Kirkpatrick and Hamilton: "Record of an Interview with Herr Hess on May 14", 15.5.41 (ND, M118 (=GB-271)).

p. 91 Sheppard: letter Hunter to Churchill, 15.5.41, endorsed "WSC, 15.5."; and Hunter, "Report on the Custody and Movements of Rudolph Hess", 14–20.5.41; 22.5.41 (PRO, PREM3/219/7).

p. 91 Gentleman: letter Hunter to J. Peck, WSC's secretary, 17.5.41 (ibid.).

p. 92 Propaganda: FO circular Weekly News Guidance No. 18, 14.5.41, confidential (PRO, FO371/26565). The telegram sent by the Dominions Office to the UK High Commissioners in Canada, etc., 19.15 hrs, 13.5.41, had said the same: "Hess appeared [to Kirkpatrick] to be completely calm and collected and gave no sign of insanity" (ibid.). And William Lyon Mackenzie King diary, 11–17.5.41 (Public Archives of Canada, Ottawa).

p. 93 Cadogan diary, 14.5.41.

p. 93 Eden, op. cit., 256, diary: 14.5.41.

p. 93 Letter Duff Cooper to Churchill, 15.5.41 (PRO, PREM3/219/7). Churchill noted on it: "Wait a few days, he is on the move. WSC, 16.5."

p. 93 Mytchett Place: Hunter letters to Number 10 (WSC and his secretaries), 15.5, and Report, 22.5.41 (PRO, PREM3/219/7).

p. 93 Cabinet discussion: Cadogan diary, 15.5.41; and War Cabinet minutes, 15.5.41, 12 noon, WC50 (41) (PRO, CAB65/18).

p. 93 A. Cadogan minute, handwritten, 15.5.41 (PRO, FO371/26565).

p. 94 Hess to be held as PoW: Cabinet minutes, loc. cit.

p. 94 Cadogan diary, 15.5.41.

p. 94 Two handwritten reports by Maj. Sheppard submitted to Churchill, dated 17.5. and 21.5.41 (PRO, PREM3/219/7).

p. 94 I. A. K[irkpatrick], "Record of a Conversation with Herr Hess on May 15th, 1941", undated (ND, M119 (=GB-272)).

p. 95 Hamilton visit to FO: unpublished portion of Cadogan diary, 15.5.41. Douglas-Hamilton, op. cit., 175, suggests: "On the same day [16 May] Hamilton had been asked to lunch with the King at Windsor. George VI was very curious to know what had happened." Evidently WSC had not informed him at their luncheon on 13 May, therefore. It is unlikely that the Duke would have asked permission of Cadogan if the King *had* "asked" him to lunch.

p. 95 Cadogan diary, 16.5.41.

p. 95 Churchill's minute to Cadogan, 16.5.41, in PRO, PREM3/219/7.

p. 95 Col. R. A. Lennie, OC Military Hospital, Drymen, Special Report, Prisoner of War, No. 3, 17.5.41 (PRO, WO199/3288A).

p. 96 Gibson Graham's report, in Rees, op. cit, 16.

p. 96 Major J. J. Sheppard, "My Impressions of 'X' (Herr Rudolph Hess)", 21.5.41; and his report of 17.5.41 (PRO, PREM3/219/7).

Chapter 7

p. 97 Letter from LM & SR Co. to Col. J. P. Duke, Asst. Adj. General, Headquarters, Scottish Command, Edinburgh, 19.41 (PRO, WO199/3288a 106028). And report by Hunter on Hess's movements 15–21.5.41 op. cit.

p. 97 Sleeping: Sheppard, "Report on the Conduct of 'X'", loc. cit.

p. 97 Ambulance: Sheppard report, loc. cit.

p. 98 Gerlach: Letter Hunter to J. Peck, loc. cit.

p. 98 Letter Rudolf Hess to Ilse Hess, Spandau, 8.1.48 (Ilse Hess, op. cit., 165).

p. 98 Cadogan diary, original text, 18.5.41.

p. 98 Kirkpatrick: Gibson Graham report, loc. cit.

p. 98 Sheppard "Report on the Conduct of 'X'", loc. cit.

p. 98 Rees, op. cit.

p. 98 Draft letter, English text only, found in file of Lt-Col. A. J. B. Larcombe (probably in OMGUS files in USA), and published, without date, etc., in *Sunday Telegraph*, 13.12.81.

p. 99 Sheppard, "My Impressions of 'X'", loc. cit. "To sum up," concluded Sheppard, "he is, I consider, a man lacking in personality, which is only offset by the power invested in him by his Master, and used ruthlessly without regard for the finer instincts of humanity."

p. 99 Hamilton rumours: Letter from Sinclair to Duff Cooper, 22.5.41, PRO, INF1/912.

p. 99 War Cabinet minutes, 5 p.m., 19.5.41, PRO, CAB65/18.

p. 100 Cadogan diary, original text, 1.5.41.

p. 100 Ibid., 19.5.41.

p. 100 Eden: Bruce Lockhart diary, quoting Rex Leeper quoting Eden, 28.5.41: "[Hess] wants peace – We are to have a pseudo-negotiator, Lord Simon." *The Diaries of Sir Robert Bruce Lockhart*, vol. ii: *1939–1945* (London, 1984).

p. 100 House of Commons Debates, Hansard, extract dated 22.5.41, in PRO, FO371/26565.

p. 100 Personal note by Lt-Col. A. H. C. Swinton, in 1941 commanding Pirbright Camp; in A. M. Scott Papers, IWM [a diary of events 17.5–20.5.41].

p. 102 Diary of Lt-Col. A. M. Scott 16.5.41– Feb. 42, in IWM, Scott papers.

p. 102 Hunter report, loc. cit.

p. 102 The Scott diary lists these three Companions on the title page as "attendants", identifies Foley in an index as Major F. Foley, CMG (MI6); states that Capt. "Barnes" "returned to duty with M.I." on 19 June and that Lt-Col. "Wallace" "returned to duty at Cockfosters" on 20 June. In the diary of Sir Robert Bruce Lockhart (of SO1) under 28.5.41 is Eden's statement that "Hess is becoming disillusioned and more useful – now being examined by Kendrick and Foley. [Has] been shown what Germans say about him. Wants peace . . ." (Bruce Lockhart, op. cit., 101).

p. 103 Christopher Andrew, *On His Majesty's Secret Service: The Making of the British Intelligence Community* (New York), 347, 349, 379f., 395f.

p. 103 Foley, Maj. Francis Edward, CMG 1941, b. Somerset 24.11.1884, died 8.5.1958; m. Katharine Eva 1921, one daughter. Capt. (mentioned in despatches) in France 1914–18; PCO Berlin 1920–39; PCO Scandinavia 1939–40; recommissioned 1940, attached to C.-in-C. Norwegian Forces in the Field 1940, ret'd 1949.

Chapter 8

p. 104 "Mytchett Place, a Short History and List of Occupants", 1780–1960.

p. 109 This is known from Sir Robert Bruce-Lockhart's diary.

p. 109 The diaries of A. Leo Kennedy, *The Times* diplomatic correspondent, are in Churchill College, Cambridge (LKEN24). Eden repeated the phrase about Hess being "very serious" on 11.6.41 (ibid.).

p. 109 Records of Swinton Committee meetings are in RG84, US Embassy in London records.

p. 109 Minute by Melville on Sinclair file, PRO, AIR19/564.

p. 114 Typescript of Churchill's draft statement to the House (not used), in PRO, PREM3/219/4.

p. 114 Rees, John Rawlings, CBE 1946. b. 25.6.1890, d. 11.4.1969; 116 Bickenhall Mansions, Baker St, W1. Data from *Who Was Who* and *The Medical Directory*.

p. 114 Dicks, Henry Victor, b. 27.4.1900, Pernau, Estonia; d. 12.7.77. He became adviser to the British Army on German morale, was with SHAEF on psychological warfare, and with the Control Commission on German personnel. See obituary by J. D. Sutherland in *Bulletin of the Royal College of Psychiatrists*, October 1977, pp.6f. Wartime papers by Dicks include "The Psychological Foundation of the Wehrmacht" (PRO, WO241/1); "The German Deserter: A Psychiatric Study" (WO241/2), and "National Socialism as a Psychiatric Problem" (WO241/6).

p. 115 "Hess's Version of Events", written *c.* June 1945, published in English by J. Bernard Hutton, in *Hess: The Man and His Mission* (New York, 1970), 136.

p. 117 Fear of German émigré: as Hess himself stated a few days later to Dicks.

This and the previous page are closely based on Major Dicks's initial report on this first meeting with Hess, in Rees, op. cit., 28ff.

p. 119 Letter Eden to Simon, 27.5.41, in BL, Ms. Simon 88.

p. 119 Minute Eden to Churchill, 27.5.41, in PRO, PREM3/219/7.

p. 120 Letter Eden to Simon, 28.5.41, in BL, Ms. Simon 88.

p. 120 Letter Eden to Simon, handwritten, 28.5.41, in BL, Ms. Simon 88.

p. 120 Cadogan diary, original text.

p. 121 Memorandum by A. C[adogan] to Prime Minister, 6.6.41 in PRO, PREM3/219/7.

p. 122 Major H.V. Dicks, report, quoted in Rees, op. cit., 37f. His chronology appears to be from memory; I have adjusted it to the Commandant's diary.

p. 123 There were two "witnesses" to the Hess–Simon talks referred to in the documents, Kurt Maass and Dr E. Semelbauer, both asked for by Hess on 15.5.41 from Huyton Internment Camp, Liverpool. There were difficulties afterwards in repatriating them in view of what they knew.

Chapter 9

p. 124 The watch, linen: referred to by Dicks as evidence of Hess's schizophrenic nature (Rees, op. cit.).

p. 124 Gilbert, op. cit., gives the documents on Austrian-born Sir Henry Strakosch; I found the Last Will & Testament in *The Times*, 1.2.44.

p. 124 Summary liquidation: Simon signed the Cabinet document submitted to Truman (and given to R. H. Jackson, chief US prosecutor at Nuremberg) recommending the execution without trial of the main Nazi leaders. (Copy in NA, RG238, Jackson papers.)

p. 124 Handwritten slip from J. M. M[artin] to PM, 9.6.41 (PRO, PREM3/219/7).

p. 124 Thompson biography of Desmond Morton; and Morton's (heavily pruned) files in the PRO.

p. 124 Morton's role as mole: in Gilbert, op. cit.; also several minutes by him in PRO, FO371 series. He was chief of IIC, the Industrial Intelligence Centre, which became a forerunner of SOE.

p. 125 Minute from Morton to PM, 9.6.41. It seems Morton had been asked to make recommendations on future treatment and propaganda uses of Hess (PRO, PREM3/219/7).

p. 125 Rudolf Hess, Basis for an Understanding, translation dated 10.6.41. Mentioned by Simon in his paper of 10.6.41 as having been prepared by Hess in advance and handed to him during their meeting of 9.6.41 (PRO, PREM3/219/7). There was a postscript about Iraq, about which "the Führer declared solely that Iraq must not be abandoned" (by the German cause).

p. 125 Verbatim German and English transcript of the meeting between "Dr Guthrie" (Simon), "Dr Mackenzie" (Kirkpatrick), "Jonathan" (Hess), German witness (Maass), "Captain Barnes" (interpreter), Lieutenant Reade (Secretary), 9.6.41, 14.30–17.30 hrs, "No. 28" in PRO, PREM3/219/5.

There is a note in Churchill's file saying that the other Part will follow (it is not in his file, however). Further extracts are printed as Document Hess-15 in *IMT*.

In Box 88 of Viscount Simon's private papers, now in BL, I found a blue carbon copy ("Copy No. 2") of the entire transcript (78 pages) and of the subsequent 9-page transcript (No. 29) of Hess's private talk in English with Simon beginning at 17.30 hrs.

p. 126 "You know I am [the Lord Chancellor]": in original, "Dr Guthrie" (but obviously Hess knew who Simon was).

p. 128 The book Hess had read would have been J. A. Farrer, *England Under Edward VII*.

p. 135 Lord Chancellor, Most Secret: Rudolf Hess – Preliminary Report. [Initialled] "S. 10.6.41," Marked "top of the box", and "read, WSC" (PRO, PREM3/219/7).

p. 136 Genuine effort: Lord Simon wrote, "One proof that Hess is merely trying to reproduce what he has heard from Hitler is that Hess breaks down as soon as he is asked for details" (ibid.).

p. 136 Prime Minister's Personal Minute No. M645/1 to Foreign Secretary, 14.6.41, in PRO, PREM3/219/5.

p. 136 German invasion of Soviet Union: in fact Eden briefed Soviet Ambassador Maisky in general terms on 14.6.41.

Göring had informed Birger Dahlerus in several stages, first about "Barbarossa" (telegram Mallett to FO, Stockholm, 9.6.41) then about the date on 15.6.41.

p. 136 Letter from Desmond Morton, on 10 Downing St paper, to H[enry] L. d'A. Hopkinson at the FO, 13.6.41; significantly in Lord Beaverbrook's papers, HLRO, file D443.

p. 136 Cadogan diary, 11.6.41.

p. 137 Suicide attempt: based on the rationale as set out by Rudolf Hess in his memorandum to Lord Beaverbrook, 5.9.41 (Beaverbrook papers, HLRO, file, D443).

p. 138 Rudolf Hess to Adolf Hitler, date not stated [June 1941], cited in Rees, op. cit., 44.

p. 140 Malone wrote an immediate transcript of the conversation from memory, partly in recorded speech; it is in the Scott diary.

p. 142 Cadogan diary, original text.

p. 142 Dicks, in Rees, op. cit., 46.

p. 142 The most reliable account of the suicide attempt is in the immediate written report by Lt-Col. Scott to Col. N. Coates, DDPW, on 16.6.41 (copy in Scott diary).

p. 142 Dicks's account is in Rees, op. cit., 47ff.

p. 142 Hess gave his version of the suicide attempt in several later conversations, among others with Malone, Beaverbrook etc.

Chapter 10

p. 143 Letter Scott to Coates, loc. cit.

p. 143 Dicks, in Rees, op. cit., 48ff.

p. 144 Cadogan diary, 16.6.41.

p. 147 Scott diary, 18.6.41.

p. 148 Letter from Col. J. R. Rees, "Consultant in Psychological Medicine to the Army", 3 Devonshire Place, W1, to DDPW [Coates], 19.6.41. He added: "The decision to allow him news is, I think, very wise. It may help to make him rather more co-operative and biddable. . . ." From this letter is seems that Major Dicks came under DGAMS (PRO, PREM3/219/3).

p. 149 The orderlies' daily reports contain a wealth of intimate data on Hess's excretory functions, which are not reproduced here but would be of significance for a psychiatrist; Dicks believed that Hess was unduly concerned with his bodily functions, and that it was possible to draw psychiatric conclusions from this.

p. 149 In editing the orderlies' diaries, I have corrected obvious spelling errors and improved the punctuation, but I have not denoted omissions (. . .) unless of major passages. The logic behind including seemingly trivial episodes is (a) Hess was not out of supervision at any moment; (b) nobody could have switched this Rudolf Hess for another one without these worthy gentlemen spotting it. I have, however, given instances where there *do* seem to be symptoms of schizophrenic behaviour or hallucinations (on which see Dicks, in Rees, op. cit. 52).

p. 151 Libel: Minute WSC to Secretary of State for War, 22.6.41, replying to latter's minute of 21.6.41 (PRO, PREM3/219/3). And Sinclair to Hamilton 21.6.41, and other correspondence in Sinclair's Private Office file, "Duke of Hamilton, Allegations concerning Rudolph Hess" (PRO, AIR19/564).

p. 152 ORB, RAF Turnhouse, 23–24.6.41 in PRO, AIR28/861; and appendices, AIR28/864.

p. 152 Letter Sinclair to Churchill, 26.6.41 (PRO, AIR19/564).

p. 158 The following pages are constructed from "2nd Lieut. W. B. Malone's report, Statements made by Z in the Course of Conversations 13–14 July 1941", in Scott diary.

Chapter 11

p. 165 Johnston, Munro Kennedy, [1940:] Surrey County Mental Hospital, Brook-wood, Woking, Surrey. Data from *The Medical Directory*.

p. 171 All this is in the deposition of Rudolf Hess, of which a handwritten copy in English is in the Scott diary and a typed copy in the Beaverbrook file, HI.RO.

p. 171 Johnston, contribution to Rees, op. cit., 60f.

p. 171 Capt. Munro Johnston, report on Rudolf Hess, handwritten copy in Scott diary.

p. 172 Dicks report, handwritten copy in Scott diary.

p. 172 German syntax: *"es gibt"*=there is.

p. 172 Rudolf Hess, "Deutschland-England unter dem Gesichtswinkel des Krieges gegen die Sowjet-Union" ("Lord Beaverbrook übergeben 9.9.41") in Beaverbrook file dated 6.9.41 (HLRO, D443); and handwritten English translation in Scott diary (which I have not always followed here), dated 7.8.41.

p. 176 Col. J. R. Rees, "The Future of 'Z'", 22.8.41, in Scott diary.

p. 178 Beaverbrook's opposition to the war is evident from various letters in the Beaverbrook files.

p. 178 Cadogan diary, original text, 2.9.41.

p. 178 Letter Rudolf Hess to Lord Beaverbrook, 4.9.41, in Beaverbrook papers, HLRO, D443.

p. 180 [Transcript] Most Secret, bedroom No. 98, Dr Livingstone and Jonathan, 19.30 hrs, 9.9.41, in Beaverbrook papers, HLRO, D443. Significantly, Beaverbrook told Hess (p. 9), "I've been meaning to write to you for some time." And (p. 15): "I look at the English with a very detached eye. I am, as you know, a Canadian."

Chapter 12

p. 185 Rudolf Hess, Statement and Protest, Appendix I, 18.9.41 (Beaverbrook papers, HLRO, D443).

p. 187 Rudolf Hess, Statement of Evidence and Protest, 5.9.41 [translation into English], signed in his own hand, with typed insertions dated 14 and 30.9.41 (Beaverbrook papers, HLRO, D443).

p. 187 German casualties: *The Times*, 20.9.41.

p. 189 Letter Rudolf Hess to Prof. Dr Fr. Gerl, of Hindelang, Allgäu, 29.9.41, forwarded by Himmler to Bormann on 13.4.42 (NA film T175/125/9926, 9934f.).

p. 191 Minute from Desmond Morton to Churchill, 28.7.41, in PRO, PREM3/219/2.

p. 191 There had been a major reshuffle at Hobart House. Visiting there on 16.9.41 Lt-Col. A. M. Scott learned that the entire PoW Directorate – Gen. Sir Alan Hunter, Gen. Sir Oswald Barrett and Col. N. Coates – had all resigned.

p. 193 Letter Cadogan to Beaverbrook, 1.11.41, and dictated comments by Beaver-brook in his file D433 (HLRO).

p. 194 [Record of] conference at the Foreign Office on 29.10.41, 16.00 hrs, attended by Cadogan, Loxley, Sir G. Thomas, Maj.-Gen. Gepp, Lt-Col. Scott, Col. Rees, Capt. Johnston, Brig. Stuart Menzies, Major F. Foley. Cf. Johnston, in Rees, op. cit., 61.

p. 194 Only English text available.

p. 195 Documents of Bayer. Staatsministerium für Unterricht und Kultus, in BA, Slg Schumacher, /236; Vertraul. Informationen v. 7.9.41 (ibid.).

p. 197 This 1945 recollection is "Hess's Version of Events" as printed in Hutton, op. cit., 131. "Translated by an American at Nuremberg".

p. 197 Scott diary, 1–2.12.41.

p. 201 Thurnheer report in Swiss archives, Berne.

Chapter 13

p. 208 Rees 'phone call: Scott diary, 18.2.42. Shortly after this entry the Scott diary ends, with his transfer to the Isle of Man. Chronological entries after this are mostly from the orderlies' reports in Suitland archives.

p. 209 Rees's report, quoted (without date) in Rees, op. cit., 64.

p. 212 Thurnheer report in Swiss archives, Berne.

p. 213 Letter from A. E[den] to WSC, 20.5.42, in PRO, PREM3/219/7.

p. 214 Churchill broadcast, 10.5.42; printed in full in *The Times*, 11.5.42, under headline: "MR CHURCHILL ON GROWING AIR OFFENSIVE. 'NOW IS THE TIME TO STRIKE'."

Chapter 14

p. 216 Capt. Johnston, in his report in Rees, op. cit., 66, states that the journey to Wales was on 25.6.42; Dr Ellis Jones also stated in his report that Hess was admitted to Maindiff Court on 25.6.42. The orderlies' reports are consistent in stating he arrived at 15.45 hrs on 26.6.41; Eden's October 1942 letter to WSC makes plain that 26.6.42 is the correct date of admission.

p. 216 Ellis Jones, David, died 1967; author, "Rudolf Hess, a Problem in Forensic Psychiatry". Data in *The Medical Directory*.

p. 216 Rubber stamp: described in ND, Hess-15.

p. 216 Military strengths: table in PRO, FO371/46777.

p. 217 "Hess's Version of Events", written at Maindiff Court, in Hutton, op. cit., 146.

p. 218 Minute Eden to PM, 8.10.42, initialled "WSC, 12.x." and marked "(seen by Major Morton)" (PRO, PREM3/219/7).

p. 220 There is no reference to Rees in the orderlies' daily reports on 4.8.42.

p. 221 Thurnheer report in Swiss archives, Berne.

p. 221 "Hess's Version of Events", in Hutton, op. cit.

p. 221 Thurnheer report in Swiss archives, Berne.

p. 223 Author's correspondence with Cadw, Welsh Historic Monuments, 1986–7, and with Mr Hodges at White Castle.

p. 223 Article in *News Chronicle*, 20.12.44; [The Old Codgers] Live Letters in the *Daily Mirror*, 5.2.45; and correspondence between Col. Evelyn Smith (War Office) and P. N. Loxley (FO), 30.12.44 and attached minutes in PRO, FO371/46777.

p. 223 Letter Rudolf Hess to Ilse Hess, Spandau, 23.1.49 (Ilse Hess, op. cit., 191).

p. 224 Brig. J. R. Rees, Consulting Psychiatrist to the Army, report to DPW, Most Secret, 29.9.41. Forwarded by Eden to WSC, Oct. 1942 (PRO, PREM3/219/7).

p. 226 Article in *Pravda*, 19.10.42; Reuter telex summarizing, and minutes by G. M. Wilson, F. K. Roberts *et al.* in PRO, FO371/33036.

p. 226 Clark Kerr's views: in telegram 262 to FO, 19.10.42, in PRO, PREM3/219/6, with WSC handwritten minute quoted, 21.10.

p. 227 War Cabinet meeting in PM's Room at House of Commons, 20.10.42, 12 noon; item 1 has been blanked out; item 2 was Hess (PRO, CAB65/28).

p. 228 Clark Kerr, telegram 280 to FO, 25.10.42, in PRO, FO371/33036.

p. 228 Eden opposed: FO to Clark Kerr, telegram 313, 30.10.42, in ibid.

p. 228 War Cabinet meeting at 10 Downing St., 26.10.42, item 2, in PRO, CAB65/28.

p. 228 War Cabinet meeting at 10 Downing St., 29.10.42, in ibid.

p. 228 War Cabinet meeting at 10 Downing St., 4.11.42, in ibid.

p. 228 FO [initialled by F. K. Roberts] to Clark Kerr, telegram 331, 4.11.42, instructing him to deliver statement included in No. 332 (PRO, FO371/30920).

p. 229 footnote Cripps, "Facts as Regards Herr Hess' Arrival in Great Britain so far as known to His Majesty's Government", draft dated 2.11.42 (PRO, FO371/30920).

p. 231 Clark Kerr to FO, telegrams 1444 and 1445 (Stalin "revealed surprising anxiety lest Hess should be sent home at the end of the war"), 6.11.42 (PRO, FO371/30920).

p. 231 Letter Rudolf to Ilse Hess, published 24.11.42.

p. 231 Stott's and Rees's visit is confirmed by the orderly's record book, 26.10.42: "occupied himself writing until he received visitors, Gen. Stott and Brig. Rees, who stayed with him for a while; during the cleaning up of his room food from his dinner the previous night was found concealed in paper behind the curtains."

p. 232 Supplement by Cripps to WP(42)520, "The Facts about Rudolf Hess", 10.11.42; quoting Rees's general conclusions, dated 6.11.42 (cf. Rees, op. cit., 75f.) (PRO, PREM3/219/6).

p. 232 FO to Lord Halifax, telegram 7227, 20.11.42; initialled by Cadogan, 19.11.42 (PRO, FO371/); the attached summary was taken by Halifax to FDR, and is in PSF file Great Britain; handed to FDR at Halifax's luncheon with him on 8.12.42 (FDR appointment diary), FDRL; cf. letter Halifax to FDR, 9.3.43, in PRO, FO115/3544.106028.

p. 233 Letters from Lord Halifax to President Roosevelt, 9.3.43 and 30.6.43 (stating that they had also gone to Mr Stalin in this form) in PRO, FO115/3544.106028).

Chapter 15

p. 234 Major Ellis Jones, report on "J", 14.1.43, in Rees, op. cit., 76f. Ellis Jones begins, "I beg to submit a report on 'J' since your last visit on 26.10.42." However, Rees also saw Hess on 10.1.43, according to the orderly reports.

p. 234 Socks: this is based on Ellis Jones's report of 14.1.43. The only reference in the orderlies' records is on 2.2.43, however: "Complained that someone had torn one of his socks while he was taking his morning toilet."

p. 234 Orderly's report, 22.12.42.

p. 237 Letter Rudolf Hess to Ilse Hess, 14.2.43 (Ilse Hess, op. cit., 95f.).

p. 237 Letter Rudolf Hess to Ilse Hess, 26.3.43 (ibid., 96f.).

p. 241 SS-Obersturmführer Günther Sorof had been Hess's adjutant. On 2 March 1943 he was released from Sachsenhausen concentration camp and sent to the front. (BDC file.)

p. 241 And letters in BDC, files on Alfred Leitgen (b. 1.9.02), Karl-Heinz Pintsch (b. 3.6.09), and Laura Schrödl (b. 26.2.15).

p. 241 Letters from Reichsschatzmeister Schwarz to Reichsleiter M. Bormann, 3.4, and replies, 11.4, 17.4.43 (BA, Slg Schumacher, /236).

p. 242 An FO minute dated 22.9.43 states that an officer was arrested for talking to the *Daily Mail*, and was to be court-martialled. The only officer whose name vanishes from the orderly report books at this time was Lt May. One item has been withdrawn from the PRO file, presumably about the court martial: C14797/5311/18.

p. 243 *Daily Mail* article, 1.9.41: "THE STORY ALL BRITAIN HAS AWAITED. THE DAILY LIFE OF HESS IN PRISON CAMP: HOW HE ACTS, TALKS AND THINKS". The FO minutes by P. N. Loxley, F. K. Roberts, W. Strang, O. Sargent, A. Eden are in PRO, FO371/34484. Loxley stated that locals knew Hess was there (though some believed it was Arnim, not Hess).

p. 243 War Cabinet meeting, 2.9.43, 11.30 a.m., in PRO, CAB65/35.

p. 243 *The Times*, 13.9.41, leading article, p. 5, col. 4.

p. 243 War Cabinet meeting, 20.9.43, 5.30 p.m., in PRO, CAB65/28.

p. 243 Letter R. I. Campbell, British Embassy, Washington, to Cordell Hull, 21.9.43, in US St. Dept file 862.00/4469, enclosing letter R. I. Campbell to FDR, 21.9.43 (PRO, FO115/3544).

p. 243 Eden made his statement on 22.9.43: cf. *The Times*, 23.9.43, p. 2, col. 4.

p. 244 There is a long report by the orderly, in Suitland diaries, on the visit by the Swiss Minister, 27.11.43, but no detail of what was discussed.

p. 245 Thurnheer report in Swiss archives, Berne.

p. 245 Report by Brigadier J. R. Rees, 3.2.44 (in Rees, op. cit.).

Chapter 16

p. 248 Lt-Col. H. V. Dicks, report to Brig. Rees, 3.3.44, in Rees, op. cit., 80ff.

p. 251 Last Word statement, prepared for delivery at IMT, but cut short before he could read it out. Cf. Bird, op. cit., 23ff.

p. 252 Dicks report, 10.5.44, and appendix: "Full Medical Notes on Evipan Narcosis Administered at Maindiff Court on May 7th, 1944" (Rees, op. cit., 87ff.).

p. 254 Evipan: the notes taken by Dicks on 7.5.44 and attached as an appendix (pp. 87ff.) to his report of 10.5.44, refer to Evipan injection. Rees himself in the text of his book (p. 70) stated: "Permission was obtained from the War Office to make an attempt during the injection of intravenous pentothal to elicit . . ." etc.

Chapter 17

p. 257 [Text, with original errors:] *Keine Injektionen mehr!* Die erste Injektionen haben das Gestadtnis in keiner Weise gebessert dafür grosche nervosität hervorgerufin. Bei Beantwortung der während der Experiments gestellter Fragen hat bewiesen, daß das Gedächtnis doch vorhanden und nur vorübergehend gestörtist. Dir Arzte sind rüberzeugt daß es in Deutschland wiederkehrt also keine Sorge und Aufregung wenn das Gedächtnis augenblick – wen noch so schlecht ist und Du sogar Personen nicht wiedererkennst die Du vorher schon einmal gesehen hast.
Auf alle Falle
Keine 2te Injektion!

p. 259 The saga with the underpants began on 8.4.45 (Sgt Everatt: "[Hess] wanted me to write a statement that I had seen the powder flying as he beats them on his wardrobe door. He appeared to be very sarcastic. I did not write a statement").

p. 261 Specialists in Switzerland: referred to by Hess in his Maindiff Court manuscript, cf. Hutton, op. cit., 159.

p. 261 Rees report, 19.12.44, in Rees, op. cit., 91, and Swiss files, Berne.

p. 264 Captain Benjamin Hurewitz (US) on 10.11.45 noticed the "scars over the 6th left rib 2″ from the lateral margin on the sternum. The point of maximum impulse of the heart was in the 5th left interspace, ½″ medial to the left nipple line." Rees, op. cit., 136f.

p. 264 Summary of medical record of Hess, prepared by Ellis Jones and Phillips, 4–12.2.45, in Rees, op. cit., 70ff.

p. 264 footnote Abendtafel am Dienstag dem 26. März 1935, in Haushofer papers.

p. 267 Report by Lt-Col. H. V. Dicks, 15.2.45, in Rees, op. cit., 91f.

p. 267 3-page foolscap letter from Rudolf Hess to Ilse Hess, 9.3.45, quoted in Rees, op. cit., 93; and letter to aunt Frau Rothacker in Zürich. Rees agrees, op. cit., 93, "The epistles written in March [1945] are so different in their tone and quality and length as to provide reassuring proof, if it were needed, of the genuineness of what had happened."

p. 268 On 2.4.45 Hess drafted his own dietary instructions to the staff:

1. I request that I be given minced meat every other day (a small quantity) and more vegetables;

2. Vegetable soup on the days that I don't have minced meat; if possible, neither should be made with rotten meat, not smelling of either petroleum or carbolic. No condiments (salt or pepper) to be used.

3. For the evening meal I should like fish and vegetables.

p. 270 From "Hess's Version of Events", in Hutton, op. cit., 161.

p. 271 Hess quoted the two passages from Guenther's *Natural Life* in a letter to Ilse Hess, 21.6.45, adding: "gerade in den ersten tagen des Mai kam ich auf folgende Stellen im Guenther."

p. 271 Letter O. Sargent to PM re Hess, PM/OS/45/101, dated 12.5.45 (PRO, PREM3/219/7).

Chapter 18

p. 277 Minutes of the Second Meeting between British War Crimes Executive and the Representatives of the USA at Church House, Westminster, on 21.6.45 at 10.45 a.m. (LC, R. H. Jackson papers).

p. 277 Rees report, 22.6.45, in Rees, op. cit.

p. 277 Letter R. H. Jackson to Dr Millet, 23.6.45, in LC, R. H. Jackson papers, box 107, file: "Psychiatric and Personality Studies of Nazi Leaders".

p. 278 The long-suffering Dr Ellis Jones had to sign a note for Hess on 9.7.45: "I certify that it is absolutely impossible without my knowledge for Herr Hess to be supplied with poison in his food or medicine. Neither are laxatives or any other form of deleterious matter placed in his food."

p. 278 Letter Ellis Jones to Rees, 19.7.45, in Rees, op. cit.

p. 280 Ellis Jones, in Rees, op. cit., 73f.

p. 280 *The Times*, 12 and 17.9.45.

Chapter 19

p. 282 2-page list by OUSCC, Interrogation Division, Analysis Section: received from Col. J. H. Amen the following material pertaining to Rudolf Hess . . . sgd Counsel, Dr Günther von Rohrscheidt, 19.12.45. On NA, film M1270, roll 6. It agrees closely with the list published at the beginning of Exhibit Hess-15, in *IMT*, vol. xxxx, pp. 279ff.

p. 282 Kelley, op. cit., 26f.

p. 283 US Signals Corps photo Neg. # 111-SC.

p. 283 Testimony of Rudolf Hess, taken at Nuremberg, Germany, on 9.10.45, 1045–1215, by Col. John H. Amen, IGD, OUSCC. Also present: Pfc Richard W. Sonnenfeldt, Interpreter, and Pvt Clair Van Vleck, Court Reporter (NA, film M1270, roll 6).

p. 288 Testimony of Rudolf Hess, taken at Nuremberg, Germany, on 9.10.45, 1430–1510, by Col. John H. Amen, IGD, OUSCC. Also present: Hermann Göring, Dr Karl Haushofer, Fritz [*sic*] von Papen, Ernst [*sic*] Bohle (for the purpose of identification), Pfc Richard W. Sonnenfeldt, Interpreter, and Pvt Clair Van Vleck, Court Reporter (NA film M1270, roll 6).

p. 289 CIOS Evaluation Report #55, 5.6.45, Interrogation of Dr Karl Haushofer (NA, RG226, OSS report XL-11080). I have used especially the documents in Jacobsen, op. cit.

p. 290 For Haushofer's very different view on Walsh, see his letter to Martha 3.10.45 (Jacobsen, op. cit., 438ff.): "The increasing warmth and really touching concern shown by Mentor [i.e. Walsh] reinforce my belief that people don't act like this towards those whom they intend to harm, but only those to whom they intend to benefit."

In his memoirs, written at the end of 1945, Haushofer wrote of the "humanity, goodness and wisdom" that Walsh had displayed and which he had "not expected to encounter on earth ever again. Ever since the finest middle oak of the finest grove of oaks bears the name of Colonel Edmund A. Walsh." He also wrote that on 9 October 1945 he had entrusted himself "to the safekeeping of my chivalrous, great, scientific rival in the U.S.A.," Walsh, at Nuremberg.

For Walsh's *real* intentions towards Haushofer and his account of the confrontation with Hess on 9.10.45: Walsh, "Report on Professor Karl Haushofer of the University of Munich, and the influence of his Geopolitics", prepared for Justice Jackson, Nuremberg, 6.2.46 (original in LC, R. H. Jackson papers, box 104, file: "Individual Responsibility: Karl Haushofer").

p. 291 Haushofer used *Du* the whole time to Hess in the conversation. Once again, I have tidied the English translation.

p. 294 In a summary written for Hofweber on 14.11.45 Haushofer referred to this meeting with his friend as one of "the most painful impressions" in his entire life. (Jacobsen, op. cit., 442n.)

p. 294 Colonel John Harlan Amen, Chief, Interrogation division: interrogation of Hermann Göring, 9.10.45, 15.30–17.00 (NA, film M1270, roll 5).

p. 296 Testimony of Papen, 12.10.45, 14.40–16.10, by Mr Thomas J. Dodd (NA, film M1270, roll 14).

p. 296 Jackson Oral History, ch. xxxix, on DI film 87.

p. 297 Conversation held between Hess (Rudolf) and Hermann Göring on Monday, 15.10.45, in room 167, Court House, Nuremberg, Germany, from 14.28 to 15.45. Court Reporter, Frances Karr; Monitor, Richard Sonnenfeldt. On p. 6 occurs the sentence, "(At this point the record was inaudible.)" and p. 9, "Conversation is drowned out by paper rustling and other noises" and "at this stage in the proceedings telephone rings and drowns out all conversation" (NA, film M1270, roll 6).

p. 299 R. H. Jackson: letter to Dr John A. P. Millet, 12.10.45, and memorandum to Ensign William E. Jackson, 12.10.45: both in LC, R. H. Jackson papers, box 107, file: "Psychiatric and Personality Studies of Nazi Leaders", and box 103, file: "Office Files, Jackson, William E.", respectively.

p. 299 Rorschach test: Kelley, op. cit., 28ff.

p. 300 Major Douglas Kelley memo to Commanding Officer, Internal Security Detachment, 16.10.45: "Psychiatric Status of Internee" (LC, R. H. Jackson papers, box 107, file: "Psychiatric and Personality Studies of Nazi Leaders").

p. 301 Relaxing drugs: "I didn't dare approve that," wrote Jackson. "I was afraid that if Hess died within a year or two, no matter what on earth he died of, it would be charged that we had killed him by poison."Oral History, ch. xxxix (DI film 87).

p. 301 Letter from Andrus to Jackson, for Col. Gill, 17.10.45, copy in LC, R. H. Jackson papers.

p. 301 Hess diary, 13.10.45.

p. 301 Letter Col. Gill, CMP, Executive, in OUSCC office, to Andrus, 20.10.1945 (NA, RG238, box 180, file: "Hess"; and LC, R. H. Jackson papers, box 107, file: "Psychiatric and Personality Studies of Nazi Leaders").

p. 302 Statement by Rudolf Hess taken at Nuremberg, Germany, on 19.10.45, 4.46 p.m. to 4.48 p.m., by Colonel John H. Amen, IGB, OUSCC, reporter: Nancy M. Schields, BCV; interpreter: Pfc Richard W. Sonnenfeldt (NA, film M1270, roll 6).

Chapter 20

p. 303 Memo Erich M. Lipman to Lt Blumenstein, "Rudolf Hess correspondence and my visit to Mrs Hess", 29.10.45 (NA, film M1270, roll 6).

p. 304 Hess diary, Oct. 1945 (Bird, op. cit., 36f.).

p. 304 Memo Major Douglas Kelley to Commanding Officer, Internal Security Detachment, 25.10.45, in Burton C. Andrus Papers, folder III (Colorado Springs).

p. 304 Letter W. Donovan to Col. R. G. Storey, Board of Review, 25.10.45, in LC, R. H. Jackson papers, box 107, file: "Psychiatric and Personality Studies of Nazi Leaders".

p. 305 Testimony of Rudolf Hess, taken at Nuremberg, Germany, on 30.10.45, 10.30 a.m. to 12.00 noon by Colonel John H. Amen, IGD, OUSCC. Also present: Major Teich, F.C., Major Kelley, D.M., Pfc Ruppert Waare, Pfc Harold Fredland, Pfc Richard W. Sonnenfeldt, Interpreter; and Frances Karr, Court Reporter (NA, film M1270, roll 6).

p. 308 Jackson, Oral History, ch. xxxix, on DI film 87.

p. 309 Report by Capt. Benjamin Hurewitz, 10.11.45, in Rees, op. cit, 136f.

p. 309 Rohrscheidt's application (not found) was dated 7.11.45.

p. 310 Rohrscheidt's second motion: Der Internationale Militärgerichtshof. Antrag des Verteidigers RA Dr von Rohrscheidt für den Angeklagten Rudolf Heß, 13.11.45 (NA, film M1270, roll 6).

p. 311 Col. B. C. Andrus, Suggestions to Major Kelly [sic] concerning interrogation of Hess, 15.11.45 (Burton C. Andrus papers, folder II).

p. 312 Testimony of Rudolf Hess, Miss Ingeborg Sperr, Miss Hildegard Fath, taken at Nuremberg, Germany, on 16.11.45, 1450–1550, by Col. John Amen, JAGD, OUSCC. Also present: Col. Paul Schroeder, Major Douglas Kelley, Hon. Claude Pepper, senator from Florida, Leo Katz, official interpreter, John H. Murtha, Court Reporter (NA, film M1270, roll 6).

p. 312 Undated transcript, headed: "Translation. Dialogue between Rudolf Hess and his secretary" (ibid.).

Chapter 21

p. 316 Reports on press conferences at Nuremberg courthouse, 9 and 19.11.45 in Burton C. Andrus papers.

p. 316 Kelley, op. cit., 17.

p. 316 Two different typed copies of the "List of Books Hess Read in the Last 10 days", 26.11.45, are in the archives (Burton C. Andrus papers; and NA, RG238, entry 199: HQ Nuremberg Military Post, #6850 Internal Security Detachment: OCCPAC, OCCWC, box 1). The full list is: Lena Christ, *Farmers*; Hans Fitz, *Loisl*; Edgar Wallace, *In the Face of All Europe*; Josef Ziermayr, *The Bruck Farm*; Ernest Claes, *Youth*; Bruno Buergel, *From a Laborer to an Astronomer*; Ludwig Thoma, *The Widower*; Kurt Faber, *With the Knapsack to India*; Kurt Faber, *Globetrotters Last Travels and Adventures*; Otto Ludwig, *Heitherethei*; Margret zur Bentlage, *The Engaged Couple*; Conte Corti, *Refusal to a Prince*; Rudolf Pechel, *Goethe and Goethe's Places*.

p. 317 Letter Ilse Hess to Martha Haushofer, wife of Karl, 14.2.46, in Jacobsen, op. cit., 442.

p. 317 English translation of affidavit of Hildegard Fath, "Memorandum about Rudolf Hess", 20.11.45, in HL, Ms. DD247H3F22 ("Gift of Mrs Douglas Kelley, Oct. 1963").

p. 318 footnote International Herald Tribune, 8.7.1984, section: "Fifty years ago".

• *p. 318* Gustave M. Gilbert, *Nuremberg Diary* (New York, 1947), 35f.

Letter Andrus to Public Relations Officer, War Dept, 6.9.46, re Misconduct of Dr Douglas M. Kelley, former major, Medical Corps. Andrus stated that Kelley served as his prison psychiatrist 21.11.45 [*sic*] to 6.2.46, had more than once been rebuked for violating prison security (granting newspaper interviews), and "left here under more or less of a cloud"; Kelley had granted an interview to an (unknown) Howard Whitman of the London *Sunday Express* published on 25.8.46 reporting verbatim interviews with the IMT prisoners (Burton C. Andrus papers).

p. 320 Jackson, Oral History, ch. xxxix, on DI film 87.

p. 321 Report on Rudolf Hess, telephoned from London, 19.11.45: sgd Moran, Rees, Riddoch (NA, RG238, box 180, "Hess"). Cf. Rees, op. cit., 143 and 217.

p. 321 The French report is not available. Results are referred to in Soviet joint report of 16.11.45, which rather puzzlingly opens with indirect quote of British report (which the British dated the 19th, "telephoned from London"). Rees, op. cit., 143, talks of the report "which Dr Rees and Dr Riddoch prepared and sent through from England", from which it seems Lord Moran was faced with a *fait accompli*.

p. 321 Record of Examination of Rudolf Hess, signed by Krasnushkin, Sepp and Kurshakov, 17.11.45 (NA, RG238, box, 180, "Hess"). Cf. Soviet memorandum to IMT, 17.11.45 (NA, RG238, box 180, file: "Hess"), with appendix (i) conclusions and (ii) report on examination of Hess (as above).

p. 322 American psychiatric commission was Dr Nolan D. C. Lewis of Columbia University; Dr Donald E. Cameron of McGill University; Colonel Paul Schroeder of Chicago (Gilbert, *Nuremberg, Diary*, op. cit., 11).

The three Americans, in this mid-trial report, "Additional Psychiatric Comment on the Rudolf Hess Case", suggested: "That the ten designated scientists came to unanimous conclusions on the main issues involved in the case is proof that the science of psychiatry is sound . . ." (NA, RG238, box 180, "Hess"). The conclusions, however, were *not* unanimous. The Russians had clearly copied the British interim findings, and Lord Moran was press-ganged into agreeing.

p. 322 Memorandum to Brig.-Gen. William L. Mitchell, General Secretary for the IMT, 20.11.45, signed Delay, Lewis, Cameron, Schroeder (NA, RG238, box 180, "Hess").

p. 326 Hess statement, 30.11.45, afternoon session; the text of the simultaneous translation shows a very poor translation job (NA, RG238, box 180, "Hess"). In Burton C. Andrus papers is a better translation of the original document, "Statement before the IMT at Nuremberg delivered on 30.11.45, /s/ Rudolf Hess". I have used this.

Epilogue

p. 327 Haensel, op. cit.

p. 327 R. H. Jackson, Oral History, ch. xxxix, on DI film 87.

p. 327 E. I. Parrant [initialled: E.I.P.] minute, 21.12.45, in reply to file note by P[atrick] Dean, 14.12, stating that Hess speech of 30.11 "convinced every hearer that Hess is mad, quite apart from his alleged amnesia. It was a typical example of his lunatic exhibitionism inspired by deep fear that he might be pronounced unfit to plead . . ." (PRO, FO371/51001).

p. 327 Affidavits of Hess, Nuremberg 7 and 12.2.46 in NA, R. H. Jackson papers, RG238, box 180, "Hess".

p. 327 Hess to Dönitz: Hess diary, 1.12.45, cited in Bird, op. cit.

p. 327 Göring to Hess: ibid.

p. 328 The case against Dönitz: Admiralty memorandum in R. H. Jackson papers, Aug. 1945. And PRO, LCO2/2980, including handwritten notes during the Anglo-US prosecutors' meeting in London, 29.5.45 (showing question marks), and note by E. I. Parrant, 23.8.45, re plans to include Keitel, Dönitz, Schacht and Krupp on the list of war criminals, "The case against Dönitz is very much weaker" and all except Keitel "should be acquitted".

p. 328 Griffith-Jones interrogation of Laura Schrödl at Nuremberg, 3.46 (IWM, FO645, box 31).

p. 331 Feldm. Erhard Milch, Gefangenschaft Tagebücher, 1947, on DI film 59.

p. 331 Constantine Brown, "The World After the War" series, "Inhuman Treatment of Nazis in Berlin Jail Poses Problem", in newspaper in file RG153 (JAG), box 1393.

p. 331 Staatsminister a.D. Rechtsanwalt Dr Alfred Seidl, *Die rechtlichen Hintergründe zum Fall Rudolf Hess* (Munich, 1980).

Archival Sources

BERLIN DOCUMENT CENTER
Biographical and SS files on Rudolf Hess, Alfred Leitgen, Karlheinz Pintsch, Laura Schrödl.
BDC-File No. 236: Rudolf Hess.
BDC-File No. 240: Jewish Question.

BERNE, SWITZERLAND: BUNDESARCHIV
Akten des Eidgenössischen Departements für Auswärtige Angelegenheiten:
    E2200 London 44/4 (Schweizerische Gesandtschaft in London).
    E2300 London   /35 (Politische Berichte betr. R. Hess).
    E2300 London   /40 (Politische Berichte betr. R. Hess).

BOSTON, MASSACHUSETTS: UNIVERSITY LIBRARY, SPECIAL MS. COLLECTION
Cecil King diaries: May 1941.
Béla Fromm papers: Karl Haushofer correspondence.

CAMBRIDGE, ENGLAND: CHURCHILL COLLEGE ARCHIVES
Sir Alexander Cadogan papers, ACAD1/10: handwritten diaries.
A. L. Kennedy papers, LKEN24: diary, 1941.

COLORADO SPRINGS, COLORADO
Burton C. Andrus Jr papers.

FREIBURG IM BREISGAU, BUNDESARCHIV-MILITÄRARCHIV
General Maximilian Freiherr von Weichs, papers.
Naval Staff war diary, August 1940, May 1941.

FREIBURG IM BREISGAU, MILITÄRGESCHICHTLICHES FORSCHUNGSAMT
Field Marshal Wilhelm Ritter von Leeb, diary, August 1940.

HYDE PARK, NEW YORK: FRANKLIN D. ROOSEVELT LIBRARY
President's Safe File "Great Britain 1942": correspondence with Lord Halifax.
Roosevelt–Churchill correspondence, Microfilm 1.

KOBLENZ: BUNDESARCHIV
Sammlung Schumacher, File 236: R. Hess.
Karl and Albrecht Haushofer papers, HX832.
Adjutantur des Führers, papers, NS10.
Parteiamtliche Prüfungskommission, papers, NS16.
Kleine Erwerbungen, No. 501: list of interpreter Paul Schmidt's pre-war notes on Hitler's
    conferences.

LONDON, ENGLAND: DAVID IRVING, AUTHOR'S ARCHIVES
Winston Churchill, desk diary (appointment cards).
General Karl Bodenschatz, author's interview, 30 November 1970.
Heinrich Heim, author's interview, 25 June 1971.
Ambassador Walther Hewel, diary, 1941, and papers.
Sir John Martin (Churchill's Private Secretary), diary, 1941.
Julius Schaub papers.

Christa Schroeder (Hitler's Private Secretary), letters and papers.
Albert Speer, office chronicle, 1941.

LONDON, ENGLAND: HOUSE OF LORDS RECORDS OFFICE
  Lord Beaverbrook papers: file D443, Rudolf Hess.

LONDON, ENGLAND: IMPERIAL WAR MUSEUM
Geoffrey Shakespeare papers, GHS2.
Lieutenant-Colonel A. Malcolm Scott papers: Camp Z diary, 1941–2, and Lieutenant-Colonel
  A. H. C. Swinton diary of events.
Professor Willi Messerschmitt papers (Handakten), FD4355/45, vol. 4, box S206.
Hans Frank minute of 19 May 1941, AL2525.
Nuremberg files FO645: interrogation of Laura Schrödl (box 161), Alfred Rosenberg (box 160),
  Ingeborg Sperr (box 31).
Miscellaneous files: letter of Graham Donald, May 1941.

LONDON, ENGLAND: PUBLIC RECORD OFFICE
AIR14/775	Bomber Command directives 1940.
AIR14/1930	Bombing policy 1940.
AIR16/698	Fighter Command, War Room Log.
AIR19/564	Sir A. Sinclair's file, "Duke of Hamilton, Allegations concerning Rudolf Hess".
AIR25/233	Operational Record Book, No. 13 Group Fighter Command.
AIR27/969	Operational Record Book, No. 141 Squadron.
AIR27/1481	Operational Record Book, No. 245 Squadron.
AIR27/2079	Operational Record Book, No. 603 Squadron.
AIR28/40	Operational Record Book, RAF Station Ayr.
AIR28/861	Operational Record Book, RAF Station Turnhouse.
AIR28/864	Ditto, appendices.
CAB65/18	War Cabinet meetings, May 1941.
CAB65/28	War Cabinet meetings, October 1942.
CAB65/35	War Cabinet meetings, September 1943.
	[NB: DEFE1/134, "Censorship of Mail", a file on Hess, is closed for fifty years.]
FO115/3544	British Embassy in Washington: R. Hess.
FO371/26565	Central Department, 1941, Germany: R. Hess [many items still closed].
FO371/26566	Ditto. Includes intercepted letters of Rudolf and Ilse Hess to his parents in Egypt 1935–8.
FO371/30919	Central Department, 1942, Germany: *Pravda* slur.
FO371/30920	Ditto, November 1942; Cripps report on Hess.
FO371/30941	Central Department, 1942, Germany: Nazi explanation of Hess mission.
FO371/33036	Northern Department, 1942, Soviet Union: Soviet criticism of British policy on Hess.
FO371/34484	Central Department, 1943, Germany: Rudolf Hess (including court martial of [Lieutenant May] for talking to the *Daily Mail*).
FO371/46777	The treatment of Rudolf Hess [at Maindiff Court; newspaper allegations of pampering].
INF1/912	Ministry of Information file on Rudolf Hess including censorship, propaganda, monitoring reports and history of intercept of 23 September 1940 Haushofer letter.
LCO2/2980	Attorney-General's Committee and British War Crimes Executive, 1945 meetings.
LCO2/2981	As above.
PREM3/14/2	Bombing policy 1940.
PREM3/14/4	Bombing policy 1940.
PREM3/219/1	Churchill's file, Hess: effect in the USA.
	[These files are photostatic copies, not originals, and have been heavily "sanitized" as the blank-page inserts show.]
PREM3/219/2	Churchill's file, Hess, medical, etc.
PREM3/219/3	Churchill's file, Hess, medical report, Duke of Hamilton libel action, etc.
PREM3/219/4	Churchill's file, Hess; public statements, etc.
PREM3/219/5	Churchill's file, Hess; interview with Simon.

PREM3/219/6   Churchill's file, Hess; Soviet attitude and report by Lord Privy Seal
               (Cripps) October–November 1942.
PREM3/219/7   Churchill's file, Hess; various, May 1941–May 1945.
PREM3/434/7   Churchill's conference with Stalin, October 1944.
FO898/1–37   Political Warfare Intelligence Directorate.
TS27/510   Treasury Solicitor's file: could Hess be subpoenaed in Hamilton libel action?
WO199/3288A   Scottish Command (British Army) file: The Capture of Rudolf Hess,
               Reports and Minutes, May–July 1941.
               [The other section of this file, WO199/3288B, is closed for seventy-five
               years, possibly because it contains court-martial proceedings].
WO208/4170   Intelligence reports: CSDIC interrogations.
WO222/885   Miliatry Hospital Drymen, quarterly reports.
WO241/1   The Directorate of Army Psychiatry: The Psychological Foundation of the
               Wehrmacht by H. V. Dicks.
WO241/2   Ibid.: The German deserter, a psychiatric study, by H. V. Dicks.
WO241/6   Ibid.: National Socialism as a Psychiatric Problem, by H. V. Dicks.

MUNICH, GERMANY: INSTITUT FÜR ZEITGESCHICHTE
Hermann Göring diary, 1941.
Testimonies (*Zeugenschriften*) of Alfred Leitgen and Julius Schaub.

OXFORD, ENGLAND: THE BODLEIAN LIBRARY
Lord Simon, papers.
Walter Monckton, papers.

STANFORD, CALIFORNIA: THE HOOVER LIBRARY
Eduard Beneš, desk diary, 1941.
Martin Bormann diary, 1934–43 (roll 1, NSDAP Hauptarchiv).
Hildegard Fath, affidavit (Ms.DD247 H3F22).
Daniel Lerner papers: DIS202 reports, No. DE404.
Walter L. Leschander collection, box 3, No. 8.
Ingeborg Sperr affidavit (Ms.DD247 H3S75).
Edvard Táborsky collection: diary 1941 (box 4), account of Hess affair by Beneš (box 4) and by
   Táborsky (box 6).

SUITLAND, MARYLAND: FEDERAL RECORDS CENTER
Office of Military Government of US for Germany; Office of the Chief of Counsel for War
   Crimes; Secretariat of the International Military Tribunal; General Records: Box 113, pieces
   5021 and 5022, two parcels, "Data on Hess compiled in Great Britain", marked Hess #1 and
   Hess #2 respectively, containing eighteen numbered report books kept by RAMC orderlies
   from 17 June 1941 to 8 October 1945 (approximately 2000 pages).
[Presumably the original file Hess-15 brought by Colonel A. J. B. Larcombe to Nuremberg is
   also here, but no longer locatable: see *Sunday Telegraph*, 13 December 1981.]

WASHINGTON, DC: LIBRARY OF CONGRESS
Martin Bormann, diary, 1934–43 (Ac9705).
Robert H. Jackson, private papers:
   Box 100   OSS and FO reports on Hess, 1945.
   Box 103   Office file, William E. Jackson.
   Box 104   Individual Responsibility: Karl Haushofer.
   Box 107   Psychiatric and Personality Studies of Nazi Leaders.
   Oral History, chap. xxxix, "Rudolf Hess: Balmy Exhibitionist".

WASHINGTON, DC: NATIONAL ARCHIVES AND RECORDS ADMINISTRATION
Record Group 228. OSS file XL 11080, interrogation of Karl Haushofer.
Record Group 238: R. H. Jackson Main Office files, box 180: "Hess".
Record Group 238, entry 199: HQ Nuremberg Military Post, No. 6850. Internal Security
   Department.
USSBS interrogation of Professor Willi Messerschmitt.
State Department files 862.00/4016 *et seq.*, 4469.
Heinrich Himmler files, Microcopy T175, roll 125.
Albrecht and Karl Haushofer papers, Microcopy T253, roll 46.
Nuremberg interrogations of Bohle, Göring, Haushofer, Hess, Papen on Microcopy M1270.

Nuremberg documents

1395-PS	Extracts from *Reichsgesetzblatt*.
1456-PS	Georg Thomas memoranda 1940.
1866-PS	Ribbentrop–Duce talk 13 May 1941.
2018-PS	Führer decree of 30 August 1939.
2124-PS	Hess Verordnung of 20 May 1938.
2639-PS	Hess Anordnungen.
2787-PS	Hess Anordnungen.
3674-PS	Hess speech, Stockholm, 14 May 1935.
M116	Hamilton–Hess talk, 11 May 1941.
M117	Kirkpatrick–Hess talk, 13 May 1941.
M118	Kirkpatrick–Hess talk, 14 May 1941.
M119	Kirkpatrick–Hess talk, 15 May 1941.

Select Bibliography

Ahnentafeln grosser Deutschen: Die Ahnentafel von Rudolf Hess (Berlin, 1934).

Anordnungen des Stellvertreters des Führers (Munich, 1937).

Akten zur deutschen Auswärtigen Politik, Serie D (1937–45), Bd. ix.

Andrew, Christopher: *On His Majesty's Secret Service: The Making of the British Intelligence Community* (New York, 1986).

Bird, Eugene K. (Lieutenant-Colonel): *Prisoner No. 7: Rudolf Hess, The Thirty Years in Jail of Hitler's Deputy Führer* (New York, 1974).

Collier, Basil: *The Defence of the United Kingdom* (London, 1957).

Das deutsche Führerlexikon 1934/37 (Berlin, 1935).

Dicks, Henry V.: *Clinical Studies in Psychopathology* (London, 1939).

—: *Fifty Years of the Tavistock Clinic* (London, 1970).

—: *Licensed Mass Murder* (London, 1972).

Dokumente der deutschen Politik, 1939 (Berlin, 1940), Bd. vii.

Eden, Anthony: *Facing the Dictators* (London, 1962).

—: *The Reckoning* (London, 1965).

Gilbert, Gustave M.: *Nuremberg Diary* (New York, 1947).

Gilbert, Martin: *Winston Churchill*, vol. vi: *Finest Hour, 1939–1941* (London, 1983).

Grenfell, Russell (Commander, "T124"): *Sea Power* (London, 1922).

Haensel, Carl: *Das Gericht vertagt sich. Aus dem Tagebuch eines Nürnberger Verteidigers* (Hamburg, n.d.).

Halder, Franz (Generaloberst): *Kriegstagebuch*, ed. Hans-Adolf Jacobsen (Stuttgart 1962).

Hamilton, James Douglas-: *Motive for a Mission: The Story Behind Hess's Flight to Britain* (London, 1972).

Hassell, Ulrich von: *Vom anderen Deutschland. Tagebücher 1938–1944* (Frankfurt, 1964).

"Heiden, Konrad": *Der Führer* (Boston, 1944).

Heim, Heinrich: *Monologe im Führerhauptquartier* (Hamburg, 1980).

Hess, Ilse: *Antwort aus Zelle Sieben. Briefwechsel mit dem Spandauer Gefangenen* (Leoni, 1967).

—: *Hess. Ein Schicksal in Briefen* (Leoni, 1984).

—: Hess, Wolf Rüdiger: *Mein Vater Rudolf Hess. Englandflug und Gefangenschaft* (Munich, 1985).

Höhne, Heinz. *Mordsache Röhm. Hitlers Durchbruch zur Alleinherrschaft* (Hamburg, 1984).

Hutton, J. Bernard: *Hess: The Man and His Mission* (New York, 1970).

Irving, David: *Hitler's War* (London, 1977).

—: *The War Path* (London, 1978).

Jacobsen, Hans-Adolf: *Karl Haushofer. Leben und Werk*, bd. i and ii (Boppard am Rhein, 1984).

Kelley, Douglas McG: *Twenty-two Cells in Nuremberg: A Psychiatrist Examines the Nazi Criminals* (New York, 1947).

Kempner, Robert: *Das Dritte Reich im Kreuzverhör* (München, 1969).

Kirkpatrick, Ivone: *The Inner Circle* (London, 1959).

Kotze, Hildegard von (ed.): *Tagebücher eines Abwehroffiziers* (Stuttgart, 1970).

Krebs, Albert: *Tendenzen und Gestalten der N.S.D.A.P. Erinnerungen an die Frühzeit der Partei* (Stuttgart, 1959).

Laack-Michel, U.: *Albrecht Haushofer und der Nationalsozialismus* (Stuttgart, 1974).

Leasor, James: *The Uninvited Envoy* (London, 1962).

Lockhart, Robert Bruce: *The Diaries of Sir Robert Bruce Lockhart*, vol. ii: *1939–1945* (London, 1984).

Martin, Bernd: *Friedensinitiativen und Machtpolitik im Zweiten Weltkrieg* (Düsseldorf, 1976).

Medical Directory, The, 1940 passim.

NS Jahrbuch. 1935 passim.

Picker, Henry: *Hitlers Tischegespräche* (Stuttgart, 1963).

Rees, John Rawlings: *The Case of Rudolf Hess* (London, 1948).

Reichsgesetzblatt, Teil I, 1933–41.

Schwarzwälder, W.: *Der Stellvertreter des Führers Rudolf Hess. Der Mann in Spandau* (Vienna, Munich, 1974).

Sutherland, J. D.; Obituary of Dicks in *Bulletin of the Royal College of Psychiatrists*, October 1977.

The Trial of the Major War Criminals Before the International Military Tribunal (Nuremberg, 1948).

Volz, Hans: *Daten der Geschichte der N.S.D.A.P.*, 9th ed (Berlin, 1939).

Zeitschrift für Geopolitik, 1935 passim.

Zoller, Albert: *Hitler Privat. Erlebnisbericht einer Geheimsekretärin* [Christa Schroeder]. (Düsseldorf, 1949).

Index

Picture Acknowledgements

BBC Hulton Picture Library: plate 5 top right, below left and right. Camera Press: plate 1 right, plate 4 above, plate 8 below. Imperial War Museum, London: plate 4 below, page 111 (X-ray) top right. National Archives, Washington: plate 1 left, plate 2 above, plate 3 above, plate 6, plate 7. Billy F. Price Collection: plate 2 below, plate 3 below. Reproduced by courtesy of University of Leeds Brotherton Library: plate 5 above left.

Jacket photographs: Camera Press. Photograph of author by Susanna Scott-Gall.